Everyman, I will go with thee,
and be thy guide

THE EVERYMAN
LIBRARY

*The Everyman Library was founded by J. M. Dent
in 1906. He chose the name Everyman because he wanted
to make available the best books ever written in every field
to the greatest number of people at the cheapest possible
price. He began with Boswell's 'Life of Johnson';
his one-thousandth title was Aristotle's 'Metaphysics',
by which time sales exceeded forty million.*

*Today Everyman paperbacks remain true to
J. M. Dent's aims and high standards, with a wide range
of titles at affordable prices in editions which address
the needs of today's readers. Each new text is reset to give
a clear, elegant page and to incorporate the latest thinking
and scholarship. Each book carries the pilgrim logo,
the character in 'Everyman', a medieval mystery play,
a proud link between Everyman
past and present.*

THE SECRET SELF 1

Short Stories by Women

Selected and Introduced by

HERMIONE LEE

'One tries to go deep –
to speak to the secret self we all have'
Katherine Mansfield

EVERYMAN
J. M. DENT · LONDON

*The 1993 reissue of this selection
is for Fiona Shaw*

This selection first published in Great Britain by
J. M. Dent 1985
Reprinted 1986, 1988, 1989

First published in Everyman's Library 1991
Reprinted 1993, 1994, 1995

Introduction, Selection and Biographical Notes
© Hermione Lee 1985

J. M. Dent
Orion Publishing Group
Orion House
5 Upper St Martin's Lane, London WC2H 9EA

Printed by The Guernsey Press Co. Ltd, Guernsey, C.I.

British Library Cataloguing in Publication Data
is available upon request.

ISBN 0 460 87348 2

CONTENTS

- 37

- 2

- 27

NOTE ON THE EDITOR

HERMIONE LEE grew up in London and read English at Oxford. She has lectured at the College of William and Mary in Virginia, at Liverpool University, and at York University, where she is Professor of English Literature. She is well known as a critic, broadcaster and reviewer, and is a fellow of the Royal Society of Literature. Her books include *The Novels of Virginia Woolf* (1977), *Elizabeth Bowen: An Estimation* (1981), *Philip Roth* (1982), *Stevie Smith: A Selection* (1983), *The Mulberry Tree: Writings of Elizabeth Bowen* (1986), *Willa Cather: A Life Saved Up* (1989) an edition of Willa Cather's stories, and editions of Virginia Woolf's *To the Lighthouse* (1992) and *The Years* (1992). She is now working on a new life of Virginia Woolf.

INTRODUCTION

Short-story writers who are analysts of the art emphasize three things: concentration, suggestiveness and enfranchisement. The short story requires a special kind of intensity and subtlety, but it also allows for liberties to be taken. Elizabeth Bowen said of her own work that 'each new story (if it is of any value) will make a whole fresh set of demands: no preceding story can be of any help'. Writing admiringly about Katherine Mansfield, she draws attention to the radical, adventurous qualities of her stories: 'Her sense of the possibilities of the story was bounded by no hard-and-fast horizons . . . Perception and language could not be kept too fresh, too alert, too fluid. Each story entailed a beginning right from the start, unknown demands, new risks, unforeseeable developments.' That sense of discovery is echoed by Elizabeth Bowen's friend Eudora Welty, looking back in *One Writer's Beginnings* (1984) over a lifetime's work: 'What one story may have pointed out to me is of no avail in the writing of another. But "avail" is not what I want; freedom ahead is what each story promises—beginning anew.'

'Fresh demands', 'new risks', 'freedom ahead': the phrases suggest pioneering and emancipation, a movement against established empires. In the nineteenth century it's notable that American writers, eager to escape from English and European traditions, made the short story their own long before the influence of Flaubert and Maupassant and Chekhov provoked short story writing in England. Walter Allen, in *The Short Story in English* (1981), suggests that 'the nature of the nineteenth-century novel in England was such as to make it very difficult for the short story as we know it to flourish or even to exist. It was too deeply entrenched in English cultural life; its supremacy was unchallenged.' It wasn't until the end of the century, with Kipling and Stevenson, that the short story, as a form to be respected, wriggled out from under the novel. Sean O'Faolain, in his jocularly anti-British book *The Short*

Story (1948), claimed that the form suits the French, the Americans and the Irish, but not the English, because they are temperamentally alien to 'the essential personal freedom' of the short story. It is 'an emphatically personal exposition', he says. 'What one searches for and what one enjoys in a short story is a special distillation of personality, a unique sensibility.'

It is tempting to draw parallels here with the woman's liberation movement, especially as the two high points of the woman's short story written in English—from about 1890 to 1930, and from the late 1960s onwards—coincide and are involved with the most active phases of twentieth-century feminism. Like nineteenth-century America (or modern Canada, Africa and India, where the short story is thriving) women short-story writers, it could be argued, are coming out from under a history of literary colonization. Their 'fresh demands', their 'unique sensibilities', find new expression in what Elizabeth Bowen calls the 'free zone' of the short story.

I would like to be able to pursue this argument with more confidence. Certainly it seemed to me, making this selection, that there are more and more good stories being written by women. Walter Allen's otherwise useful book, whose bibliography of eighty-five short-story writers includes only sixteen women (and who omits from consideration such writers as Jean Rhys, Jean Stafford, Grace Paley and Elizabeth Taylor), is quickly beginning to look out-of-date. There are now numerous feminist anthologies of short stories, which appropriate the form as the special property of women writers. A recent anthology of Canadian short stories by women, for instance, describes the strength of the collection as coming from 'women who are engaged in creating new worlds both in the imagination and in reality, women who have found new ways of countering various forms of oppression'. There is persuasive reasoning behind such polemics. It seems quite likely that the origins and characteristics of the short story—its relation to folk-lore and fairytale (narratives told to children), its suitability for part-time writers or writers likely to be interrupted, its friendliness to subjective expression and domestic materials—make it a form especially suited to women, and which women writers can thus make particularly their own, as they emerge from a long history of obscurity and silence.

But the case is not so simple. It is not possible, for one thing, to equate the supremacy of the nineteenth-century novel in England with male supremacy. If the short story in English began as a liberated colony breaking away from that old empire, then it broke away as much from Jane Austen and George Eliot as from Dickens or Trollope. It would be absurd, too, to argue that women write better short stories than men. Even the most random of lists, which would need to include Henry James, James Joyce, D. H. Lawrence, Rudyard Kipling, Somerset Maugham, Walter de la Mare, M. R. James, Frank O'Connor, Liam O'Flaherty, V. S. Pritchett, William Trevor and Sean O'Faolain, would put paid to that notion. Nor can one ignore the crucial influence of male writers on some of the best women short-story writers. Willa Cather would not have written as she did without Flaubert, Elizabeth Bowen without Sheridan LeFanu, Doris Lessing without Lawrence, or Katherine Mansfield without Chekhov.

It doesn't seem profitable, then, to pursue a separatist aesthetic theory of the twentieth-century woman's short story. But it might be more useful to try to characterize that story. Again, I doubt whether a 'psychological sentence of the feminine gender' (Virginia Woolf's phrase for Dorothy Richardson's writing) can always be distinguished, or whether a woman's story can always be identified by its subject-matter. (The case for a distinct woman's story or woman's subject seems to me reactionary rather than enfranchising. Virginia Woolf's argument, that writers should reconcile or transcend sexual difference, rather than asserting it, is a powerful one.) But it could be said that some distinctive angles of vision and ways of expression are apparent in this selection, which would not be found in an anthology of stories by men.

In *One Writer's Beginnings*, Eudora Welty recalls as characteristic an early story of hers, 'A Memory', in which a young girl visits a park on a weekday and looks at it with her hands squared over her eyes. 'Ever since I had begun taking painting lessons' (says the narrator in the story) 'I had made small frames with my fingers to look out on everything.' What she sees through her 'small frame'—down-and-outs and children in the park—depresses her. Welty comments, looking back on the story:

> The tableau discovered through the young girl's framing hands is an unwelcome realism. How can she accommo-date the existence of this view to the dream of love, which

she carried already inside her? Amorphous and tender, from now on it will have to remain hidden, her own secret imagining. The frame only raises the question of the vision.'

This passage—which is as much about the form as the subject of the story—can be set beside two other interesting remarks. One is by Willa Cather, writing about Katherine Mansfield's New Zealand stories, 'Prelude' and 'At the Bay'. What makes these her best stories, Cather says, is the struggle they depict between the group life of the family and the secret life of the individual. The other is Elizabeth Bowen's description of her own wartime collection, *The Demon Lover and Other Stories*, in which, she says, private fantasy and hallucination serve as a form of 'resistance' to the abnormal conditions of war.

These three women writers' very different remarks about short stories by women point to a shared idea. Inside the 'small frame', the particular vantage point with its local peculiarities and temperamental bias, there is a form of conflict: between secret visions and unwelcome realities, between personal desires and family restrictions, between consolatory dreams and hostile circumstances. A great many of the stories in this anthology are energized by such conflicts, whether the outcome is victory or defeat.

That Eudora Welty's 'small frame' story is told by a young girl suggests a characteristic of these conflicts. Very often, the tension is between a child's perceptions and the adult world. This subject is not, of course, a female prerogative (think of Joyce's 'Araby', or Kipling's 'Baa Baa Black Sheep'), but it does occur in women's stories over and over again. The susceptibility and literalness of children, their matter-of-fact but unsocialized behaviour, their imaginative play with what is immediately to hand, seems to be a particularly sympathetic and useful subject for women writers. Alice Munro's bossy slum-child reacting unaccountably to the horrible death of her backward brother; Grace Paley's pleased, over-confident Jewish schoolgirl, lapping up the neighbourhood comments on her large part in the nativity play; Jean Stafford's lonely journeying Indian boy; Janet Frame's excited, bewildered family outing to the wrong seaside; Ellen Gilchrist's ferocious wartime adolescent, in furious rivalry with her boy cousins; and Joyce Carol Oates' bored, callous, frightened Colorado girl, all use the perspective of children as the centre and focus of the stories.

The conflict between adult expectations and demands and the children's concealed or extreme reactions can also be extended to characters who have not properly grown up, and whose secret selves are ill-adapted to the grown-up world they are supposed to belong to. Two of the stories by women which I most admire, Katherine Mansfield's 'The Daughters of the Late Colonel' and Elizabeth Bowen's 'Her Table Spread', comically and feelingly present this sort of retardation. Constantia and Josephine, ageing victims of a ferocious paternal régime, will always be frightened daughters, even though their lifetime of 'looking after father and at the same time keeping out of father's way' is over. So precisely does the story invoke their childishness (in their terror of going through 'father's things', their guilt at having him buried, their nervousness of the housemaid and the hired nurse) that it seems quite possible to us, as to them, that 'father' should be lurking inside his huge wardrobe, or that the barrel-organ might still disturb him. The lost possibility of another life—not as 'daughters' but as women, not inside the house but in a world of space and freedom—is just glimpsed, but we can see that it cannot be theirs. In Elizabeth Bowen's story, the statuesque and embarrassing Valeria Cuffe is also a kind of prisoner, 'still detained in childhood' like an enchanted princess, in her peculiar, damp Anglo-Irish castle. Her infatuated expectation of a romantic suitor from the English destroyer in the estuary is discharged on her real visitor, the disappointed, asexual, unhopeful Mr Alban. An impossible juvenile romanticism is jostled against sad adulthood and melancholy realities. It's part of the story's brilliance that this can also stand, without intrusiveness, for a study in Anglo–Irish relations.

Other 'retarded' misfits—the furious ugly girl in the doctor's waiting-room in Flannery O'Connor's 'Revelation', the dopey unfavoured sister in Alice Walker's 'Everyday Use', the sloppy child-bride in Doris Lessing's 'The De Wets Come to Kloof Grange'—are sent as messengers or warnings to the 'grown-ups' who think they are in full, privileged control of the world they inhabit. Mrs Turpin's sublime complacency in 'Revelation', and Mrs Gale's self-protective compromise with her exile in Rhodesia in the Lessing story, are shattered by the assault of characters who can't accommodate, and who make the older women aware of what they have done with their lives.

Such confrontations between child and adult, the asocial and the habituated, the extreme and the compromised, are more than merely personal. It's very often the case with these women's stories that a detailed, inward, localized study of a character or a marriage or a family will carry the weight of a larger idea. Doris Lessing's story is not just a comparison of an old and a young marriage, or a study of women's behaviour in a country where men do the work; the clear, severe characterization of Mrs Gale is also a powerful demonstration of what is wrong with colonialism. Nadine Gordimer's 'Six Feet of the Country' similarly uses her worthless (but well-understood) suburban Johannesburg couple as a way of penetrating the catastrophic gulf between whites and blacks under apartheid. The marriage is played off against the political relationships with great subtlety. Alice Walker's 'Everyday Use', in which the Georgia mother chooses which of her daughters to give her quilts to, is a fine wry family story, but it's also a lesson in the proper value of the Southern black inheritance. Jean Stafford shows without comment what is wrong with 'Uncle Sam's' treatment of the Indians; a savage attack on sexism and racism bubbles underneath Jean Rhys's apparently feckless, slapdash narrative of a Caribbean girl in squalid London, and Jayne Anne Phillips takes only one ferocious paragraph to 'do' the New York underworld where a woman survives brutishness only through brutality. All these are political stories, though they make no 'statements'.

Some of these women writers, like Ruth Prawer Jhabvala with her high-spirited mockery of the trendy ashram in Southern India, or Muriel Spark making a glitteringly malevolent judgement (through highly eccentric means) on the England of 1919, are coldly distanced from their subject. Others, like Anita Desai, and especially the English writers (Sylvia Townsend Warner, Elizabeth Taylor, Elizabeth Jane Howard), immerse themselves in normal, everyday minutiae as a way of describing the behaviour of a particular class at a particular time. But whatever the strategy, local detail and exactness are always essential qualities. By this I don't mean, necessarily, a small scale or a domestic subject. 'Local colour' has tended to be used as a rather demeaning term, often associated with glum turn-of-the-century Zolaesque determinism, where the characters must endure whatever their 'local colour' happens to be, because that's their fate. (Pauline Smith shows, though, how strong this can be.) Most of these women writers, however, give a sense of space and potential opening up behind the constricted province of the story, even where, like Jean Rhys or Jean Stafford or Katherine Mansfield, they are dealing with captivity. Willa Cather wrote in 1938 of wanting to create the feeling of a Dutch interior, where the sea is glimpsed through the window of a warmly furnished room. This quality is there in her marvellous novella, 'Coming, Aphrodite!', which gives a rich description of bohemian life in late nineteenth-century Washington Square, but keeps floating off from there to Paris and Mexico and the future, like Molly, her lady balloonist—the first feminist heroine in this selection. Ultimately it is not an elegant, nostalgic period piece, but an exceptional love story, which invokes classical and Indian mythic archetypes, and a meditation on the necessary conditions for the artist, especially the woman artist.

Some of the most intensely 'local' of the stories, like Eudora Welty's Mississippi marriage between an old man and a young girl, deep in the Natchez Trace country, or Flannery O'Connor's violently absurd collection of misfits in her Georgia waiting-room, work towards mystical conclusions which entirely transcend the local setting. Some end with deliberate glimpses of 'a world elsewhere', as with Jean Stafford's sleeping boy and Alice Munro's Joycean falling snow. Some use an unnamed provincial context (Elspeth Davie's ghostly Edinburgh, Mary Lavin's claustrophobic small-town Ireland) for discomforting ends which make the reader feel anything but 'at home'. The most extreme translation of local materials into something rich and strange is Gertrude Stein's experiment in re-appropriating syntax, which uses homely, normal items (wife, cow, love story, 15th October, preparing, busy) and standard ingredients of narrative suspense (to be, when he can, not now, soon, what is it, happening) to make a secret, playful tone poem which refuses to be categorized or explained.

If there is always, in these stories, a negotiation between the private and particular, and the external and universal, then the selection of detail and the establishing of a point of view are always crucial. I have tried to give as much variety here as possible. There are some fine examples of first-person narrative, especially interesting when the speaker's imperceptiveness and limitations (as in the Gordimer and the Jhabvala) are played off against an implied alternative point-of-view, or when the 'I' is an exuberant comic device, as with the Grace Paley, splendidly vigorous, and the Muriel Spark. By contrast, there are a number of stories which enter into a character through a flexible, chameleon-like third-person narrative, notably Katherine Mansfield's, Elizabeth Taylor's (marvellously subdued and skilful), Katherine Anne Porter's and Flannery O'Connor's. I have chosen some writers partly for their dialogue—O'Connor again, Mary Lavin, Grace Paley—and some for their specialized tone of voice, whether weighted with Biblical cadences like Pauline Smith, or formally measured and detached like Elspeth Davie, or invoking fairytale and folklore, like Angela Carter or Ahdaf Soueif. I wanted to include writers who confounded all expectations of how the short story ought to behave: hence the Gertrude Stein, the Jayne Anne Phillips, and Margaret Atwood's ironically conclusive set of propositions. I wanted variety in length, since the brief story with a sting in the tail (like Sylvia Townsend Warner's or Janet Frame's) or the comic sketch (like Dorothy Parker's) are quite different from what Henry James called 'the beautiful and blest *nouvelle*'. There could only be room, though, for one novella, and I chose the Willa Cather.

A selection such as this is bound to be partial and personal. It's not been possible, for instance, to suggest the importance of sequences to writers such as Alice Munro, Eudora Welty or Katherine Anne Porter, whose characters, like Joyce's or Sherwood Anderson's, often move from one story to another. (My only gesture towards story-sequences or collections has been the inclusion of Ahdaf Soueif's 'The Wedding of Zeina', which comes from what might as well be called a novel as a book of stories.) Chronology and nationality have obviously needed to be balanced. The selection is 'modern' in that it begins after the First World War and covers every decade up to the mid-eighties. There are no translations, but, while trying to avoid a consciously 'token' regionalism, I have looked for stories outside England and America. It would have been easy to fill the book with first-rate American stories, and the omissions I've made here for the sake of range and variety, of writers such as Kate Chopin, Edith Wharton, Caroline Gordon, Ann Beattie, Anne Leaton and Cynthia Ozick, have been the most difficult. I wanted to include a story by Elizabeth Bishop, the American poet, but she left behind her an aversion to 'women's anthologies' which made this impossible.

The irony of this embargo is that I share Elizabeth Bishop's wariness of the 'ghettoizing' of women writers. In that it is not bristling with manifestos, this is not a feminist selection. But it is so, perhaps, in wanting to resist (or alter) predictable assumptions about women writers and their stories. There are a number of painful examples in this book (in the stories of Jean Rhys, Katherine Mansfield, Pauline Smith, Elizabeth Jane Howard) of women as the victims of men. But there are also stories which sympathetically enter into male feelings (Dorothy Parker, Katherine Anne Porter, Mary Lavin, Nadine Gordimer, Willa Cather, and, most touchingly, Anita Desai), or whose female characters are tough, powerful, jolly, exuberant, cruel or reckless, as in Muriel Spark, Grace Paley, Angela Carter, Joyce Carol Oates, Ahdaf Soueif and Bobbie Ann Mason, who brings us firmly up to date with a modern, marital version of the Civil War. Above all, what I have wanted to find are stories by women which are 'revelations' of hidden areas of the self, which evoke a unique response and make 'fresh demands' on the reader, and which have that quality of disclosure and privacy described by Katherine Mansfield, in a letter written to Dorothy Brett in 1921, when she had just finished 'At the Bay': 'One tries to go deep—to speak to the secret self we all have—to acknowledge that. I mustn't say any more about it.'

HERMIONE LEE

KATHERINE MANSFIELD

The Daughters of the Late Colonel

I

The week after was one of the busiest weeks of their lives. Even when they went to bed it was only their bodies that lay down and rested; their minds went on, thinking things out, talking things over, wondering, deciding, trying to remember where . . .

Constantia lay like a statue, her hands by her sides, her feet just overlapping each other, the sheet up to her chin. She stared at the ceiling.

'Do you think father would mind if we gave his top-hat to the porter?'

'The porter?' snapped Josephine. 'Why ever the porter? What a very extraordinary idea!'

'Because,' said Constantia slowly, 'he must often have to go to funerals. And I noticed at—at the cemetery that he only had a bowler.' She paused. 'I thought then how very much he'd appreciate a top-hat. We ought to give him a present, too. He was always very nice to father.'

'But,' cried Josephine, flouncing on her pillow and staring across the dark at Constantia, 'father's head!' And suddenly, for one awful moment, she nearly giggled. Not, of course, that she felt in the least like giggling. It must have been habit. Years ago, when they had stayed awake at night talking, their beds had simply heaved. And now the porter's head, disappearing, popped out, like a candle, under father's hat. . . . The giggle mounted, mounted; she clenched her hands; she fought it down; she frowned fiercely at the dark and said 'Remember' terribly sternly.

'We can decide tomorrow,' she said.

Constantia had noticed nothing; she sighed.

'Do you think we ought to have our dressing-gowns dyed as well?'

'Black?' almost shrieked Josephine.

'Well, what else?' said Constantia. 'I was thinking—it doesn't seem quite sincere, in a way, to wear black out of doors and when we're fully dressed, and then when we're at home—'

'But nobody sees us,' said Josephine. She gave the bedclothes such a twitch that both her feet became uncovered and she had to creep up the pillows to get them well under again.

'Kate does,' said Constantia. 'And the postman very well might.'

Josephine thought of her dark-red slippers, which matched her dressing-gown, and of Constantia's favourite indefinite green ones which went with hers. Black! Two black dressing-gowns and two pairs of black woolly slippers, creeping off to the bathroom like black cats.

'I don't think it's absolutely necessary,' said she.

Silence. Then Constantia said, 'We shall have to post the papers with the notice in them tomorrow to catch the Ceylon mail. . . . How many letters have we had up till now?'

'Twenty-three.'

Josephine had replied to them all, and twenty-three times when she came to 'We miss our dear father so much' she had broken down and had to use her handkerchief, and on some of them even to soak up a very light-blue tear with an edge of blotting-paper. Strange! She couldn't have put it on—but twenty-three times. Even now, though, when she said over to herself sadly 'We miss our dear father *so* much,' she could have cried if she'd wanted to.

'Have you got enough stamps?' came from Constantia.

'Oh, how can I tell?' said Josephine crossly. 'What's the good of asking me that now?'

'I was just wondering,' said Constantia mildly.

Silence again. There came a little rustle, a scurry, a hop.

'A mouse,' said Constantia.

'It can't be a mouse because there aren't any crumbs,' said Josephine.

'But it doesn't know there aren't,' said Constantia.

A spasm of pity squeezed her heart. Poor little thing! She wished she'd left a tiny piece of biscuit on the dressing-table. It was awful to think of it not finding anything. What would it do?

'I can't think how they manage to live at all,' she said slowly.

'Who?' demanded Josephine.

And Constantia said more loudly than she meant to, 'Mice.'

Josephine was furious. 'Oh, what nonsense, Con!' she said. 'What have mice got to do with it? You're asleep.'

'I don't think I am,' said Constantia. She shut her eyes to make sure. She was.

Josephine arched her spine, pulled up her knees, folded her arms so that her fists came under her ears, and pressed her cheek hard against the pillow.

II

Another thing which complicated matters was they had Nurse Andrews staying on with them that week. It was their own fault; they had asked her. It was Josephine's idea. On the morning—well, on the last morning, when the doctor had gone, Josephine had said to Constantia, 'Don't you think it would be rather nice if we asked Nurse Andrews to stay on for a week as our guest?'

'Very nice,' said Constantia.

'I thought,' went on Josephine quickly, 'I should just say this afternoon, after I've paid her, "My sister and I would be very pleased, after all you've done for us, Nurse Andrews, if you would stay on for a week as our guest." I'd have to put that in about being our guest in case—'

'Oh, but she could hardly expect to be paid!' cried Constantia.

'One never knows,' said Josephine sagely.

Nurse Andrews had, of course, jumped at the idea. But it was a bother. It meant they had to have regular sit-down meals at the proper times, whereas if they'd been alone they could just have asked Kate if she wouldn't have minded bringing them a tray wherever they were. And meal-times now that the strain was over were rather a trial.

Nurse Andrews was simply fearful about butter. Really they couldn't help feeling that about butter, at least, she took advantage of their kindness. And she had that maddening habit of asking for just an inch more bread to finish what she had on her plate, and then, at the last mouthful, absent-mindedly—of course it wasn't absent-mindedly—taking another helping. Josephine got very red when this happened, and she fastened her small, bead-like eyes on the tablecloth as if she saw a minute strange insect creeping through the web of it. But Constantia's long, pale face lengthened and set, and she gazed away—away—far over the desert, to where that line of camels unwound like a thread of wool. . . .

'When I was with Lady Tukes,' said Nurse Andrews, 'she had such a dainty little contrayvance for the buttah. It was a silvah

3

Cupid balanced on the—on the bordah of a glass dish, holding a tayny fork. And when you wanted some buttah you simply pressed his foot and he bent down and speared you a piece. It was quite a gayme.'

Josephine could hardly bear that. But 'I think those things are very extravagant' was all she said.

'But whey?' asked Nurse Andrews, beaming through her eyeglasses. 'No one, surely, would take more buttah than one wanted —would one?'

'Ring, Con,' cried Josephine. She couldn't trust herself to reply.

And proud young Kate, the enchanted princess, came in to see what the old tabbies wanted now. She snatched away their plates of mock something or other and slapped down a white, terrified blancmange.

'Jam, please, Kate,' said Josephine kindly.

Kate knelt and burst open the sideboard, lifted the lid of the jam-pot, saw it was empty, put it on the table, and stalked off.

'I'm afraid,' said Nurse Andrews a moment later, 'there isn't any.'

'Oh, what a bother!' said Josephine. She bit her lip. 'What had we better do?'

Constantia looked dubious. 'We can't disturb Kate again,' she said softly.

Nurse Andrews waited, smiling at them both. Her eyes wandered, spying at everything behind her eyeglasses. Constantia in despair went back to her camels. Josephine frowned heavily— concentrated. If it hadn't been for this idiotic woman she and Con would, of course, have eaten their blancmange without. Suddenly the idea came.

'I know,' she said. 'Marmalade. There's some marmalade in the sideboard. Get it, Con.'

'I hope,' laughed Nurse Andrews—and her laugh was like a spoon tinkling against a medicine-glass—'I hope it's not very bittah marmalayde.'

III

But, after all, it was not long now, and then she'd be gone for good. And there was no getting over the fact that she had been very kind to father. She had nursed him day and night at the end. Indeed, both Constantia and Josephine felt privately she had rather overdone the not leaving him at the very last. For when they had gone in

4

to say good-bye Nurse Andrews had sat beside his bed the whole time, holding his wrist and pretending to look at her watch. It couldn't have been necessary. It was so tactless, too. Supposing father had wanted to say something—something private to them. Not that he had. Oh, far from it! He lay there, purple, a dark, angry purple in the face, and never even looked at them when they came in. Then, as they were standing there, wondering what to do, he had suddenly opened one eye. Oh, what a difference it would have made, what a difference to their memory of him, how much easier to tell people about it, if he had only opened both! But no—one eye only. It glared at them a moment and then . . . went out.

IV

It had made it very awkward for them when Mr Farolles, of St John's, called the same afternoon.

'The end was quite peaceful, I trust?' were the first words he said as he glided towards them through the dark drawing-room.

'Quite,' said Josephine faintly. They both hung their heads. Both of them felt certain that eye wasn't at all a peaceful eye.

'Won't you sit down?' said Josephine.

'Thank you, Miss Pinner,' said Mr Farolles gratefully. He folded his coat-tails and began to lower himself into father's arm-chair, but just as he touched it he almost sprang up and slid into the next chair instead.

He coughed. Josephine clasped her hands; Constantia looked vague.

'I want you to feel, Miss Pinner,' said Mr Farolles, 'and you, Miss Constantia, that I'm trying to be helpful. I want to be helpful to you both, if you will let me. These are the times,' said Mr Farolles, very simply and earnestly, 'when God means us to be helpful to one another.'

'Thank you very much, Mr Farolles,' said Josephine and Constantia.

'Not at all,' said Mr Farolles gently. He drew his kid gloves through his fingers and leaned forward. 'And if either of you would like a little Communion, either or both of you, here *and* now, you have only to tell me. A little Communion is often very help—a great comfort,' he added tenderly.

But the idea of a little Communion terrified them. What! In the drawing-room by themselves—with no—no altar or anything! The piano would be much too high, thought Constantia, and Mr Farolles could not possibly lean over it with the chalice. And Kate would be sure to come bursting in and interrupt them, thought Josephine. And supposing the bell rang in the middle? It might be somebody important—about their mourning. Would they get up reverently and go out, or would they have to wait . . . in torture?

'Perhaps you will send round a note by your good Kate if you would care for it later,' said Mr Farolles.

'Oh yes, thank you very much!' they both said.

Mr Farolles got up and took his black straw hat from the round table.

'And about the funeral,' he said softly. 'I may arrange that—as your dear father's old friend and yours, Miss Pinner—and Miss Constantia?'

Josephine and Constantia got up too.

'I should like it to be quite simple,' said Josephine firmly, 'and not too expensive. At the same time, I should like—'

'A good one that will last,' thought dreamy Constantia, as if Josephine were buying a night-gown. But, of course, Josephine didn't say that. 'One suitable to our father's position.' She was very nervous.

'I'll run round to our good friend Mr Knight,' said Mr Farolles soothingly. 'I will ask him to come and see you. I am sure you will find him very helpful indeed.'

v

Well, at any rate, all that part of it was over, though neither of them could possibly believe that father was never coming back. Josephine had had a moment of absolute terror at the cemetery, while the coffin was lowered, to think that she and Constantia had done this thing without asking his permission. What would father say when he found out? For he was bound to find out sooner or later. He always did. 'Buried. You two girls had me *buried*!' She heard his stick thumping. Oh, what would they say? What possible excuse could they make? It sounded such an appallingly heartless thing to do. Such a wicked advantage to take of a person because he happened to be helpless at the moment. The other people seemed to treat it all as a matter of course. They were strangers; they couldn't be expected to understand that father was the very last person for such a thing to happen to. No, the entire blame for it all would fall on her and Constantia. And the expense, she thought, stepping into the tight-buttoned cab. When she had to show him the bills. What would he say then?

She heard him absolutely roaring. 'And do you expect me to pay for this gimcrack excursion of yours?'

'Oh,' groaned poor Josephine aloud, 'we shouldn't have done it, Con!'

And Constantia, pale as a lemon in all that blackness, said in a frightened whisper, 'Done what, Jug?'

'Let them bu-bury father like that,' said Josephine, breaking down and crying into her new, queer-smelling mourning handkerchief.

'But what else could we have done?' asked Constantia wonderingly. 'We couldn't have kept him, Jug—we couldn't have kept him unburied. At any rate, not in a flat that size.'

Josephine blew her nose; the cab was dreadfully stuffy.

'I don't know,' she said forlornly. 'It is all so dreadful. I feel we ought to have tried to, just for a time at least. To make perfectly sure. One thing's certain'—and her tears sprang out again—'father will never forgive us for this—never!'

VI

Father would never forgive them. That was what they felt more than ever when, two mornings later, they went into his room to go through his things. They had discussed it quite calmly. It was even down on Josephine's list of things to be done. *Go through father's things and settle about them.* But that was a very different matter from saying after breakfast:

'Well, are you ready, Con?'

'Yes, Jug—when you are.'

'Then I think we'd better get it over.'

It was dark in the hall. It had been a rule for years never to disturb father in the morning, whatever happened. And now they were going to open the door without knocking even. . . . Constantia's eyes were enormous at the idea; Josephine felt weak in the knees.

'You—you go first,' she gasped, pushing Constantia.

But Constantia said, as she always had said on those occasions, 'No, Jug, that's not fair. You're eldest.'

Josephine was just going to say—what at other times she wouldn't have owned to for the world—what she kept for her very

7

last weapon, 'But you're tallest,' when they noticed that the kitchen door was open, and there stood Kate. . . .

'Very stiff,' said Josephine, grasping the door-handle and doing her best to turn it. As if anything ever deceived Kate!

It couldn't be helped. That girl was . . . Then the door was shut behind them, but—but they weren't in father's room at all. They might have suddenly walked through the wall by mistake into a different flat altogether. Was the door just behind them? They were too frightened to look. Josephine knew that if it was it was holding itself tight shut; Constantia felt that, like the doors in dreams, it hadn't any handle at all. It was the coldness which made it so awful. Or the whiteness—which? Everything was covered. The blinds were down, a cloth hung over the mirror, a sheet hid the bed; a huge fan of white paper filled the fire-place. Constantia timidly put out her hand; she almost expected a snowflake to fall. Josephine felt a queer tingling in her nose, as if her nose was freezing. Then a cab klop-klopped over the cobbles below, and the quiet seemed to shake into little pieces.

'I had better pull up a blind,' said Josephine bravely.

'Yes, it might be a good idea,' whispered Constantia.

They only gave the blind a touch, but it flew up and the cord flew after, rolling round the blind-stick, and the little tassel tapped as if trying to get free. That was too much for Constantia.

'Don't you think—don't you think we might put it off for another day?' she whispered.

'Why?' snapped Josephine, feeling, as usual, much better now that she knew for certain that Constantia was terrified. 'It's got to be done. But I do wish you wouldn't whisper, Con.'

'I didn't know I was whispering,' whispered Constantia.

'And why do you keep on staring at the bed?' said Josephine, raising her voice almost defiantly. 'There's nothing *on* the bed.'

'Oh, Jug, don't say so!' said poor Connie. 'At any rate, not so loudly.'

Josephine felt herself that she had gone too far. She took a wide swerve over to the chest of drawers, put out her hand, but quickly drew it back again.

'Connie!' she gasped, and she wheeled round and leaned with her back against the chest of drawers.

'Oh, Jug—what?'

Josephine could only glare. She had the most extraordinary

feeling that she had just escaped something simply awful. But how could she explain to Constantia that father was in the chest of drawers? He was in the top drawer with his handkerchiefs and neckties, or in the next with his shirts and pyjamas, or in the lowest of all with his suits. He was watching there, hidden away—just behind the door-handle—ready to spring.

She pulled a funny old-fashioned face at Constantia, just as she used to in the old days when she was going to cry.

'I can't open,' she nearly wailed.

'No, don't, Jug,' whispered Constantia earnestly. 'It's much better not to. Don't let's open anything. At any rate, not for a long time.'

'But—but it seems so weak,' said Josephine, breaking down.

'But why not be weak for once, Jug?' argued Constantia, whispering quite fiercely. 'If it is weak.' And her pale stare flew from the locked writing-table—so safe—to the huge glittering wardrobe, and she began to breathe in a queer, panting way. 'Why shouldn't we be weak for once in our lives, Jug? It's quite excusable. Let's be weak—be weak, Jug. It's much nicer to be weak than to be strong.'

And then she did one of those amazingly bold things that she'd done about twice before in their lives: she marched over to the wardrobe, turned the key, and took it out of the lock. Took it out of the lock and held it up to Josephine, showing Josephine by her extraordinary smile that she knew what she'd done—she'd risked deliberately father being in there among his overcoats.

If the huge wardrobe had lurched forward, had crashed down on Constantia, Josephine wouldn't have been surprised. On the contrary, she would have thought it the only suitable thing to happen. But nothing happened. Only the room seemed quieter than ever, and bigger flakes of cold air fell on Josephine's shoulders and knees. She began to shiver.

'Come, Jug,' said Constantia, still with that awful callous smile; and Josephine followed just as she had that last time, when Constantia had pushed Benny into the round pond.

VII

But the strain told on them when they were back in the dining-room. They sat down, very shaky, and looked at each other.

'I don't feel I can settle to anything,' said Josephine, 'until I've had something. Do you think we could ask Kate for two cups of hot water?'

'I really don't see why we shouldn't,' said Constantia carefully. She was quite normal again. 'I won't ring. I'll go to the kitchen door and ask her.'

'Yes, do,' said Josephine, sinking down into a chair. 'Tell her, just two cups, Con, nothing else—on a tray.'

'She needn't even put the jug on, need she?' said Constantia, as though Kate might very well complain if the jug had been there.

'Oh no, certainly not! The jug's not at all necessary. She can pour it direct out of the kettle,' cried Josephine, feeling that would be a labour-saving indeed.

Their cold lips quivered at the greenish brims. Josephine curved her small red hands round the cup; Constantia sat up and blew on the wavy steam, making it flutter from one side to the other.

'Speaking of Benny,' said Josephine.

And though Benny hadn't been mentioned Constantia immediately looked as though he had.

'He'll expect us to send him something of father's, of course. But it's so difficult to know what to send to Ceylon.'

'You mean things get unstuck so on the voyage,' murmured Constantia.

'No, lost,' said Josephine sharply. 'You know there's no post. Only runners.'

Both paused to watch a black man in white linen drawers running through the pale fields for dear life, with a large brown paper parcel in his hands. Josephine's black man was tiny; he scurried along glistening like an ant. But there was something blind and tireless about Constantia's tall, thin fellow, which made him, she decided, a very unpleasant person indeed. . . . On the verandah, dressed all in white and wearing a cork helmet, stood Benny. His right hand shook up and down, as father's did when he was impatient. And behind him, not in the least interested, sat Hilda, the unknown sister-in-law. She swung in a cane rocker and flicked over the leaves of the *Tatler*.

'I think his watch would be the most suitable present,' said Josephine.

Constantia looked up; she seemed surprised.

'Oh, would you trust a gold watch to a native?'

'But, of course, I'd disguise it,' said Josephine. 'No one would know it was a watch.' She liked the idea of having to make a parcel such a curious shape that no one could possibly guess what it was. She even thought for a moment of hiding the watch in a narrow cardboard corset-box that she'd kept by her for a long time, waiting for it to come in for something. It was such beautiful, firm cardboard. But, no, it wouldn't be appropriate for this occasion. It had lettering on it: *Medium Women's 28. Extra Firm Busks.* It would be almost too much of a surprise for Benny to open that and find father's watch inside.

'And, of course, it isn't as though it would be going—ticking, I mean,' said Constantia, who was still thinking of the native love of jewellery. 'At least,' she added, 'it would be very strange if after all that time it was.'

VIII

Josephine made no reply. She had flown off on one of her tangents. She had suddenly thought of Cyril. Wasn't it more usual for the only grandson to have the watch? And then dear Cyril was so appreciative and a gold watch meant so much to a young man. Benny, in all probability, had quite got out of the habit of watches; men so seldom wore waistcoats in those hot climates. Whereas Cyril in London wore them from year's end to year's end. And it would be so nice for her and Constantia, when he came to tea, to know it was there. 'I see you've got on grandfather's watch, Cyril.' It would be somehow so satisfactory.

Dear boy! What a blow his sweet, sympathetic little note had been! Of course they quite understood; but it was most unfortunate.

'It would have been such a point, having him,' said Josephine.

'And he would have enjoyed it so,' said Constantia, not thinking what she was saying.

However, as soon as he got back he was coming to tea with his aunties. Cyril to tea was one of their rare treats.

'Now, Cyril, you mustn't be frightened of our cakes. Your Auntie Con and I bought them at Buszard's this morning. We know what a man's appetite is. So don't be ashamed of making a good tea.'

Josephine cut recklessly into the rich dark cake that stood for her winter gloves or the soling and heeling of Constantia's only respectable shoes. But Cyril was most unmanlike in appetite.

'I say, Aunt Josephine, I simply can't. I've only just had lunch, you know.'

'Oh, Cyril, that can't be true! It's after four,' cried Josephine. Constantia sat with her knife poised over the chocolate-roll.

'It is, all the same,' said Cyril. 'I had to meet a man at Victoria, and he kept me hanging about till . . . there was only time to get lunch and to come on here. And he gave me—phew'—Cyril put his hand to his forehead—'a terrific blow-out,' he said.

It was disappointing—today of all days. But still he couldn't be expected to know.

'But you'll have a meringue, won't you, Cyril?' said Aunt Josephine. 'These meringues were bought specially for you. Your dear father was so fond of them. We were sure you are, too.'

'I *am*, Aunt Josephine,' cried Cyril ardently. 'Do you mind if I take half to begin with?'

'Not at all, dear boy; but we mustn't let you off with that.'

'Is your dear father still so fond of meringues?' asked Auntie Con gently. She winced faintly as she broke through the shell of hers.

'Well, I don't quite know, Auntie Con,' said Cyril breezily.

At that they both looked up.

'Don't know?' almost snapped Josephine. 'Don't know a thing like that about your own father, Cyril?'

'Surely,' said Auntie Con softly.

Cyril tried to laugh it off. 'Oh, well,' he said, 'it's such a long time since—' He faltered. He stopped. Their faces were too much for him.

'Even *so*,' said Josephine.

And Auntie Con looked.

Cyril put down his teacup. 'Wait a bit,' he cried. 'Wait a bit, Aunt Josephine. What am I thinking of?'

He looked up. They were beginning to brighten. Cyril slapped his knee.

'Of course,' he said, 'it was meringues. How could I have forgotten? Yes, Aunt Josephine, you're perfectly right. Father's most frightfully keen on meringues.'

They didn't only beam. Aunt Josephine went scarlet with pleasure; Auntie Con gave a deep, deep sigh.

'And now, Cyril, you must come and see father,' said Josephine. 'He knows you were coming today.'

'Right,' said Cyril, very firmly and heartily. He got up from his chair; suddenly he glanced at the clock.

'I say, Auntie Con, isn't your clock a bit slow? I've got to meet a man at—at Paddington just after five. I'm afraid I shan't be able to stay very long with grandfather.'

'Oh, he won't expect you to stay *very* long!' said Aunt Josephene.

Constantia was still gazing at the clock. She couldn't make up her mind if it was fast or slow. It was one or the other, she felt almost certain of that. At any rate, it had been.

Cyril still lingered. 'Aren't you coming along, Auntie Con?'

'Of course,' said Josephine, 'we shall all go. Come on, Con.'

IX

They knocked at the door, and Cyril followed his aunts into grandfather's hot, sweetish room.

'Come on,' said Grandfather Pinner. 'Don't hang about. What is it? What've you been up to?'

He was sitting in front of a roaring fire, clasping his stick. He had a thick rug over his knees. On his lap there lay a beautiful pale yellow silk handkerchief.

'It's Cyril, father,' said Josephine shyly. And she took Cyril's hand and led him forward.

'Good afternoon, grandfather,' said Cyril, trying to take his hand out of Aunt Josephine's. Grandfather Pinner shot his eyes at Cyril in the way he was famous for. Where was Auntie Con? She stood on the other side of Aunt Josephine; her long arms hung down in front of her; her hands were clasped. She never took her eyes off grandfather.

'Well,' said Grandfather Pinner, beginning to thump, 'what have you got to tell me?'

What had he, what had he got to tell him? Cyril felt himself smiling like a perfect imbecile. The room was stifling, too.

But Aunt Josephine came to his rescue. She cried brightly, 'Cyril says his father is still very fond of meringues, father dear.'

'Eh?' said Grandfather Pinner, curving his hand like a purple meringue-shell over one ear.

Josephine repeated, 'Cyril says his father is still very fond of meringues.'

'Can't hear,' said old Colonel Pinner. And he waved Josephine away with his stick, then pointed with his stick to Cyril. 'Tell me what she's trying to say,' he said.

(My God!) 'Must I?' said Cyril, blushing and staring at Aunt Josephine.

'Do, dear,' she smiled. 'It will please him so much.'

'Come on, out with it!' cried Colonel Pinner testily, beginning to thump again.

And Cyril leaned forward and yelled, 'Father's still very fond of meringues.'

At that Grandfather Pinner jumped as though he had been shot.

'Don't shout!' he cried. 'What's the matter with the boy? *Meringues!* What about 'em?'

'Oh, Aunt Josephine, must we go on?' groaned Cyril desperately.

'It's quite all right, dear boy,' said Aunt Josephine, as though he and she were at the dentist's together. 'He'll understand in a minute.' And she whispered to Cyril, 'He's getting a bit deaf, you know.' Then she leaned forward and really bawled at Grandfather Pinner, 'Cyril only wanted to tell you, father dear, that *his* father is still very fond of meringues.'

Colonel Pinner heard that time, heard and brooded, looking Cyril up and down.

'What an esstrordinary thing!' said old Grandfather Pinner. 'What an esstrordinary thing to come all this way here to tell me!'

And Cyril felt it *was*.

'Yes, I shall send Cyril the watch,' said Josephine.

'That would be very nice,' said Constantia. 'I seem to remember last time he came there was some little trouble about the time.'

x

They were interrupted by Kate bursting through the door in her usual fashion, as though she had discovered some secret panel in the wall. 'Fried or boiled?' asked the bold voice.

Fried or boiled? Josephine and Constantia were quite bewildered for the moment. They could hardly take it in.

'Fried or boiled what, Kate?' asked Josephine, trying to begin to concentrate.

Kate gave a loud sniff. 'Fish.'

'Well, why didn't you say so immediately?' Josephine reproached her gently. 'How could you expect us to understand,

Kate? There are a great many things in this world, you know, which are fried or boiled.' And after such a display of courage she said quite brightly to Constantia, 'Which do you prefer, Con?'

'I think it might be nice to have it fried,' said Constantia. 'On the other hand, of course, boiled fish is very nice. I think I prefer both equally well . . . Unless you . . . In that case—'

'I shall fry it,' said Kate, and she bounced back, leaving their door open and slamming the door of her kitchen.

Josephine gazed at Constantia; she raised her pale eyebrows until they rippled away into her pale hair. She got up. She said in a very lofty, imposing way, 'Do you mind following me into the drawing-room, Constantia? I've something of great importance to discuss with you.'

For it was always to the drawing-room they retired when they wanted to talk over Kate.

Josephine closed the door meaningly. 'Sit down, Constantia,' she said, still very grand. She might have been receiving Constantia for the first time. And Con looked round vaguely for a chair, as though she felt indeed quite a stranger.

'Now the question is,' said Josephine, bending forward, 'whether we shall keep her or not.'

'That is the question,' agreed Constantia.

'And this time,' said Josephine firmly, 'we must come to a definite decision.'

Constantia looked for a moment as though she might begin going over all the other times, but she pulled herself together and said, 'Yes, Jug.'

'You see, Con,' explained Josephine, 'everything is so changed now.' Constantia looked up quickly. 'I mean,' went on Josephine, 'we're not dependent on Kate as we were.' And she blushed faintly. 'There's not father to cook for.'

'That is perfectly true,' agreed Constantia. 'Father certainly doesn't want any cooking now whatever else—'

Josephine broke in sharply, 'You're not sleepy, are you, Con?'

'Sleepy, Jug?' Constantia was wide-eyed.

'Well, concentrate more,' said Josephine sharply, and she returned to the subject. 'What it comes to is, if we did'—and this she barely breathed, glancing at the door—'give Kate notice'—she raised her voice again—'we could manage our own food.'

'Why not?' cried Constantia. She couldn't help smiling. The idea was so exciting. She clasped her hands. 'What should we live on, Jug?'

'Oh, eggs in various forms!' said Jug, lofty again. 'And, besides, there are all the cooked foods.'

'But I've always heard,' said Constantia, 'they are considered so very expensive.'

'Not if one buys them in moderation,' said Josephine. But she tore herself away from this fascinating bypath and dragged Constantia after her.

'What we've got to decide now, however, is whether we really do trust Kate or not.'

Constantia leaned back. Her flat little laugh flew from her lips.

'Isn't it curious, Jug,' said she, 'that just on this one subject I've never been able to quite make up my mind?'

XI

She never had. The whole difficulty was to prove anything. How did one prove things, how could one? Suppose Kate had stood in front of her and deliberately made a face. Mightn't she very well have been in pain? Wasn't it impossible, at any rate, to ask Kate if she was making a face at her? If Kate answered 'No'—and, of course, she would say 'No'—what a position! How undignified! Then, again, Constantia suspected, she was almost certain that Kate went to her chest of drawers when she and Josephine were out, not to take things but to spy. Many times she had come back to find her amethyst cross in the most unlikely places, under her lace ties or on top of her evening bertha. More than once she had laid a trap for Kate. She had arranged things in a special order and then called Josephine to witness.

'You see, Jug?'

'Quite, Con.'

'Now we shall be able to tell.'

But, oh dear, when she did go to look, she was as far off from a proof as ever! If anything was displaced, it might so very well have happened as she closed the drawer; a jolt might have done it so easily.

'You come, Jug, and decide. I really can't. It's too difficult.'

But after a pause and a long glare Josephine would sigh, 'Now you've put the doubt into my mind, Con, I'm sure I can't tell myself.'

* * *

'Well, we can't postpone it again,' said Josephine. 'If we postpone it this time—'

XII

But at that moment in the street below a barrel-organ struck up. Josephine and Constantia sprang to their feet together.

'Run, Con,' said Josephine. 'Run quickly. There's sixpence on the—'

Then they remembered. It didn't matter. They would never have to stop the organ-grinder again. Never again would she and Constantia be told to make that monkey take his noise somewhere else. Never would sound that loud, strange bellow when father thought they were not hurrying enough. The organ-grinder might play there all day and the stick would not thump.

> It never will thump again,
> It never will thump again,

played the barrel-organ.

What was Constantia thinking? She had such a strange smile; she looked different. She couldn't be going to cry.

'Jug, Jug,' said Constantia softly, pressing her hands together. 'Do you know what day it is? It's Saturday. It's a week today, a whole week.'

> A week since father died,
> A week since father died,

cried the barrel-organ. And Josephine, too, forgot to be practical and sensible; she smiled faintly, strangely. On the Indian carpet there fell a square of sunlight, pale red; it came and went and came—and stayed, deepened—until it shone almost golden.

'The sun's out,' said Josephine, as though it really mattered.

A perfect fountain of bubbling notes shook from the barrel-organ, round, bright notes, carelessly scattered.

Constantia lifted her big, cold hands as if to catch them, and then her hands fell again. She walked over to the mantelpiece to her favourite Buddha. And the stone and gilt image, whose smile always gave her such a queer feeling, almost a pain and yet a pleasant pain, seemed today to be more than smiling. He knew something; he had a secret. 'I know something that you don't know,' said her Buddha. Oh, what was it, what could it

17

be? And yet she had always felt there was . . . something.

The sunlight pressed through the windows, thieved its way in, flashed its light over the furniture and the photographs. Josephine watched it. When it came to mother's photograph, the enlargement over the piano, it lingered as though puzzled to find so little remained of mother, except the earrings shaped like tiny pagodas and a black feather boa. Why did the photographs of dead people always fade so? wondered Josephine. As soon as a person was dead their photograph died too. But, of course, this one of mother was very old. It was thirty-five years old. Josephine remembered standing on a chair and pointing out that feather boa to Constantia and telling her that it was a snake that had killed their mother in Ceylon. . . . Would everything have been different if mother hadn't died? She didn't see why. Aunt Florence had lived with them until they had left school, and they had moved three times and had their yearly holiday and . . . and there'd been changes of servants, of course.

Some little sparrows, young sparrows they sounded, chirped on the window-ledge. *Yeep—eyeep—yeep*. But Josephine felt they were not sparrows, not on the window-ledge. It was inside her, that queer little crying noise. *Yeep—eyeep—yeep*. Ah, what was it crying, so weak and forlorn?

If mother had lived, might they have married? But there had been nobody for them to marry. There had been father's Anglo-Indian friends before he quarrelled with them. But after that she and Constantia never met a single man except clergymen. How did one meet men? Or even if they'd met them, how could they have got to know men well enough to be more than strangers? One read of people having adventures, being followed, and so on. But nobody had ever followed Constantia and her. Oh yes, there had been one year at Eastbourne a mysterious man at their boarding-house who had put a note on the jug of hot water outside their bedroom door! But by the time Connie had found it the steam had made the writing too faint to read; they couldn't even make out to which of them it was addressed. And he had left next day. And that was all. The rest had been looking after father and at the same time keeping out of father's way. But now? But now? The thieving sun touched Josephine gently. She lifted her face. She was drawn over to the window by gentle beams. . . .

Until the barrel-organ stopped playing Constantia stayed before the Buddha, wondering, but not as usual, not vaguely. This time her wonder was like longing. She remembered the times she had come in here, crept out of bed in her night-gown when the moon was full, and lain on the floor with her arms outstretched, as though she was crucified. Why? The big, pale moon had made her do it. The horrible dancing figures on the carved screen had leered at her and she hadn't minded. She remembered too how, whenever they were at the seaside, she had gone off by herself and got as close to the sea as she could, and sung something, something she had made up, while she gazed all over that restless water. There had been this other life, running out, bringing things home in bags, getting things on approval, discussing them with Jug, and taking them back to get more things on approval, and arranging father's trays and trying not to annoy father. But it all seemed to have happened in a kind of tunnel. It wasn't real. It was only when she came out of the tunnel into the moonlight or by the sea or into a thunderstorm that she really felt herself. What did it mean? What was it she was always wanting? What did it all lead to? Now? Now?

She turned away from the Buddha with one of her vague gestures. She went over to where Josephine was standing. She wanted to say something to Josephine, something frightfully important, about—about the future and what . . .

'Don't you think perhaps—' she began.

But Josephine interrupted her. 'I was wondering if now—' she murmured. They stopped; they waited for each other.

'Go on, Con,' said Josephine.

'No, no, Jug; after you,' said Constantia.

'No, say what you were going to say. You began,' said Josephine.

'I . . . I'd rather hear what you were going to say first,' said Constantia.

'Don't be absurd, Con.'

'Really, Jug.'

'Connie!'

'Oh, *Jug*!'

A pause. Then Constantia said faintly, 'I can't say what I was going to say, Jug, because I've forgotten what it was . . . that I was going to say.'

Josephine was silent for a moment. She stared at a big cloud where the sun had been. Then she replied shortly, 'I've forgotten too.'

Pauline Smith

The Sisters

Marta was the eldest of my father's children, and she was sixteen years old when our mother died and our father lost the last of his water-cases to old Jan Redlinghuis of Bitterwater. It was the water-cases that killed my mother. Many, many times she had cried to my father to give in to old Jan Redlinghuis whose water-rights had been fixed by law long before my father built his water furrow from the Ghamka river. But my father could not rest. If he could but get a fair share of the river water for his furrow, he would say, his farm of Zeekoegatt would be as rich as the farm of Bitterwater and we should then have a town house in Platkops dorp and my mother should wear a black cashmere dress all the days of her life. My father could not see that my mother did not care about the black cashmere dress or the town house in Platkops dorp. My mother was a very gentle woman with a disease of the heart, and all she cared about was to have peace in the house and her children happy around her. And for so long as my father was at law about his water-rights there could be no peace on all the farm of Zeekoegatt. With each new water-case came more bitterness and sorrow to us all. Even between my parents at last came bitterness and sorrow. And in bitterness and sorrow my mother died.

In his last water-case my father lost more money than ever before, and to save the farm he bonded some of the lands to old Jan Redlinghuis himself. My father was surely mad when he did this, but he did it. And from that day Jan Redlinghuis pressed him, pressed him, pressed him, till my father did not know which way to turn. And then, when my father's back was up against the wall and he thought he must sell the last of his lands to pay his bond, Jan Redlinghuis came to him and said:

'I will take your daughter, Marta Magdalena, instead.'

Three days Jan Redlinghuis gave my father, and in three days, if Marta did not promise to marry him, the lands of Zeekoegatt must be sold. Marta told me this late that same night. She said to me:

'Sukey, my father has asked me to marry old Jan Redlinghuis. I am going to do it.'

And she said again: 'Sukey, my darling, listen now! If I marry old Jan Redlinghuis he will let the water into my father's furrow, and the lands of Zeekoegatt will be saved. I am going to do it, and God will help me.'

I cried to her: 'Marta! Old Jan Redlinghuis is a sinful man, going at times a little mad in his head. God must help you before you marry him. Afterwards it will be too late.'

And Marta said: 'Sukey, if I do right, right will come of it, and it is right for me to save the lands for my father. Think now, Sukey, my darling! There is not one of us that is without sin in the world and old Jan Redlinghuis is not always mad. Who am I to judge Jan Redlinghuis? And can I then let my father be driven like a poor white to Platkops dorp?' And she drew me down on to the pillow beside her, and took me into her arms, and I cried there until far into the night.

The next day I went alone across the river to old Jan Redlinghuis's farm. No one knew that I went, or what it was in my heart to do. When I came to the house Jan Redlinghuis was out on the *stoep* smoking his pipe.

I said to him: 'Jan Redlinghuis, I have come to offer myself.'

Jan Redlinghuis took his pipe out of his mouth and looked at me. I said again: 'I have come to ask you to marry me instead of my sister Marta.'

Old Jan Redlinghuis said to me: 'And why have you come to do this thing, Sukey de Jager?'

I told him: 'Because it is said that you are a sinful man, Jan Redlinghuis, going at times a little mad in your head, and my sister Marta is too good for you.'

For a little while old Jan Redlinghuis looked at me, sitting there with his pipe in his hand, thinking the Lord knows what. And presently he said:

'All the same, Sukey de Jager, it is your sister Marta that I will marry and no one else. If not, I will take the lands of Zeekoegatt as is my right, and I will make your father bankrupt. Do now as you like about it.'

And he put his pipe in his mouth, and not one other word would he say.

I went back to my father's house with my heart heavy like lead.

And all that night I cried to God: 'Do now what you will with me, but save our Marta.' Yes, I tried to make a bargain with the Lord so that Marta might be saved. And I said also: 'If He does not save our Marta I will know that there is no God.'

In three weeks Marta married old Jan Redlinghuis and went to live with him across the river. On Marta's wedding day I put my father's Bible before him and said:

'Pa, pray if you like, but I shall not pray with you. There is no God or surely He would have saved our Marta. But if there is a God as surely will He burn our souls in Hell for selling Marta to old Jan Redlinghuis.'

From that time I could do what I would with my father, and my heart was bitter to all the world but my sister Marta. When my father said to me:

'Is it not wonderful, Sukey, what we have done with the water that old Jan Redlinghuis lets pass to my furrow?'

I answered him: 'What is now wonderful? It is blood that we lead on our lands to water them. Did not my mother die for it? And was it not for this that we sold my sister Marta to old Jan Redlinghuis?'

Yes, I said that. It was as if my heart must break to see my father water his lands while old Jan Redlinghuis held my sister Marta up to shame before all Platkops.

I went across the river to my sister Marta as often as I could, but not once after he married her did old Jan Redlinghuis let Marta come back to my father's house.

'Look now, Sukey de Jager,' he would say to me, 'your father has sold me his daughter for his lands. Let him now look to his lands and leave me his daughter.' And that was all he would say about it.

Marta had said that old Jan Redlinghuis was not always mad, but from the day that he married her his madness was to cry to all the world to look at the wife that Burgert de Jager had sold to him.

'Look,' he would say, 'how she sits in her new tent-cart—the wife that Burgert de Jager sold to me.'

And he would point to the Zeekoegatt lands and say: 'See now, how green they are, the lands that Burgert de Jager sold me his daughter to save.'

Yes, even before strangers would he say these things, stopping his cart in the road to say them, with Marta sitting by his side.

My father said to me: 'Is it not wonderful, Sukey, to see how Marta rides through the country in her new tent-cart?'

22

I said to him: 'What is now wonderful? It is to her grave that she rides in the new tent-cart, and presently you will see it.'

And I said to him also: 'It took you many years to kill my mother, but believe me it will not take as many months for old Jan Redlinghuis to kill my sister Marta.' Yes, God forgive me, but I said that to my father. All my pity was for my sister Marta, and I had none to give my father.

And all this time Marta spoke no word against old Jan Redlinghuis. She had no illness that one might name, but every day she grew a little weaker, and every day Jan Redlinghuis inspanned the new tent-cart and drove her round the country. This madness came at last so strong upon him that he must drive from sun-up to sun-down crying to all whom he met:

'Look now at the wife that Burgert de Jager sold to me!'

So it went, day after day, day after day, till at last there came a day when Marta was too weak to climb into the cart and they carried her from where she fell into the house. Jan Redlinghuis sent for me across the river.

When I came to the house old Jan Redlinghuis was standing on the *stoep* with his gun. He said to me: 'See here, Sukey de Jager! Which of us now had the greatest sin—your father who sold me his daughter Marta, or I who bought her? Marta who let herself be sold, or you who offered yourself to save her?'

And he took up his gun and left the *stoep* and would not wait for an answer.

Marta lay where they had put her on old Jan Redlinghuis's great wooden bed, and only twice did she speak. Once she said:

'He was not always mad, Sukey, my darling, and who am I that I should judge him?'

And again she said: 'See how it is, my darling! In a little while I shall be with our mother. So it is that God has helped me.'

At sun-down Marta died, and when they ran to tell Jan Redlinghuis they could not find him. All that night they looked for him, and the next day also. We buried Marta in my mother's grave at Zeekoegatt. . . . And still they could not find Jan Redlinghuis. Six days they looked for him, and at last they found his body in the mountains. God knows what madness had driven old Jan Redlinghuis to the mountains when his wife lay dying, but there it was they found him, and at Bitterwater he was buried.

That night my father came to me and said: 'It is true what you said to me, Sukey. It is blood that I have led on my lands to water them, and this night will I close the furrow that I built from the Ghamka river. God forgive me, I will do it.'

It was in my heart to say to him: 'The blood is already so deep in the lands that nothing we can do will now wash it out.' But I did not say this. I do not know how it was, but there came before me the still, sad face of my sister, Marta, and it was as if she herself answered for me.

'Do now as it seems right to you,' I said to my father. 'Who am I that I should judge you?'

Dorothy Parker

Here We Are

The young man in the new blue suit finished arranging the glistening luggage in tight corners of the Pullman compartment. The train had leaped at curves and bounced along straightaways, rendering balance a praiseworthy achievement and a sporadic one; and the young man had pushed and hoisted and tucked and shifted the bags with concentrated care.

Nevertheless, eight minutes for the settling of two suitcases and a hat-box is a long time.

He sat down, leaning back against bristled green plush, in the seat opposite the girl in beige. She looked as new as a peeled egg. Her hat, her fur, her frock, her gloves were glossy and stiff with novelty. On the arc of the thin, slippery sole of one beige shoe was gummed a tiny oblong of white paper, printed with the price set and paid for that slipper and its fellow, and the name of the shop that had dispensed them.

She had been staring raptly out of the window, drinking in the big weathered signboards that extolled the phenomena of codfish without bones and screens no rust could corrupt. As the young man sat down, she turned politely from the pane, met his eyes, started a smile and got it about half done, and rested her gaze just above his right shoulder.

'Well!' the young man said.

'Well!' she said.

'Well, here we are,' he said.

'Here we are,' she said. 'Aren't we?'

'I should say we were,' he said. 'Eeyop. Here we are.'

'Well!' she said.

'Well!' he said. 'Well. How does it feel to be an old married lady?'

'Oh, it's too soon to ask me that,' she said. 'At least—I mean. Well, I mean, goodness, we've only been married about three hours, haven't we?'

The young man studied his wrist-watch as if he were just acquiring the knack of reading time.

'We have been married,' he said, 'exactly two hours and twenty-six minutes.'

'My,' she said. 'It seems like longer.'

'No,' he said. 'It isn't hardly half-past six yet.'

'It seems like later,' she said. 'I guess it's because it starts getting dark so early.'

'It does, at that,' he said. 'The nights are going to be pretty long from now on. I mean. I mean—well, it starts getting dark early.'

'I didn't have any idea what time it was,' she said. 'Everything was so mixed up, I sort of don't know where I am, or what it's all about. Getting back from the church, and then all those people, and then changing all my clothes, and then everybody throwing things, and all. Goodness, I don't see how people do it every day.'

'Do what?' he said.

'Get married,' she said. 'When you think of all the people, all over the world, getting married just as if it was nothing. Chinese people and everybody. Just as if it wasn't anything.'

'Well, let's not worry about people all over the world,' he said. 'Let's don't think about a lot of Chinese. We've got something better to think about. I mean. I mean—well, what do we care about them?'

'I know,' she said. 'But I just sort of got to thinking of them, all of them, all over everywhere, doing it all the time. At least, I mean—getting married, you know. And it's—well, it's sort of such a big thing to do, it makes you feel queer. You think of them, all of them, all doing it just like it wasn't anything. And how does anybody know what's going to happen next?'

'Let them worry,' he said. 'We don't have to. We know darn well what's going to happen next. I mean. I mean—well, we know it's going to be great. Well, we know we're going to be happy. Don't we?'

'Oh, of course,' she said. 'Only you think of all the people, and you have to sort of keep thinking. It makes you feel funny. An awful lot of people that get married, it doesn't turn out so well. And I guess they all must have thought it was going to be great.'

'Come on, now,' he said. 'This is no way to start a honeymoon, with all this thinking going on. Look at us—all married and everything done. I mean. The wedding all done and all.'

'Ah, it was nice, wasn't it?' she said. 'Did you really like my veil?'

'You looked great,' he said. 'Just great.'

'Oh, I'm terribly glad,' she said. 'Ellie and Louise looked lovely, didn't they? I'm terribly glad they did finally decide on pink. They looked perfectly lovely.'

'Listen,' he said. 'I want to tell you something. When I was standing up there in that old church waiting for you to come up, and I saw those two bridesmaids, I thought to myself, I thought, "Well, I never knew Louise could look like that!" Why, she'd have knocked anybody's eye out.'

'Oh, really?' she said. 'Funny. Of course, everybody thought her dress and hat were lovely, but a lot of people seemed to think she looked sort of tired. People have been saying that a lot, lately. I tell them I think it's awfully mean of them to go around saying that about her. I tell them they've got to remember that Louise isn't so terribly young any more, and they've got to expect her to look like that. Louise can say she's twenty-three all she wants to, but she's a good deal nearer twenty-seven.'

'Well, she was certainly a knock-out at the wedding,' he said. 'Boy!'

'I'm terribly glad you thought so,' she said. 'I'm glad someone did. How did you think Ellie looked?'

'Why, I honestly didn't get a look at her,' he said.

'Oh, really?' she said. 'Well, I certainly think that's too bad. I don't suppose I ought to say it about my own sister, but I never saw anybody look as beautiful as Ellie looked today. And always so sweet and unselfish, too. And you didn't even notice her. But you never pay attention to Ellie, anyway. Don't think I haven't noticed it. It makes me feel just terrible. It makes me feel just awful, that you don't like my own sister.'

'I do like her!' he said. 'I'm crazy for Ellie. I think she's a great kid.'

'Don't think it makes any difference to Ellie!' she said. 'Ellie's got enough people crazy about her. It isn't anything to her whether you like her or not. Don't flatter yourself she cares! Only, the only thing is, it makes it awfully hard for me you don't like her, that's the only thing. I keep thinking, when we come back and get in that apartment and everything, it's going to be awfully hard for me that you won't want my own sister to come and see me. It's going to make it awfully hard for me that you won't ever want my family around. I know how you feel about my family. Don't think I haven't seen it. Only, if you don't ever want to see them, that's your loss. Not theirs. Don't flatter yourself!'

'Oh, now, come on!' he said. 'What's all this talk about not wanting your family around? Why, you know how I feel about your family. I think your old lady—I think your mother's swell. And Ellie. And your father. What's all this talk?'

'Well, I've seen it,' she said. 'Don't think I haven't. Lots of people they get married, and they think it's going to be great and everything, and then it all goes to pieces because people don't like people's families, or something like that. Don't tell me! I've seen it happen.'

'Honey,' he said, 'what is all this? What are you getting all angry about? Hey, look, this is our honeymoon. What are you trying to start a fight for? Ah, I guess you're just feeling sort of nervous.'

'Me?' she said. 'What have I got to be nervous about? I mean. I mean, goodness, I'm not nervous.'

'You know, lots of times,' he said, 'they say that girls get kind of nervous and yippy on account of thinking about—I mean. I mean— well, it's like you said, things are all so sort of mixed up and everything, right now. But afterwards, it'll be all right. I mean. I mean—well, look, honey, you don't look any too comfortable. Don't you want to take your hat off? And let's don't ever fight, ever. Will we?'

'Ah, I'm sorry I was cross,' she said. 'I guess I did feel a little bit funny. All mixed up, and then thinking of all those people all over everywhere, and then being sort of 'way off here, all alone with you. It's so sort of different. It's sort of such a big thing. You can't blame a person for thinking, can you? Yes, don't let's ever, ever fight. We won't be like a whole lot of them. We won't fight or be nasty or anything. Will we?'

'You bet your life we won't,' he said.

'I guess I will take this darned old hat off,' she said. 'It kind of presses. Just put it up on the rack, will you, dear? Do you like it, sweetheart?'

'Looks good on you,' he said.

'No, but I mean,' she said, 'do you really like it?'

'Well, I'll tell you,' he said. 'I know this is the new style and everything like that, and it's probably great. I don't know anything

28

about things like that. Only I like the kind of a hat like that blue hat you had. Gee, I liked that hat.'

'Oh, really?' she said. 'Well, that's nice. That's lovely. The first thing you say to me, as soon as you get me off on a train away from my family and everything, is that you don't like my hat. The first thing you say to your wife is you think she has terrible taste in hats. That's nice, isn't it?'

'Now, honey,' he said, 'I never said anything like that. I only said—'

'What you don't seem to realize,' she said, 'is this hat cost twenty-two dollars. Twenty-two dollars. And that horrible old blue thing you think you're so crazy about, that cost three ninety-five.'

'I don't give a darn what they cost,' he said. 'I only said—I said I liked that blue hat. I don't know anything about hats. I'll be crazy about this one as soon as I get used to it. Only it's kind of not like your other hats. I don't know about the new styles. What do I know about women's hats?'

'It's too bad,' she said, 'you didn't marry somebody that would get the kind of hats you'd like. Hats that cost three ninety-five. Why didn't you marry Louise? You always think she looks so beautiful. You'd love her taste in hats. Why didn't you marry her?'

'Ah, now, honey,' he said. 'For heaven's sakes!'

'Why didn't you marry her?' she said. 'All you've done, ever since we got on this train, is talk about her. Here I've sat and sat, and just listened to you saying how wonderful Louise is. I suppose that's nice, getting me all off here alone with you, and then raving about Louise right in front of my face. Why didn't you ask her to marry you? I'm sure she would have jumped at the chance. There aren't so many people asking her to marry them. It's too bad you didn't marry her. I'm sure you'd have been much happier.'

'Listen, baby,' he said, 'while you're talking about things like that, why didn't you marry Joe Brooks? I suppose he could have given you all the twenty-two-dollar hats you wanted, I suppose!'

'Well, I'm not so sure I'm not sorry I didn't,' she said. 'There! Joe Brooks wouldn't have waited until he got me all off alone and then sneered at my taste in clothes. Joe Brooks wouldn't ever hurt my feelings. Joe Brooks has always been fond of me. There!'

'Yeah,' he said. 'He's fond of you. He was so fond of you he didn't even send a wedding present. That's how fond of you he was.'

'I happen to know for a fact,' she said, 'that he was away on business, and as soon as he comes back he's going to give me anything I want, for the apartment.'

'Listen,' he said. 'I don't want anything he gives you in our apartment. Anything he gives you, I'll throw right out the window. That's what I think of your friend Joe Brooks. And how do you know where he is and what he's going to do, anyway? Has he been writing to you?'

'I suppose my friends can correspond with me,' she said. 'I didn't hear there was any law against that.'

'Well, I suppose they can't!' he said. 'And what do you think of that? I'm not going to have my wife getting a lot of letters from cheap travelling salesmen!'

'Joe Brooks is not a cheap travelling salesman!' she said. 'He is not! He gets a wonderful salary.'

'Oh yeah?' he said. 'Where did you hear that?'

'He told me so himself,' she said.

'Oh, he told you so himself,' he said. 'I see. He told you so himself.'

'You've got a lot of right to talk about Joe Brooks,' she said. 'You and your friend Louise. All you ever talk about is Louise.'

'Oh, for heaven's sakes!' he said. 'What do I care about Louise? I just thought she was a friend of yours, that's all. That's why I ever even noticed her.'

'Well, you certainly took an awful lot of notice of her today,' she said. 'On our wedding day! You said yourself when you were standing there in the church you just kept thinking of her. Right up at the altar. Oh, right in the presence of God! And all you thought about was Louise.'

'Listen, honey,' he said, 'I never should have said that. How does anybody know what kind of crazy things come into their heads when they're standing there waiting to get married? I was just telling you that because it was so kind of crazy. I thought it would make you laugh.'

'I know,' she said. 'I've been all sort of mixed up today, too. I told you that. Everything so strange and everything. And me all the time thinking about all those people all over the world, and now us here all alone, and everything. I know you get all mixed up. Only I did think, when you kept talking about how beautiful Louise looked, you did it with malice and forethought.'

'I never did anything with malice and forethought!' he said. 'I just told you that about Louise because I thought it would make you laugh.'

'Well, it didn't,' she said.

'No, I know it didn't,' he said. 'It certainly did not. Ah, baby, and we ought to be laughing, too. Hell, honey lamb, this is our honeymoon. What's the matter?'

'I don't know,' she said. 'We used to squabble a lot when we were going together and then engaged and everything, but I thought everything would be so different as soon as you were married. And now I feel so sort of strange and everything. I feel so sort of alone.'

'Well, you see, sweetheart,' he said, 'we're not really married yet. I mean. I mean—well, things will be different afterwards. Oh, hell. I mean, we haven't been married very long.'

'No,' she said.

'Well, we haven't got much longer to wait now,' he said. 'I mean—well, we'll be in New York in about twenty minutes. Then we can have dinner, and sort of see what we feel like doing. Or I mean. Is there anything special you want to do tonight?'

'What?' she said.

'What I mean to say,' he said, 'would you like to go to a show or something?'

'Why, whatever you like,' she said. 'I sort of didn't think people went to theatres and things on their—I mean, I've got a couple of letters I simply must write. Don't let me forget.'

'Oh,' he said. 'You're going to write letters tonight?'

'Well, you see,' she said. 'I've been perfectly terrible. What with all the excitement and everything. I never did thank poor old Mrs Sprague for her berry spoon, and I never did a thing about those book ends the McMasters sent. It's just too awful of me. I've got to write them this very night.'

'And when you've finished writing your letters,' he said, 'maybe I could get you a magazine or a bag of peanuts.'

'What?' she said.

'I mean,' he said, 'I wouldn't want you to be bored.'

'As if I could be bored with you!' she said. 'Silly! Aren't we married? Bored!'

'What I thought,' he said, 'I thought when we got in, we could go right up to the Biltmore and anyway leave our bags, and maybe have a little dinner in the room, kind of quiet, and then do whatever we wanted. I mean. I mean—well, let's go right up there from the station.'

'Oh, yes, let's,' she said. 'I'm so glad we're going to the Biltmore. I just love it. The twice I've stayed in New York we've always stayed there, Papa and Mamma and Ellie and I, and I was crazy about it. I always sleep so well there. I go right off to sleep the minute I put my head on the pillow.'

'Oh, you do?' he said.

'At least, I mean,' she said. 'Way up high it's so quiet.'

'We might go to some show or other tomorrow night instead of tonight,' he said. 'Don't you think that would be better?'

'Yes, I think it might,' she said.

He rose, balanced a moment, crossed over and sat down beside her.

'Do you really have to write those letters tonight?' he said.

'Well,' she said, 'I don't suppose they'd get there any quicker than if I wrote them tomorrow.'

There was a silence with things going on in it.

'And we won't ever fight any more, will we?' he said.

'Oh, no,' she said. 'Not ever! I don't know what made me do like that. It all got so sort of funny, sort of like a nightmare, the way I got thinking of all those people getting married all the time; and so many of them, everything spoils on account of fighting and everything. I got all mixed up thinking about them. Oh, I don't want to be like them. But we won't be, will we?'

'Sure we won't,' he said.

'We won't go all to pieces,' she said. 'We won't fight. It'll all be different, now we're married. It'll all be lovely. Reach me down my hat, will you, sweetheart? It's time I was putting it on. Thanks. Ah, I'm so sorry you don't like it.'

'I do so like it!' he said.

'You said you didn't,' she said. 'You said you thought it was perfectly terrible.'

'I never said any such thing,' he said. 'You're crazy.'

'All right, I may be crazy,' she said. 'Thank you very much. But that's what you said. Not that it matters—it's just a little thing. But it makes you feel pretty funny to think you've gone and married somebody that says you have perfectly terrible taste in hats. And then goes and says you're crazy, beside.'

'Now, listen here,' he said. 'Nobody said any such thing. Why, I love that hat. The more I look at it the better I like it. I think it's great.'

'That isn't what you said before,' she said.

'Honey,' he said. 'Stop it, will you? What do you want to start all this for? I love the damned hat. I mean, I love your hat. I love anything you wear. What more do you want me to say?'

'Well, I don't want you to say it like that,' she said.

'I said I think it's great,' he said. 'That's all I said.'

'Do you really?' she said. 'Do you honestly? Ah, I'm so glad. I'd hate you not to like my hat. It would be—I don't know, it would be sort of such a bad start.'

'Well, I'm crazy for it,' he said. 'Now we've got that settled, for heaven's sakes. Ah, baby. Baby lamb. We're not going to have any bad starts. Look at us—we're on our honeymoon. Pretty soon we'll be regular old married people. I mean. I mean, in a few minutes we'll be getting in to New York, and then we'll be going to the hotel, and then everything will be all right. I mean—well, look at us! Here we are married! Here we are!'

'Yes, here we are,' she said. 'Aren't we?'

WILLA CATHER

Coming, Aphrodite!

I

Don Hedger had lived for four years on the top floor of an old house on the south side of Washington Square, and nobody had ever disturbed him. He occupied one big room with no outside exposure except on the north, where he had built in a many-paned studio window that looked upon a court and upon the roofs and walls of other buildings. His room was very cheerless, since he never got a ray of direct sunlight; the south corners were always in shadow. In one of the corners was a clothes closet, built against the partition, in another a wide divan, serving as a seat by day and a bed by night. In the front corner, the one farther from the window, was a sink, and a table with two gas burners where he sometimes cooked his food. There, too, in the perpetual dusk, was the dog's bed, and often a bone or two for his comfort.

The dog was a Boston bull terrier, and Hedger explained his surly disposition by the fact that he had been bred to the point where it told on his nerves. His name was Caesar III, and he had taken prizes at very exclusive dog shows. When he and his master went out to prowl about University Place or to promenade along West Street, Caesar III was invariably fresh and shining. His pink skin showed through his mottled coat, which glistened as if it had just been rubbed with olive oil, and he wore a brass-studded collar, bought at the smartest saddler's. Hedger, as often as not, was hunched up in an old striped blanket coat, with a shapeless felt hat pulled over his bushy hair, wearing black shoes that had become grey, or brown ones that had become black, and he never put on gloves unless the day was biting cold.

Early in May, Hedger learned that he was to have a new neighbour in the rear apartment—two rooms, one large and one small, that faced the west. His studio was shut off from the larger of these rooms by double doors, which, though they were fairly tight, left him a good deal at the mercy of the occupant. The rooms had been leased, long before he came there, by a trained nurse who

34

considered herself knowing in old furniture. She went to auction sales and bought up mahogany and dirty brass and stored it away here, where she meant to live when she retired from nursing. Meanwhile, she sub-let her rooms, with their precious furniture, to young people who came to New York to 'write' or to 'paint'—who proposed to live by the sweat of the brow rather than of the hand, and who desired artistic surroundings. When Hedger first moved in, these rooms were occupied by a young man who tried to write plays,—and who kept on trying until a week ago, when the nurse had put him out for unpaid rent.

A few days after the playwright left, Hedger heard an ominous murmur of voices through the bolted double doors: the lady-like intonation of the nurse—doubtless exhibiting her treasures—and another voice, also a woman's, but very different; young, fresh, unguarded, confident. All the same, it would be very annoying to have a woman in there. The only bathroom on the floor was at the top of the stairs in the front hall, and he would always be running into her as he came or went from his bath. He would have to be more careful to see that Caesar didn't leave bones about the hall, too; and she might object when he cooked steak and onions on his gas burner.

As soon as the talking ceased and the women left, he forgot them. He was absorbed in a study of paradise fish at the Aquarium, staring out at people through the glass and green water of their tank. It was a highly gratifying idea; the incommunicability of one stratum of animal life with another,—though Hedger pretended it was only an experiment in unusual lighting. When he heard trunks knocking against the sides of the narrow hall, then he realized that she was moving in at once. Toward noon, groans and deep gasps and the creaking of ropes, made him aware that a piano was arriving. After the tramp of the movers died away down the stairs, somebody touched off a few scales and chords on the instrument, and then there was peace. Presently he heard her lock her door and go down the hall humming something; going out to lunch, probably. He stuck his brushes in a can of turpentine and put on his hat, not stopping to wash his hands. Caesar was smelling along the crack under the bolted doors; his bony tail stuck out hard as a hickory withe, and the hair was standing up about his elegant collar.

Hedger encouraged him. 'Come along, Caesar. You'll soon get used to a new smell.'

In the hall stood an enormous trunk, behind the ladder that led to the roof, just opposite Hedger's door. The dog flew at it with a growl of hurt amazement. They went down three flights of stairs and out into the brilliant May afternoon.

Behind the Square, Hedger and his dog descended into a basement oyster house where there were no tablecloths on the tables and no handles on the coffee cups, and the floor was covered with sawdust, and Caesar was always welcome,—not that he needed any such precautionary flooring. All the carpets of Persia would have been safe for him. Hedger ordered steak and onions absent-mindedly, not realizing why he had an apprehension that this dish might be less readily at hand hereafter. While he ate, Caesar sat beside his chair, gravely disturbing the sawdust with his tail.

After lunch Hedger strolled about the Square for the dog's health and watched the stages pull out;—that was almost the very last summer of the old horse stages on Fifth Avenue. The fountain had but lately begun operations for the season and was throwing up a mist of rainbow water which now and then blew south and sprayed a bunch of Italian babies that were being supported on the outer rim by older, very little older, brothers and sisters. Plump robins were hopping about on the soil; the grass was newly cut and blindingly green. Looking up the Avenue through the Arch, one could see the young poplars with their bright, sticky leaves, and the Brevoort glistening in its spring coat of paint, and shining horses and carriages,—occasionally an automobile, misshapen and sullen, like an ugly threat in a stream of things that were bright and beautiful and alive.

While Caesar and his master were standing by the fountain, a girl approached them, crossing the Square. Hedger noticed her because she wore a lavender cloth suit and carried in her arms a big bunch of fresh lilacs. He saw that she was young and handsome,—beautiful, in fact, with a splendid figure and good action. She, too, paused by the fountain and looked back through the Arch up the Avenue. She smiled rather patronizingly as she looked, and at the same time seemed delighted. Her slowly curving upper lip and half-closed eyes seemed to say: 'You're gay, you're exciting, you are quite the right sort of thing; but you're none too fine for me.'

In the moment she tarried, Caesar stealthily approached her and sniffed at the hem of her lavender skirt, then, when she went south like an arrow, he ran back to his master and lifted a face full of emotion and alarm, his lower lip twitching under his sharp white teeth and his hazel eyes pointed with a very definite discovery. He stood thus, motionless, while Hedger watched the lavender girl go up the steps and through the door of the house in which he lived.

'You're right, my boy, it's she! She might be worse looking, you know.'

When they mounted to the studio, the new lodger's door, at the back of the hall, was a little ajar, and Hedger caught the warm perfume of lilacs just brought in out of the sun. He was used to the musty smell of the old hall carpet. (The nurse-lessee had once knocked at his studio door and complained that Caesar must be somewhat responsible for the particular flavour of that mustiness, and Hedger had never spoken to her since.) He was used to the old smell, and he preferred it to that of the lilacs, and so did his companion, whose nose was so much more discriminating. Hedger shut his door vehemently, and fell to work.

Most young men who dwell in obscure studios in New York have had a beginning, come out of something, have somewhere a home town, a family, a paternal roof. But Don Hedger had no such background. He was a foundling, and had grown up in a school for homeless boys, where book-learning was a negligible part of the curriculum. When he was sixteen, a Catholic priest took him to Greensburg, Pennsylvania, to keep house for him. The priest did something to fill in the large gaps in the boy's education,—taught him to like 'Don Quixote' and 'The Golden Legend', and encouraged him to mess with paints and crayons in his room up under the slope of the mansard. When Don wanted to go to New York to study at the Art League, the priest got him a night job as packer in one of the big department stores. Since then, Hedger had taken care of himself; that was his only responsibility. He was singularly unencumbered; had no family duties, no social ties, no obligations toward anyone but his landlord. Since he travelled light, he had travelled rather far. He had got over a good deal of the earth's surface, in spite of the fact that he never in his life had more than three hundred dollars ahead at any one time, and he had already outlived a succession of convictions and revelations about his art.

Though he was not but twenty-six years old, he had twice been on the verge of becoming a marketable product; once through some studies of New York streets he did for a magazine, and once through a collection of pastels he brought home from New Mexico, which Remington, then at the height of his popularity, happened to see, and generously tried to push. But on both occasions Hedger decided that this was something he didn't wish to carry further,— simply the old thing over again and got nowhere,—so he took enquiring dealers experiments in a 'later manner', that made them put him out of the shop. When he ran short of money, he could always get any amount of commercial work; he was an expert draughtsman and worked with lightning speed. The rest of his time he spent in groping his way from one kind of painting into another, or travelling about without luggage, like a tramp, and he was chiefly occupied with getting rid of ideas he had once thought very fine.

Hedger's circumstances, since he had moved to Washington Square, were affluent compared to anything he had ever known before. He was now able to pay advance rent and turn the key on his studio when he went away for four months at a stretch. It didn't occur to him to wish to be richer than this. To be sure, he did without a great many things other people think necessary, but he didn't miss them, because he had never had them. He belonged to no clubs, visited no houses, had no studio friends, and he ate his dinner alone in some decent little restaurant, even on Christmas and New Year's. For days together he talked to nobody but his dog and the janitress and the lame oysterman.

After he shut the door and settled down to his paradise fish on that first Tuesday in May, Hedger forgot all about his new neighbour. When the light failed, he took Caesar out for a walk. On the way home he did his marketing on West Houston Street, with a one-eyed Italian woman who always cheated him. After he had cooked his beans and scallopini, and drunk half a bottle of Chianti, he put his dishes in the sink and went up on the roof to smoke. He was the only person in the house who ever went to the roof, and he had a secret understanding with the janitress about it. He was to have 'the privilege of the roof', as she said, if he opened the heavy trapdoor on sunny days to air out the upper hall, and was watchful to close it when rain threatened. Mrs Foley was fat and dirty and hated to climb stairs,—besides, the roof was reached by a perpendicular iron ladder, definitely inaccessible to a woman of her bulk, and the iron door at the top of it was too heavy for any but Hedger's strong arm to lift. Hedger was not above medium height, but he practised with weights and dumb-bells, and in the shoulders he was as strong as a gorilla.

So Hedger had the roof to himself. He and Caesar often slept up there on hot nights, rolled in blankets he had brought home from Arizona. He mounted with Caesar under his left arm. The dog had never learned to climb a perpendicular ladder, and never did he feel so much his master's greatness and his own dependence upon him, as when he crept under his arm for this perilous ascent. Up there was even gravel to scratch in, and a dog could do whatever he liked, so long as he did not bark. It was a kind of Heaven, which no one was strong enough to reach but his great, paint-smelling master.

On this blue May night there was a slender, girlish looking young moon in the west, playing with a whole company of silver stars. Now and then one of them darted away from the group and shot off into the gauzy blue with a soft little trail of light, like laughter. Hedger and his dog were delighted when a star did this. They were quite lost in watching the glittering game, when they were suddenly diverted by a sound,—not from the stars, though it was music. It was not the Prologue to Pagliacci, which rose ever and anon on hot evenings from an Italian tenement on Thompson Street, with the gasps of the corpulent baritone who got behind it; nor was it the hurdy-gurdy man, who often played at the corner in the balmy twilight. No, this was a woman's voice, singing the tempestuous, overlapping phrases of Signor Puccini, then comparatively new in the world, but already so popular that even Hedger recognized his unmistakable gusts of breath. He looked about over the roofs; all was blue and still, with the well-built chimneys that were never used now standing up dark and mournful. He moved softly toward the yellow quadrangle where the gas from the hall shone up through the half-lifted trapdoor. Oh yes! It came up through the hole like a strong draught, a big, beautiful voice, and it sounded rather like a professional's. A piano had arrived in the morning, Hedger remembered. This might be a very great nuisance. It would be pleasant enough to listen to, if you could turn it on and off as you wished; but you couldn't. Caesar, with the gas light shining on his collar and his ugly but sensitive face, panted and looked up for information. Hedger put down a reassuring hand.

'I don't know. We can't tell yet. It may not be so bad.'

He stayed on the roof until all was still below, and finally descended, with quite a new feeling about his neighbour. Her voice, like her figure, inspired respect,—if one did not choose to call it admiration. Her door was shut, the transom was dark; nothing remained of her but the obtrusive trunk, unrightfully taking up room in the narrow hall.

II

For two days Hedger didn't see her. He was painting eight hours a day just then, and only went out to hunt for food. He noticed that she practised scales and exercises for about an hour in the morning; then she locked her door, went humming down the hall, and left him in peace. He heard her getting her coffee ready at about the same time he got his. Earlier still, she passed his room on her way to her bath. In the evening she sometimes sang, but on the whole she didn't bother him. When he was working well he did not notice anything much. The morning paper lay before his door until he reached out for his milk bottle, then he kicked the sheet inside and it lay on the floor until evening. Sometimes he read it and sometimes he did not. He forgot there was anything of importance going on in the world outside of his third floor studio. Nobody had ever taught him that he ought to be interested in other people; in the Pittsburgh steel strike, in the Fresh Air Fund, in the scandal about the Babies' Hospital. A grey wolf, living in a Wyoming canyon, would hardly have been less concerned about these things than was Don Hedger.

One morning he was coming out of the bathroom at the front end of the hall, having just given Caesar his bath and rubbed him into a glow with a heavy towel. Before the door, lying in wait for him, as it were, stood a tall figure in a flowing blue silk dressing-gown that fell away from her marble arms. In her hands she carried various accessories of the bath.

'I wish,' she said distinctly, standing in his way, 'I wish you wouldn't wash your dog in the tub. I never heard of such a thing! I've found his hair in the tub, and I've smelled a doggy smell, and now I've caught you at it. It's an outrage!'

Hedger was badly frightened. She was so tall and positive, and was fairly blazing with beauty and anger. He stood blinking, holding on to his sponge and dog-soap, feeling that he ought to bow very low to her. But what he actually said was:

'Nobody has ever objected before. I always wash the tub,—and, anyhow, he's cleaner than most people.'

'Cleaner than me?' her eyebrows went up, her white arms and neck and her fragrant person seemed to scream at him like a band of outraged nymphs. Something flashed through his mind about a man who was turned into a dog, or was pursued by dogs, because he unwittingly intruded upon the bath of beauty.

'No, I didn't mean that,' he muttered, turning scarlet under the bluish stubble of his muscular jaws. 'But I know he's cleaner than I am.'

'That I don't doubt!' Her voice sounded like a soft shivering of crystal, and with a smile of pity she drew the folds of her voluminous blue robe close about her and allowed the wretched man to pass. Even Caesar was frightened; he darted like a streak down the hall, through the door and to his own bed in the corner among the bones.

Hedger stood still in the doorway, listening to indignant sniffs and coughs and a great swishing of water about the sides of the tub. He had washed it; but as he had washed it with Caesar's sponge, it was quite possible that a few bristles remained; the dog was shedding now. The playwright had never objected, nor had the jovial illustrator who occupied the front apartment,—but he, as he admitted, 'was usually pye-eyed, when he wasn't in Buffalo'. He went home to Buffalo sometimes to rest his nerves.

It had never occurred to Hedger that anyone would mind using the tub after Caesar;—but then, he had never seen a beautiful girl caparisoned for the bath before. As soon as he beheld her standing there, he realized the unfitness of it. For that matter, she ought not to step into a tub that any other mortal had bathed in; the illustrator was sloppy and left cigarette ends on the moulding.

All morning as he worked he was gnawed by a spiteful desire to get back at her. It rankled that he had been so vanquished by her disdain. When he heard her locking her door to go out for lunch, he stepped quickly into the hall in his messy painting coat, and addressed her.

'I don't wish to be exigent, Miss,'—he had certain grand words that he used upon occasion—'but if this is your trunk, it's rather in the way here.'

'Oh, very well!' she exclaimed carelessly, dropping her keys into her handbag. 'I'll have it moved when I can get a man to do it,' and she went down the hall with her free, roving stride.

Her name, Hedger discovered from her letters, which the postman left on the table in the lower hall, was Eden Bower.

*   *   *

III

In the closet that was built against the partition separating his room from Miss Bower's, Hedger kept all his wearing apparel, some of it on hooks and hangers, some of it on the floor. When he opened his closet door now-a-days, little dust-coloured insects flew out on downy wing, and he suspected that a brood of moths were hatching in his winter overcoat. Mrs Foley, the janitress, told him to bring down all his heavy clothes and she would give them a beating and hang them in the court. The closet was in such disorder that he shunned the encounter, but one hot afternoon he set himself to the task. First he threw out a pile of forgotten laundry and tied it up in a sheet. The bundle stood as high as his middle when he had knotted the corners. Then he got his shoes and overshoes together. When he took his overcoat from its place against the partition, a long ray of yellow light shot across the dark enclosure,—a knot hole, evidently, in the high wainscoting of the west room. He had never noticed it before, and without realizing what he was doing, he stooped and squinted through it.

Yonder, in a pool of sunlight, stood his new neighbour, wholly unclad, doing exercises of some sort before a long gilt mirror. Hedger did not happen to think how unpardonable it was of him to watch her. Nudity was not improper to anyone who had worked so much from the figure, and he continued to look, simply because he had never seen a woman's body so beautiful as this one,—positively glorious in action. As she swung her arms and changed from one pivot of motion to another, muscular energy seemed to flow through her from her toes to her finger-tips. The soft flush of exercise and the gold of afternoon sun played over her flesh together, enveloped her in a luminous mist which, as she turned and twisted, made now an arm, now a shoulder, now a thigh, dissolve in pure light and instantly recover its outline with the next gesture. Hedger's fingers curved as if he were holding a crayon; mentally he was doing the whole figure in a single running line, and the charcoal seemed to explode in his hand at the point where the energy of each gesture was discharged into the whirling disc of light, from a foot or shoulder, from the up-thrust chin or the lifted breasts.

He could not have told whether he watched her for six minutes or sixteen. When her gymnastics were over, she paused to catch up a lock of hair that had come down, and examined with solicitude a little reddish mole that grew under her left arm-pit. Then, with her hand on her hip, she walked unconcernedly across the room and disappeared through the door into her bedchamber.

Disappeared—Don Hedger was crouching on his knees, staring at the golden shower which poured in through the west windows, at the lake of gold sleeping on the faded Turkish carpet. The spot was enchanted; a vision out of Alexandria, out of the remote pagan past, had bathed itself there in Helianthine fire.

When he crawled out of his closet, he stood blinking at the grey sheet stuffed with laundry, not knowing what had happened to him. He felt a little sick as he contemplated the bundle. Everything here was different; he hated the disorder of the place, the grey prison light, his old shoes and himself and all his slovenly habits. The black calico curtains that ran on wires over his big window were white with dust. There were three greasy frying pans in the sink, and the sink itself— He felt desperate. He couldn't stand this another minute. He took up an armful of winter clothes and ran down four flights into the basement.

'Mrs Foley,' he began, 'I want my room cleaned this afternoon, thoroughly cleaned. Can you get a woman for me right away?'

'Is it company you're having?' the fat, dirty janitress enquired. Mrs Foley was the widow of a useful Tammany man, and she owned real estate in Flatbush. She was huge and soft as a feather bed. Her face and arms were permanently coated with dust, grained like wood where the sweat had trickled.

'Yes, company. That's it.'

'Well, this is a queer time of the day to be asking for a cleaning woman. It's likely I can get you old Lizzie, if she's not drunk. I'll send Willy round to see.'

Willy, the son of fourteen, roused from the stupor and stain of his fifth box of cigarettes by the gleam of a quarter, went out. In five minutes he returned with old Lizzie,—she smelling strong of spirits and wearing several jackets which she had put on one over the other, and a number of skirts, long and short, which made her resemble an animated dish-clout. She had, of course, to borrow her equipment from Mrs Foley, and toiled up the long flights, dragging mop and pail and broom. She told Hedger to be of good cheer, for he had got the right woman for the job, and showed him a great leather strap she wore about her wrist to prevent dislocation of tendons. She swished about the place, scattering dust and splashing soapsuds, while he watched her in nervous despair. He stood over

43

WILLA CATHER

Lizzie and made her scour the sink, directing her roughly, then paid her and got rid of her. Shutting the door on his failure, he hurried off with his dog to lose himself among the stevedores and dock labourers on West Street.

A strange chapter began for Don Hedger. Day after day, at that hour in the afternoon, the hour before his neighbour dressed for dinner, he crouched down in his closet to watch her go through her mysterious exercises. It did not occur to him that his conduct was detestable; there was nothing shy or retreating about this unclad girl,—a bold body, studying itself quite coolly and evidently well pleased with itself, doing all this for a purpose. Hedger scarcely regarded his action as conduct at all; it was something that had happened to him. More than once he went out and tried to stay away for the whole afternoon, but at about five o'clock he was sure to find himself among his old shoes in the dark. The pull of that aperture was stronger than his will,—and he had always considered his will the strongest thing about him. When she threw herself upon the divan and lay resting, he still stared, holding his breath. His nerves were so on edge that a sudden noise made him start and brought out the sweat on his forehead. The dog would come and tug at his sleeve, knowing that something was wrong with his master. If he attempted a mournful whine, those strong hands closed about his throat.

When Hedger came slinking out of his closet, he sat down on the edge of the couch, sat for hours without moving. He was not painting at all now. This thing, whatever it was, drank him up as ideas had sometimes done, and he sank into a stupor of idleness as deep and dark as the stupor of work. He could not understand it; he was no boy, he had worked from models for years, and a woman's body was no mystery to him. Yet now he did nothing but sit and think about one. He slept very little, and with the first light of morning he awoke as completely possessed by this woman as if he had been with her all the night before. The unconscious operations of life went on in him only to perpetuate this excitement. His brain held but one image now—vibrated, burned with it. It was a heathenish feeling; without friendliness, almost without tenderness.

Women had come and gone in Hedger's life. Not having had a mother to begin with, his relations with them, whether amorous or friendly, had been casual. He got on well with janitresses and

44

wash-women, with Indians and with the peasant women of foreign countries. He had friends among the silk-skirt factory girls who came to eat their lunch in Washington Square, and he sometimes took a model for a day in the country. He felt an unreasoning antipathy toward the well-dressed women he saw coming out of big shops, or driving in the Park. If, on his way to the Art Museum, he noticed a pretty girl standing on the steps of one of the houses on upper Fifth Avenue, he frowned at her and went by with his shoulders hunched up as if he were cold. He had never known such girls, or heard them talk, or seen the inside of the houses in which they lived; but he believed them all to be artificial and, in an aesthetic sense, perverted. He saw them enslaved by desire of merchandise and manufactured articles, effective only in making life complicated and insincere and in embroidering it with ugly and meaningless trivialities. They were enough, he thought, to make one almost forget woman as she existed in art, in thought, and in the universe.

He had no desire to know the woman who had, for the time at least, so broken up his life,—no curiosity about her everyday personality. He shunned any revelation of it, and he listened for Miss Bower's coming and going, not to encounter, but to avoid her. He wished that the girl who wore shirt-waists and got letters from Chicago would keep out of his way, that she did not exist. With her he had naught to make. But in a room full of sun, before an old mirror, on a little enchanted rug of sleeping colours, he had seen a woman who emerged naked through a door, and disappeared naked. He thought of that body as never having been clad, or as having worn the stuffs and dyes of all the centuries but his own. And for him she had no geographical associations; unless with Crete, or Alexandria, or Veronese's Venice. She was the immortal conception, the perennial theme.

The first break in Hedger's lethargy occurred one afternoon when two young men came to take Eden Bower out to dine. They went into her music room, laughed and talked for a few minutes, and then took her away with them. They were gone a long while, but he did not go out for food himself; he waited for them to come back. At last he heard them coming down the hall, gayer and more talkative than when they left. One of them sat down at the piano, and they all began to sing. This Hedger found absolutely unendurable. He snatched up his hat and went running down the stairs.

Caesar leaped beside him, hoping that old times were coming back. They had supper in the oysterman's basement and then sat down in front of their own doorway. The moon stood full over the Square, a thing of regal glory; but Hedger did not see the moon; he was looking, murderously, for men. Presently two, wearing straw hats and white trousers and carrying canes, came down the steps from his house. He rose and dogged them across the Square. They were laughing and seemed very much elated about something. As one stopped to light a cigarette, Hedger caught from the other:

'Don't you think she has a beautiful talent?'

His companion threw away his match. 'She has a beautiful figure.' They both ran to catch the stage.

Hedger went back to his studio. The light was shining from her transom. For the first time he violated her privacy at night, and peered through that fatal aperture. She was sitting, fully dressed, in the window, smoking a cigarette and looking out over the house-tops. He watched her until she rose, looked about her with a disdainful, crafty smile, and turned out the light.

The next morning, when Miss Bower went out, Hedger followed her. Her white skirt gleamed ahead of him as she sauntered about the Square. She sat down behind the Garibaldi statue and opened a music book she carried. She turned the leaves carelessly, and several times glanced in his direction. He was on the point of going over to her, when she rose quickly and looked up at the sky. A flock of pigeons had risen from somewhere in the crowded Italian quarter to the south, and were wheeling rapidly up through the morning air, soaring and dropping, scattering and coming together, now grey, now white as silver, as they caught or intercepted the sunlight. She put up her hand to shade her eyes and followed them with a kind of defiant delight in her face.

Hedger came and stood beside her. 'You've surely seen them before?'

'Oh, yes,' she replied, still looking up. 'I see them every day from my windows. They always come home about five o'clock. Where do they live?'

'I don't know. Probably some Italian raises them for the market. They were here long before I came, and I've been here four years.'

'In that same gloomy room? Why didn't you take mine when it was vacant?'

'It isn't gloomy. That's the best light for painting.'

'Oh, is it? I don't know anything about painting. I'd like to see your pictures sometime. You have such a lot in there. Don't they get dusty, piled up against the wall like that?'

'Not very. I'd be glad to show them to you. Is your name really Eden Bower? I've seen your letters on the table.'

'Well, it's the name I'm going to sing under. My father's name is Bowers, but my friend Mr Jones, a Chicago newspaper man who writes about music, told me to drop the "s". He's crazy about my voice.'

Miss Bower didn't usually tell the whole story,—about anything. Her first name, when she lived in Huntington, Illinois, was Edna, but Mr Jones had persuaded her to change it to one which he felt would be worthy of her future. She was quick to take suggestions, though she told him she 'didn't see what was the matter with "Edna" '.

She explained to Hedger that she was going to Paris to study. She was waiting in New York for Chicago friends who were to take her over, but who had been detained. 'Did you study in Paris?' she asked.

'No, I've never been in Paris. But I was in the south of France all last summer, studying with C——. He's the biggest man among the moderns,—at least I think so.'

Miss Bower sat down and made room for him on the bench. 'Do tell me about it. I expected to be there by this time, and I can't wait to find out what it's like.'

Hedger began to relate how he had seen some of this Frenchman's work in an exhibition, and deciding at once that this was the man for him, he had taken a boat for Marseilles the next week, going over steerage. He proceeded at once to the little town on the coast where his painter lived, and presented himself. The man never took pupils, but because Hedger had come so far, he let him stay. Hedger lived at the master's house and every day they went out together to paint, sometimes on the blazing rocks down by the sea. They wrapped themselves in light woollen blankets and didn't feel the heat. Being there and working with C—— was being in Paradise, Hedger concluded; he learned more in three months than in all his life before.

Eden Bower laughed. 'You're a funny fellow. Didn't you do anything but work? Are the women very beautiful? Did you have awfully good things to eat and drink?'

Hedger said some of the women were fine looking, especially one girl who went about selling fish and lobsters. About the food there was nothing remarkable,—except the ripe figs, he liked those. They drank sour wine, and used goat-butter, which was strong and full of hair, as it was churned in a goat skin.

'But don't they have parties or banquets? Aren't there any fine hotels down there?'

'Yes, but they are all closed in summer, and the country people are poor. It's a beautiful country, though.'

'How, beautiful?' she persisted.

'If you want to go in, I'll show you some sketches, and you'll see.'

Miss Bower rose. 'All right. I won't go to my fencing lesson this morning. Do you fence? Here comes your dog. You can't move but he's after you. He always makes a face at me when I meet him in the hall, and shows his nasty little teeth as if he wanted to bite me.'

In the studio Hedger got out his sketches, but to Miss Bower, whose favourite pictures were Christ Before Pilate and a redhaired Magdalen of Henner, these landscapes were not at all beautiful, and they gave her no idea of any country whatsoever. She was careful not to commit herself, however. Her vocal teacher had already convinced her that she had a great deal to learn about many things.

'Why don't we go out to lunch somewhere?' Hedger asked, and began to dust his fingers with a handkerchief—which he got out of sight as swiftly as possible.

'All right, the Brevoort,' she said carelessly. 'I think that's a good place, and they have good wine. I don't care for cocktails.'

Hedger felt his chin uneasily. 'I'm afraid I haven't shaved this morning. If you could wait for me in the Square? It won't take me ten minutes.'

Left alone, he found a clean collar and handkerchief, brushed his coat and blacked his shoes, and last of all dug up ten dollars from the bottom of an old copper kettle he had brought from Spain. His winter hat was of such a complexion that the Brevoort hall boy winked at the porter as he took it and placed in on the rack in a row of fresh straw ones.

IV

That afternoon Eden Bower was lying on the couch in her music room, her face turned to the window, watching the pigeons.

Reclining thus she could see none of the neighbouring roofs, only the sky itself and the birds that crossed and recrossed her field of vision, white as scraps of paper blowing in the wind. She was thinking that she was young and handsome and had had a good lunch, that a very easy-going, light-hearted city lay in the streets below her; and she was wondering why she found this queer painter chap, with his lean, bluish cheeks and heavy black eyebrows, more interesting than the smart young men she met at her teacher's studio.

Eden Bower was, at twenty, very much the same person that we all know her to be at forty, except that she knew a great deal less. But one thing she knew: that she was to be Eden Bower. She was like someone standing before a great show window full of beautiful and costly things, deciding which she will order. She understands that they will not all be delivered immediately, but one by one they will arrive at her door. She already knew some of the many things that were to happen to her; for instance, that the Chicago millionaire who was going to take her abroad with his sister as chaperone, would eventually press his claim in quite another manner. He was the most circumspect of bachelors, afraid of everything obvious, even of women who were too flagrantly handsome. He was a nervous collector of pictures and furniture, a nervous patron of music, and a nervous host; very cautious about his health, and about any course of conduct that might make him ridiculous. But she knew that he would at last throw all his precautions to the winds.

People like Eden Bower are inexplicable. Her father sold farming machinery in Huntington, Illinois, and she had grown up with no acquaintances or experiences outside of that prairie town. Yet from her earliest childhood she had not one conviction or opinion in common with the people about her,—the only people she knew. Before she was out of short dresses she had made up her mind that she was going to be an actress, that she would live far away in great cities, that she would be much admired by men and would have everything she wanted. When she was thirteen, and was already singing and reciting for church entertainments, she read in some illustrated magazine a long article about the late Czar of Russia, then just come to the throne or about to come to it. After that, lying in the hammock on the front porch on summer evenings, or sitting through a long sermon in the family pew, she amused herself by trying to make up her mind whether she would or would not be the Czar's mistress when she played in his Capital. Now Edna had met this fascinating word only in the novels of Ouida,—her hard-worked little mother kept a long row of them in the upstairs storeroom, behind the linen chest. In Huntington, women who bore that relation to men were called by a very different name, and their lot was not an enviable one; of all the shabby and poor, they were the shabbiest. But then, Edna had never lived in Huntington, not even before she began to find books like 'Sappho' and 'Mademoiselle de Maupin', secretly sold in paper covers throughout Illinois. It was as if she had come into Huntington, into the Bowers family, on one of the trains that puffed over the marshes behind their back fence all day long, and was waiting for another train to take her out.

As she grew older and handsomer, she had many beaux, but these small-town boys didn't interest her. If a lad kissed her when he brought her home from a dance, she was indulgent and she rather liked it. But if he pressed her further, she slipped away from him, laughing. After she began to sing in Chicago, she was consistently discreet. She stayed as a guest in rich people's houses, and she knew that she was being watched like a rabbit in a laboratory. Covered up in bed, with the lights out, she thought her own thoughts, and laughed.

This summer in New York was her first taste of freedom. The Chicago capitalist, after all his arrangements were made for sailing, had been compelled to go to Mexico to look after oil interests. His sister knew an excellent singing master in New York. Why should not a discreet, well-balanced girl like Miss Bower spend the summer there, studying quietly? The capitalist suggested that his sister might enjoy a summer on Long Island; he would rent the Griffiths' place for her, with all the servants, and Eden could stay there. But his sister met this proposal with a cold stare. So it fell out, that between selfishness and greed, Eden got a summer all her own,— which really did a great deal toward making her an artist and whatever else she was afterward to become. She had time to look about, to watch without being watched; to select diamonds in one window and furs in another, to select shoulders and moustaches in the big hotels where she went to lunch. She had the easy freedom of obscurity and the consciousness of power. She enjoyed both. She was in no hurry.

While Eden Bower watched the pigeons, Don Hedger sat on the other side of the bolted doors, looking into a pool of dark turpentine, at his idle brushes, wondering why a woman could do this to him. He, too, was sure of his future and knew that he was a chosen man. He could not know, of course, that he was merely the first to fall under a fascination which was to be disastrous to a few men and pleasantly stimulating to many thousands. Each of these two young people sensed the future, but not completely. Don Hedger knew that nothing much would ever happen to him. Eden Bower understood that to her a great deal would happen. But she did not guess that her neighbour would have more tempestuous adventures sitting in his dark studio than she would find in all the capitals of Europe, or in all the latitude of conduct she was prepared to permit herself.

V

One Sunday morning Eden was crossing the Square with a spruce young man in a white flannel suit and a panama hat. They had been breakfasting at the Brevoort and he was coaxing her to let him come up to her rooms and sing for an hour.

'No, I've got to write letters. You must run along now. I see a friend of mine over there, and I want to ask him about something before I go up.'

'That fellow with the dog? Where did you pick him up?' the young man glanced toward the seat under a sycamore where Hedger was reading the morning paper.

'Oh, he's an old friend from the West,' said Eden easily. 'I won't introduce you, because he doesn't like people. He's a recluse. Good-bye. I can't be sure about Tuesday. I'll go with you if I have time after my lesson.' She nodded, left him, and went over to the seat littered with newspapers. The young man went up the Avenue without looking back.

'Well, what are you going to do today? Shampoo this animal all morning?' Eden enquired teasingly.

Hedger made room for her on the seat. 'No, at twelve o'clock I'm going out to Coney Island. One of my models is going up in a balloon this afternoon. I've often promised to go and see her, and now I'm going.'

Eden asked if models usually did such stunts. No, Hedger told her, but Molly Welch added to her earnings in that way. 'I believe,' he added, 'she likes the excitement of it. She's got a good deal of spirit. That's why I like to paint her. So many models have flaccid bodies.'

'And she hasn't, eh? Is she the one who comes to see you? I can't help hearing her, she talks so loud.'

'Yes, she has a rough voice, but she's a fine girl. I don't suppose you'd be interested in going?'

'I don't know.' Eden sat tracing patterns on the asphalt with the end of her parasol. 'Is it any fun? I got up feeling I'd like to do something different today. It's the first Sunday I've not had to sing in church. I had that engagement for breakfast at the Brevoort, but it wasn't very exciting. That chap can't talk about anything but himself.'

Hedger warmed a little. 'If you've never been to Coney Island, you ought to go. It's nice to see all the people; tailors and bartenders and prize-fighters with their best girls, and all sorts of folks taking a holiday.'

Eden looked sidewise at him. So one ought to be interested in people of that kind, ought one? He was certainly a funny fellow. Yet he was never, somehow, tiresome. She had seen a good deal of him lately, but she kept wanting to know him better, to find out what made him different from men like the one she had just left—whether he really was as different as he seemed. 'I'll go with you,' she said at last, 'if you'll leave that at home.' She pointed to Caesar's flickering ears with her sunshade.

'But he's half the fun. You'd like to hear him bark at the waves when they come in.'

'No, I wouldn't. He's jealous and disagreeable if he sees you talking to anyone else. Look at him now.'

'Of course, if you make a face at him. He knows what that means, and he makes a worse face. He likes Molly Welch, and she'll be disappointed if I don't bring him.'

Eden said decidedly that he couldn't take both of them. So at twelve o'clock when she and Hedger got on the boat at Desbrosses Street, Caesar was lying on his pallet, with a bone.

Eden enjoyed the boat-ride. It was the first time she had been on the water, and she felt as if she were embarking for France. The light warm breeze and the plunge of the waves made her very wide awake, and she liked crowds of any kind. They went to the balcony of a big, noisy restaurant and had a shore dinner, with tall steins of beer. Hedger had got a big advance from his advertising firm since he first lunched with Miss Bower ten days ago, and he was ready for anything.

After dinner they went to the tent behind the bathing beach, where the tops of two balloons bulged out over the canvas. A red-faced man in a linen suit stood in front of the tent, shouting in a hoarse voice and telling the people that if the crowd was good for five dollars more, a beautiful young woman would risk her life for their entertainment. Four little boys in dirty red uniforms ran about taking contributions in their pill-box hats. One of the balloons was bobbing up and down in its tether and people were shoving forward to get nearer the tent.

'Is it dangerous, as he pretends?' Eden asked.

'Molly says it's simple enough if nothing goes wrong with the balloon. Then it would be all over, I suppose.'

'Wouldn't you like to go up with her?'

'I? Of course not. I'm not fond of taking foolish risks.'

Eden sniffed. 'I shouldn't think sensible risks would be very much fun.'

Hedger did not answer, for just then everyone began to shove the other way and shout, 'Look out. There she goes!' and a band of six pieces commenced playing furiously.

As the balloon rose from its tent enclosure, they saw a girl in green tights standing in the basket, holding carelessly to one of the ropes with one hand and with the other waving to the spectators. A long rope trailed behind to keep the balloon from blowing out to sea.

As it soared, the figure in green tights in the basket diminished to a mere spot, and the balloon itself, in the brilliant light, looked like a big silver-grey bat, with its wings folded. When it began to sink, the girl stepped through the hole in the basket to a trapeze that hung below, and gracefully descended through the air, holding to the rod with both hands, keeping her body taut and her feet close together. The crowd, which had grown very large by this time, cheered vociferously. The men took off their hats and waved, little boys shouted, and fat old women, shining with the heat and a beer lunch, murmured admiring comments upon the balloonist's figure. 'Beautiful legs, she has!'

'That's so,' Hedger whispered. 'Not many girls would look well in that position.' Then, for some reason, he blushed a slow, dark, painful crimson.

The balloon descended slowly, a little way from the tent, and the red-faced man in the linen suit caught Molly Welch before her feet touched the ground, and pulled her to one side. The band struck up 'Blue Bell' by way of welcome, and one of the sweaty pages ran forward and presented the ballonist with a large bouquet of artificial flowers. She smiled and thanked him, and ran back across the sand to the tent.

'Can't we go inside and see her?' Eden asked. 'You can explain to the door man. I want to meet her.' Edging forward, she herself addressed the man in the linen suit and slipped something from her purse into his hand.

They found Molly seated before a trunk that had a mirror in the lid and a 'make-up' outfit spread upon the tray. She was wiping the cold cream and powder from her neck with a discarded chemise.

'Hello, Don,' she said cordially. 'Brought a friend?'

Eden liked her. She had an easy, friendly manner, and there was something boyish and devil-may-care about her.

'Yes, it's fun. I'm mad about it,' she said in reply to Eden's questions. 'I always want to let go, when I come down on the bar. You don't feel your weight at all, as you would on a stationary trapeze.'

The big drum boomed outside, and the publicity man began shouting to newly arrived boatloads. Miss Welch took a last pull at her cigarette. 'Now you'll have to get out, Don. I change for the next act. This time I go up in a black evening dress, and lose the skirt in the basket before I start down.'

'Yes, go along,' said Eden. 'Wait for me outside the door. I'll stay and help her dress.'

Hedger waited and waited, while women of every build bumped into him and begged his pardon, and the red pages ran about holding out their caps for coins, and the people ate and perspired and shifted parasols against the sun. When the band began to play a two-step, all the bathers ran up out of the surf to watch the ascent. The second balloon bumped and rose, and the crowd began shouting to the girl in a black evening dress who stood leaning against the ropes and smiling. 'It's a new girl,' they called. 'It ain't the-Countess this time. You're a peach, girlie!'

The balloonist acknowledged these compliments, bowing and looking down over the sea of upturned faces,—but Hedger was determined she should not see him, and he darted behind the tent-fly. He was suddenly dripping with cold sweat, his mouth was full of the bitter taste of anger and his tongue felt stiff behind his teeth. Molly Welch, in a shirt-waist and a white tam-o'-shanter cap, slipped out from the tent under his arm and laughed up in his face. 'She's a crazy one you brought along. She'll get what she wants!'

'Oh, I'll settle with you, all right!' Hedger brought out with difficulty.

'It's not my fault, Donnie. I couldn't do anything with her. She bought me off. What's the matter with you? Are you soft on her? She's safe enough. It's as easy as rolling off a log, if you keep cool.' Molly Welch was rather excited herself, and she was chewing gum at a high speed as she stood beside him, looking up at the floating silver cone. 'Now watch,' she exclaimed suddenly. 'She's coming down on the bar. I advised her to cut that out, but you see she does it first-rate. And she got rid of the skirt, too. Those black tights show off her legs very well. She keeps her feet together like I told her, and makes a good line along the back. See the light on those silver slippers,—that was a good idea I had. Come along to meet her. Don't be a grouch; she's done it fine!'

Molly tweaked his elbow, and then left him standing like a stump, while she ran down the beach with the crowd.

Though Hedger was sulking, his eye could not help seeing the low blue welter of the sea, the arrested bathers, standing in the surf, their arms and legs stained red by the dropping sun, all shading their eyes and gazing upward at the slowly falling silver star.

Molly Welch and the manager caught Eden under the arms and lifted her aside, a red page dashed up with a bouquet, and the band struck up 'Blue Bell'. Eden laughed and bowed, took Molly's arm, and ran up the sand in her black tights and silver slippers, dodging the friendly old women, and the gallant sports who wanted to offer their homage on the spot.

When she emerged from the tent, dressed in her own clothes, that part of the beach was almost deserted. She stepped to her companion's side and said carelessly: 'Hadn't we better try to catch this boat? I hope you're not sore at me. Really, it was lots of fun.'

Hedger looked at his watch. 'Yes, we have fifteen minutes to get to the boat,' he said politely.

As they walked toward the pier, one of the pages ran up panting. 'Lady, you're carrying off the bouquet,' he said, aggrievedly.

Eden stopped and looked at the bunch of spotty cotton roses in her hand. 'Of course. I want them for a souvenir. You gave them to me yourself.'

'I give 'em to you for looks, but you can't take 'em away. They belong to the show.'

'Oh, you always use the same bunch?'

'Sure we do. There ain't too much money in this business.'

She laughed and tossed them back to him. 'Why are you angry?' she asked Hedger. 'I wouldn't have done it if I'd been with some fellows, but I thought you were the sort who wouldn't mind. Molly didn't for a minute think you would.'

'What possessed you to do such a fool thing?' he asked roughly.

'I don't know. When I saw her coming down, I wanted to try it. It looked exciting. Didn't I hold myself as well as she did?'

Hedger shrugged his shoulders, but in his heart he forgave her.

The return boat was not crowded, though the boats that passed them, going out, were packed to the rails. The sun was setting. Boys and girls sat on the long benches with their arms about each other, singing. Eden felt a strong wish to propitiate her companion, to be alone with him. She had been curiously wrought up by her balloon trip; it was a lark, but not very satisfying unless one came back to something after the flight. She wanted to be admired and adored. Though Eden said nothing, and sat with her arms limp on the rail in front of her, looking languidly at the rising silhouette of the city and the bright path of the sun, Hedger felt a strange drawing near to her. If he but brushed her white skirt with his knee, there was an instant communication between them, such as there had never been before. They did not talk at all, but when they went over the gangplank she took his arm and kept her shoulder close to his. He felt as if they were enveloped in a highly charged atmosphere, an invisible network of subtle, almost painful sensibility. They had somehow taken hold of each other.

An hour later, they were dining in the back garden of a little French hotel on Ninth Street, long since passed away. It was cool and leafy there, and the mosquitoes were not very numerous. A party of South Americans at another table were drinking champagne, and Eden murmured that she thought she would like some, if it were not too expensive. 'Perhaps it will make me think I am in the balloon again. That was a very nice feeling. You've forgiven me, haven't you?'

Hedger gave her a quick straight look from under his black

eyebrows, and something went over her that was like a chill, except that it was warm and feathery. She drank most of the wine; her companion was indifferent to it. He was talking more to her tonight than he had ever done before. She asked him about a new picture she had seen in his room; a queer thing full of stiff, supplicating female figures. 'It's Indian, isn't it?'

'Yes. I call it Rain Spirits, or maybe, Indian Rain. In the Southwest, where I've been a good deal, the Indian traditions make women have to do with the rain-fall. They were supposed to control it, somehow, and to be able to find springs, and make moisture come out of the earth. You see I'm trying to learn to paint what people think and feel; to get away from all that photographic stuff. When I look at you, I don't see what a camera would see, do I?'

'How can I tell?'

'Well, if I should paint you, I could make you understand what I see.' For the second time that day Hedger crimsoned unexpectedly, and his eyes fell and steadily contemplated a dish of little radishes. 'That particular picture I got from a story a Mexican priest told me; he said he found it in an old manuscript book in a monastery down there, written by some Spanish Missionary, who got his stories from the Aztecs. This one he called "The Forty Lovers of the Queen", and it was more or less about rain-making.'

'Aren't you going to tell it to me?' Eden asked.

Hedger fumbled among the radishes. 'I don't know if it's the proper kind of story to tell a girl.'

She smiled; 'Oh, forget about that! I've been balloon riding today. I like to hear you talk.'

Her low voice was flattering. She had seemed like clay in his hands ever since they got on the boat to come home. He leaned back in his chair, forgot his food, and, looking at her intently, began to tell his story, the theme of which he somehow felt was dangerous tonight.

The tale began, he said, somewhere in Ancient Mexico, and concerned the daughter of a king. The birth of this Princess was preceded by unusual portents. Three times her mother dreamed that she was delivered of serpents, which betokened that the child she carried would have power with the rain gods. The serpent was the symbol of water. The Princess grew up dedicated to the gods, and wise men taught her the rain-making mysteries. She was with difficulty restrained from men and was guarded at all times, for it was the law of the Thunder that she be maiden until her marriage. In the years of her adolescence, rain was abundant with her people. The oldest man could not remember such fertility. When the Princess had counted eighteen summers, her father went to drive out a war party that harried his borders on the north and troubled his prosperity. The King destroyed the invaders and brought home many prisoners. Among the prisoners was a young chief, taller than any of his captors, of such strength and ferocity that the King's people came a day's journey to look at him. When the Princess beheld his great stature, and saw that his arms and breast were covered with the figures of wild animals, bitten into the skin and coloured, she begged his life from her father. She desired that he should practise his art upon her, and prick upon her skin the signs of Rain and Lightning and Thunder, and stain the wounds with herb-juices, as they were upon his own body. For many days, upon the roof of the King's house, the Princess submitted herself to the bone needle, and the women with her marvelled at her fortitude. But the Princess was without shame before the Captive, and it came about that he threw from him his needles and his stains, and fell upon the Princess to violate her honour; and her women ran down from the roof screaming, to call the guard which stood at the gateway of the King's house, and none stayed to protect their mistress. When the guard came, the Captive was thrown into bonds, and he was gelded, and his tongue was torn out, and he was given for a slave to the Rain Princess.

The country of the Aztecs to the east was tormented by thirst, and their king, hearing much of the rain-making arts of the Princess, sent an embassy to her father, with presents and an offer of marriage. So the Princess went from her father to be the Queen of the Aztecs, and she took with her the Captive, who served her in everything with entire fidelity and slept upon a mat before her door.

The King gave his bride a fortress on the outskirts of the city, whither she retired to entreat the rain gods. This fortress was called the Queen's House, and on the night of the new moon the Queen came to it from the palace. But when the moon waxed and grew toward the round, because the god of Thunder had had his will of her, then the Queen returned to the King. Drought abated in the country and rain fell abundantly by reason of the Queen's power with the stars.

When the Queen went to her own house she took with her no servant but the Captive, and he slept outside her door and brought her food after she had fasted. The Queen had a jewel of great value, a turquoise that had fallen from the sun, and had the image of the sun upon it. And when she desired a young man whom she had seen in the army or among the slaves, she sent the Captive to him with the jewel, for a sign that he should come to her secretly at the Queen's House upon business concerning the welfare of all. And some, after she had talked with them, she sent away with rewards; and some she took into her chamber and kept them by her for one night or two. Afterward she called the Captive and bade him conduct the youth by the secret way he had come, underneath the chambers of the fortress. But for the going away of the Queen's lovers the Captive took out the bar that was beneath a stone in the floor of the passage, and put in its stead a rush-reed, and the youth stepped upon it and fell through into a cavern that was the bed of an underground river, and whatever was thrown into it was not seen again. In this service nor in any other did the Captive fail the Queen.

But when the Queen sent for the Captain of the Archers, she detained him four days in her chamber, calling often for food and wine, and was greatly content with him. On the fourth day she went to the Captive outside her door and said: 'Tomorrow take this man up by the sure way, by which the King comes, and let him live.'

In the Queen's door were arrows, purple and white. When she desired the King to come to her publicly, with his guard, she sent him a white arrow; but when she sent the purple, he came secretly, and covered himself with his mantle to be hidden from the stone gods at the gate. On the fifth night that the Queen was with her lover, the Captive took a purple arrow to the King, and the King came secretly and found them together. He killed the Captain with his own hand, but the Queen he brought to public trial. The Captive, when he was put to the question, told on his fingers forty men that he had let through the underground passage into the river. The Captive and the Queen were put to death by fire, both on the same day, and afterward there was scarcity of rain.

Eden Bower sat shivering a little as she listened. Hedger was not trying to please her, she thought, but to antagonize and frighten her by his brutal story. She had often told herself that his lean, big-boned lower jaw was like his bull-dog's, but tonight his face made Caesar's most savage and determined expression seem an affectation. Now she was looking at the man he really was. Nobody's eyes had ever defied her like this. They were searching her and seeing everything; all she had concealed from Livingston, and from the millionaire and his friends, and from the newspaper men. He was testing her, trying her out, and she was more ill at ease than she wished to show.

'That's quite a thrilling story,' she said at last, rising and winding her scarf about her throat. 'It must be getting late. Almost everyone has gone.'

They walked down the Avenue like people who have quarrelled, or who wish to get rid of each other. Hedger did not take her arm at the street crossings, and they did not linger in the Square. At her door he tried none of the old devices of the Livingston boys. He stood like a post, having forgotten to take off his hat, gave her a harsh, threatening glance, muttered 'goodnight', and shut his own door noisily.

There was no question of sleep for Eden Bower. Her brain was working like a machine that would never stop. After she undressed, she tried to calm her nerves by smoking a cigarette, lying on the divan by the open window. But she grew wider and wider awake, combating the challenge that had flamed all evening in Hedger's eyes. The balloon had been one kind of excitement, the wine another; but the thing that had roused her, as a blow rouses a proud man, was the doubt, the contempt, the sneering hostility with which the painter had looked at her when he told his savage story. Crowds and balloons were all very well, she reflected, but woman's chief adventure is man. With a mind over active and a sense of life over strong, she wanted to walk across the roofs in the starlight, to sail over the sea and face at once a world of which she had never been afraid.

Hedger must be asleep; his dog had stopped sniffing under the double doors. Eden put on her wrapper and slippers and stole softly down the hall over the old carpet; one loose board creaked just as she reached the ladder. The trapdoor was open, as always on hot nights. When she stepped out on the roof she drew a long breath and walked across it, looking up at the sky. Her foot touched something soft; she heard a low growl, and on the instant Caesar's sharp little teeth caught her ankle and waited. His breath was like steam on her leg. Nobody had ever intruded upon his roof before, and he panted for the movement or the word that would let him spring his jaw. Instead, Hedger's hand seized his throat.

'Wait a minute. I'll settle with him,' he said grimly. He dragged the dog toward the manhole and disappeared. When he came back, he found Eden standing over by the dark chimney, looking away in an offended attitude.

'I caned him unmercifully,' he panted. 'Of course you didn't hear anything; he never whines when I beat him. He didn't nip you, did he?'

'I don't know whether he broke the skin or not,' she answered aggrievedly, still looking off into the west.

'If I were one of your friends in white pants, I'd strike a match to find whether you were hurt, though I know you are not, and then I'd see your ankle, wouldn't I?'

'I suppose so.'

He shook his head and stood with his hands in the pockets of his old painting jacket. 'I'm not up to such boy-tricks. If you want the place to yourself, I'll clear out. There are plenty of places where I can spend the night, what's left of it. But if you stay here and I stay here—' He shrugged his shoulders.

Eden did not stir, and she made no reply. Her head drooped slightly, as if she were considering. But the moment he put his arms about her they began to talk, both at once, as people do in an opera. The instant avowal brought out a flood of trivial admissions. Hedger confessed his crime, was reproached and forgiven, and now Eden knew what it was in his look that she had found so disturbing of late.

Standing against the black chimney, with the sky behind and blue shadows before, they looked like one of Hedger's own paintings of that period; two figures, one white and one dark, and nothing whatever distinguishable about them but that they were male and female. The faces were lost, the contours blurred in shadow, but the figures were a man and a woman, and that was their whole concern and their mysterious beauty,—it was the rhythm in which they moved, at last, along the roof and down into the dark hole; he first, drawing her gently after him. She came down very slowly. The excitement and bravado and uncertainty of that long day and night seemed all at once to tell upon her. When his feet were on the carpet and he reached up to lift her down, she twined her arms about his neck as after a long separation, and turned her face

61

to him, and her lips, with their perfume of youth and passion.

One Saturday afternoon Hedger was sitting in the window of Eden's music room. They had been watching the pigeons come wheeling over the roofs from their unknown feeding grounds.

'Why,' said Eden suddenly, 'don't we fix those big doors into your studio so they will open? Then, if I want you, I won't have to go through the hall. That illustrator is loafing about a good deal of late.'

'I'll open them, if you wish. The bolt is on your side.'

'Isn't there one on yours, too?'

'No. I believe a man lived there for years before I came in, and the nurse used to have these rooms herself. Naturally, the lock was on the lady's side.'

Eden laughed and began to examine the bolt. 'It's all stuck up with paint.' Looking about, her eye lighted upon a bronze Buddha which was one of the nurse's treasures. Taking him by his head, she struck the bolt a blow with his squatting posteriors. The two doors creaked, sagged, and swung weakly inward a little way, as if they were too old for such escapades. Eden tossed the heavy idol into a stuffed chair. 'That's better,' she exclaimed exultantly. 'So the bolts are always on the lady's side? What a lot society takes for granted!'

Hedger laughed, sprang up and caught her arms roughly. 'Whoever takes you for granted— Did anybody, ever?'

'Everybody does. That's why I'm here. You are the only one who knows anything about me. Now I'll have to dress if we're going out for dinner.'

He lingered, keeping his hold on her. 'But I won't always be the only one, Eden Bower. I won't be the last.'

'No, I suppose not,' she said carelessly. 'But what does that matter? You are the first.'

As a long, despairing whine broke in the warm stillness, they drew apart. Caesar, lying on his bed in the dark corner, had lifted his head at this invasion of sunlight, and realized that the side of his room was broken open, and his whole world shattered by change. There stood his master and this woman, laughing at him! The woman was pulling the long black hair of this mightiest of men, who bowed his head and permitted it.

*　　*　　*

VI

In time they quarrelled, of course, and about an abstraction,—as young people often do, as mature people almost never do. Eden came in late one afternoon. She had been with some of her musical friends to lunch at Burton Ives' studio, and she began telling Hedger about its splendours. He listened a moment and then threw down his brushes. 'I know exactly what it's like,' he said impatiently. 'A very good department-store conception of a studio. It's one of the show places.'

'Well, it's gorgeous, and he said I could bring you to see him. The boys tell me he's awfully kind about giving people a lift, and you might get something out of it.'

Hedger started up and pushed his canvas out of the way. 'What could I possibly get from Burton Ives? He's almost the worst painter in the world; the stupidest, I mean.'

Eden was annoyed. Burton Ives had been very nice to her and had begged her to sit for him. 'You must admit that he's a very successful one,' she said coldly.

'Of course he is! Anybody can be successful who will do that sort of thing. I wouldn't paint his pictures for all the money in New York.'

'Well, I saw a lot of them, and I think they are beautiful.'

Hedger bowed stiffly.

'What's the use of being a great painter if nobody knows about you?' Eden went on persuasively. 'Why don't you paint the kind of pictures people can understand, and then, after you're successful, do whatever you like?'

'As I look at it,' said Hedger brusquely, 'I am successful.'

Eden glanced about. 'Well, I don't see any evidences of it,' she said, biting her lip. 'He has a Japanese servant and a wine cellar, and keeps a riding horse.'

Hedger melted a little. 'My dear, I have the most expensive luxury in the world, and I am much more extravagant than Burton Ives, for I work to please nobody but myself.'

'You mean you could make money and don't? That you don't try to get a public?'

'Exactly. A public only wants what has been done over and over. I'm painting for painters,—who haven't been born.'

'What would you do if I brought Mr Ives down here to see your things?'

'Well, for God's sake, don't! Before he left I'd probably tell him what I thought of him.'

Eden rose. 'I give you up. You know very well there's only one kind of success that's real.'

'Yes, but it's not the kind you mean. So you've been thinking me a scrub painter, who needs a helping hand from some fashionable studio man? What the devil have you had anything to do with me for, then?'

'There's no use talking to you,' said Eden walking slowly toward the door. 'I've been trying to pull wires for you all afternoon, and this is what it comes to.' She had expected that the tidings of a prospective call from the great man would be received very differently, and had been thinking as she came home in the stage how, as with a magic wand, she might gild Hedger's future, float him out of his dark hole on a tide of prosperity, see his name in the papers and his pictures in the windows on Fifth Avenue.

Hedger mechanically snapped the midsummer leash on Caesar's collar and they ran downstairs and hurried through Sullivan Street off toward the river. He wanted to be among rough, honest people, to get down where the big drays bumped over stone paving blocks and the men wore corduroy trousers and kept their shirts open at the neck. He stopped for a drink in one of the sagging bar-rooms on the water front. He had never in his life been so deeply wounded; he did not know he could be so hurt. He had told this girl all his secrets. On the roof, in these warm, heavy summer nights, with her hands locked in his, he had been able to explain all his misty ideas about an unborn art the world was waiting for; had been able to explain them better than he had ever done to himself. And she had looked away to the chattels of this uptown studio and coveted them for him! To her he was only an unsuccessful Burton Ives.

Then why, as he had put it to her, did she take up with him? Young, beautiful, talented as she was, why had she wasted herself on a scrub? Pity? Hardly; she wasn't sentimental. There was no explaining her. But in this passion that had seemed so fearless and so fated to be, his own position now looked to him ridiculous; a poor dauber without money or fame,—it was her caprice to load him with favours. Hedger ground his teeth so loud that his dog, trotting beside him, heard him and looked up.

While they were having supper at the oysterman's, he planned his escape. Whenever he saw her again, everything he had told her, that he should never have told anyone, would come back to him; ideas he had never whispered even to the painter whom he worshipped and had gone all the way to France to see. To her they must seem his apology for not having horses and a valet, or merely the puerile boastfulness of a weak man. Yet if she slipped the bolt tonight and came through the doors and said, 'Oh, weak man, I belong to you!' what could he do? That was the danger. He would catch the train out to Long Beach tonight, and tomorrow he would go on to the north end of Long Island, where an old friend of his had a summer studio among the sand dunes. He would stay until things came right in his mind. And she could find a smart painter, or take her punishment.

When he went home, Eden's room was dark; she was dining out somewhere. He threw his things into a holdall he had carried about the world with him, strapped up some colours and canvases, and ran downstairs.

VII

Five days later Hedger was a restless passenger on a dirty, crowded Sunday train, coming back to town. Of course he saw now how unreasonable he had been in expecting a Huntington girl to know anything about pictures; here was a whole continent full of people who knew nothing about pictures and he didn't hold it against them. What had such things to do with him and Eden Bower? When he lay out on the dunes, watching the moon come up out of the sea, it had seemed to him that there was no wonder in the world like the wonder of Eden Bower. He was going back to her because she was older than art, because she was the most over-whelming thing that had ever come into his life.

He had written her yesterday, begging her to be at home this evening, telling her that he was contrite, and wretched enough.

Now that he was on his way to her, his stronger feeling un-accountably changed to a mood that was playful and tender. He wanted to share everything with her, even the most trivial things. He wanted to tell her about the people on the train, coming back tired from their holiday with bunches of wilted flowers and dirty daisies; to tell her that the fish-man, to whom she had often sent him for lobsters, was among the passengers, disguised in a silk shirt and a spotted tie, and how his wife looked exactly like a fish, even to her eyes, on which cataracts were forming. He could tell her, too,

65

that he hadn't as much as unstrapped his canvases,—that ought to convince her.

In those days passengers from Long Island came into New York by ferry. Hedger had to be quick about getting his dog out of the express car in order to catch the first boat. The East River, and the bridges, and the city to the west, were burning in the conflagration of the sunset; there was that great home-coming reach of evening in the air.

The car changes from Thirty-fourth Street were too many and too perplexing; for the first time in his life Hedger took a hansom cab for Washington Square. Caesar sat bolt upright on the worn leather cushion beside him, and they jogged off, looking down on the rest of the world.

It was twilight when they drove down lower Fifth Avenue into the Square, and through the Arch behind them were the two long rows of pale violet lights that used to bloom so beautifully against the grey stone and asphalt. Here and yonder about the Square hung globes that shed a radiance not unlike the blue mists of evening, emerging softly when daylight died, as the stars emerged in the thin blue sky. Under them the sharp shadows of the trees fell on the cracked pavement and the sleeping grass. The first stars and the first lights were growing silver against the gradual darkening, when Hedger paid his driver and went into the house,—which, thank God, was still there! On the hall table lay his letter of yesterday, unopened.

He went upstairs with every sort of fear and every sort of hope clutching at his heart; it was as if tigers were tearing him. Why was there no gas burning in the top hall? He found matches and the gas bracket. He knocked, but got no answer; nobody was there. Before his own door were exactly five bottles of milk, standing in a row. The milk-boy had taken spiteful pleasure in thus reminding him that he forgot to stop his order.

Hedger went down to the basement; it, too, was dark. The janitress was taking her evening airing on the basement steps. She sat waving a palm-leaf fan majestically, her dirty calico dress open at the neck. She told him at once that there had been 'changes'. Miss Bower's room was to let again, and the piano would go tomorrow. Yes, she left yesterday, she sailed for Europe with friends from Chicago. They arrived on Friday, heralded by many telegrams. Very rich people they were said to be, though the man had refused to pay the nurse a month's rent in lieu of notice,—which would have been only right, as the young lady had agreed to take the rooms until October. Mrs Foley had observed, too, that he didn't overpay her or Willy for their trouble, and a great deal of trouble they had been put to, certainly. Yes, the young lady was very pleasant, but the nurse said there were rings on the mahogany table where she had put tumblers and wine glasses. It was just as well she was gone. The Chicago man was uppish in his ways, but not much to look at. She supposed he had poor health, for there was nothing to him inside his clothes.

Hedger went slowly up the stairs—never had they seemed so long, or his legs so heavy. The upper floor was emptiness and silence. He unlocked his room, lit the gas, and opened the windows. When he went to put his coat in the closet, he found, hanging among his clothes, a pale, flesh-tinted dressing-gown he had liked to see her wear, with a perfume—oh, a perfume that was still Eden Bower! He shut the door behind him and there, in the dark, for a moment he lost his manliness. It was when he held this garment to him that he found a letter in the pocket.

The note was written with a lead pencil, in haste: She was sorry that he was angry, but she still didn't know just what she had done. She had thought Mr Ives would be useful to him; she guessed he was too proud. She wanted awfully to see him again, but Fate came knocking at her door after he had left her. She believed in Fate. She would never forget him, and she knew he would become the greatest painter in the world. Now she must pack. She hoped he wouldn't mind her leaving the dressing-gown; somehow, she could never wear it again.

After Hedger read this, standing under the gas, he went back into the closet and knelt down before the wall; the knot hole had been plugged up with a ball of wet paper,—the same blue note-paper on which her letter was written.

He was hard hit. Tonight he had to bear the loneliness of a whole lifetime. Knowing himself so well, he could hardly believe that such a thing had ever happened to him, that such a woman had lain happy and contented in his arms. And now it was over. He turned out the light and sat down on his painter's stool before the big window. Caesar, on the floor beside him, rested his head on his master's knee. We must leave Hedger thus, sitting in his tank with his dog, looking up at the stars.

* * *

COMING, APHRODITE! This legend, in electric lights over the Lexington Opera House, had long announced the return of Eden Bower to New York after years of spectacular success in Paris. She came at last, under the management of an American Opera Company, but bringing her own *chef d'orchestre*.

One bright December afternoon Eden Bower was going down Fifth Avenue in her car, on the way to her broker, in Williams Street. Her thoughts were entirely upon stocks,—Cerro de Pasco, and how much she should buy of it,—when she suddenly looked up and realized that she was skirting Washington Square. She had not seen the place since she rolled out of it in an old-fashioned four-wheeler to seek her fortune, eighteen years ago.

'*Arrêtez, Alphonse. Attendez moi,*' she called, and opened the door before he could reach it. The children who were streaking over the asphalt on roller skates saw a lady in a long fur coat, and short, high-heeled shoes, alight from a French car and pace slowly about the Square, holding her muff to her chin. This spot, at least, had changed very little, she reflected; the same trees, the same fountain, the white arch, and over yonder, Garibaldi, drawing the sword for freedom. There, just opposite her, was the old red brick house.

'Yes, that is the place,' she was thinking. 'I can smell the carpets now, and the dog,—what was his name? That grubby bathroom at the end of the hall, and that dreadful Hedger—still, there was something about him, you know—' She glanced up and blinked against the sun. From somewhere in the crowded quarter south of the Square a flock of pigeons rose, wheeling quickly upward into the brilliant blue sky. She threw back her head, pressed her muff closer to her chin, and watched them with a smile of amazement and delight. So they still rose, out of all that dirt and noise and squalor, fleet and silvery, just as they used to rise that summer when she was twenty and went up in a balloon on Coney Island!

Alphonse opened the door and tucked her robes about her. All the way down town her mind wandered from Cerro de Pasco, and she kept smiling and looking up at the sky.

When she had finished her business with the broker, she asked him to look in the telephone book for the address of M. Gaston Jules, the picture dealer, and slipped the paper on which he wrote it into her glove. It was five o'clock when she reached the French Galleries, as they were called. On entering she gave the attendant her card, asking him to take it to M. Jules. The dealer appeared very promptly and begged her to come into his private office, where he pushed a great chair toward his desk for her and signalled his secretary to leave the room.

'How good your lighting is in here,' she observed, glancing about. 'I met you at Simon's studio, didn't I? Oh, no! I never forget anybody who interests me.' She threw her muff on his writing table and sank into the deep chair. 'I have come to you for some information that's not in my line. Do you know anything about an American painter named Hedger?'

He took the seat opposite her. 'Don Hedger? But, certainly! There are some very interesting things of his in an exhibition at V——'s. If you would care to—'

She held up her hand. 'No, no. I've no time to go to exhibitions. Is he a man of any importance?'

'Certainly. He is one of the first men among the moderns. That is to say, among the very moderns. He is always coming up with something different. He often exhibits in Paris, you must have seen—'

'No, I tell you I don't go to exhibitions. Has he had great success? That is what I want to know.'

M. Jules pulled at his short grey moustache. 'But, Madame, there are many kinds of success,' he began cautiously.

Madame gave a dry laugh. 'Yes, so he used to say. We once quarrelled on that issue. And how would you define his particular kind?'

M. Jules grew thoughtful. 'He is a great name with all the young men, and he is decidedly an influence in art. But one can't definitely place a man who is original, erratic, and who is changing all the time.'

She cut him short. 'Is he much talked about at home? In Paris, I mean? Thanks. That's all I want to know.' She rose and began buttoning her coat. 'One doesn't like to have been an utter fool, even at twenty.'

'*Mais, non!*' M. Jules handed her her muff with a quick, sympathetic glance. He followed her out through the carpeted showroom, now closed to the public and draped in cheesecloth, and put her into her car with words appreciative of the honour she had done him in calling.

Leaning back in the cushions, Eden Bower closed her eyes, and her face, as the street lamps flashed their ugly orange light upon it, became hard and settled, like a plaster cast; so a sail, that has been filled by a strong breeze, behaves when the wind suddenly dies. Tomorrow night the wind would blow again, and this mask would be the golden face of Aphrodite. But a 'big' career takes its toll, even with the best of luck.

GERTRUDE STEIN

As A Wife Has A Cow: A Love Story

Nearly all of it to be as a wife has a cow, a love story. All of it to be as a wife has a cow, all of it to be as a wife has a cow, a love story.

As to be all of it as to be a wife as a wife has a cow, a love story, all of it as to be all of it as a wife all of it as to be as a wife has a cow a love story, all of it as a wife has a cow as a wife has a cow a love story.

Has made, as it has made as it has made, has made has to be as a wife has a cow, a love story. Has made as to be as a wife has a cow a love story. As a wife has a cow, as a wife has a cow, a love story. Has to be as a wife has a cow a love story. Has made as to be as a wife has a cow a love story.

When he can, and for that when he can, for that. When he can and for that when he can. For that. When he can. For that when he can. For that. And when he can and for that. Or that, and when he can. For that and when he can.

And to in six and another. And to and in and six and another. And to and in and six and another. And to in six and and to and in and six and another. And to and in and six and another. And to and six and in and another and and to and six and another and and to and in and six and to and six and in and another.

In came in there, came in there come out of there. In came in come out of there. Come out there in came in there. Come out of there and in and come out of there. Came in there, come out of there.

Feeling or for it, as feeling or for it, came in or come in or come out of there or feeling as feeling or feeling as for it.

As a wife has a cow.

Came in and come out.

As a wife has a cow a love story.

As a love story, as a wife has a cow, a love story.

Not and now, now and not, not and now, by and by not and now, as not, as soon as not not and now, now as soon now now as soon,

71

now as soon as soon as now. Just as soon just now just now just as soon just as soon as now. Just as soon as now.

And in that, as and in that, in that and and in that, so that, so that and in that, and in that and so that and as for that and as for that and that. In that. In that and and for that as for that and in that. Just as soon and in that. In that as that and just as soon. Just as soon as that.

Even now, now and even now and now and even now. Not as even now, therefore, even now and therefore, therefore and even now and even now and therefore even now. So not to and moreover and even now and therefore and moreover and even now and so and even now and therefore even now.

Do they as they do so. And do they do so.

We feel we feel. We feel or if we feel if we feel or if we feel. We feel or if we feel. As it is made made a day made a day or two made a day, as it is made a day or two, as it is made a day. Made a day. Made a day. Not away a day. By day. As it is made a day.

On the fifteenth of October as they say, said anyway, what is it as they expect, as they expect it or as they expected it, as they expect it and as they expected it, expect it or for it, expected it and it is expected of it. As they say said anyway. What is it as they expect for it, what is it and it is as they expect of it. What is it. What is it the fifteenth of October as they say as they expect or as they expected as they expect for it. What is it as they say the fifteenth of October as they say and as expected of it, the fifteenth of October as they say, what is it as expected of it. What is it and the fifteenth of October as they say and expected of it.

And prepare and prepare so prepare to prepare and prepare to prepare to prepare and prepare so as to prepare, so to prepare and prepare to prepare to prepare for and to prepare for it to prepare, to prepare for it, in preparation, as preparation in preparation by preparation. They will be too busy afterwards to prepare. As preparation prepare, to prepare, as to preparation and to prepare. Out there.

Have it as having having it as happening, happening to have it as having, having to have it as happening. Happening and have it as happening and having it happen as happening and having to have it happen as happening, and my wife has a cow as now, my wife having a cow as now, my wife having a cow as now and having a cow as now and having a cow and having a cow now, my wife has a cow and now. My wife has a cow.

ELIZABETH BOWEN

Her Table Spread

Alban had few opinions on the subject of marriage; his attitude to women was negative, but in particular he was not attracted to Miss Cuffe. Coming down early for dinner, red satin dress cut low, she attacked the silence with loud laughter before he had spoken. He recollected having heard that she was abnormal—at twenty-five, of statuesque development, still detained in childhood. The two other ladies, in beaded satins, made entrances of a surprising formality. It occurred to him, his presence must constitute an occasion: they certainly sparkled. Old Mr Rossiter, uncle to Mrs Treye, came last, more sourly. They sat for some time without the addition of lamplight. Dinner was not announced; the ladies by remaining on guard, seemed to deprecate any question of its appearance. No sound came from other parts of the Castle.

Miss Cuffe was an heiress to whom the Castle belonged and whose guests they all were. But she carefully followed the movements of her aunt, Mrs Treye; her ox-eyes moved from face to face in happy submission rather than expectancy. She was continually preoccupied with attempts at gravity, as though holding down her skirts in a high wind. Mrs Treye and Miss Carbin combined to cover her excitement; still, their looks frequently stole from the company to the windows, of which there were too many. He received a strong impression someone outside was waiting to come in. At last, with a sigh they got up: dinner had been announced.

The Castle was built on high ground, commanding the estuary; a steep hill, with trees, continued above it. On fine days the view was remarkable, of almost Italian brilliance, with that constant reflection up from the water that even now prolonged the too-long day. Now, in continuous evening rain, the winding wooded line of the further shore could be seen and, nearer the windows, a smothered island with the stump of a watch-tower. Where the Castle stood, a higher tower had answered the island's. Later a keep, then wings, had been added; now the fine peaceful residence had French windows opening on to the terrace. Invasions from the water would henceforth be social, perhaps amorous. On the slope down from the terrace, trees began again; almost, but not quite concealing the destroyer. Alban, who knew nothing, had not yet looked down.

It was Mr Rossiter who first spoke of the destroyer—Alban meanwhile glancing along the table; the preparations had been stupendous. The destroyer had come today. The ladies all turned to Alban: the beads on their bosoms sparkled. So this was what they had here, under their trees. Engulfed by their pleasure, from now on he disappeared personally. Mr Rossiter, rising a note, continued. The estuary, it appeared, was deep, with a channel buoyed up it. By a term of the Treaty, English ships were permitted to anchor in these waters.

'But they've been afraid of the rain!' chimed in Valeria Cuffe.

'Hush,' said her aunt, 'that's silly. Sailors would be accustomed to getting wet.'

But, Miss Carbin reported, that spring there *had* already been one destroyer. Two of the officers had been seen dancing at the hotel at the head of the estuary.

'So,' said Alban, 'you are quite in the world.' He adjusted his glasses in her direction.

Miss Carbin—blonde, not forty, and an attachment of Mrs Treye's—shook her head despondently. 'We were all away at Easter. Wasn't it curious they should have come then? The sailors walked in the demesne but never touched the daffodils.'

'As though I should have cared!' exclaimed Valeria passionately.

'Morale too good,' stated Mr Rossiter.

'But next evening,' continued Miss Carbin, 'the officers did not go to the hotel. They climbed up here through the trees to the terrace—you see, they had no idea. Friends of ours were staying here at the Castle, and they apologized. Our friends invited them in to supper . . .'

'Did they accept?'

The three ladies said in a breath: 'Yes, they came.'

Valeria added urgently, 'So don't you *think*—?'

'So tonight we have a destroyer to greet you,' Mrs Treye said quickly to Alban. 'It is quite an event; the country people are coming down from the mountains. These waters are very lonely;

the steamers have given up since the bad times; there is hardly a pleasure-boat. The weather this year has driven visitors right away.'

'You are beautifully remote.'

'Yes,' agreed Miss Carbin. 'Do you know much about the Navy? Do you think, for instance, that this is likely to be the same destroyer?'

'*Will they remember?*' Valeria's bust was almost on the table. But with a rustle Mrs Treye pressed Valeria's toe. For the dining-room also looked out across the estuary, and the great girl had not once taken her eyes from the window. Perhaps it was unfortunate that Mr Alban should have coincided with the destroyer. Perhaps it was unfortunate for Mr Alban too.

For he saw now he was less than half the feast; unappeased, the party sat looking through him, all grouped at an end of the table—to the other, chairs had been pulled up. Dinner was being served very slowly. Candles—possible to see from the water—were lit now; some wet peonies glistened. Outside, day still lingered hopefully. The bushes over the edge of the terrace were like heads—you could have sworn sometimes you saw them mounting, swaying in manly talk. Once, wound up in the rain, a bird whistled, seeming hardly a bird.

'Perhaps since then they have been to Greece, or Malta?'

'That would be the Mediterranean fleet,' said Mr Rossiter.

They were sorry to think of anything out in the rain tonight.

'The decks must be streaming,' said Miss Carbin.

Then Valeria, exclaiming. 'Please excuse me!' pushed her chair in and ran from the room.

'She is impulsive,' explained Mrs Treye. 'Have *you* been to Malta, Mr Alban?'

In the drawing-room, empty of Valeria, the standard lamps had been lit. Through their ballet-skirt shades, rose and lemon, they gave out a deep, welcoming light. Alban, at the ladies' invitation, undraped the piano. He played, but they could see he was not pleased. It was obvious he had always been a civilian, and when he had taken his place on the piano-stool—which he twirled round three times, rather fussily—his dinner-jacket wrinkled across the shoulders. It was sad they should feel so indifferent, for he came from London. Mendelssohn was exasperating to them—they opened all four windows to let the music downhill. They preferred

75

not to draw the curtains; the air, though damp, being pleasant tonight, they said.

The piano was damp, but Alban played almost all his heart out. He played out the indignation of years his mild manner concealed. He had failed to love; nobody did anything about this; partners at dinner gave him less than half their attention. He knew some spring had dried up at the root of the world. He was fixed in the dark rain, by an indifferent shore. He played badly, but they were unmusical. Old Mr Rossiter, who was not what he seemed, went back to the dining-room to talk to the parlourmaid.

Valeria, glittering vastly, appeared in a window.

'Come *in*!' her aunt cried in indignation. She would die of a chill, childless, in fact unwedded; the Castle would have to be sold and where would they all be?

But—'Lights down there!' Valeria shouted above the music.

They had to run out for a moment, laughing and holding cushions over their bare shoulders. Alban left the piano; they looked boldly down from the terrace. Indeed, there they were: two lights like arc-lamps, blurred by rain and drawn down deep in reflection into the steady water. There were, too, ever so many portholes, all lit up.

'Perhaps they are playing bridge,' said Miss Carbin.

'Now I wonder if Uncle Robert ought to have called,' said Mrs Treye. 'Perhaps we have seemed remiss—one calls on a regiment.'

'Patrick could row him out tomorrow.'

'He hates the water.' She sighed. 'Perhaps they will be gone.'

'Let's go for a row now—let's go for a row with a lantern,' besought Valeria, jumping and pulling her aunt's elbow. They produced such indignation she disappeared again—wet satin skirts and all—into the bushes. The ladies could do no more: Alban suggested the rain might spot their dresses.

'They must lose a great deal, playing cards throughout an evening for high stakes,' Miss Carbin said with concern as they all sat down again.

'Yet, if you come to think of it, somebody must win.'

But the naval officers who so joyfully supped at Easter had been, Miss Carbin knew, a Mr Graves, and a Mr Garrett: *they* would certainly lose. 'At all events, it is better than dancing at the hotel; there would be nobody of their type.'

'There is nobody there at all.'

'I expect they are best where they are . . . Mr Alban, a Viennese waltz?'

He played while the ladies whispered, waving the waltz time a little distractedly. Mr Rossiter, coming back, momentously stood: they turned in hope: even the waltz halted. But he brought no news. 'You should call Valeria in. You can't tell who may be round the place. She's not fit to be out tonight.'

'Perhaps she's not out.'

'She is,' said Mr Rossiter crossly. 'I just saw her racing past the window with a lantern.'

Valeria's mind was made up: she was a princess. Not for nothing had she had the dining-room silver polished and all set out. She would pace around in red satin that swished behind, while Mr Alban kept on playing a loud waltz. They would be dazed at all she had to offer—also her two new statues and the leopard-skin from the auction.

When he and she were married (she inclined a little to Mr Garrett) they would invite all the Navy up the estuary and give them tea. Her estuary would be filled up, like a regatta, with loud excited battleships tooting to one another and flags flying. The terrace would be covered with grateful sailors, leaving room for the band. She would keep the peacocks her aunt did not allow. His friends would be surprised to notice that Mr Garrett had meanwhile become an admiral, all gold. He would lead the other admirals into the Castle and say, while they wiped their feet respectfully: 'These are my wife's statues; she has given them to me. One is Mars, one is Mercury. We have a Venus, but she is not dressed. And wait till I show you our silver and gold plates . . .' The Navy would be unable to tear itself away.

She had been excited for some weeks at the idea of marrying Mr Alban, but now the lovely appearance of the destroyer put him out of her mind. He would not have done; he was not handsome. But she could keep him to play the piano on quiet afternoons.

Her friends had told her Mr Garrett was quite a Viking. She was so very familiar with his appearance that she felt sometimes they had already been married for years—though still, sometimes, he could not realize his good luck. She still had to remind him the island was hers too . . . Tonight, Aunt and darling Miss Carbin had so fallen in with her plans, putting on their satins and decorating the drawing-room, that the dinner became a betrothal feast. There was some little hitch about the arrival of Mr Garrett—she had heard that gentlemen sometimes could not tie their ties. And now he was late and would be discouraged. So she must now go half-way down to the water and wave a lantern.

But she put her two hands over the lantern, then smothered it in her dress. She had a panic. Supposing she should prefer Mr Graves?

She had heard Mr Graves was stocky, but very merry; when he came to supper at Easter he slid in the gallery. He would teach her to dance, and take her to Naples and Paris . . . Oh, dear, oh, dear, then they must fight for her; that was all there was to it . . . She let the lantern out of her skirts and waved. Her fine arm with bangles went up and down, up and down, with the staggering light; the trees one by one jumped up from the dark, like savages.

Inconceivably, the destroyer took no notice.

Undisturbed by oars, the rain stood up from the water; not a light rose to peer, and the gramophone, though it remained very faint, did not cease or alter.

In mackintoshes, Mr Rossiter and Alban meanwhile made their way to the boat-house, Alban did not know why. 'If that goes on,' said Mr Rossiter, nodding towards Valeria's lantern, 'they'll fire one of their guns at us.'

'Oh, no. Why?' said Alban. He buttoned up, however, the collar of his mackintosh.

'Nervous as cats. It's high time that girl was married. She's a nice girl in many ways, too.'

'Couldn't we get the lantern away from her?' They stepped on a paved causeway and heard the water nibble the rocks.

'She'd scream the place down. She's of age now, you see.'

'But if—'

'Oh, she won't do that; I was having a bit of fun with you.' Chuckling equably, Mrs Treye's uncle unlocked and pulled open the boat-house door. A bat whistled out.

'Why are we here?'

'She might come for the boat; she's a fine oar,' said Mr Rossiter wisely. The place was familiar to him; he lit an oil-lamp and, sitting down on a trestle with a staunch air of having done what he could, reached a bottle of whisky out of the boat. He motioned the bottle to Alban. 'It's a wild night,' he said. 'Ah, well, we don't have these destroyers every day.'

'That seems fortunate.'

'Well, it is and it isn't.' Restoring the bottle to the vertical, Mr Rossiter continued: 'It's a pity you don't want a wife. You'd be the better for a wife, d'you see, a young fellow like you. She's got a nice character; she's a girl you could shape. She's got a nice income.' The bat returned from the rain and knocked round the lamp. Lowering the bottle frequently, Mr Rossiter talked to Alban (whose attitude remained negative) of women in general and the parlourmaid in particular . . .

'*Bat!*' Alban squealed irrepressibly, and with his hand to his ear—where he still felt it—fled from the boat-house. Mr Rossiter's conversation continued. Alban's pumps squelched as he ran; he skidded along the causeway and balked at the upward steps. His soul squelched equally: he had been warned, he had been warned. He had heard they were all mad; he had erred out of headiness and curiosity. A degree of terror was agreeable to his vanity: by express wish he had occupied haunted rooms. Now he had no other pumps in this country, no idea where to buy them, and a ducal visit ahead. Also, wandering as it were among the apples and amphoras of an art school, he had blundered into the life room: woman revolved gravely.

'Hell,' he said to the steps, mounting, his mind blank to the outcome.

He was nerved for the jumping lantern, but half-way up to the Castle darkness was once more absolute. Her lantern had gone out; he could orientate himself—in spite of himself—by her sobbing. Absolute desperation. He pulled up so short that, for balance, he had to cling to a creaking tree.

'Hi!' she croaked. Then: 'You *are* there! I hear you!'

'Miss Cuffe—'

'How too bad you are! I never heard you rowing. I thought you were never coming—'

'Quietly, my dear girl.'

'Come up quickly. I haven't seen you. Come up to the windows—'

'Miss Cuffe—'

'Don't you remember the way?' As sure but not so noiseless as a cat in the dark, Valeria hurried to him.

'Mr Garrett—' she panted. 'I'm Miss Cuffe. Where have you been? I've destroyed my beautiful red dress and they've eaten up your dinner. But we're still waiting. Don't be afraid; you'll soon be there now. I'm Miss Cuffe; this is my Castle—'

'Listen, it's I, Mr Alban—.'

'Ssh, ssh, Mr Alban: *Mr Garrett has landed.*'

Her cry, his voice, some breath of the joyful intelligence, brought the others on to the terrace, blind with lamplight.

'Valeria?'

'Mr Garrett has landed!'

Mrs Treye said to Miss Carbin under her breath, 'Mr Garrett has come.'

Miss Carbin, half weeping with agitation, replied, 'We must go in.' But uncertain who was to speak next, or how to speak, they remained leaning over the darkness. Behind, through the windows, lamps spread great skirts of light, and Mars and Mercury, unable to contain themselves, stooped from their pedestals. The dumb keyboard shone like a ballroom floor.

Alban, looking up, saw their arms and shoulders under the bright rain. Close by, Valeria's fingers creaked on her warm wet satin. She laughed like a princess, magnificently justified. Their unseen faces were all three lovely, and, in the silence after the laughter, such a strong tenderness reached him that, standing there in full manhood, he was for a moment not exiled. For the moment, without moving or speaking, he stood, in the dark, in a flame, as though all three said: 'My darling . . .'

Perhaps it was best for them all that early, when next day first lightened the rain, the destroyer steamed out—below the extinguished Castle where Valeria lay with her arms wide, past the boat-house where Mr Rossiter lay insensible and the bat hung masked in its wings—down the estuary into the open sea.

Sylvia Townsend Warner

A Correspondence in *The Times*

My Aunt Angel was paying one of her visits to London, a winter visit in her skunk. As usual, she had a little shopping to do, and my mother and I went shopping with her.

On this afternoon we had been to Marshall & Snelgrove, Penberthy (for gloves), D. H. Evans, Waring & Gillow, Peter Robinson, Liberty's (for a wedding present), The Goldsmiths' Company (repair to Aunt Angel's teapot), and Robinson & Cleaver. We had also visited a very small shop in an alley off Great Marlborough Street, where Aunt Angel always buys buttons, and an exhibition of garden water colours, and we had looked in at Burlington House. Now we were having tea at Stewart's, at a small table so beset with boxes, parcels, and small chintz-paper bags that the waitress who brought the toast and the tea had the greatest difficulty placing them on the table. Indeed, there was a moment when it seemed that the neat gentleman at the next table, who for his part had no entanglements save with an umbrella, was likely to get Aunt Angel's toast before she did.

'After tea,' said Aunt Angel, 'I want to see those California floods at the cinema.'

'I only hope,' said my mother, 'that we shan't be seeing our own. I don't know what's come over the Thames. It seems to be much further up the Embankment than it used to be.'

'It's the moon. Don't you remember Flora's face in India?'

The family voice is loud, the family diction is clear. The gentleman at the next table looked up with interest. I was interested too, and asked, 'What happened to Flora's face?'

'She went to sleep in the moonlight,' Aunt Angel explained. 'I suppose the ayah had not closed the shutters properly. Anyhow, it was a full moon and she slept in it, and when she woke, one side of her face was so swelled that she couldn't open that eye.'

'Which Flora was that?' inquired my mother, pretty calmly.

'Flora McCuddy. In Madras.'

'It can't have been Flora McCuddy. Flora McCuddy never was in Madras. It must have been Flora Popham. Or else it was at Jubbulpore, not Madras.'

'Nonsense, Nora. It was Flora McCuddy, because I can distinctly remember her telling me about the mad dog that nearly bit Captain Kimmins. And that was at Madras.'

'Flora Popham,' repeated my mother. 'I suppose you know that Tottie Larpent is dead?'

Two days later Aunt Angel exclaimed, 'Have you seen this extraordinary coincidence in *The Times*?'

The letter was headed 'Lunar Gravity', and ran as follows:

Sir:

The recent level of the Thames at Westminster Bridge suggests to me that your readers might be interested in another example of the power which can be exercised by the moon at its full. A lady of my acquaintance, now unfortunately no more, told me that when she was in Madras she inadvertently slept with the light of the brilliant full moon of Southern India upon one side of her face. In the morning the cheek on which the moonlight had rested was distended and highly painful, and so perceptible was the influence of lunar gravity that for some time she was unable to open one eye. I should be interested to know if any of your readers have had similar experiences.

Junior Carlton Club   Autolycus

'Just what I told you, Nora. Flora McCuddy.'

'Flora Popham,' said my mother.

They argued with some briskness. Flora McCuddy and Flora Popham and Captain Kimmins and the mad dog and several other figures from the family past were whirled round in the debate, and Aunt Angel regretted that a photograph album which would, she said, have settled everything was in Devonshire, so carefully put away that it was not possible to indicate its whereabouts by a telegram. On the morrow they rustled through *The Times* but found nothing more to the point than a letter from some crank or other about sowing turnips in the wax of the moon. The next day brought a much better bag. Besides two letters on turnips and a letter from a lady in Cheltenham saying that an Indian full moon was something which those who had only viewed the moon from Europe could not imagine, Ethelberta Woolley-Wallis added her important testimony:

> SIR,
>
> On my first visit to Madras, now many years ago, I was warned by my ayah never to sleep in the light of a full moon. The result of doing this was not made quite clear, and I understood that a severe headache would be my portion if I were unwary enough to do so. But in the light of Autolycus's letter I now feel convinced that a swelling of the face might have resulted, and this, in those bygone days, would have been a serious matter to a young bride. My ayah was a most devoted and intelligent creature. I wonder, a little sadly, if a present-day ayah would be so devoted to the welfare of her mem-sahib, for there has been a most regrettable change for the worse in the relations of the white and coloured races, due (in my humble opinion) entirely to ill-advised kow-towing to misguided, if not worse, sedition-mongers.

'There, you see! Madras,' exclaimed Aunt Angel.

Meanwhile my mother's eye had gone further down the column, and she uttered a cry of triumph.

> SIR:
>
> I can add my corroboration to the story told by your correspondent, 'Autolycus'. I personally had a somewhat similar experience of the Indian full moon when I was in the Central Provinces in 1898. In my case I was 'sleeping rough' while on shikar, and as I closed my eyes and composed myself to slumber, hearing all round me the howlings and barkings of the jungle excited by the full moon, I remarked to my companion that I wondered if we should not find ourselves mauled before daylight. His reply was on somewhat fatalistic lines, and we were speedily asleep. The light of our fire and the noise made by our beaters kept the animal life at a respectful distance. But on awaking I found myself in possession of the worst

stiff neck it has ever been my lot to experience in the course of a pretty arduous and adventurous life, and my companion told me it was caused by the moon. Repressing a natural impulse to reply 'Moonshine', I made further enquiries which fully bore out his diagnosis. No doubt only the difference between my tough skin and a lady's more delicate epidermis stood between me and such a swelling as described by 'Autolycus'.

CHOLMONDELEY COFFIN,
Lieut. Col. retd.

UNITED SERVICES CLUB

'Central Provinces! Jubbulpore! Of course it was Flora Popham,' said my mother. Aunt Angel seemed unconvinced by this reasoning, even when my mother added that everyone admitted that the heat in India grew hotter and hotter as one went inland and that therefore the inland moon must be stronger too. When Aunt Angel left by the 2:15 for Exeter, one would have thought that the two sisters, championing their respective Floras, would never again transcend terms of armed neutrality. Yet at that very moment, perhaps, the words had been penned which would unite them in a single thought, a single reaction. For the next day's *Times* carried (in addition to a trifling communication from the gentleman who had read the Thirty-nine Articles in Cornwall by the light of the aurora borealis) a letter suggesting that a mosquito and not the moon might have been responsible for the swelled cheek of the lady in Madras. And in addition to this outrage, the third editorial, headed 'O, Swear Not by the Moon', poked fun at the whole story in a demure, satirical way and insinuated that there might be a good deal to be said for the hypothesis of the mosquito.

The family honour was at stake. My mother and my Aunt Angel sprang to its defence. There was no leisure for consultation, no leisure for reconciliation even. But in Monday's *Times* they met.

SIR:

Your correspondent, J. Wilkins Metcalf, doubts the accuracy of the incident related by Autolycus. I am in a position to substantiate it, since the lady in question, Mrs Wolf McCuddy, was my first cousin once removed. I can well recollect Mrs McCuddy telling me of this experience

and describing it as one of the most remarkable things
that happened to her in Madras.

17 ROUGEMONT ROAD, EXETER   ANGEL BURBECK

SIR:

As regards the letter by Autolycus and the subsequent
suggestion by Mr Wilkins Metcalf that a mosquito and
not the full moon was responsible, I happen to be able to
settle the matter. The lady was my aunt by marriage, Mrs
Algernon Popham, and I have often heard the story from
her lips, exactly as told by Autolycus except for one detail.
Mrs Popham was never in Madras. India is a continent, a
fact often overlooked by those who have never been there,
and contains many things quite as strange as this story
which Mr Wilkins Metcalf finds improbable. My aunt by
marriage, who knew India well, would have been much
amused at this suggestion that she had mistaken a moon-
stroke for a mosquito bite.

32 SHEEPCOT TERRACE, W.8   NORA WARNER

'I think your letter is the more convincing,' I said to my mother.
'Aunt Angel has overdone the formality. Yours seems to me to ring
truer.'

'I should hope so,' replied my mother. 'Poor Flora McCuddy!
Why should Flora Popham's lies be fathered on her like that?'

'Flora Popham's lies?' said I.

'Just because she's been in India! As if no one else in the family
had ever been in India. Full moon, indeed! If the full moon could
bulge a brazen kettle, then I might believe that it bulged Flora
Popham's cheek.'

'But, Mother, you said right along it was Flora Popham! Did she
tell you this story?'

'Of course not,' said my mother. 'It's just one of Angel's wool-
gatherings. But I couldn't have such a silly story fastened on poor,
honest, simple-hearted old Flora McCuddy.'

KATHERINE ANNE PORTER

Rope

On the third day after they moved to the country he came walking back from the village carrying a basket of groceries and a twenty-four-yard coil of rope. She came out to meet him, wiping her hands on her green smock. Her hair was tumbled, her nose was scarlet with sunburn; he told her that already she looked like a born country woman. His grey flannel shirt stuck to him, his heavy shoes were dusty. She assured him he looked like a rural character in a play.

Had he brought the coffee? She had been waiting all day long for coffee. They had forgot it when they ordered at the store the first day.

Gosh, no, he hadn't. Lord, now he'd have to go back. Yes, he would if it killed him. He thought, though, he had everything else. She reminded him it was only because he didn't drink coffee himself. If he did he would remember it quick enough. Suppose they ran out of cigarettes? Then she saw the rope. What was that for? Well, he thought it might do to hang clothes on, or something. Naturally she asked him if he thought they were going to run a laundry? They already had a fifty-foot line hanging right before his eyes. Why, hadn't he noticed it, really? It was a blot on the landscape to her.

He thought there were a lot of things a rope might come in handy for. She wanted to know what, for instance. He thought a few seconds, but nothing occurred. They could wait and see, couldn't they? You need all sorts of strange odds and ends around a place in the country. She said, yes, that was so; but she thought just at that time, when every penny counted, it seemed funny to buy more rope. That was all. She hadn't meant anything else. She hadn't just seen, not at first, why he felt it was necessary.

Well, thunder, he had bought it because he wanted to, and that was all there was to it. She thought that was reason enough, and couldn't understand why he hadn't said so at first. Undoubtedly it would be useful, twenty-four yards of rope, there were hundreds of things—she couldn't think of any at the moment—but it would come in. Of course. As he had said, things always did in the country.

But she was a little disappointed about the coffee, and oh, look, look, look at the eggs! Oh, my, they're all running! What had he put on top of them? Hadn't he known eggs mustn't be squeezed? Squeezed, who had squeezed them, he wanted to know. What a silly thing to say. He had simply brought them along in the basket with the other things. If they got broke it was the grocer's fault. He should know better than to put heavy things on top of eggs.

She believed it was the rope. That was the heaviest thing in the pack, she saw him plainly when he came in from the road, the rope was a big package on top of everything. He desired the whole wide world to witness that this was not a fact. He had carried the rope in one hand and the basket in the other, and what was the use of her having eyes if that was the best they could do for her.

Well, anyhow, she could see one thing plain: no eggs for breakfast. They'd have to scramble them now, for supper. It was too damned bad. She had planned to have steak for supper. No ice, meat wouldn't keep. He wanted to know why she couldn't finish breaking the eggs in a bowl and set them in a cool place.

Cool place! If he could find one for her, she'd be glad to set them there. Well, then, it seemed to him they might very well cook the meat at the same time they cooked the eggs and then warm up the meat for tomorrow. The idea simply choked her. Warmed-up meat, when they might as well have had it fresh. Second best and scraps and makeshifts, even to the meat! He rubbed her shoulder a little. It doesn't really matter so much, does it, darling? Sometimes when they were playful, he would rub her shoulder and she would arch and purr. This time she hissed and almost clawed. He was getting ready to say that they could surely manage somehow when she turned on him and said, if he told her they could manage somehow she would certainly slap his face.

He swallowed the words red hot, his face burned. He picked up the rope and started to put it on the top shelf. She would not have it on the top shelf, the jars and tins belonged there; positively she would not have the top shelf cluttered up with a lot of rope. She had borne all the clutter she meant to bear in the flat in town, there was space here at least and she meant to keep things in order.

Well, in that case, he wanted to know what the hammer and nails were doing up there? And why had she put them there when she knew very well he needed that hammer and those nails upstairs to fix the window sashes? She simply slowed down everything and made double work on the place with her insane habit of changing things around and hiding them.

She was sure she begged his pardon, and if she had had any reason to believe he was going to fix the sashes this summer she would have left the hammer and nails right where he put them: in the middle of the bedroom floor where they could step on them in the dark. And now if he didn't clear the whole mess out of there she would throw them down the well.

Oh, all right, all right—could he put them in the closet? Naturally not, there were brooms and mops and dustpans in the closet, and why couldn't he find a place for his rope outside her kitchen? Had he stopped to consider there were seven God-forsaken rooms in the house, and only one kitchen?

He wanted to know what of it? And did she realize she was making a complete fool of herself? And what did she take him for, a three-year-old idiot? The whole trouble with her was she needed something weaker than she was to heckle and tyrannize over. He wished to God now they had a couple of children she could take it out on! Maybe he'd get some rest.

Her face changed at this, she reminded him he had forgot the coffee and had bought a worthless piece of rope. And when she thought of all the things they actually needed to make the place even decently fit to live in, well, she could cry, that was all. She looked so forlorn, so lost and despairing he couldn't believe it was only a piece of rope that was causing all the racket. What *was* the matter, for God's sake?

Oh, would he please hush and go away, and *stay* away, if he could, for five minutes? By all means, yes, he would. He'd stay away indefinitely if she wished. Lord, yes, there was nothing he'd like better than to clear out and never come back. She couldn't for the life of her see what was holding him, then. It was a swell time. Here she was, stuck, miles from a railroad, with a half-empty house on her hands, and not a penny in her pocket, and everything on earth to do; it seemed the God-sent moment for him to get out from under. She was surprised he hadn't stayed in town as it was until she had come out and done the work and got things straightened out. It was his usual trick.

It appeared to him that this was going a little far. Just a touch out of bounds, if she didn't mind his saying so. Why the hell had he stayed in town the summer before? To do a half-dozen extra jobs to get the money he had sent her. That was it. She knew perfectly well they couldn't have done it otherwise. She had agreed with him at the time. And that was the only time, so help him, he had ever left her to do anything by herself.

Oh, he could tell that to his great-grandmother. She had her notion of what had kept him in town. Considerably more than a notion, if he wanted to know. So, she was going to bring all that up again, was she? Well, she could just think what she pleased. He was tired of explaining. It may have looked funny but he had simply got hooked in, and what could he do? It was impossible to believe that she was going to take it seriously. Yes, yes, she knew how it was with a man: if he was left by himself a minute, some woman was certain to kidnap him. And naturally he couldn't hurt her feelings by refusing!

Well, what was she raving about? Did she forget she had told him those two weeks alone in the country were the happiest she had known for four years? And how long had they been married when she said that? All right, shut up! If she thought that hadn't stuck in his craw.

She hadn't meant she was happy because she was away from him. She meant she was happy getting the devilish house nice and ready for him. That was what she had meant, and now look! Bringing up something she had said a year ago simply to justify himself for forgetting her coffee and breaking the eggs and buying a wretched piece of rope they couldn't afford. She really thought it was time to drop the subject, and now she wanted only two things in the world. She wanted him to get that rope from underfoot, and go back to the village and get her coffee, and if he could remember it, he might bring a metal mitt for the skillets, and two more curtain rods, and if there were any rubber gloves in the village, her hands were simply raw, and a bottle of milk of magnesia from the drugstore.

He looked out at the dark blue afternoon sweltering on the slopes, and mopped his forehead and sighed heavily and said, if only she could wait a minute for *anything*, he was going back. He had said so, hadn't he, the very instant they found he had overlooked it?

Oh, yes, well . . . run along. She was going to wash windows. The country was so beautiful! She doubted they'd have a moment to enjoy it. He meant to go, but he could not until he had said that if she wasn't such a hopeless melancholiac she might see that this was only for a few days. Couldn't she remember anything pleasant about the other summers? Hadn't they ever had any fun? She hadn't time to talk about it, and now would he please not leave that rope lying around for her to trip on? He picked it up, somehow it had toppled off the table, and walked out with it under his arm.

Was he going this minute? He certainly was. She thought so. Sometimes it seemed to her he had second sight about the precisely perfect moment to leave her ditched. She had meant to put the mattresses out to sun; if they put them out this minute they would get at least three hours; he must have heard her say that morning she meant to put them out. So of course he would walk off and leave her to it. She supposed he thought the exercise would do her good.

Well, he was merely going to get her coffee. A four-mile walk for two pounds of coffee was ridiculous, but he was perfectly willing to do it. The habit was making a wreck of her, but if she wanted to wreck herself there was nothing he could do about it. If he thought it was coffee that was making a wreck of her, she congratulated him: he must have a damned easy conscience.

Conscience or no conscience, he didn't see why the mattresses couldn't very well wait until tomorrow. And anyhow, for God's sake! were they living *in* the house, or were they were going to let the house ride them to death? She paled at this, her face grew livid about the mouth, she looked quite dangerous, and reminded him that housekeeping was no more her work than it was his: she had other work to do as well, and when did he think she was going to find time to do it at this rate?

Was she going to start on that again? She knew as well as he did that his work brought in the regular money, hers was only occasional, if they depended on what *she* made—and she might as well get this question straight once for all!

That was positively not the point. The question was, when both of them were working on their own time, was there going to be a division of the housework, or wasn't there? She merely wanted to know, she had to make her plans. Why, he thought that was all arranged. It was understood that he was to help. Hadn't he always, in summers?

Hadn't he, though? Oh, just hadn't he? And when, and where, and doing what? Lord, what an uproarious joke!

It was such a very uproarious joke that her face turned slightly purple, and she screamed with laughter. She laughed so hard she had to sit down, and finally a rush of tears spurted from her eyes and poured down into the lifted corners of her mouth. He dashed towards her and dragged her up to her feet and tried to pour water on her head. The dipper hung by a string on a nail and he broke it loose. Then he tried to pump water with one hand while she struggled in the other. So he gave it up and shook her instead.

She wrenched away, crying out for him to take his rope and go to hell, she had simply given him up: and ran. He heard her high-heeled bedroom slippers clattering and stumbling on the stairs.

He went out around the house and into the lane; he suddenly realized he had a blister on his heel and his shirt felt as if it were on fire. Things broke so suddenly you didn't know where you were. She could work herself into a fury about simply nothing. She was terrible, damn it: not an ounce of reason. You might as well talk to a sieve as to that woman when she got going. Damned if he'd spend his life humouring her! Well, what to do now? He would take back the rope and exchange it for something else. Things accumulated, things were mountainous; you couldn't move them or sort them out or get rid of them. They just lay around and rotted. He'd take it back. Hell, why should he? He wanted it. What was it anyhow? A piece of rope. Imagine anybody caring more about a piece of rope than about a man's feelings. What earthly right had she to say a word about it? He remembered all the useless, meaningless things she bought for herself. Why? because I wanted it, that's why! He stopped and selected a large stone by the road. He would put the rope behind it. He would put it in the tool-box when he got back. He'd heard enough about it to last him a life-time.

When he came back she was leaning against the post box beside the road, waiting. It was pretty late, the smell of broiled steak floated nose-high in the cooling air. Her face was young and smooth and fresh-looking. Her unmanageable funny black hair was all on end. She waved to him from a distance, and he speeded up. She called out that supper was ready and waiting, was he starved?

You bet he was starved. Here was the coffee. He waved it at her. She looked at his other hand. What was that he had there?

Well, it was the rope again. He stopped short. He had meant to exchange it but forgot. She wanted to know why he should exchange it, if it was something he really wanted. Wasn't the air sweet now, and wasn't it fine to be here?

She walked beside him with one hand hooked into his leather belt. She pulled and jostled him a little as he walked, and leaned against him. He put his arm clear around her and patted her stomach. They exchanged wary smiles. Coffee, coffee for the Ootsum-Wootsums! He felt as if he were bringing her a beautiful present.

He was a love, she firmly believed, and if she had had her coffee in the morning, she wouldn't have behaved so funny . . . There was a whip-poor-will still coming back, imagine, clear out of season, sitting in the crab-apple tree calling all by himself. Maybe his girl stood him up. Maybe she did. She hoped to hear him once more, she loved whip-poor-wills . . . He knew how she was, didn't he?

Sure, he knew how she was.

MARY LAVIN

Love Is For Lovers

At the non-committal age of forty-five, Mathew Simmins began to think about marriage. Somehow or other he had never thought about it before. It took up nearly all his time and energy to get the day's work done in the day, because only for him, Mahaffy's Stores would have gone to the wall long ago. Paid hands never really put their heart into their work the way he did. Mathew drew a salary, too, of course, but it was how he felt about the shop that made the difference between him and the shop boys. He was like one of the family. For instance, the shop boys stopped work on the dot of six—actually stopped on the first stroke of the hour, and although Mathew could not himself swear to whether it was the first or the last stroke which indicated *exactly* the termination of one hour and the commencement of another, common courtesy would seem to have demanded that they wait for the last stroke before rushing to grab their coats and get away. For years Mathew had had it in mind to consult a jeweller on this delicate point, but there was no jeweller in the town, and gradually he let the matter slide. All the same he never quite lost a mild irritation at six o'clock when assistants and apprentices alike raced to the storehouse door behind which they hung their coats and caps. They always seemed to manage things in such a way that they were down at that end of the shop tipping up to six. And those of them who were held up by a customer coming in at the last minute, gave the customer short shrift and raced to make up the lost time. Mathew had more than once seen an apprentice—one of the cheekier sort—who, having got into the clutches of an admittedly inconsiderate customer, actually vaulted over a counter in his haste to get out of the place. As if to make it known that once six had gone he owed no deference to anyone!

At precisely five minutes past six the blinds were down, the counters at the grocery end were covered with dust sheets, and Mathew alone remained to turn down the wicks of the lamps, and lock up for the night before leaving for his lodgings. On one.

memorable occasion when the shop door had shut on the last of the assistants, a mouse popped out from a hole in the wainscot and ran across the floor. Mathew thought at first it was a toy mouse on a string, a silly prank played by one of the apprentices. But it was a real mouse, and it took advantage of his hesitancy to get up on the counter and go at the cheese right under his very eyes. That meant another delay, laying down traps, as well as coming in earlier next morning to get rid of the dead mouse and block up the hole. There was always something over and above the day's work to be done in a big shop like Mahaffy's, if you had a proper sense of responsibility. It was almost unbelievable the odd jobs Mathew had to do. Once or twice he had found the day-book open, with a list of a last customer's purchases—a credit customer of course—properly entered, and with a neat line under the figures—but whoever made the entry had not waited to tot up the total. And he frequently found the till open, where someone hadn't taken the time to push the drawer back after flinging in the last coin of the day. Naturally, on these occasions Mathew did what was to be done, and moreover he said nothing about it next morning. He was not the type to be eternally picking on people over trifles. The assistants were almost all young and people nowadays could never be got to do a tap more than they were paid to do. They gave satisfaction from nine to six and that was what counted. In his quiet way Mathew kept order during shop hours. He prided himself that he gave his apprentices as good a training as they'd get in any shop in the town. Perhaps better? And it gave him real gratification on Friday evenings when he stayed behind, purposely and of his own volition, to make up the pay packets and have them in the safe ready for handing out on Saturday evening. He would have been quite within his rights to make them up during shop hours, but it was these small scruples that gave him what he considered a justifiable pride and self-respect. As he'd put each boy's pay into the separate paper packets, specially ordered for this purpose, with the name of the Store on one side and an advertisement for tea on the other, Mathew often felt exactly the same as if he was a partner—the active partner! Old Mahaffy—God rest his soul—had been extremely active, but when he died, Young Mr Mahaffy, who took over, was more of a sleeping partner. This was a private joke, of course, which Mathew enjoyed with himself alone, chuckling over it silently many a time. On those Friday evenings he sometimes indulged in these silent chuckles all the way up the street to the Mahaffy residence. For it was a custom established after the death of old Mahaffy that Mathew would call around in person to receive his cheque direct from the hands of Young Mr Mahaffy. It gave a nice touch to his association with the firm, Mathew felt. Sometimes in the big gloomy dining-room, seated opposite the young man, Mathew often felt that young Mr Mahaffy too regarded him in the light of a partner. There was never any open reference to a partnership. And Mathew was quite satisfied to leave things as they were. It was enough for him to know that he had the gratitude of the Mahaffys. Yes. Yes. The gratitude was there all right. On his side too, there was also considerable gratitude. Where would he be if it were not for the Stores? He never let himself forget that he had not had one penny to rub against another the day he first put on his brown shop-coat and took his place behind Mahaffy's counter. Well he remembered that day—he began in the haberdashery, but he had done his stint behind the grocery and hardware also, a fact to which he attributed his overall knowledge of shopkeeping and management. He had a nice little sum tucked away in the bank today, but where had he made the money? In Mahaffy's! Where else? Young Mr Mahaffy might not have his father's ability, and Mathew had to work hard to make up for some of the young man's deficiencies, but he liked Young Mahaffy. He thought him an exceedingly nice man, and knew him to be one of the best chess players in the county, although he never entered for any competitions or contests. Mathew made a point of being just as deferential to the son as he had been to the father, who had always demanded the deference of everyone in his employment, from the highest to the lowest. The old man had been the glum type, testy and demanding, even with those who had served him for the whole of their lives. Young Mr Mahaffy was a gracious man, a man of great simplicity. No other words could so aptly describe him. Every Friday evening—after exchanging a few words of a more or less similar kind each week—he always made the exact same remark when it came time for him to slide the glossy white vellum envelope, with Mathew's cheque inside it, across the broad mahogany tabletop.

'You are Mahaffy's Mathew and Mahaffy's is you,' he'd say. 'I am a good-for-nothing. I only rake in the profits.'

And Mathew felt it to be in keeping with their relationship that his reply too be the same as always.

'Don't forget you write the cheques as well, sir.'

Those words of Mathews usually gave Young Mahaffy his cue for standing up and shaking hands with him. There was a sort of ritual touch to their encounters that Mathew liked. He liked to know precisely when to come and when to go. He liked to know for certain where he stood with people. It made it easier to deal with them. That, no doubt, was why it upset him so much when one of his best customers, a widow, a Mrs Rita Cooligan, became so forgetful she was forever leaving something behind on one of the counters, and coming back in a state to look for it. To make matters worse she insisted on calling for him.

'Mr Simmins! Where is he? I must see Mr Simmins,' she'd call out as she'd come running back into the shop, regardless of whether or not there were other customers present. And when she'd see him, she'd rush up to him, pushing her hat back from her forehead in a manner that made her look younger and more helpless than she had seemed to Mathew when she first brought her custom to Mahaffy's. Then, he thought of her as a mature woman, and certainly strong-minded, and well balanced. But here she was arousing such feelings of protectiveness in him that he let the shop be turned upside down in his efforts to pacify her. For one thing, he'd send the shop boys scurrying hither and thither all over the place, although he knew well they'd make it an excuse for tricking and fooling around under the counters. The tops of the counters he took care of himself, lifting up every blessed thing and looking under it, in search of whatever it was she had lost, although once it was only a handkerchief. Sometimes, however, Mrs Cooligan mislaid something less easily replaced—like a key-ring with the key of her house on it. She really was a featherhead, as indeed she called herself, when almost always, and with a rich, warm laugh, she would suddenly produce the missing article from somewhere on her own person, or from an inside pocket of her handbag which Mathew could have sworn she had searched, not indeed once, but several times. She was in such a state, however, one had to excuse her. And to show her that he did, Mathew always permitted himself to smile. The shop boys of course would have gone on screeching with laughter for the rest of the day, if he hadn't sent them about their business. Not that a little simple fun did anyone any harm, but it couldn't be carried too far. Mrs Cooligan herself almost carried the thing too far. When she'd finally leave the shop she'd still be laughing, as she went up the street. Mathew shook his head. Featherhead! he said to himself again, but he meant it in a kindly way. How long, he wondered, was it since her husband died? It was sad to see a woman like that so full of life left to live out the best years of her life alone. Here, however, Mathew put a strong rein on himself. It didn't seem proper to think about the poor woman's private life, such thoughts bordered on coarseness, and that was something he had always guarded against.

Then one day in early spring when the sun, for the time of year, was so strong, Mathew had thought he had better take the butter out of the window. Mahaffy's was giving a special offer in butter and a nice little display had been arranged to attract attention to it. His landlady had kindly made up a number of butter pats and Mathew had arranged them on a glass butter-dish from stock. But it would be disastrous if the unseasonable heat of the sun melted the butter. He just put his head into the window to take out the glass dish when he saw Mrs Cooligan coming down the street. What a fine figure she had, though to be truthful he had never considered himself a judge of such matters. Indeed, some of the young things that came into the shop these days looked so thin, so downright peaky, he often felt like commenting on their condition when talking to their parents, because one could not know people from the pram up—even in business—without taking a friendly interest in them. But to his astonishment these were the very girls he'd hear the shop boys gassing about as they were going out into the street in the evening, or when in the morning they would arrive at the door and he would be inside struggling with the lock to open up and let them in. Well, as the saying went, it took all kinds to make a world. And watching Mrs Rita Cooligan come sailing down the street, Mathew felt even a blind man could see that she was a well built woman. At this point he took out his handkerchief and vehemently blew his nose.

Meanwhile his customer was advancing rapidly, considering how highly arched were her shoes. She was wearing the same coat as usual, and although yesterday he could not have told what colour it was—not if his life depended on it—today in the spring sunlight he saw it was a nice colour. A sort of plum? It was tight, or perhaps he should say neat-fitting, and he liked the way she had pulled the belt tight like a man would, only of course, unlike a man her top rose up from it in a way that put him in mind of a swan on a pond. There again of course, swans were white and cold and Mrs Rita Cooligan exuded nothing but richness and warmth, being dark, and her complexion being the sort he understood to be called olive complexion.

But Mrs Cooligan had now almost arrived at the door and was clearly coming into the shop, since it was the end shop in the street. Realizing that having watched her, when she had not known she was being watched, might make it hard for him to appear natural, Mathew made a lightning decision to stay where he was with his back turned. In fact when he heard the shop door open, he poked his head still further into the aperture of the window and busied himself with making slight alterations on the window display, moving things around a bit and trying to fill the space made by the removal of the butter. But he couldn't keep up this charade for long. There was one thing he could do. The sun was really strong. Even though he had taken out the butter, it would be quite reasonable to lower the window blind. He reached out for the cord, but his mind unfortunately was not properly centred on what he was doing and after he had lowered the blind, he let the cord slip from his grasp and the blind shot up again with a sound so loud and shocking that it brought the blood to his head. He didn't dare to turn around and see what Mrs Cooligan had made of his clumsiness. To hide this new flux of embarrassment he had no other course open to him but bury his head still deeper into the opening of the window and continue to fiddle about with various articles and wait until she left the premises.

At last Mrs Cooligan concluded her purchases. Mathew knew when she was leaving by the tap-tap of her heels, and by a breath of heavy perfume that travelled through the shop, like a ring of smoke puffed into the air. He was almost relieved to find that as it neared him this intoxicating wreath of scent had begun to dissolve. Preoccupied in this way, he was still not giving his full attention to what he was doing and so when Mrs Cooligan, having gained the street, happened to stop and look in the window, he was struck dumb when he found himself staring straight into her face—that is to say, as clearly as he could see it with a fly paper hanging down between them, encrusted with dead flies. And immediately he had the uneasy feeling that she had known all along that he had been trying to avoid her, and this was her way of punishing him. He was contrite beyond words. Mrs Cooligan was one of Mahaffy's best customers. He resolved at once to make amends for having offended her, next time she came into the shop—if she ever did come in again. He might perhaps open a tin of biscuits and invite her to sample a new variety? Nothing pleased customers more than flattery like that—and his innocent little ruse served a double purpose, because most customers bought a pound or so of the biscuits, and the over-independent types, who felt obliged to give it as their opinion that the new variety was a bit on the sweet side, or else a bit on the plain side, nevertheless bought some sort of biscuits, if only to prove their point. It was a good business move in either case. In either case Mathew knew he was showing respect for the customer as well as putting a few more shillings in the till. There was no duplicity involved. After all, one man's meat was another man's poison.

Reassuring himself that Mrs Cooligan had really gone, Mathew was about to return to his station behind the desk, when, of a sudden, the shop door was thrown open with such violent force that a pile of empty biscuit tins that had been left near the door, ready when the van would arrive to collect returns, came toppling to the floor, making an indescribable din.

'Oh what have I done?' Mrs Cooligan cried as Mathew rushed forward to assist her in stepping over the wretched tins. In his attempts to be of assistance Mathew had to lift one of his legs with both hands over the heap of tins. But at least he was in command of the situation.

'What is the matter?' he cried.

'Oh Mr Simmins,' Mrs Cooligan was almost in tears. 'This time it's my handbag I've lost! I left it behind in some shop or other, but it's not in the butchers because I called there first of all. And it's not in the drapers, I didn't leave it there either. And I could not possibly have dropped it in the street on my way down here, or else the new chemist would have seen me drop it, because he assured me he never took his eyes off me for one moment—not for one second, if you want his exact words.'

'Please, please, Mrs Cooligan,' Mathew cried. 'Please don't get excited. Perhaps you didn't bring your bag out with you? Perhaps you left it at home?'

'No, no, no,' Mrs Cooligan cried with extraordinary firmness. 'You must understand that I took my bag with me expressly because it contained a sum of money that I intended to lodge to my account in the bank.'

99

'Ah,' Mathew said, steadying himself still more to cope with this new aspect of the situation. 'Perhaps you left it behind in the bank?'

'I haven't been to the bank yet,' Mrs Cooligan replied with singular simplicity.

Mathew saw the matter, this time, was really serious. 'I hope there wasn't a large amount of money in the bag?' he asked, as he sent the shop boys scurrying off to look for it, and he having begun his usual lifting of things and putting them down again, not even bothering to rub a dab of butter off his cuff as he took his hand from behind the butter-slab although it was improbable that the hand-bag could have got there, his intention having been to reassure her, nothing more. But she really was a strange woman.

'I don't care a rap about the money, Mr Simmins,' she said. 'What grieves me is the loss of a souvenir that was in an inner pocket of the bag—a paper knife—a little paper knife with an ivory handle that I've treasured ever since it was given to me years ago by someone I dearly loved.'

Mathew was struck to the heart, when her eyes filled with tears, he was so bewildered he didn't know what to say to her: but it did occur to him that it must have been given to her by that other fellow, her husband, and unaccountably he felt less sorry for her. Why didn't she keep things like that at home, instead of hawking them around in her handbag? His sympathy towards her lessened so much he went over and attended in person to another customer, although he seldom attended any customer in person any more. But, as if she had read his mind, at that very instant he overheard her talking to one of the shop boys and explaining that the paper knife had been given to her by her best friend when they had both been schoolgirls together before her friend married and went to Australia and was never heard from again!

Mathew could have kicked himself for being so hasty in misjudging her.

'Don't despair!' he cried. 'I believe we'll find it yet. If necessary I will paste a notice on the window.' Indeed, there and then he grabbed one of the assistants by the sleeve. 'Get a pencil!' he ordered. 'Say we are offering a reward.' He turned back to Mrs Cooligan. 'This is not meant to convey that I have given up hope of yet finding it on the premises.' Here he plucked another of the boys by the sleeve. 'Did you try the sugar bin?' he demanded. The boy seemed a bit nonplussed but Mathew had turned away and was addressing himself to Mrs Cooligan. 'We lost one of the weights belonging to the scales, a few months ago—I forget which weight it was, the half hundredweight or the eight-ounce, but whichever it was we were put to great inconvenience without it. We searched everywhere to no avail, and I myself was on the point of giving up and sending away to replace it, when I happened to pass the sugar bin and, partly to take my mind off my annoyance, I stopped to ascertain if there was sufficient sugar to last the weekend without sending out for more to the storeroom—something I usually do by eye, but which incredibly, I did that day by diving in my hand and running it through the sugar. And what do you suppose! Guess! I felt my hand hit against something hard on the bottom of the bin. "Come here, Joe," I cried. "There's something here in this bin. Put in your hand and see what it is!" Never did I suspect it to be the missing weight, but when Joe delved in his hand that was the very thing he pulled up and showed me. Isn't that right, Joe?' he asked, but Joe, instead of confirming the story, had already dived his hand into the bin and began to sift the sugar between his fingers.

'Any luck, Joe?' Mrs Cooligan cried, as she leaned over the counter in such a way that Mathew was overwhelmed by her resemblance to a swan, with her top part swelling up over the counter and the rest of her hidden below it.

In the end, however, it had to be acknowledged by all that the handbag had vanished. It was not to be seen high up or low down. And Mrs Cooligan was forced to depart without it, although at the door she paused and called back to Mathew.

'Somehow or other I cannot help feeling that it is here somewhere,' she said.

Mathew felt that the shop boys must have been proud of the way he rose to the occasion.

'Rest assured, Mrs Cooligan,' he said. 'If we find it, I will send Joe, here, down with it to your house. Immediately.'

'You're more than kind,' Mrs Cooligan said, and then instead of going out, she came back into the shop. 'I do hope you believe me, Mr Simmins, when I say it's not the loss of the money that matters to me, but the loss of my little paper knife. I never took it out of the house before. I don't know what possessed me to take it with me today. It's a sort of a talisman, a charm. I always keep it on my bedside table. For luck! And if I think I hear a noise in the middle of the night, I put out my hand and feel around for it, and always,

always, it gives me courage.' Then she left, having given Mathew a smile, a brave smile.

'I still believe we will find it,' Mathew said very solemnly, because it was, as far as he could recollect, the first lie he had ever told. The last he thought to see of her that day was when she smiled in at him again through the shop window before going bravely up the street. She was a woman of great self control, he thought, as he set about tidying up the counters. He could not but admire her sentiments towards an old friend, although he did, quite frankly, find it hard to understand how sentiment could take precedence over the loss of good money.

All that afternoon Mathew kept his eyes open for the missing handbag, while he went around readying up the mess that had been made in their search for it by those giddy shop boys. It was hard to see why they had to empty out three boxes of shoe laces. And it was harder still to explain why they had considered it necessary to unravel several balls of twine. Indeed, by the time six o'clock struck Mathew was almost as much put out by the state of the shop as he was by Mrs Cooligan's loss. And when the shop boys had gone gallivanting off, and as he himself went down to the storehouse door to get his outdoor clothes, he was actually frowning.

Mathew kept his coat and hat in the same place as his assistants, for convenience, but on a separate nail from the nails on which they hung their coats. There had to be some distinctions made in the interests of authority! But this evening, as he reached up to take down his coat, his foot hit against something and sent it sliding across the floorboards. As he said to himself in bed that night, he knew, or to be accurate, he partly guessed, before stooping to pick it up, that it was Rita Cooligan's handbag. And so it was.

Mathew was as pleased as Punch. To think of how the shop boys had monkeyed about for hours looking for it, with no success, whereas he had only to walk down to the end of the shop and there it was under his feet as if placed there by magic. He picked it up. And seeing, that the clasp was open, he carefully closed it, although mind you, it took him some minutes to master that catch. There was a little trick to it—a very clever little trick. But he got it.

'Very clever!' he said out loud when he had ascertained that the clasp was well and truly closed, and he went over to put the bag into the safe. Before closing the safe he took a last look at it, and he marvelled at how extraordinary it was for women to feel the need of a contraption like it, whereas a man's wallet was so uncompli-cated. Really, women were strange creatures.

This, therefore, may have been the point at which for the first time Mathew thought about marriage, but of course it was in a very negative way, because although other differences between women and men kept popping into his head, he assumed that by and large they were differences that he, personally, would never explore. However, after he had let himself out into the street, checking the shop door several times, due to the unusual tension caused by the events of the day, it crossed his mind that it was odd he had never thought about marriage—or, rather, never thought of it as being for him, within his province. Otherwise he felt no differently from any other evening as he plodded his way towards his lodgings, a little stiff after a long day's work, a trifle chilly in spite of his having on his heavy top-coat.

It was only by the merest chance, as he passed the entrance to a small road—a cul-de-sac really—where Mrs Cooligan lived—that he happened to look down at the terrace of small houses and saw that although most of the front windows were dark, there was one window so brightly lit that in spite of the curtains being drawn, a soft glow came through into the small front garden. Mathew stood for a moment. He knew that colour. Plum! It crossed his mind immediately that the house must be her house, Mrs Cooligan's. It was a pity he had not found her bag before closing time, or certainly he would, as he had promised, have Joe or one of the boys down with it to her. Or would he? On consideration, it would have been better perhaps—had he found it in time—to send word that he had put it in the safe until such time as it could be passed from his hand to hers. Not that the assistants were untrustworthy! They would not be employed in Mahaffy's were that so, but that was solely with regard to money. With things of purely sentimental value they might not be so scrupulous. Supposing the paper knife were to be let fall out of the bag, unnoticed, into the gutter, to be picked up by some other careless person who in turn might toss it into a rubbish can. Yes, it would have been preferable to simply send word that the article had been found, just to put her out of suspense. Too bad he had not found it earlier.

Mathew was about to continue on his way when it struck him like a bolt from the blue that there was nothing to stop him from calling to her door himself, right there and then, and put her mind at ease. But now, Mathew was disturbed by the realization that he was not certain of the number of her house, a fact for which he felt specially culpable since he often sent special deliveries to her door, and needless to say, as was only fitting in a place like Mahaffy's, that all labels on parcels should be in his own hand which he had perfected until it was copperplate. How could he have forgotten her number? Then, with a little spurt of jauntiness, he decided to take a shot in the dark, even if it was a long shot, and so next moment found him striding down the road, making for the house with the plum-coloured curtains. As he stepped up to the hall door, Mathew thought again what a pity it was he had not brought the bag with him. What a triumph it would have been when she'd open the door to hold it up without a word, just a knowing look, a telling smile! As he raised his hand to lift the iron door-knocker, however, Mathew was disconcerted to see it was fashioned in the shape of a mailed fist and he was overcome by an understandable timidity. He would feel as if he was banging on her door with his own fist. Fortunately there was a bell. And, assuming the bell to be one of the common, ordinary sorts, where you pushed a button with your finger, he was about to ring when another complication arose. The mechanism of the bell was most unusual. It consisted of two metal wings, like the wings of an ornamental butterfly, which presumably you pressed together. There was something vaguely familiar about the mechanism of the bell, he thought, as he gingerly pressed on the two bits of metal. Next minute he nearly fell off the doorstep with the twitter of sound just inside the door. For a moment he thought the sound was inside his ear, and that an insect had got into the ear and was trapped there. Before he was fully recovered the door was flung open.

'Your handbag, I found it,' Mathew said, summoning up the whole stock of his presence of mind to bring out the words.

Mrs Cooligan was quite composed.

'Mr Simmins! What a surprise! Do come inside!' she said, holding open the door and standing back. 'How nice of you to call. Welcome!' He had decidedly done the right thing by calling. She made it seem the most natural thing in the world. And now, no doubt to put him still more at ease, she was drawing his attention to something on the back of the door. 'How do you like my bell, Mr Simmins. It's my own invention. It's just a bicycle-bell fastened to the inside, with a hole bored so the two lugs can be squeezed from outside. So economical! And quite ingenious, don't you think? Listen!' she commanded, and before she closed the door she filled the hallway with twitter after twitter. Then she threw open the door of the front room, the room with the plum curtains, which was certainly comfortable, and hot. Mathew had not intended to do more than stand on the doorstep, but he was a bit confused by Mrs Cooligan's chatter, and the twittering of the bell, but above all by the incessant barking of a large liver-and-white spotted dog sitting on a plum coloured sofa. In two ticks Mathew was sitting on the sofa too.

'It was *so* nice of you to come,' Mrs Cooligan said, with such cordiality, she made it seem like a social call. He wondered if perhaps she had not heard what he'd said at the door?

'Your bag! I found it,' he said, and he almost had to shout to be heard above the din the dog was making.

'Be quiet, Pete!' Mrs Cooligan said. 'Be quiet.' And when the dog didn't stop she picked it up and held it in her arms. 'Nice Petey!' she coaxed. 'Petey mustn't bark at this kind gentleman. The kind gentleman brought back my bag, Petey.'

Mathew was relieved to see she had in fact registered the reason for his call, and he was even more relieved when the old dog yielded to the warmth of her arms and stopped yapping. Seemingly it had taken in what she'd said, because it looked at Mathew now with rich brown eyes, moist and red-brimmed. A well-meaning poor dog, Mathew thought, and forgave it the noise it had made.

'Isn't he sweet?' Mrs Cooligan was asking. 'He understands every word I say to him. You'll be firm friends, the two of you, from now on. You'll see! Pat him, Mr Simmins! Pat him! Take his paw. Make him shake hands! He won't bite. He's full of love, once he gets to know people. Make him give the paw.'

It was touching to see her devotion to the dog and its devotion to her, but Mathew had not patted a dog since he was a boy, and he was a bit nervous. Nevertheless he put out his hand and stroked Pete whose coat was certainly soft and silky. A very well kept animal! Stroking Pete's coat was like stroking human hair. Not that Mathew had ever done that in all his life, and involuntarily he glanced at Mrs Cooligan's hair that, seen without a hat, seemed to ripple like waves of the sea, ripple after ripple after ripple. When Mathew looked back quickly at the dog, Mrs Cooligan took its paw and began to pull it gently, making the loose flesh wobble. A most peculiar sensation went through Mathew—quite as if she was touching him. He stopped stroking the dog, but he went on looking into its wet eyes.

Mrs Cooligan saw at once that he was uncomfortable about something, and with a tact for which Mathew was more grateful than he could say, she tried to make him feel at home by talking to him playfully through the dog.

'Well, Pete? What do you think of Mr Simmins? Isn't he a nice man, Pete?'

And Pete understood every word, or so it would seem from the way he put out his tongue and tried to lick Mathew's hand.

'A wonderfully intelligent little creature,' Mrs Cooligan said, 'and with a heart brimful of human kindness. When poor Arthur—my husband, now dead, as I think you know, Mr Simmins—when he knew that his days were numbered, he picked up Pete one day and looking into his eyes, he told him he was leaving me in his charge. "Pete will take care of you, Rita my darling," he said.'

From that moment Mathew found himself thinking of her not as Mrs Cooligan, but as Rita. It was upsetting. He stood up at once.

'About your bag,' he said, in as practical a manner as possible.

Mrs Cooligan did not stand up, but she dropped Pete on the floor and she too become practical.

'I will call for it tomorrow,' she said.

Immediately Mathew recalled how she felt about her little keepsake. She'd be without it all night. Ah well, he thought, it might not be right to proffer to go back to the shop, it could make him appear altogether too accommodating, make him look as if he wanted to put her under a compliment to him. Nothing was further from his mind. Then she herself brought up the subject of the paper knife, if indirectly.

'You do realize, don't you, Mr Simmins, it was never the loss of the ten pounds that bothered me, it was only—'

Mathew, however, heard no more.

'Ten pounds!' He was thunderstruck. 'You don't mean to say there was an amount of that size in the bag? Why didn't you tell me. I found it on the floor! The clasp was open! The money could have fallen out. I didn't look inside.' So great was his consternation that he had to mop his forehead with his handkerchief.

'Oh, I didn't mean to upset you, Mr Simmins,' Mrs Cooligan said. 'On the contrary! Do please sit down again.'

What a strange woman! She didn't care about losing ten pounds, and yet for the sake of economy she had installed that diabolical, twittering doorbell. It was almost irresponsible. He put away his handkerchief and returned to the subject of the money.

'May I ask if this money was in a single note, or if it was in two five-pound notes?' he asked.

Rita shrugged her firm, rounded shoulders, which Mathew only now noticed were bare, but then the room was very hot. He himself was perspiring, but that may have been due to worry over the money.

'I really don't remember whether it was singles or fivers,' she said. Then she concentrated hard. 'Wait a minute. I think it was two fivers. I know that last week it was a tenner, but it could have been two fivers this time.'

Evidently a regular income, Mathew thought. A pension perhaps? An annuity?

'Mrs Cooligan,' he said. He nearly said Rita! 'You must understand that although *you* may not be concerned about the safety of this money, I cannot remain unconcerned. Once the bag passed into my hands I hold myself responsible for it and also for whatever it contained. I think I simply must go back to the shop and make sure the money is alright.'

Rita sprang to her feet at that.

'You will do no such thing,' she cried. 'Not on my account, you won't! How could you think I'd be so inconsiderate, as to let you go back all that way—without your supper—which I'm sure you'd find flat and tasteless when you'd finally get it.' She was right there, Mathew thought, but all the same he went resolutely toward the door. 'No, I won't allow it,' Rita cried, and pushing past him, she stood with her back against the door, and threw out her arms as if physically to prevent his leaving. She sounded in deadly earnest, but again Mathew thought he detected a playfulness about her. A strange woman!

He, however, remained grave and earnest.

'I'm afraid I must insist,' he said. 'You don't understand, the money may be lying about on the floor.'

'Let it lie there,' she said. 'Aren't you always the first one into the shop in the morning? What could happen to it during the night?'

She'd nearly got him there! But he had his wits about him.

'A mouse might chew it up,' he said.

'A mouse? A mouse!' She was so taken by surprise she lowered her arms, which must have been tired stretched out like that, and she began to laugh so much and so heartily that she had to cross her arms over her bosom to prevent herself shaking to bits. Then, quite suddenly she gave way. 'Very well,' she said quietly. 'I will permit you to go and fetch it, but I warn you I don't like to be disobeyed and when you come back with it you may find yourself faced with paying me a forfeit.'

Mathew hadn't the foggiest idea what she was talking about. He was on edge to get back to the shop.

'Don't be long!' she called from the doorway.

'I don't intend to dally,' he called back gaily. And in fact he was striding along like a twenty year old, so fast he wasn't in the least chilly, and he didn't feel as stiff in the joints as usual either. What he did feel was hungry—famished in fact. He could hear his stomach rumbling. And to make matters worse when he got back to Rita's with the bag—in which the money was safe and sound, tucked away and zipped into an inner pocket—a tantalizing smell of food rushed out into the air when she threw open the door. He held out the bag, coughing loudly to cover up the rumbling in his gut and preparing to dash off.

'Oh no, you don't!' Rita cried. She caught his arm and literally pulled him into the hall. Taking the bag she tossed it on the hall table and threw open the door of the front room where a small table, drawn up to the fire, was laid with places for two. 'Now you must pay your forfeit! You must keep me company for supper. Give me your coat,' she cried, and gave him a push that sent him into the middle of the room. As she took his coat she was talking ten to the dozen and Pete was beating the floor with his stubby tail. 'I love having people for a meal, specially in the evening. I never eat properly when I'm alone. Pete here always gets the best part of the meal. On top of his own share!' She picked up the dog. 'Isn't that so, Pete?' Then she put the dog down. 'Most evenings it doesn't seem worth while cooking for one person alone. I keep thinking how much Arthur loved my steak and kidney pie. That's what we're having tonight. I hope it's one of your favourite dishes?' It was. Mathew sat down beside Pete, who had scrambled back up on the plush sofa.

She was full of surprises. He would never have thought her the domesticated type. Only this morning he'd been thinking of her as a swan! Cooking was something he associated with landladies and downtrodden wives.

That night, however, after he had been invited to come again and try another of her culinary specialities, he felt it would have been boorish to refuse. And when in the course of the following weeks he had sampled several dishes and they'd got around to steak and kidney for the second time, Mathew discovered plenty of other differences, that he had not thought about, between men and women, only now he was beginning to think it might not be too late for him to investigate some of them more closely.

For although he hadn't thought of marriage ever, or certainly not for years, this did not mean that Mathew was not romantic at the white-hot core. As a young man, when he first came to Mahaffy's, he used to spend a lot of time looking at the girls in the town as they strolled about the streets, and thought how much nicer they were than big fat country girls. He would not have objected to making the acquaintance of one of these girls, but they seemed so quick, so smart, he didn't dare to speak to them. And it wasn't as if he knew anyone who would introduce him! Besides that, he was soon so wrapped up in Mahaffy's he was too tired after shop hours to do much more than crawl back to the lodging house for his evening meal and read the evening newspaper. Later in the night he might perhaps take a short walk, but by then there were no girls in the streets, they'd all have gone off somewhere. To the cinema perhaps? Or to the dance hall, from which, when he'd pass it, the music came out in gusts like wind blowing at gale force, against which he knew he would never push his way. He began then to content himself with looking at girls on the posters that were pasted to hoardings and the gable end of disused buildings, advertising some commodity like scented soap, or a camera. In his more fanciful moments he used to try to imagine what it would be like if they were real flesh and blood girls who might at any moment step down out of the poster and take his arm. Together, then, he and that girl would go up the street linked and laughing into each other's eyes.

There was one particular poster on a hoarding opposite Mahaffy's, which advertised a well known make of bicycle, and the girl on that poster was the one who really took Mathew's fancy. She wore a blue tam—blue was a nice colour—and she had blue eyes as well, and as she pedalled towards him, she rode right into the cool summer breeze, not caring that her golden hair got blown about. Indeed one golden strand of it blew right across her face. After a time he confined himself to that girl and it was always her, and not the others, that he'd dream of as stepping down and suggesting that he buy a bicycle and go for a spin with her. He was not in love with her. Needless to say! A girl on a poster! If he hadn't been a steady chap he would never have got where he got in Mahaffy's. Not in a million years!

All this, of course, was long ago. Girls never wore tams now. They never let their hair blow about. They sprayed something on it to keep the ripples in place. And most girls nowadays looked coarse on a bicycle. Anyway he had, quite properly, been brought up to understand that you couldn't have everything in this life. He had a good job in Mahaffy's and a nice little nest egg in the bank. What more could he have asked of life, not ever having thought that some women could be lonely too—not until the day one, of her own accord, flew down on to the path in front of him, asking to be caught. For Mathew was not as backward as he might seem. He knew what Rita had in mind. He didn't blame her either, and he made full acknowledgement that, if left to himself, he would never have come forward the way she did. She had made the blessings of marriage seem much more easily obtainable than he would ever have believed possible.

In other words Mathew decided to let events take their course. And in due time he and Rita were both overtaken by summer.

In the full heat of summer, an exceptionally hot Saturday in the middle of July, when he and Rita were having a cup of tea, Rita suddenly had one of her brainwaves. Running out into the garden she looked up into the sun. Then running back into the house, she pushed a cushion into Mathew's hand, and gave Pete an old newspaper to carry out in his mouth—just to please the dog. 'We're going to have tea in the garden,' she said. It seemed a good idea, but as they drank their tea in the small garden, which was almost burnt-up with the heat of that summer sun, Mathew found himself wondering why she had never planted a few trees, as a neighbour down the road had done. Trees—even bushes—could cast a nice shade in summer. And in Rita's garden no cool shade fell. Mathew was soon uncomfortably hot, and he wondered if she might not have looked cooler in some colour other than that eternal plum colour? Blue? Green? They were nice colours. He liked them better than that plum.

Putting his hand over his cup, as she went to pour more tea for him, Mathew casually remarked that in America people, or so he heard, drank iced tea.

'America?' Rita cried. 'That's a place I'd give anything to visit!'

'Who wouldn't!' Mathew said. 'The fare is over a hundred and fifty pounds.'

'Oh well,' Rita said with a pout. 'As far as I am concerned, I might as well spend the money Arthur left me one way as another. After all, he did tell me that I was to spend it any way I liked, and put a recommendation into his will that I was to have as good a time as was possible for a woman alone. I'd have no hesitation at all in going to America, and seeing Niagara Falls, and the Statue of Liberty and all that, only I'm not really sure that I'd enjoy it on my own. What do you think, Mathew?'

'I don't know,' Mathew said, mopping his brow.

'Well? Would you enjoy going there all alone?' Rita challenged.

'I don't know,' Mathew repeated. 'I have never considered taking such a step.'

'Well, consider it now!' Rita said. 'Wouldn't you be lonely going off to America all alone?'

'But who said I was going?' Mathew asked. He was frankly bewildered by this turn the conversation had taken. In courtesy towards Rita, he felt obliged to give the prospect some consideration.

'I don't know anybody in America,' he said at last.

'But if you went there with a friend, what then?' she asked, leaning forward towards him.

'Since there isn't any question of my going, I don't see the point of all this discussion.' Mathew was becoming unbearably hot.

'Do have another cup of tea, Mat?' Rita asked, as she reached for and took his cup. 'Will I pour away the dregs?'

'Don't bother,' Mathew said listlessly.

But Rita looked into the cup and gave a little screech.

'There's a fly in your cup,' she said, and she spilled the cold slop out on the grass. The fly was not quite dead though, and feeling the firm ground under its feet, it shook the tea leaves from its wings and, crawling up onto a blade of grass, rubbed its forefeet together exactly as if clapping at its release. Alas, the celebration was premature, for Pete had spotted the fly. And Pete made a snap at it. In a desperate effort to save the fly Mathew aimed a kick at Pete's rump, but fat and all as Pete was, he was quicker than Mathew and Mathew missed. The fly went down Pete's gullet.

'Why didn't you take it out on a spoon?' he demanded of Rita. 'You could have put it down somewhere safe, where that damned dog wouldn't have got it.'

'Who are you talking about?' Rita was genuinely bewildered.

'That fly,' Mathew said.

Rita stared at him.

'But flies are a nuisance, Mathew. They get into the jam and into the honey—they get into everything. And if they land on meat they lay eggs and—'

Mathew's stomach turned upside down.

'Please!' he cried. 'Please,' and to settle his stomach he stared up into the sky, that was so blue and cool and remote.

'Mathew, you weren't listening to me a minute ago when I was talking about America,' Rita said. 'Wouldn't it be fun if we were both there at the same time, or better still if we went on the same ship? You may not know it, but you are very good company. And so efficient! You'd see to everything. You'd make such a success of the trip. Not like poor little me! I am no use at all outside my own little nest. I'd get lost within two seconds of walking down the gangplank.'

'I'd say you'd make out alright anywhere you'd go,' Mathew said, so stoutly, and so sure of what he was saying, Rita took another tack.

'Did I ever tell you about a cousin of mine who went over there, once? I didn't. Well, let me tell you, Mathew, she met her Fate on board the ship.'

'What do you mean by that?' Matthew asked, roused at last to a small degree of interest.

'Oh Mathew! You are so funny! Did you never hear that old expression? It means she met the man Destiny had laid out for her to marry. As a matter of fact, they were married as soon as the ship docked.' Then, seeing by his face that Mathew still didn't appear to get her meaning, Rita threw back her head and laughed so loudly the tea cups rattled in their saucers. 'You are so innocent, my pet,' she said. But she wagged her finger at him. 'At least you pretend to be innocent, you cunning old fox!'

She meant to be flattering, and that is the way Mathew would have taken her remarks, if only Pete hadn't started to bark again for no good reason that Mathew could see. Rita grabbed him up again and hugged him tight.

'He thinks I'm upset about something. Poor Pete! He wants to show he's here to protect me. He's a marvellous watch dog. Put him to the test, Mathew, if you don't believe me. Pretend to hit me! Go on. Please do. Just pretend. You'll see the state he'll get himself into, poor fellow. He'll bark his head off! You'll die laughing. Go on! Hit me. It's only make-believe!'

But Mathew was too hot for playing games of any kind. Anyway, Pete must have been too hot in Rita's arms because he was struggling to free his head, and Mathew thought the dog only wanted to reach out and lick him—lick his face—with its big, fat tongue that was disgustingly like a greasy slice of ham. He rapidly returned his gaze to the blue sky over them all, and stared up into it as hard as he could stare.

'Don't you think it's too hot to hold that dog in your arms?' he asked at last, when Pete began to pant.

'Too hot to cuddle my Petey? Nonsense!' Rita put a plump white hand on the old dog's fat, white belly, and she began to roll its belly round and round like a ball. 'I told you what Arthur said to me in the last moments before he left me.' She leant forward. 'Oh, Mathew, I do wish you had known Arthur. You two would have taken to each other on sight. But now it's too late. Poor Arthur!'

A tear, only one tear, ran down her face, but Mathew hoped that would be all.

'Arthur is happy wherever he is, Rita,' he said hastily. 'He is at peace. There's no reason to feel sorry for him.' Mathew was hot and tired, but he always endeavoured to be honest. He did not feel that Arthur had gone to a Better Place. At worst he was under the sod, his eyeballs stopped with clay. But when at that moment Pete took a notion and awkwardly jumped from Rita's lap on to Mathew's knees, that were tightly pressed together, and made a really determined effort to lick his face, Mathew, who put out his hand to fend off the dog, could feel its internal organs working inside the dog's baggy belly, and he thought he'd throw up.

'Get down! Get down!' he cried, perhaps too roughly, because Pete looked deeply hurt.

'Why Mathew!' Rita exclaimed. 'I'm beginning to think you don't like poor old Pete.'

'I don't dislike him,' Mathew said.

'That's not the point,' Rita said, gathering the dog up into her arms again. Then she stood up and went over and sat on one of the stone steps leading into the house. 'Come over here, Mathew,' she said. 'It's much nicer sitting here than on those deck chairs.'

'No, thank you,' Mathew said. He never felt safe in a deck chair, but he certainly didn't feel like sitting on a hot stone. There was a short silence, after which Rita suggested clearing away the tea things. Could she never sit still for a second? 'Let's leave them until later,' he said.

'What if it rains?' she asked, and held her hand palm upwards to the cloudless heavens.

'It won't rain,' Mathew said, without needing to raise his eyes. No such luck, he thought. Cool, sweet rain was a long way from falling on them. 'It won't rain,' he said again, and then, rather than try to think of anything else to say, he had an insane desire to go on repeating himself like a gramophone record with a crack in it.

At that moment he only wanted one thing from life and that was to be left alone—to sit still, with his eyes closed, and not have to say another word until he felt good and like it! And it occurred to him that perhaps if they were married—Rita and him—they would not have to keep talking all the time. If they were married she surely wouldn't be hurt if he wanted to be silent now and then? Wasn't it only before marriage one had to be over-polite? Marriage would surely allow for an occasional slump, even in an uncomfortable deck chair?

As he turned over these thoughts in his mind, Mathew noticed that Rita had put out her hand to tweak Pete's ear. Pete, with a frantic wriggle, got off her lap to lay himself out flat on the grass. And Mathew put himself another question. Could he be sure that Rita felt the same as him, about marriage? He would like to have asked her there and then, point blank, how she felt about it, but he warned himself that such enquiries might compromise him, so he just stole a look at her from under his burning eyelids. She had reached out again and tweaked Pete's ear.

'Isn't he an old dote?' she said. 'He sleeps on the foot of my bed. Did you know that, Mathew?'

He didn't, but he might have guessed, Mathew thought.

'Why don't you let the poor brute sleep now?' he said irritably.

'Why would he want to sleep in the middle of a lovely hot summer afternoon?' Rita asked, and she stood up as if to come over closer to Mathew himself.

'The butter is melting,' Mathew said. 'I think maybe you should take it into the house.'

'True for you,' Rita said. 'Let's clear the table while we're at it. Give me a hand, Mat,' she said, as she herself took up the butter to go inside. Pete got up too and waddled after her. But Mathew sat tight. It was getting hotter instead of cooler as the afternoon wore on. He looked at Poor Pete's fat rump disappearing into the house. Pete was no pup. Mathew felt sorry for Pete. But when he looked at the step where Pete had sprawled a short time before he saw that the stone was still wet with the grease marks left by Pete's lolling tongue, and all of a sudden he knew he'd be sick if he didn't get away from the sight of them. The fit of nausea that had been coming on for some time was about to peak. He'd have to get away, alone somewhere, and fight off the attack. The sky was no longer blue. His eyes must have become affected by the heat. Now, not only the sky but the grass and even the trees in the garden farther down the street, were all the one colour, a horrible brownish hue like in an old fashioned sepia photograph, that would fade into nothingness if exposed any longer to this sun. His head began to spin. He didn't dare call out for help, although he could scarcely make his way to the door. If Rita thought he was sick, she would want him to take something, she'd want to rub his forehead; make him lie down. The thought of swallowing anything made his stomach do another somersault. The thought of lying down on that awful plush sofa appalled him. The dog was on it the first night he came to the house. It smelled of dog.

Mathew ran. He ran through the house, without Rita hearing him, because she was talking to Pete. And when he got out into the road, he crossed to the shady side. Immediately he felt cool again. Immediately he could see better. The sky regained its blue. The trees got back their green. And the railings along which he ran his hand were wonderfully cold.

When he reached his lodgings, Mathew, who couldn't wait to forage in his pocket for his keys, never felt so grateful for anything as for the clear clarion of the bell that sent a single peal and no more through the blessedly silent house, creating no echo. He appreciated the distant manner of the landlady when she opened the door. He liked the chilliness of the house. And when he repaired to his room, he liked the cold white glaze on the counterpane and the cold feel of it as he turned it back and lay down. And just as he had not thought about marriage for many a day, he realized that he had never thought about death either. He thought of it now, though. And the coldness and darkness of the grave didn't seem as bad as it once had seemed. It had its own appeal, like the shade of a tree on a stifling day. Life itself at that moment seemed as hot and pulsing as marriage. Sweat broke out again on Mathew's face.

He hoped, naturally, that he had a certain way to go yet before death's green shadow reached out over him, but meanwhile he told himself that he had better steer clear of the Rita Cooligans of this life, who could expect incessant chat all day long—and God knows how long into the night as well! A husband wouldn't be enough for Rita. She'd want to keep that smelly dog as well—sleeping on the foot of their bed. Mathew wouldn't be any use to a woman like Rita. To begin with, his feet were always icy, and he never minded it. In fact, in summer he often slept with his feet sticking out from under the covers. No. Marriage was not for him.

Late that night, however, when he lay between the sheets, Mathew remembered the girl on the poster with the blue tam, and the slender legs and the golden hair blown across her face in the breeze. Perhaps if he had met a girl like that in real life, a girl made of flesh and blood, instead of paper pasted to a board, he might have found marriage sweet and fragrant. But she had cycled away and left him. He could never see her again. Perhaps there were marriages in which people asked love to be no warmer than it ought to be, but he had not been one of the lucky ones. Death was the next step, for him, and as he was dropping off to sleep, he thought of stepping through green cemetery grass, and across cold grave-slabs. In his last wakeful moment Mathew looked up at the moon that was in its first quarter. It could be called gold no doubt, but it was the strange greenish gold of a young, young moon.

EUDORA WELTY

Livvie

Solomon carried Livvie twenty-one miles away from her home when he married her. He carried her away up on the Old Natchez Trace into the deep country to live in his house. She was sixteen—only a girl, then. Once people said he thought nobody would ever come along there. He told her himself that it had been a long time, and a day she did not know about, since that road was a travelled road with *people* coming and going. He was good to her, but he kept her in the house. She had not thought that she could not get back. Where she came from, people said an old man did not want anybody in the world to ever find his wife, for fear they would steal her back from him. Solomon asked her before he took her, would she be happy?—very dignified, for he was a coloured man that owned his land and had it written down in the courthouse; and she said, 'Yes, sir,' since he was an old man and she was young and just listened and answered. He asked her, if she was choosing winter, would she pine for spring, and she said, 'No indeed.' Whatever she said, always, was because he was an old man . . . while nine years went by. All the time, he got older, and he got so old he gave out. At last he slept the whole day in bed, and she was young still.

It was a nice house, inside and outside both. In the first place, it had three rooms. The front room was papered in holly paper, with green palmettos from the swamp spaced at careful intervals over the walls. There was fresh newspaper cut with fancy borders on the mantelshelf, on which were propped photographs of old or very young men printed in faint yellow—Solomon's people. Solomon had a houseful of furniture. There was a double settee, a tall scrolled rocker and an organ in the front room, all around a three-legged table with a pink marble top, on which was set a lamp with three gold feet, besides a jelly glass with pretty hen feathers in it. Behind the front room, the other room had the bright iron bed with the polished knobs like a throne, in which Solomon slept all day. There were snow-white curtains of wiry lace at the window, and a lace bedspread belonged on the bed. But what old Solomon slept so sound under was a big feather-stitched piece-quilt in the pattern 'Trip Around the World,' which had twenty-one different colours, four hundred and forty pieces, and a thousand yards of thread, and that was what Solomon's mother made in her life and old age. There was a table holding the Bible, and a trunk with a key. On the wall were two calendars, and a diploma from somewhere in Solomon's family, and under that, Livvie's one possession was nailed, a picture of the little white baby of the family she worked for, back in Natchez before she was married. Going through that room and on to the kitchen, there was a big wood stove and a big round table always with a wet top and with the knives and forks in one jelly glass and the spoons in another, and a cut-glass vinegar bottle between, and going out from those, many shallow dishes of pickled peaches, fig preserves, watermelon pickles and blackberry jam always sitting there. The churn sat in the sun, the doors of the safe were always both shut, and there were four baited mousetraps in the kitchen, one in every corner.

The outside of Solomon's house looked nice. It was not painted, but across the porch was an even balance. On each side there was one easy chair with high springs, looking out, and a fern basket hanging over it from the ceiling, and a dishpan of zinnia seedlings growing at its foot on the floor. By the door was a plough-wheel, just a pretty iron circle, nailed up on one wall, and a square mirror on the other, a turquoise-blue comb stuck up in the frame, with the wash-stand beneath it. On the door was a wooden knob with a pearl in the end, and Solomon's black hat hung on that, if he was in the house.

Out front was a clean dirt yard and with every vestige of grass patiently uprooted and the ground scarred in deep whorls from the strike of Livvie's broom. Rose bushes with tiny blood-red roses blooming every month grew in threes on either side of the steps. On one side was a peach tree, on the other a pomegranate. Then coming around up the path from the deep cut of the Natchez Trace below was a line of bare crape-myrtle trees with every branch of them ending in a coloured bottle, green or blue. There was no word that fell from Solomon's lips to say what they were for, but Livvie knew that there could be a spell put in trees, and she was familiar from the time she was born with the way bottle trees kept evil spirits from coming into the house—by luring them inside the coloured bottles, where they cannot get out again. Solomon had made the bottle trees with his own hands over the nine years, in labour amounting to about a tree a year, and without a sign that he had any uneasiness in his heart, for he took as much pride in his precautions against spirits coming in the house as he took in the house, and sometimes in the sun the bottle trees looked prettier than the house did.

It was a nice house. It was in a place where the days would go by and surprise anyone that they were over. The lamplight and the firelight would shine out the door after dark, over the still and breathing country, lighting the roses and the bottle trees, and all was quiet there.

But there was nobody, nobody at all, not even a white person. And if there had been anybody, Solomon would not have let Livvie look at them, just as he would not let her look at a field hand, or a field hand look at her. There was no house near, except for the cabins of the tenants that were forbidden to her, and there was no house as far as she had been, stealing away down the still, deep Trace. She felt as if she waded a river when she went, for the dead leaves on the ground reached as high as her knees, and when she was all scratched and bleeding she said it was not like a road that went anywhere. One day, climbing up the high bank, she had found a graveyard without a church, with ribbon-grass growing about the foot of an angel (she had climbed up because she thought she saw angel wings), and in the sun, trees shining like burning flames through the great caterpillar nets which enclosed them. Scarey thistles stood looking like the prophets in the Bible in Solomon's house. Indian paint-brushes grew over her head, and the mourning dove made the only sound in the world. Oh, for a stirring of the leaves, and a breaking of the nets! But not by a ghost, prayed Livvie, jumping down the bank. After Solomon took to his bed, she never went out, except one more time.

Livvie knew she made a nice girl to wait on anybody. She fixed things to eat on a tray like a surprise. She could keep from singing when she ironed, and to sit by a bed and fan away the flies, she could be so still she could not hear herself breathe. She could clean up the house and never drop a thing, and wash the dishes without a sound, and she would step outside to churn, for churning sounded too sad to her, like sobbing, and if it made her homesick and not Solomon, she did not think of that.

But Solomon scarcely opened his eyes to see her, and scarcely tasted his food. He was not sick or paralysed or in any pain that he mentioned, but he was surely wearing out in the body, and no matter what nice hot thing Livvie would bring him to taste, he would only look at it now, as if he were past seeing how he could add anything more to himself. Before she could beg him, he would go fast asleep. She could not surprise him any more, if he would not taste, and she was afraid that he was never in the world going to taste another thing she brought him—and so how could he last?

But one morning it was breakfast time and she cooked his eggs and grits, carried them in on a tray, and called his name. He was sound asleep. He lay in a dignified way with his watch beside him, on his back in the middle of the bed. One hand drew the quilt up high, though it was the first day of spring. Through the white lace curtains a little puffy wind was blowing as if it came from round cheeks. All night the frogs had sung out in the swamp, like a commotion in the room, and he had not stirred, though she lay wide awake and saying 'Shh, frogs!' for fear he would mind them.

He looked as if he would like to sleep a little longer; and so she put back the tray and waited. When she tiptoed and stayed so quiet, she surrounded herself with a little reverie, and sometimes it seemed to her when she was so stealthy that the quiet she kept was for a sleeping baby, and that she had a baby and was its mother. When she stood at Solomon's bed and looked down at him, she would be thinking, 'He sleeps so well', and she would hate to wake him up. And in some other way, too, she was afraid to wake him up because even in his sleep he seemed to be such a strict man.

Of course, nailed to the wall over the bed—only she would forget who it was—there was a picture of him when he was young. Then he had a fan of hair over his forehead like a king's crown. Now his hair lay down on his head, the spring had gone out of it. Solomon had a lightish face, with eyebrows scattered but rugged, the way privet grows, strong eyes, with second sight, a strict mouth, and a little gold smile. This was the way he looked in his clothes, but in bed in the daytime he looked a different and smaller man, even when he was wide awake, and holding the Bible. He looked like somebody kin to himself. And then sometimes when he lay in sleep and she stood fanning the flies away, and the light came in, his face was like new, so smooth and clear that it was like a glass of jelly held to the window, and she could almost look through his forehead and see what he thought.

She fanned him and at length he opened his eyes and spoke her name, but he would not taste the nice eggs she had kept warm under a pan.

Back in the kitchen she ate heartily, his breakfast and hers, and looked out the open door at what went on. The whole day, and the whole night before, she had felt the stir of spring close to her. It was as present in the house as a young man would be. The moon was in the last quarter and outside they were turning the sod and planting peas and beans. Up and down the red fields, over which smoke from the brush-burning hung showing like a little skirt of sky, a white horse and a white mule pulled the plough. At intervals hoarse shouts came through the air and roused her as if she dozed neglectfully in the shade, and they were telling her, 'Jump up!' She could see how over each ribbon of field were moving men and girls, on foot and mounted on mules, with hats set on their heads and bright with tall hoes and forks as if they carried streamers on them and were going to some place on a journey—and how as if at a signal now and then they would all start at once shouting, hollering, cajoling, calling and answering back, running, being leaped on and breaking away, flinging to earth with a shout and lying motionless in the trance of twelve o'clock. The old women came out of the cabins and brought them the food they had ready for them, and then all worked together, spread evenly out. The little children came too, like a bouncing stream overflowing the fields, and set upon the men, the women, the dogs, the rushing birds, and the wave-like rows of earth, their little voices almost too high to be heard. In the middle distance like some white and gold towers were the haystacks, with black cows coming around to eat their edges. High above everything, the wheel of fields, house, and cabins, and the deep road surrounding like a moat to keep them in, was the turning sky, blue with long, far-flung white mare's-tail clouds, serene and still as high flames. And sound asleep while all this went around him that was his, Solomon was like a little still spot in the middle.

Even in the house the earth was sweet to breathe. Solomon had never let Livvie go any farther than the chicken house and the well. But what if she would walk now into the heart of the fields and take a hoe and work until she fell stretched out and drenched with her efforts, like other girls, and laid her cheek against the laid-open earth, and shamed the old man with her humbleness and delight? To shame him! A cruel wish could come in uninvited and so fast while she looked out the back door. She washed the dishes and scrubbed the table. She could hear the cries of the little lambs. Her mother, that she had not seen since her wedding day, had said one time, 'I rather a man be anything, than a woman be mean.'

So all morning she kept tasting the chicken broth on the stove, and when it was right she poured off a nice cupful. She carried it in to Solomon, and there he lay having a dream. Now what did he dream about? For she saw him sigh gently as if not to disturb some whole thing he held round in his mind, like a fresh egg. So even an old man dreamed about something pretty. Did he dream of her, while his eyes were shut and sunken, and his small hand with the wedding ring curled close in sleep around the quilt? He might be dreaming of what time it was, for even through his sleep he kept track of it like a clock, and knew how much of it went by, and waked up knowing where the hands were even before he consulted the silver watch that he never let go. He would sleep with the watch in his palm, and even holding it to his cheek like a child that loves a plaything. Or he might dream of journeys and travels on a steamboat to Natchez. Yet she thought he dreamed of her; but even while she scrutinized him, the rods of the foot of the bed seemed to rise up like a rail fence between them, and she could see that people never could be sure of anything as long as one of them was asleep and the other awake. To look at him dreaming of her when he might be going to die frightened her a little, as if he might carry her with him that way, and she wanted to run out of the room. She took hold of the bed and held on, and Solomon opened his eyes and called her name, but he did not want anything. He would not taste the good broth.

Just a little after that, as she was taking up the ashes in the front room for the last time in the year, she heard a sound. It was somebody coming. She pulled the curtains together and looked through the slit.

Coming up the path under the bottle trees was a white lady. At first she looked young, but then she looked old. Marvellous to see, a little car stood steaming like a kettle out in the field-track—it had come without a road.

Livvie stood listening to the long, repeated knockings at the door, and after a while she opened it just a little. The lady came in through the crack, though she was more than middle-sized and wore a big hat.

'My name is Miss Baby Marie,' she said.

Livvie gazed respectfully at the lady and at the little suitcase she was holding close to her by the handle until the proper moment. The lady's eyes were running over the room, from palmetto to palmetto, but she was saying, 'I live at home . . . out from Natchez . . . and get out and show these pretty cosmetic things to the white people and the coloured people both . . . all around . . . years and years. . . . Both shades of powder and rouge . . . It's the kind of work a girl can do and not go clear 'way from home. . . .' And the harder she looked, the more she talked. Suddenly she turned up her nose and said, 'It is not Christian or sanitary to put feathers in a vase,' and then she took a gold key out of the front of her dress and began unlocking the locks on her suitcase. Her face drew the light, the way it was covered with intense white and red, with a little patty-cake of white between the wrinkles by her upper lip. Little red tassels of hair bobbed under the rusty wires of her picture-hat, as with an air of triumph and secrecy she now drew open her little suitcase and brought out bottle after bottle and jar after jar, which she put down on the table, the mantelpiece, the settee, and the organ.

'Did you ever see so many cosmetics in your life?' cried Miss Baby Marie.

'No'm,' Livvie tried to say, but the cat had her tongue.

'Have you ever applied cosmetics?' asked Miss Baby Marie next.

'No'm,' Livvie tried to say.

'Then look!' she said, and pulling out the last thing of all, 'Try this!' she said. And in her hand was unclenched a golden lipstick which popped open like magic. A fragrance came out of it like incense, and Livvie cried out suddenly, 'Chinaberry flowers!'

Her hand took the lipstick, and in an instant she was carried away in the air through the spring, and looking down with a half-drowsy smile from a purple cloud she saw from above a chinaberry tree, dark and smooth and neatly leaved, neat as a guinea hen in the dooryard, and there was her home that she had left. On one side of the tree was her mama holding up her heavy apron, and she could see it was loaded with ripe figs, and on the other side was her papa holding a fish-pole over the pond, and she could see it transparently, the little clear fishes swimming up to the brim.

'Oh, no, not chinaberry flowers—secret ingredients,' said Miss Baby Marie. 'My cosmetics have secret ingredients—not chinaberry flowers.'

'It's purple,' Livvie breathed, and Miss Baby Marie said, 'Use it freely. Rub it on.'

Livvie tiptoed out to the wash-stand on the front porch and before the mirror put the paint on her mouth. In the wavery surface her face danced before her like a flame. Miss Baby Marie followed her out, took a look at what she had done, and said, 'That's it.'

Livvie tried to say 'Thank you' without moving her parted lips where the paint lay so new.

By now Miss Baby Marie stood behind Livvie and looked in the mirror over her shoulder, twisting up the tassels of her hair. 'The lipstick I can let you have for only two dollars,' she said, close to her neck.

'Lady, but I don't have no money, never did have,' said Livvie.

'Oh, but you don't pay the first time. I make another trip, that's the way I do. I come back again—later.'

'Oh,' said Livvie, pretending she understood everything so as to please the lady.

'But if you don't take it now, this may be the last time I'll call at your house,' said Miss Baby Marie sharply. 'It's far away from anywhere, I'll tell you that. You don't live close to anywhere.'

'Yes'm. My husband, he keep the *money*,' said Livvie, trembling. 'He is strict as he can be. He don't know *you* walk in here—Miss Baby Marie!'

'Where is he!'

'Right now, he in yonder sound asleep, an old man. I wouldn't ever ask him for anything.'

Miss Baby Marie took back the lipstick and packed it up. She gathered up the jars for both black and white and got them all inside the suitcase, with the same little fuss of triumph with which she had brought them out. She started away.

'Good-bye,' she said, making herself look grand from the back, but at the last minute she turned around in the door. Her old hat wobbled as she whispered, 'Let me see your husband.'

Livvie obediently went on tiptoe and opened the door to the other room. Miss Baby Marie came behind her and rose on her toes and looked in.

'My, what a little tiny old, old man!' she whispered, clasping her hands and shaking her head over them. 'What a beautiful quilt! What a tiny old, old man!'

'He can sleep like that all day,' whispered Livvie proudly.

They looked at him awhile so fast asleep, and then all at once they looked at each other. Somehow that was as if they had a secret, for he had never stirred. Livvie then politely, but all at once, closed the door.

'Well! I'd certainly like to leave you with a lipstick!' said Miss Baby Marie vivaciously. She smiled in the door.

'Lady, but I told you I don't have no money, and never did have.'

'And never will?' In the air and all around, like a bright halo around the white lady's nodding head, it was a true spring day.

'Would you take eggs, lady?' asked Livvie softly.

'No, I have plenty of eggs—plenty,' said Miss Baby Marie.

'I still don't have no money,' said Livvie, and Miss Baby Marie took her suitcase and went on somewhere else.

Livvie stood watching her go, and all the time she felt her heart beating in her left side. She touched the place with her hand. It seemed as if her heart beat and her whole face flamed from the pulsing colour of her lips. She went to sit by Solomon and when he opened his eyes he could not see a change in her. 'He's fixin' to die,' she said inside. That was the secret. That was when she went out of the house for a little breath of air.

She went down the path and down the Natchez Trace a way, and she did not know how far she had gone, but it was not far, when she saw a sight. It was a man, looking like a vision—she standing on one side of the Old Natchez Trace and he standing on the other.

As soon as this man caught sight of her, he began to look himself over. Starting at the bottom with his pointed shoes, he began to look up, lifting his peg-top pants the higher to see fully his bright socks. His coat long and wide and leaf-green he opened like doors to see his high-up tawny pants and his pants he smoothed downward from the points of his collar, and he wore a luminous baby-pink satin shirt. At the end, he reached gently above his wide platter-shaped round hat, the colour of a plum, and one finger touched at the feather, emerald green, blowing in the spring winds.

No matter how she looked, she could never look so fine as he did, and she was not sorry for that, she was pleased.

He took three jumps, one down and two up, and was by her side. 'My name is Cash,' he said.

He had a guinea pig in his pocket. They began to walk along. She stared on and on at him, as if he were doing some daring spectacular thing, instead of just walking beside her. It was not simply the city way he was dressed that made her look at him and see hope in its insolence looking back. It was not only the way he moved along kicking the flowers as if he could break through everything in the way and destroy anything in the world, that made her eyes grow bright. It might be, if he had not appeared *that day* she would never have looked so closely at him, but the time people come makes a difference.

They walked through the still leaves of the Natchez Trace, the light and the shade falling through trees about them, the white irises shining like candles on the banks and the new ferns shining like green stars up in the oak branches. They came out at Solomon's house, bottle trees and all. Livvie stopped and hung her head.

Cash began whistling a little tune. She did not know what it was, but she had heard it before from a distance, and she had a revelation. Cash was a field hand. He was a transformed field hand. Cash belonged to Solomon. But he had stepped out of his overalls into this. There in front of Solomon's house he laughed. He had a round head, a round face, all of him was young, and he flung his head up, rolled it against the mare's-tail sky in his round hat, and he could laugh just to see Solomon's house sitting there. Livvie looked at it, and there was Solomon's black hat hanging on the peg on the front door, the blackest thing in the world.

'I been to Natchez,' Cash said, wagging his head around against the sky. '*I* taken a trip, I ready for Easter!'

How was it possible to look so fine before the harvest? Cash must have stolen the money, stolen it from Solomon. He stood in the path and lifted his spread hand high and brought it down again and again in his laughter. He kicked up his heels. A little chill went through her. It was as if Cash was bringing that strong hand down to beat a drum or to rain blows upon a man, such an abandon and menace were in his laugh. Frowning, she went closer to him and his swinging arm drew her in at once and the fright was crushed from her body, as a little match-flame might be smothered out by what it lighted. She gathered the folds of his coat behind him and fastened her red lips to his mouth, and she was dazzled at herself then, the way he had been dazzled at himself to begin with.

In that instant she felt something that could not be told—that Solomon's death was at hand, that he was the same to her as if he were dead now. She cried out, and uttering little cries turned and ran for the house.

At once Cash was coming, following after, he was running behind her. He came close, and half-way up the path he laughed and passed her. He even picked up a stone and sailed it into the bottle trees. She put her hands over her head, and sounds clattered through the bottle trees like cries of outrage. Cash stamped and plunged zigzag up the front steps and in at the door.

When she got there, he had stuck his hands in his pockets and was turning slowly about in the front room. The little guinea pig peeped out. Around Cash, the pinned-up palmettos looked as if a lazy green monkey had walked up and down and around the walls leaving green prints of his hands and feet.

She got through the room and his hands were still in his pockets, and she fell upon the closed door to the other room and pushed it open. She ran to Solomon's bed, calling 'Solomon! Solomon!' The little shape of the old man never moved at all, wrapped under the quilt as if it were winter still.

'Solomon!' She pulled the quilt away, but there was another one under that, and she fell on her knees beside him. He made no sound except a sigh, and then she could hear in the silence the light springy steps of Cash walking and walking in the front room, and the ticking of Solomon's silver watch, which came from the bed. Old Solomon was far away in his sleep, his face looked small, relentless, and devout, as if he were walking somewhere where she could imagine the snow falling.

Then there was a noise like a hoof pawing the floor, and the door gave a creak, and Cash appeared beside her. When she looked up, Cash's face was so black it was bright, and so bright and bare of pity that it looked sweet to her. She stood up and held up her head. Cash was so powerful that his presence gave her strength even when she did not need any.

Under their eyes Solomon slept. People's faces tell of things and places not known to the one who looks at them while they sleep, and while Solomon slept under the eyes of Livvie and Cash his face told them like a mythical story that all his life he had built, little scrap by little scrap, respect. A beetle could not have been more laborious or more ingenious in the task of its destiny. When Solomon was young, as he was in his picture overhead, it was the infinite thing with him, and he could see no end to the respect he would contrive and keep in a house. He had built a lonely house, the way he would make a cage, but it grew to be the same with him as a great monumental pyramid and sometimes in his absorption of getting it erected he was like the builder-slaves of Egypt who forgot or never knew the origin and meaning of the thing to which they gave all the strength of their bodies and used up all their days. Livvie and Cash could see that as a man might rest from a life-labour he lay in his bed, and they could hear how, wrapped in his quilt, he sighed to himself comfortably in sleep, while in his dreams he might have been an ant, a beetle, a bird, an Egyptian, assembling and carrying on his back and building with his hands, or he might have been an old man of India or a swaddled baby, about to smile and brush all away.

Then without warning old Solomon's eyes flew wide open under the hedge-like brows. He was wide awake.

And instantly Cash raised his quick arm. A radiant sweat stood on his temples. But he did not bring his arm down—it stayed in the air, as if something might have taken hold.

It was not Livvie—she did not move. As if something said 'Wait', she stood waiting. Even while her eyes burned under motionless lids, her lips parted in a stiff grimace, and with her arms stiff at her sides she stood above the prone old man and the panting young one, erect and apart.

Movement when it came came in Solomon's face. It was an old and strict face, a frail face, but behind it, like a covered light, came an animation that could play hide and seek, that would dart and escape, had always escaped. The mystery flickered in him, and invited from his eyes. It was that very mystery that Cash with his quick arm would have to strike, and that Livvie could not weep for. But Cash only stood holding his arm in the air, when the gentlest flick of his great strength, almost a puff of his breath, would have been enough, if he had known how to give it, to send the old man over the obstruction that kept him away from death.

'Young ones can't wait,' said Solomon.

Livvie shuddered violently, and then in a gush of tears she stooped for a glass of water and handed it to him, but he did not see her.

'So here come the young man Livvie wait for. Was no prevention. No prevention. Now I lay eyes on young man and it come to be somebody I know all the time, and been knowing since he were born in a cotton patch, and watched grow up year to year, Cash McCord, growed to size, growed up to come in my house in the end—ragged and barefoot.'

Solomon gave a cough of distaste. Then he shut his eyes vigorously, and his lips began to move like a chanter's.

'When Livvie married, her husband were already somebody. He had paid great cost for his land. He spread sycamore leaves over the ground from wagon to door, day he brought her home, so her foot would not have to touch ground. He carried her through his door. Then he growed old and could not lift her, and she were still young.'

Livvie's sobs followed his words like a soft melody repeating each thing as he stated it. His lips moved for a little without sound, or she cried too fervently, and unheard he might have been telling his whole life, and then he said, 'God forgive Solomon for sins great and small. God forgive Solomon for carrying away too young girl for wife and keeping her away from her people and from all the young people would clamour for her back.'

Then he lifted up his right hand toward Livvie where she stood by the bed and offered her his silver watch. He dangled it before her eyes, and she hushed crying; her tears stopped. For a moment the watch could be heard ticking as it always did, precisely in his proud hand. She lifted it away. Then he took hold of the quilt; then he was dead.

Livvie left Solomon dead and went out of the room. Stealthily, nearly without noise, Cash went beside her. He was like a shadow, but his shiny shoes moved over the floor in spangles, and the green downy feather shone like a light in his hat. As they reached the front room, he seized her deftly as a long black cat and dragged her hanging by the waist round and round him, while he turned in a circle, his face bent down to hers. The first moment, she kept one arm and its hand stiff and still, the one that held Solomon's watch. Then the fingers softly let go, all of her was limp, and the watch fell somewhere on the floor. It ticked away in the still room, and all at once there began outside the full song of a bird.

They moved around and around the room and into the brightness of the open door, then he stopped and shook her once. She rested in silence in his trembling arms, unprotesting as a bird on a nest. Outside the redbirds were flying and criss-crossing, the sun was in all the bottles on the prisoned trees, and the young peach was shining in the middle of them with the bursting light of spring.

DORIS LESSING

The De Wets Come to Kloof Grange

The verandah, which was lifted on stone pillars, jutted forward over the garden like a box in the theatre. Below were luxuriant masses of flowering shrubs, and creepers whose shiny leaves, like sequins, reflected light from a sky stained scarlet and purple and apple-green. This splendiferous sunset filled one half of the sky, fading gently through shades of mauve to a calm expanse of ruffling grey, blown over by tinted cloudlets; and in this still evening sky, just above a clump of darkening conifers, hung a small crystal moon.

There sat Major Gale and his wife, as they did every evening at this hour, side by side trimly in deck chairs, their sundowners on small tables at their elbows, critically watching, like connoisseurs, the pageant presented for them.

Major Gale said, with satisfaction: 'Good sunset tonight,' and they both turned their eyes to the vanquishing moon. The dusk drew veils across the sky and garden; and punctually, as she did every day, Mrs Gale shook off nostalgia like a terrier shaking off water and rose, saying: 'Mosquitoes!' She drew her deck chair to the wall, where she neatly folded and stacked it.

'Here is the post,' she said, her voice quickening; and Major Gale went to the steps, waiting for the native who was hastening towards them through the tall shadowing bushes. He swung a sack from his back and handed it to Major Gale. A sour smell of raw meat rose from the sack. Major Gale said with a kindly contempt he used for his native servants: 'Did the spooks get you?' and laughed. The native, who had panted the last mile of his ten-mile journey through a bush filled with unnameable phantoms, ghosts of ancestors, wraiths of tree and beast, put on a pantomime of fear and chattered and shivered for a moment like an ape, to amuse his master. Major Gale dismissed the boy. He ducked thankfully around the corner of the house to the back, where there were lights and companionship.

Mrs Gale lifted the sack and went into the front room. There she

131

lit the oil lamp and called for the houseboy, to whom she handed the groceries and meat she removed. She took a fat bundle of letters from the very bottom of the sack and wrinkled her nose slightly; blood from the meat had stained them. She sorted the letters into two piles; and then husband and wife sat themselves down opposite each other to read their mail.

It was more than the ordinary farm living-room. There were koodoo horns branching out over the fireplace, and a bundle of knobkerries hanging on a nail; but on the floor were fine rugs, and the furniture was two hundred years old. The table was a pool of softly-reflected lights; it was polished by Mrs Gale herself every day before she set on it an earthenware crock filled with thorny red flowers. Africa and the English eighteenth century mingled in this room and were at peace.

From time to time Mrs Gale rose impatiently to attend to the lamp, which did not burn well. It was one of those terrifying paraffin things that have to be pumped with air to a whiter-hot flame from time to time, and which in any case emit a continuous soft hissing noise. Above the heads of the Gales a light cloud of flying insects wooed their fiery death and dropped one by one, plop, plop, plop to the table among the letters.

Mrs Gale took an envelope from her own heap and handed it to her husband. 'The assistant,' she remarked abstractedly, her eyes bent on what she held. She smiled tenderly as she read. The letter was from her oldest friend, a woman doctor in London, and they had written to each other every week for thirty years, ever since Mrs Gale came to exile in Southern Rhodesia. She murmured half-aloud: 'Why, Betty's brother's daughter is going to study economics,' and though she had never met Betty's brother, let alone the daughter, the news seemed to please and excite her extraordinarily. The whole of the letter was about people she had never met and was not likely ever to meet—about the weather, about English politics. Indeed, there was not a sentence in it that would not have struck an outsider as having been written out of a sense of duty; but when Mrs Gale had finished reading it, she put it aside gently and sat smiling quietly: she had gone back half a century to her childhood.

Gradually sight returned to her eyes, and she saw her husband where previously she had sat looking through him. He appeared disturbed; there was something wrong about the letter from the assistant.

Major Gale was a tall and still military figure, even in his khaki bush-shirt and shorts. He changed them twice a day. His shorts were creased sharp as folded paper, and the six pockets of his shirt were always buttoned up tight. His small head, with its polished surface of black hair, his tiny jaunty black moustache, his farmer's hands with their broken but clean nails—all these seemed to say that it was no easy matter not to let oneself go, not to let this damned disintegrating gaudy easy-going country get under one's skin. It wasn't easy, but he did it; he did it with the conscious effort that had slowed his movements and added the slightest touch of caricature to his appearance: one finds a man like Major Gale only in exile.

He rose from his chair and began pacing the room, while his wife watched him speculatively and waited for him to tell her what was the matter. When he stood up, there was something not quite right—what was it? Such a spruce and tailored man he was; but the disciplined shape of him was spoiled by a curious fatness and softness: the small rounded head was set on a thickening neck; the buttocks were fattening too, and quivered as he walked. Mrs Gale, as these facts assailed her, conscientiously excluded them: she had her own picture of her husband, and could not afford to have it destroyed.

At last he sighed, with a glance at her; and when she said: 'Well, dear?' he replied at once, 'The man has a wife.'

'Dear me!' she exclaimed, dismayed.

At once, as if he had been waiting for her protest, he returned briskly: 'It will be nice for you to have another woman about the place.'

'Yes, I suppose it will,' she said humorously. At this most familiar note in her voice, he jerked his head up and said aggressively: 'You always complain I bury you alive.'

And so she did. Every so often, but not so often now, she allowed herself to overflow into a mood of gently humorous bitterness; but it had not carried conviction for many years; it was more, really, of an attention to him, like remembering to kiss him good night. In fact, she had learned to love her isolation, and she felt aggrieved that he did not know it.

'Well, but they can't come to the house. That I really couldn't put up with.' The plan had been for the new assistant—Major Gale's farming was becoming too successful and expanding for him to

133

manage any longer by himself—to have the spare room, and share the house with his employers.

'No, I suppose not, if there's a wife.' Major Gale sounded doubtful; it was clear he would not mind another family sharing with them. 'Perhaps they could have the old house?' he enquired at last.

'I'll see to it,' said Mrs Gale, removing the weight of worry off her husband's shoulders. Things he could manage: people bothered him. That they bothered her, too, now, was something she had become resigned to his not understanding. For she knew he was hardly conscious of her; nothing existed for him outside his farm. And this suited her well. During the early years of their marriage, with the four children growing up, there was always a little uneasiness between them, like an unpaid debt. Now they were friends and could forget each other. What a relief when he no longer 'loved' her! (That was how she put it.) Ah, that 'love'—she thought of it with a small humorous distaste. Growing old had its advantages.

When she said 'I'll see to it,' he glanced at her, suddenly, directly, her tone had been a little too comforting and maternal. Normally his gaze wavered over her, not seeing her. Now he really observed her for a moment; he saw an elderly Englishwoman, as thin and dry as a stalk of maize in September, sitting poised over her letters, one hand touching them lovingly, and gazing at him with her small flower-blue eyes. A look of guilt in them troubled him. He crossed to her and kissed her cheek. 'There!' she said, inclining her face with a sprightly, fidgety laugh. Overcome with embarrassment he stopped for a moment, then said determinedly: 'I shall go and have my bath.'

After his bath, from which he emerged pink and shining like an elderly baby, dressed in flannels and a blazer, they ate their dinner under the wheezing oil lamp and the cloud of flying insects. Immediately the meal was over he said 'Bed', and moved off. He was always in bed before eight and up by five. Once Mrs Gale had adapted herself to his routine. Now, with the four boys out sailing the seven seas in the navy, and nothing really to get her out of bed (her servants were perfectly trained), she slept until eight, when she joined her husband at breakfast. She refused to have that meal in bed; nor would she have dreamed of appearing in her dressing-gown. Even as things were she was guilty enough about sleeping those three daylight hours, and found it necessary to apologize for her slackness. So, when her husband had gone to bed she remained under the lamp, re-reading her letters, sewing, reading, or simply dreaming about the past, the very distant past, when she had been Caroline Morgan, living near a small country town, a country squire's daughter. That was how she liked best to think of herself.

Tonight she soon turned down the lamp and stepped on to the verandah. Now the moon was a large, soft, yellow fruit caught in the top branches of the blue-gums. The garden was filled with glamour, and she let herself succumb to it. She passed quietly down the steps and beneath the trees, with one quick solicitous glance back at the bedroom window: her husband hated her to be out of the house by herself at night. She was on her way to the old house that lay half a mile distant over the veld.

Before the Gales had come to this farm, two brothers had it, South Africans by birth and upbringing. The houses had then been separated by a stretch of untouched bush, with not so much as a fence or a road between them; and in this state of guarded independence the two men had lived, both bachelors, both quite alone. The thought of them amused Mrs Gale. She could imagine them sending polite notes to each other, invitations to meals or to spend an evening. She imagined them loaning each other books by native bearer, meeting at a neutral point between their homes. She was amused, but she respected them for a feeling she could understand. She made up all kinds of pretty ideas about these brothers, until one day she learned from a neighbour that in fact the two men had quarrelled continually, and had eventually gone bankrupt because they could not agree how the farm was to be run. After this discovery Mrs Gale ceased to think about them; a pleasant fancy had become a distasteful reality.

The first thing she did on arriving was to change the name of the farm from Kloof Nek to Kloof Grange, making a link with home. One of the houses was denuded of furniture and used as a storage space. It was a square, bare box of a place, stuck in the middle of the bare veld, and its shut windows flashed back light to the sun all day. But her own home had been added to and extended, and surrounded with verandahs and fenced; inside the fence were two acres of garden, that she had created over years of toil. And what a garden! These were what she lived for: her flowering African shrubs, her vivid English lawns, her water-garden with the goldfish and water-lilies. Not many people had such a garden.

She walked through it this evening under the moon, feeling herself grow light-headed and insubstantial with the influence of the strange greenish light, and of the perfumes from the flowers. She touched the leaves with her fingers as she passed, bending her face to the roses. At the gate, under the hanging white trumpets of the moon-flower she paused, and lingered for a while, looking over the space of empty veld between her and the other house. She did not like going outside her garden at night. She was not afraid of natives, no: she had contempt for women who were afraid, for she regarded Africans as rather pathetic children, and was very kind to them. She did not know what made her afraid. Therefore she took a deep breath, compressed her lips, and stepped carefully through the gate, shutting it behind her with a sharp click. The road before her was a glimmering white ribbon, the hard-crusted sand sending up a continuous small sparkle of light as she moved. On either side were sparse stumpy trees, and their shadows were deep and black. A nightjar cut across the stars with crooked trailing wings, and she set her mouth defiantly: why, this was only the road she walked over every afternoon, for her constitutional! There were the trees she had pleaded for, when her husband was wanting to have them cut for firewood: in a sense, they were her trees. Deliberately slowing her steps, as a discipline, she moved through the pits of shadow, gaining each stretch of clear moonlight with relief, until she came to the house. It looked dead, a dead thing with staring eyes, with those blank windows gleaming pallidly back at the moon. Nonsense, she told herself. Nonsense. And she walked to the front door, unlocked it, and flashed her torch over the floor. Sacks of grain were piled to the rafters, and the brick floor was scattered with loose mealies. Mice scurried invisibly to safety, and flocks of cockroaches blackened the walls. Standing in a patch of moonlight on the brick, so that she would not unwittingly walk into a spiderweb or a jutting sack, she drew in deep breaths of the sweetish smell of maize, and made a list in her head of what had to be done; she was a very capable woman.

Then something struck her: if the man had forgotten, when applying for the job, to mention a wife, he was quite capable of forgetting children too. If they had children it wouldn't do; no, it wouldn't. She simply couldn't put up with a tribe of children—for Afrikaners never had less than twelve—running wild over her beautiful garden and teasing her goldfish. Anger spurted in her. De Wet—the name was hard on her tongue. Her husband should not have agreed to take on an Afrikaner. Really, really, Caroline, she chided herself humorously, standing there in the deserted moonlit house, don't jump to conclusions, don't be unfair.

She decided to arrange the house for a man and his wife, ignoring the possibility of children. She would arrange things, in kindness, for a woman who might be unused to living in loneliness; she would be good to this woman; so she scolded herself, to make atonement for her short fit of pettiness. But when she tried to form a picture of this woman who was coming to share her life, at least to the extent of taking tea with her in the mornings, and swapping recipes (so she supposed), imagination failed her. She pictured a large Dutch frau, all homely comfort and sweating goodness, and was repulsed. For the first time the knowledge that she must soon, next week, take another woman into her life, came home to her; and she disliked it intensely.

Why must she? Her husband would not have to make a friend of the man. They would work together, that was all; but because they, the wives, were two women on an isolated farm, they would be expected to live in each other's pockets. All her instincts toward privacy, the distance which she had put between herself and other people, even her own husband, rebelled against it. And because she rebelled, rejecting this imaginary Dutch woman, to whom she felt so alien, she began to think of her friend Betty, as if it were she who would be coming to the farm.

Still thinking of her friend Betty she returned through the silent veld to her home, imagining them walking together over this road and talking as they had been used to do. The thought of Betty, who had turned into a shrewd, elderly woman doctor with kind eyes, sustained her through the frightening silences. At the gate she lifted her head to sniff the heavy perfume of the moon-flowers, and became conscious that something else was invading her dream: it was a very bad smell, an odour of decay mingled with the odour from the flowers. Something had died on the veld, and the wind had changed and was bringing the smell towards the house. She made a mental note: I must send the boy in the morning to see what it is. Then the conflict between her thoughts of her friend and her own life presented itself sharply to her. You are a silly woman, Caroline, she said to herself. Three years before they had gone on holiday to

England, and she had found she and Betty had nothing to say to each other. Their lives were so far apart, and had been for so long, that the weeks they spent together were an offering to a friendship that had died years before. She knew it very well, but tried not to think of it. It was necessary to her to have Betty remain, in imagination at least, as a counter-weight to her loneliness. Now she was being made to realize the truth. She resented that too, and somewhere the resentment was chalked up against Mrs De Wet, the Dutch woman who was going to invade her life with impertinent personal claims.

And next day, and the days following, she cleaned and swept and tidied the old house, not for Mrs De Wet, but for Betty. Otherwise she could not have gone through with it. And when it was all finished, she walked through the rooms which she had furnished with things taken from her own home, and said to a visionary Betty (but Betty as she had been thirty years before): 'Well, what do you think of it?' The place was bare but clean now, and smelling of sunlight and air. The floors had coloured coconut matting over the brick; the beds, standing on opposite sides of the room, were covered with gaily striped counterpanes. There were vases of flowers everywhere. 'You would like living here,' Mrs Gale said to Betty, before locking the house up and returning to her own, feeling as if she had won a victory over herself.

The De Wets sent a wire saying they would arrive on Sunday after lunch. Mrs Gale noted with annoyance that this would spoil her rest, for she slept every day, through the afternoon heat. Major Gale, for whom every day was a working day (he hated idleness and found odd jobs to occupy him on Sundays), went off to a distant part of the farm to look at his cattle. Mrs Gale laid herself down on her bed with her eyes shut and listened for a car, all her nerves stretched. Flies buzzed drowsily over the window-panes; the breeze from the garden was warm and scented. Mrs Gale slept uncomfortably, warring all the afternoon with the knowledge that she should be awake. When she woke at four she was cross and tired, and there was still no sign of a car. She rose and dressed herself, taking a frock from the cupboard without looking to see what it was: her clothes were often fifteen years old. She brushed her hair absent-mindedly; and then, recalled by a sense that she had not taken enough trouble, slipped a large gold locket round her neck, as a conscientious mark of welcome. Then she left a message with the houseboy that she would be in the garden and walked away from the verandah with a strong excitement growing in her. This excitement rose as she moved through the crowding shrubs under the walls, through the rose garden with its wide green lawns where water sprayed all the year round, and arrived at her favourite spot among the fountains and the pools of water lilies. Her water-garden was an extravagance, for the pumping of the water from the river cost a great deal of money.

She sat herself on a shaded bench; and on one side were the glittering plumes of the fountains, the roses, the lawns, the house, and beyond them the austere wind-bitten high veld; on the other, at her feet, the ground dropped hundreds of feet sharply to the river. It was a rocky shelf thrust forward over the gulf, and here she would sit for hours, leaning dizzily outwards, her short grey hair blown across her face, lost in adoration of the hills across the river. Not of the river itself, no, she thought of that with a sense of danger, for there, below her, in that green-crowded gully, were suddenly the tropics: palm trees, a slow brown river that eddied into reaches of marsh or curved round belts of reeds twelve feet high. There were crocodiles, and leopards came from the rocks to drink. Sitting there on her exposed shelf, a smell of sun-warmed green, of hot decaying water, of luxurious growth, an intoxicating heady smell, rose in waves to her face. She had learned to ignore it, and to ignore the river, while she watched the hills. They were *her* hills: that was how she felt. For years she had sat here, hours every day, watching the cloud shadows move over them, watching them turn blue with distance or come close after rain so that she could see the exquisite brushwork of trees on the lower slopes. They were never the same half an hour together. Modulating light created them anew for her as she looked, thrusting one peak forward and withdrawing another, moving them back so that they were hazed on a smoky horizon, crouched in sullen retreat, or raising them so that they towered into a brilliant cleansed sky. Sitting here, buffeted by winds, scorched by the sun or shivering with cold, she could challenge anything. They were her mountains; they were what she was; they had made her, had crystallized her loneliness into a strength, had sustained her and fed her.

And now she almost forgot the De Wets were coming, and were hours late. Almost, not quite. At last, understanding that the sun was setting (she could feel its warmth striking below her shoulders), her small irritation turned to anxiety. Something might have happened to them? They had taken the wrong road, perhaps? The car had broken down? And there was the Major, miles away with their own car, and so there was no means of looking for them. Perhaps she should send out natives along the roads? If they had taken the wrong turning, to the river, they might be bogged in mud to the axles. Down there, in the swampy heat, they could be bitten by mosquitoes and then . . .

Caroline, she said to herself severely (thus finally withdrawing from the mountains), don't let things worry you so. She stood up and shook herself, pushed the hair out of her face, and gripped her whipping skirts in a thick bunch. She stepped backwards away from the wind that raked the edges of the cliff, sighed a goodbye to her garden for that day, and returned to the house. There, outside the front door, was a car, an ancient jalopy bulging with luggage, its back doors tied with rope. And children! She could see a half-grown girl on the steps. No, really, it was too much. On the other side of the car stooped a tall, thin, fairheaded man, burnt as brown as toffee, looking for someone to come. He must be the father. She approached, adjusting her face to a smile, looking apprehensively about her for the children. The man slowly came forward, the girl after him. 'I expected you earlier,' began Mrs Gale briskly, looking reproachfully into the man's face. His eyes were cautious, blue, assessing. He looked her casually up and down and seemed not to take her into account. 'Is Major Gale about?' he asked. 'I am Mrs Gale,' she replied. Then, again: 'I expected you earlier.' Really, four hours late and not a word of apology!

'We started late,' he remarked. 'Where can I put our things?'

Mrs Gale swallowed her annoyance and said: 'I didn't know you had a family. I didn't make arrangements.'

'I wrote to the Major about my wife,' said De Wet. 'Didn't he get my letter?' He sounded offended.

Weakly Mrs Gale said: 'Your wife?' and looked in wonderment at the girl, who was smiling awkwardly behind her husband. It could be seen, looking at her more closely, that she might perhaps be eighteen. She was a small creature, with delicate brown legs and arms, a brush of dancing black curls, and large excited black eyes. She put both hands round her husband's arm, and said, giggling: 'I am Mrs De Wet.'

De Wet put her away from him, gently, but so that she pouted and said: 'We got married last week.'

'Last week,' said Mrs Gale, conscious of dislike.

The girl said, with an extraordinary mixture of effrontery and shyness: 'He met me in a cinema and we got married next day.' It seemed as if she were in some way offering herself to the older woman, offering something precious of herself.

'Really,' said Mrs Gale politely, glancing almost apprehensively at this man, this slow-moving, laconic, shrewd South African, who had behaved with such violence and folly. Distaste twisted her again.

Suddenly the man said, grasping the girl by the arm, and gently shaking her to and fro, in a sort of controlled exasperation: 'Thought I had better get myself a wife to cook for me, all this way out in the blue. No restaurants here, hey, Doodle?'

'Oh, Jack,' pouted the girl, giggling. 'All he thinks about is his stomach,' she said to Mrs Gale, as one girl to another, and then glanced with delicious fear up at her husband.

'Cooking is what I married you for,' he said, smiling down at her intimately.

There stood Mrs Gale opposite them, and she saw that they had forgotten her existence; and that it was only by the greatest effort of will that they did not kiss. 'Well,' she remarked drily, 'this is a surprise.'

They fell apart, their faces changing. They became at once what they had been during the first moments: two hostile strangers. They looked at her across the barrier that seemed to shut the world away from them. They saw a middle-aged English lady, in a shapeless old-fashioned blue silk dress, with a gold locket sliding over a flat bosom, smiling at them coldly, her blue, misted eyes critically narrowed.

'I'll take you to your house,' she said energetically. 'I'll walk, and you go in the car—no, I walk it often.' Nothing would induce her to get into the bouncing rattle-trap that was bursting with luggage and half-suppressed intimacies.

As stiff as a twig, she marched before them along the road, while the car jerked and ground along in bottom gear. She knew it was ridiculous; she could feel their eyes on her back, could feel their astonished amusement; but she could not help it.

When they reached the house, she unlocked it, showed them briefly what arrangements had been made, and left them. She walked back in a tumult of anger, caused mostly because of her picture of herself, walking along that same road, meekly followed by the car, and refusing to do the only sensible thing, which was to get into it with them.

She sat on the verandah for half an hour, looking at the sunset sky without seeing it, and writhing with various emotions, none of which she classified. Eventually she called the houseboy, and gave him a note, asking the two to come to dinner. No sooner had the boy left, and was trotting off down the bushy path to the gate, than she called him back. 'I'll go myself,' she said. This was partly to prove that she made nothing of walking the half mile, and partly from contrition. After all, it was no crime to get married, and they seemed very fond of each other. That was how she put it.

When she came to the house, the front room was littered with luggage, paper, pots and pans. All the exquisite order she had created was destroyed. She could hear voices from the bedroom.

'But, Jack, I don't want you to. I want you to stay with me.' And then his voice, humorous, proud, slow, amorous: 'You'll do what I tell you, my girl. I've got to see the old man and find out what's cooking. I start work tomorrow, don't forget.'

'But, Jack . . .' Then came sounds of scuffling, laughter, and a sharp slap.

'Well,' said Mrs Gale, drawing in her breath. She knocked on the wood of the door, and all sound ceased. 'Come in,' came the girl's voice. Mrs Gale hesitated, then went into the bedroom.

Mrs De Wet was sitting in a bunch on the bed, her flowered frock spread all around her, combing her hair. Mrs Gale noted that the two beds had already been pushed together. 'I've come to ask you to dinner,' she said briskly. 'You don't want to have to cook when you've just come.'

Their faces had already become blank and polite.

'Oh no, don't trouble, Mrs Gale,' said De Wet, awkwardly. 'We'll get ourselves something, don't worry.' He glanced at the girl, and his face softened. He said, unable to resist it: 'She'll get busy with the tin-opener in a minute, I expect. That's her idea of feeding a man.'

'Oh Jack,' pouted his wife.

De Wet turned back to the wash-stand, and proceeded to swab lather on his face. Waving the brush at Mrs Gale, he said: 'Thanks all the same. But tell the Major I'll be over after dinner to talk things over.'

'Very well,' said Mrs Gale, 'just as you like.'

She walked away from the house. Now she felt rebuffed. After all, they might have had the politeness to come; yet she was pleased they hadn't; yet if they preferred making love to getting to know the people who were to be their close neighbours for what might be years, it was their own affair . . .

Mrs De Wet was saying, as she painted her toenails, with her knees drawn up to her chin, and the bottle of varnish gripped between her heels: 'Who the hell does she think she is, anyway? Surely she could give us a meal without making such a fuss when we've just come.'

'She came to ask us, didn't she?'

'Hoping we would say no.'

And Mrs Gale knew quite well that this was what they were thinking, and felt it was unjust. She would have liked them to come: the man wasn't a bad sort, in his way; a simple soul, but pleasant enough; as for the girl, she would have to learn, that was all. They should have come; it was their fault. Nevertheless she was filled with that discomfort that comes of having done a job badly. If she had behaved differently they would have come. She was cross throughout dinner; and that meal was not half finished when there was a knock on the door. De Wet stood there, apparently surprised they had not finished, from which it seemed that the couple had, after all, dined off sardines and bread and butter.

Major Gale left his meal and went out to the verandah to discuss business, Mrs Gale finished her dinner in state, and then joined the two men. Her husband rose politely at her coming, offered her a chair, sat down and forgot her presence. She listened to them talking for some two hours. Then she interjected a remark (a thing she never did, as a rule, for women get used to sitting silent when men discuss farming) and did not know herself what made her say what she did about the cattle; but when De Wet looked round absently as if to say she should mind her own business, and her husband remarked absently, 'Yes, dear,' when a Yes dear did not fit her remark at all, she got up angrily and went indoors. Well, let them talk, then, she did not mind.

As she undressed for bed, she decided she was tired, because of her broken sleep that afternoon. But she could not sleep then, either. She listened to the sound of the men's voices, drifting brokenly round the corner of the verandah. They seemed to be thoroughly enjoying themselves. It was after twelve when she heard De Wet say, in that slow facetious way of his: 'I'd better be getting home. I'll catch it hot, as it is.' And, with rage, Mrs Gale heard her husband laugh. He actually laughed. She realized that she herself had been planning an acid remark for when he came to the bedroom; so when he did enter, smelling of tobacco smoke, and grinning, and then proceeded to walk jauntily about the room in his underclothes, she said nothing, but noted that he was getting fat, in spite of all the hard work he did.

'Well, what do you think of the man?'

'He'll do very well indeed,' said Major Gale, with satisfaction. 'Very well. He knows his stuff all right. He's been doing mixed farming in the Transvaal for years.' After a moment he asked politely, as he got with a bounce into his own bed on the other side of the room: 'And what is she like?'

'I haven't seen much of her, have I? But she seems pleasant enough.' Mrs Gale spoke with measured detachment.

'Someone for you to talk to,' said Major Gale, turning himself over to sleep. 'You had better ask her over to tea.'

At this Mrs Gale sat straight up in her own bed with a jerk of annoyance. Someone for her to talk to, indeed! But she composed herself, said good night with her usual briskness, and lay awake. Next day she must certainly ask the girl to morning tea. It would be rude not to. Besides, that would leave the afternoon free for her garden and her mountains.

Next morning she sent a boy across with a note, which read: 'I shall be so pleased if you will join me for morning tea.' She signed it: Caroline Gale.

She went herself to the kitchen to cook scones and cakes. At eleven o'clock she was seated on the verandah in the green-dappled shade from the creepers, saying to herself that she believed she was in for a headache. Living as she did, in a long, timeless abstraction of growing things and mountains and silence, she had become very conscious of her body's responses to weather and to the slow advance of age. A small ache in her ankle when rain was due was like a cherished friend. Or she would sit with her eyes shut, in the shade, after a morning's pruning in the violent sun, feeling waves of pain flood back from her eyes to the back of her skull, and say with satisfaction: 'You deserve it, Caroline!' It was right she should pay for such pleasure with such pain.

At last she heard lagging footsteps up the path, and she opened her eyes reluctantly. There was the girl, preparing her face for a social occasion, walking primly through the bougainvillaea arches, in a flowered frock as vivid as her surroundings. Mrs Gale jumped to her feet and cried gaily: 'I am so glad you had time to come.' Mrs De Wet giggled irresistibly and said: 'But I had nothing else to do, had I?' Afterwards she said scornfully to her husband: 'She's nuts. She writes me letters with stuck-down envelopes when I'm five minutes away, and says Have I the time? What the hell else did she think I had to do?' And then, violently: 'She can't have anything to do. There was enough food to feed ten.'

'Wouldn't be a bad idea if you spent more time cooking,' said De Wet fondly.

The next day Mrs Gale gardened, feeling guilty all the time, because she could not bring herself to send over another note of invitation. After a few days, she invited the De Wets to dinner, and through the meal made polite conversation with the girl while the men lost themselves in cattle diseases. What could one talk to a girl like that about? Nothing! Her mind, as far as Mrs Gale was concerned, was a dark continent, which she had no inclination to explore. Mrs De Wet was not interested in recipes, and when Mrs Gale gave helpful advice about ordering clothes from England, which was so much cheaper than buying them in the local towns, the reply came that she had made all her own clothes since she was seven. After that there seemed nothing to say, for it was hardly possible to remark that these strapped sun-dresses and bright slacks were quite unsuitable for the farm, besides being foolish, since bare shoulders in this sun were dangerous. As for her shoes! She wore corded beach sandals which had already turned dust colour from the roads.

There were two more tea parties; then they were allowed to lapse. From time to time Mrs Gale wondered uneasily what on earth the poor child did with herself all day, and felt it was her duty to go and find out. But she did not.

One morning she was pricking seedlings into a tin when the houseboy came and said the little missus was on the verandah and she was sick.

At once dismay flooded Mrs Gale. She thought of a dozen tropical diseases, of which she had had unpleasant experience, and almost ran to the verandah. There was the girl, sitting screwed up in a chair, her face contorted, her eyes red, her whole body shuddering violently. 'Malaria,' thought Mrs Gale at once, noting that trembling.

'What is the trouble, my dear?' Her voice was kind. She put her hand on the girl's shoulder. Mrs De Wet turned and flung her arms round her hips, weeping, weeping, her small curly head buried in Mrs Gale's stomach. Holding herself stiffly away from this dismaying contact, Mrs Gale stroked the head and made soothing noises.

'Mrs Gale, Mrs Gale . . .'

'What is it?'

'I can't stand it. I shall go mad. I simply can't stand it.'

Mrs Gale, seeing that this was not a physical illness, lifted her up, led her inside, laid her on her own bed, and fetched cologne and handkerchiefs. Mrs De Wet sobbed for a long while, clutching the older woman's hand, and then at last grew silent. Finally she sat up with a small rueful smile, and said pathetically: 'I am a fool.'

'But what *is* it, dear?'

'It isn't anything, really. I am so lonely. I wanted to get my mother up to stay with me, only Jack said there wasn't room, and he's quite right, only I got mad, because I thought he might at least have had my mother . . .'

Mrs Gale felt guilt like a sword: she could have filled the place of this child's mother.

'And it isn't anything, Mrs Gale, not really. It's not that I'm not happy with Jack. I am, but I never see him. I'm not used to this kind of thing. I come from a family of thirteen counting my parents, and I simply can't stand it.'

Mrs Gale sat and listened, and thought of her own loneliness when she first began this sort of life.

'And then he comes in late, not till seven sometimes, and I know he can't help it, with the farm work and all that, and then he has supper and goes straight off to bed. I am not sleepy then. And then I get up sometimes and I walk along the road with my dog . . .'

Mrs Gale remembered how, in the early days after her husband had finished with his brief and apologetic embraces, she used to rise with a sense of relief and steal to the front room, where she lighted the lamp again and sat writing letters, reading old ones, thinking of her friends and of herself as a girl. But that was before she had her first child. She thought: This girl should have a baby; and could not help glancing downwards at her stomach.

Mrs De Wet, who missed nothing, said resentfully: 'Jack says I should have a baby. That's all he says.' Then, since she had to include Mrs Gale in this resentment, she transformed herself all at once from a sobbing baby into a gauche but armoured young woman with whom Mrs Gale could have no contact. 'I am sorry,' she said formally. Then, with a grating humour: 'Thank you for letting me blow off steam.' She climbed off the bed, shook her skirts straight, and tossed her head. 'Thank you. I am a nuisance.' With painful brightness she added: 'So, that's how it goes. Who would be a woman, eh?'

Mrs Gale stiffened. 'You must come and see me whenever you are lonely,' she said, equally bright and false. It seemed to her incredible that this girl should come to her with all her defences down, and then suddenly shut her out with this facetious nonsense. But she felt more comfortable with the distance between them, she couldn't deny it.

'Oh, I will, Mrs Gale. Thank you so much for asking me.' She lingered for a moment, frowning at the brilliantly polished table in the front room, and then took her leave. Mrs Gale watched her go. She noted that at the gate the girl started whistling gaily, and smiled comically. Letting off steam! Well, she said to herself, well . . . And she went back to her garden.

That afternoon she made a point of walking across to the other house. She would offer to show Mrs De Wet the garden. The two women returned together, Mrs Gale wondering if the girl regretted her emotional lapse of the morning. If so, she showed no signs of it. She broke into bright chatter when a topic mercifully occurred to her; in between were polite silences full of attention to what she seemed to hope Mrs Gale might say.

Mrs Gale was relying on the effect of her garden. They passed the house through the shrubs. There were the fountains, sending up their vivid showers of spray, there the cool mats of water-lilies, under which the coloured fishes slipped, there the irises, sunk in green turf.

'This must cost a packet to keep up,' said Mrs De Wet. She stood at the edge of the pool, looking at her reflection dissolving among the broad green leaves, glanced obliquely up at Mrs Gale, and dabbled her exposed red toenails in the water.

Mrs Gale saw that she was thinking of herself as her husband's employer's wife. 'It does, rather,' she said drily, remembering that the only quarrels she ever had with her husband were over the cost of pumping up water. 'You are fond of gardens?' she asked. She could not imagine anyone not being fond of gardens.

Mrs De Wet said sullenly: 'My mother was always too busy having kids to have time for gardens. She had her last baby early this year.' An ancient and incommunicable resentment dulled her face. Mrs Gale, seeing that all this beauty and peace meant nothing to her companion that she would have it mean, said, playing her last card: 'Come and see my mountains.' She regretted the pronoun as soon as it was out—*so* exaggerated.

But when she had the girl safely on the rocky verge of the escarpment, she heard her say: 'There's my river.' She was leaning forward over the great gulf, and her voice was lifted with excitement. 'Look,' she was saying. 'Look, there it is.' She turned to Mrs Gale, laughing, her hair spun over her eyes in a fine iridescent rain, tossing her head back, clutching her skirts down, exhilarated by the tussle with the wind.

'Mind, you'll lose your balance.' Mrs Gale pulled her back. 'You have been down to the river, then?'

'I go there every morning.'

Mrs Gale was silent. The thing seemed preposterous. 'But it is four miles there and four back.'

'Oh, I'm used to walking.'

'But . . .' Mrs Gale heard her own sour, expostulating voice and stopped herself. There was after all no logical reason why the girl should not go to the river. 'What do you do there?'

'I sit on the edge of a big rock and dangle my legs in the water, and I fish, sometimes. I caught a barbel last week. It tasted foul, but it was fun catching it. And I pick water-lilies.'

'There are crocodiles,' said Mrs Gale sharply. The girl was wrong-headed; anyone was who could like that steamy bath of vapours, heat, smells and—what? It was an unpleasant place. 'A native girl was taken there last year, at the ford.'

'There couldn't be a crocodile where I go. The water is clear, right down. You can see right under the rocks. It is a lovely pool. There's a kingfisher, and water-birds, all colours. They are so pretty. And when you sit there and look, the sky is a long narrow slit. From here it looks quite far across the river to the other side, but really it isn't. And the trees crowding close make it narrower.

Just think how many millions of years it must have taken for the water to wear down the rock so deep.'

'There's bilharzia, too.'

'Oh, bilharzia!'

'There's nothing funny about bilharzia. My husband had it. He had injections for six months before he was cured.'

The girl's face dulled. 'I'll be careful,' she said irrationally, turning away, holding her river and her long hot dreamy mornings away from Mrs Gale, like a secret.

'Look at the mountains,' said Mrs Gale, pointing. The girl glanced over the chasm at the foothills, then bent forward again, her face reverent. Through the mass of green below were glimpses of satiny brown. She breathed deeply: 'Isn't it a lovely smell?' she said.

'Let's go and have some tea,' said Mrs Gale. She felt cross and put out; she had no notion why. She could not help being brusque with the girl. And so at last they were quite silent together; and in silence they remained on that verandah above the beautiful garden, drinking their tea and wishing it was time for them to part.

Soon they saw the two husbands coming up the garden. Mrs De Wet's face lit up; and she sprang to her feet and was off down the path, running lightly. She caught her husband's arm and clung there. He put her away from him, gently. 'Hullo,' he remarked good-humouredly. 'Eating again?' And then he turned back to Major Gale and went on talking. The girl lagged up the path behind her husband like a sulky small girl, pulling at Mrs Gale's beloved roses and scattering crimson petals everywhere.

On the verandah the men sank at once into chairs, took large cups of tea, and continued talking as they drank thirstily. Mrs Gale listened and smiled. Crops, cattle, disease; weather, crops and cattle. Mrs De Wet perched on the verandah wall and swung her legs. Her face was petulant, her lips trembled, her eyes were full of tears. Mrs Gale was saying silently under her breath, with ironical pity, in which there was also cruelty: You'll get used to it, my dear; you'll get used to it. But she respected the girl, who had courage: walking to the river and back, wandering round the dusty flower-beds in the starlight, trying to find peace—at least, she was trying to find it.

She said sharply, cutting into the men's conversation: 'Mr De Wet, did you know your wife spends her mornings at the river?'

The man looked at her vaguely, while he tried to gather the sense of her words: his mind was on the farm. 'Sure,' he said at last. 'Why not?'

'Aren't you afraid of bilharzia?'

He said laconically: 'If we were going to get it, we would have got it long ago. A drop of water can infect you, touching the skin.'

'Wouldn't it be wiser not to let the water touch you in the first place?' she enquired with deceptive mildness.

'Well, I told her. She wouldn't listen. It is too late now. Let her enjoy it.'

'But . . .'

'About that red heifer,' said Major Gale, who had not been aware of any interruption.

'No,' said Mrs Gale sharply. 'You are not going to dismiss it like that.' She saw the three of them look at her in astonishment. 'Mr De Wet, have you ever thought what it means to a woman being alone all day, with not enough to do. It's enough to drive anyone crazy.'

Major Gale raised his eyebrows; he had not heard his wife speak like that for so long. As for De Wet, he said with a slack good-humour that sounded brutal: 'And what do you expect me to do about it.'

'You don't realize,' said Mrs Gale futilely, knowing perfectly well there was nothing he could do about it. 'You don't understand how it is.'

'She'll have a kid soon,' said De Wet. 'I hope so, at any rate. That will give her something to do.'

Anger raced through Mrs Gale like a flame along petrol. She was trembling. 'She might be that red heifer,' she said at last.

'What's the matter with having kids?' asked De Wet. 'Any objection?'

'You might ask me first,' said the girl bitterly.

Her husband blinked at her, comically bewildered. 'Hey, what is this?' he enquired. 'What have I done? You said you wanted to have kids. Wouldn't have married you otherwise.'

'I never said I didn't.'

'Talking about her as if she were . . .'

'When, then?' Mrs Gale and the man were glaring at each other.

'There's more to women than having children,' said Mrs Gale at last, and flushed because of the ridiculousness of her words.

De Wet looked her up and down, up and down. 'I want kids,' he said at last. 'I want a large family. Make no mistake about that. And when I married her'—he jerked his head at his wife—'I told her I wanted them. She can't turn round now and say I didn't.'

'Who is turning round and saying anything?' asked the girl, fine and haughty, staring away over the trees.

'Well, if no one is blaming anyone for anything,' asked Major Gale, jauntily twirling his little moustache, 'what is all this about?'

'God knows, I don't,' said De Wet angrily. He glanced sullenly at Mrs Gale. 'I didn't start it.'

Mrs Gale sat silent, trembling, feeling foolish, but so angry she could not speak. After a while she said to the girl: 'Shall we go inside, my dear?' The girl, reluctantly, and with a lingering backward look at her husband, rose and followed Mrs Gale. 'He didn't mean anything,' she said awkwardly, apologizing for her husband to her husband's employer's wife. This room, with its fine old furniture, always made her apologetic. At this moment, De Wet stooped into the doorway and said: 'Come on, I am going home.'

'Is that an order?' asked the girl quickly, backing so that she came side by side with Mrs Gale: she even reached for the older woman's hand. Mrs Gale did not take it: this was going too far.

'What's got into you?' he said, exasperated. 'Are you coming, or are you not?'

'I can't do anything else, can I?' she replied, and followed him from the house like a queen who has been insulted.

Major Gale came in after a few moments. 'Lovers' quarrel,' he said, laughing awkwardly. This phrase irritated Mrs Gale. 'That man!' she exclaimed. 'That man!'

'Why, what is wrong with him?' She remained silent, pretending to arrange her flowers. This silly scene, with its hinterlands of emotion, made her furious. She was angry with herself, angry with her husband, and furious at that foolish couple who had succeeded in upsetting her and destroying her peace. At last she said: 'I am going to bed. I've such a headache I can't think.'

'I'll bring you a tray, my dear,' said Major Gale, with a touch of exaggeration in his courtesy that annoyed her even more. 'I don't want anything, thank you,' she said, like a child, and marched off to the bedroom.

There she undressed and went to bed. She tried to read, found she was not following the sense of the words, put down the book, and blew out the light. Light streamed into the room from the moon;

she could see the trees along the fence banked black against stars. From next door came the clatter of her husband's solitary meal.

Later she heard voices from the verandah. Soon her husband came into the room and said: 'De Wet is asking whether his wife has been here.'

'What!' exclaimed Mrs Gale, slowly assimilating the implications of this. 'Why, has she gone off somewhere?'

'She's not at home,' said the Major uncomfortably. For he always became uncomfortable and very polite when he had to deal with situations like this.

Mrs Gale sank back luxuriously on her pillows. 'Tell that fine young man that his wife often goes for long walks by herself when he's asleep. He probably hasn't noticed it.' Here she gave a deadly look at her husband. 'Just as I used to,' she could not prevent herself adding.

Major Gale fiddled with his moustache, and gave her a look which seemed to say: 'Oh lord, don't say we are going back to all that business again?' He went out, and she heard him saying: 'Your wife might have gone for a walk, perhaps?' Then the young man's voice: 'I know she does sometimes. I don't like her being out at night, but she just walks around the house. And she takes the dogs with her. Maybe she's gone further this time—being upset you know.'

'Yes, I know,' said Major Gale. Then they both laughed. The laughter was of a quite different quality from the sober responsibility of their tone a moment before: and Mrs Gale found herself sitting up in bed, muttering: 'How *dare* he?'

She got up and dressed herself. She was filled with premonitions of unpleasantness. In the main room her husband was sitting reading, and since he seldom read, it seemed he was also worried. Neither of them spoke. When she looked at the clock, she found it was just past nine o'clock.

After an hour of tension, they heard the footsteps they had been waiting for. There stood De Wet, angry, worried sick, his face white, his eyes burning.

'We must get the boys out,' he said, speaking directly to Major Gale, and ignoring Mrs Gale.

'I am coming too,' she said.

'No, my dear,' said the Major cajolingly. 'You stay here.'

'You can't go running over the veld at this time of night,' said De Wet to Mrs Gale, very blunt and rude.

'I shall do as I please,' she returned.

The three of them stood on the verandah, waiting for the natives. Everything was drenched in moonlight. Soon they heard a growing clamour of voices from over the ridge, and a little later the darkness there was lightened by flaring torches held high by invisible hands: it seemed as if the night were scattered with torches advancing of their own accord. Then a crowd of dark figures took shape under the broken lights. The farm natives, excited by the prospect of a night's chasing over the veld, were yelling as if they were after a small buck or a hare.

Mrs Gale sickened. 'Is it necessary to have all these natives in it?' she asked. 'After all, have we even considered the possibilities? Where can a girl run *to* on a place like this?'

'That is the point,' said Major Gale frigidly.

'I can't bear to think of her being—pursued, like this, by a crowd of natives. It's horrible.'

'More horrible still if she has hurt herself and is waiting for help,' said De Wet. He ran off down the path, shouting to the natives and waving his arms. The Gales saw them separate into three bands, and soon there were three groups of lights jerking away in different directions through the hazy dark, and the yells and shouting came back to them on the wind.

Mrs Gale thought: 'She could have taken the road back to the station, in which case she could be caught by car, even now.'

She commanded her husband: 'Take the car along the road and see.'

'That's an idea,' said the Major, and went off to the garage. She heard the car start off, and watched the rear light dwindle redly into the night.

But that was the least ugly of the possibilities. What if she had been so blind with anger, grief, or whatever emotion it was that had driven her away, that she had simply run off into the veld not knowing where she went? There were thousands of acres of trees, thick grass, gullies, *kopjes*. She might at this moment be lying with a broken arm or leg; she might be pushing her way through grass higher than her head, stumbling over roots and rocks. She might be screaming for help somewhere for fear of wild animals, for if she crossed the valley into the hills there were leopards, lions, wild dogs. Mrs Gale suddenly caught her breath in an agony of fear: the valley! What if she had mistaken her direction and walked over the edge of the escarpment in the dark? What if she had forded the river and been taken by a crocodile? There were so many things: she might even be caught in a gametrap. Once, taking her walk, Mrs Gale herself had come across a tall sapling by the path where the spine and ribs of a large buck dangled, and on the ground were the pelvis and legs, fine eroded bones of an animal trapped and forgotten by its trapper. Anything might have happened. And worse than any of the actual physical dangers was the danger of falling a victim to fear: being alone on the veld, at night, knowing oneself lost: this was enough to send anyone off balance.

The silly little fool, the silly little fool: anger and pity and terror confused in Mrs Gale until she was walking crazily up and down her garden through the bushes, tearing blossoms and foliage to pieces in trembling fingers. She had no idea how time was passing; until Major Gale returned and said that he had taken the ten miles to the station at seven miles an hour, turning his lights into the bush this way and that. At the station everyone was in bed; but the police were standing on the alert for news.

It was long after twelve. As for De Wet and the bands of searching natives, there was no sign of them. They would be miles away by this time.

'Go to bed,' said Major Gale at last.

'Don't be ridiculous,' she said. After a while she held out her hand to him, and said: 'One feels so helpless.'

There was nothing to say; they walked together under the stars, their minds filled with horrors. Later she made some tea and they drank it standing; to sit would have seemed heartless. They were so tired they could hardly move. Then they got their second wind and continued walking. That night Mrs Gale hated her garden, that highly-cultivated patch of luxuriant growth, stuck in the middle of a country that could do this sort of thing to you suddenly. It was all the fault of the country! In a civilized sort of place, the girl would have caught the train to her mother, and a wire would have put everything right. Here, she might have killed herself, simply because of a passing fit of despair. Mrs Gale began to get hysterical. She was weeping softly in the circle of her husband's arm by the time the sky lightened and the redness of dawn spread over the sky.

As the sun rose, De Wet returned alone over the veld. He said he had sent the natives back to their huts to sleep. They had found nothing. He stated that he also intended to sleep for an hour, and that he would be back on the job by eight. Major Gale nodded: he recognized this as a necessary discipline against collapse. But after the young man had walked off across the veld towards his house, the two older people looked at each other and began to move after him. 'He must not be alone,' said Mrs Gale sensibly. 'I shall make him some tea and see that he drinks it.'

'He wants sleep,' said Major Gale. His own eyes were red and heavy.

'I'll put something in his tea,' said Mrs Gale. 'He won't know it is there.' Now she had something to do, she was much more cheerful. Planning De Wet's comfort, she watched him turn in at his gate and vanish inside the house; they were some two hundred yards behind.

Suddenly there was a shout, and then a commotion of screams and yelling. The Gales ran fast along the remaining distance and burst into the front room, white-faced and expecting the worst, in whatever form it might choose to present itself.

There was De Wet, his face livid with rage, bending over his wife, who was huddled on the floor and shielding her head with her arms, while he beat her shoulders with his closed fists.

Mrs Gale exclaimed: 'Beating your wife!'

De Wet flung the girl away from him, and staggered to his feet. 'She was here all the time,' he said, half in temper, half in sheer wonder. 'She was hiding under the bed. She told me so. When I came in she was sitting on the bed and laughing at me.'

The girl beat her hands on the floor and said, laughing and crying together: 'Now you have to take some notice of me. Looking for me all night over the veld with your silly natives! You looked so stupid, running about like ants, looking for me.'

'My God,' said De Wet simply, giving up. He collapsed backwards into a chair and lay there, his eyes shut, his face twitching.

'So now you have to notice me,' she said defiantly, but beginning to look scared. 'I have to pretend to run away, but then you sit up and take notice.'

'Be quiet,' said De Wet, breathing heavily. 'Be quiet, if you don't want to get hurt bad.'

'Beating your wife,' said Mrs Gale. 'Savages behave better.'

'Caroline, my dear,' said Major Gale awkwardly. He moved towards the door.

'Take that woman out of here if you don't want me to beat her too,' said De Wet to Major Gale.

Mrs Gale was by now crying with fury. 'I'm not going,' she said. 'I'm not going. This poor child isn't safe with you.'

'But what was it all about?' said Major Gale, laying his hand kindly on the girl's shoulder. 'What was it, my dear? What did you have to do it for, and make us all so worried?'

She began to cry. 'Major Gale, I am so sorry. I forgot myself. I got so mad. I told him I was going to have a baby. I told him when I got back from your place. And all he said was: That's fine. That's the first of them, he said. He didn't love me, or say he was pleased, or nothing.'

'Dear Christ in hell,' said De Wet wearily, with the exasperation strong in his voice, 'what do you make me do these things for? Do you think I want to beat you? Did you think I wasn't pleased: I keep telling you I want kids, I love kids.'

'But you don't care about me,' she said, sobbing bitterly.

'Don't I?' he said helplessly.

'Beating your wife when she is pregnant,' said Mrs Gale. 'You ought to be ashamed of yourself.' She advanced on the young man with her own fists clenched, unconscious of what she was doing. 'You ought to be beaten yourself, that's what you need.'

Mrs De Wet heaved herself off the floor, rushed on Mrs Gale, pulled her back so that she nearly lost balance, and then flung herself on her husband. 'Jack,' she said, clinging to him desperately, 'I am so sorry, I am so sorry, Jack.'

He put his arms round her. 'There,' he said simply, his voice thick with tiredness, 'don't cry. We got mixed up, that's all.'

Major Gale, who had caught and steadied his wife as she staggered back, said to her in a low voice: 'Come, Caroline. Come. Leave them to sort it out.'

'And what if he loses his temper again and decides to kill her this time?' demanded Mrs Gale, her voice shrill.

De Wet got to his feet, lifting his wife with him. 'Go away now, Mrs Major,' he said. 'Get out of here. You've done enough damage.'

'I've done enough damage?' she gasped. 'And what have I done?'

'Oh nothing, nothing at all,' he said with ugly sarcasm. 'Nothing at all. But please go and leave my wife alone in future, Mrs Major.'

'Come, Caroline, *please*,' said Major Gale.

She allowed herself to be drawn out of the room. Her head was aching so that the vivid morning light invaded her eyes in a wave of pain. She swayed a little as she walked.

'Mrs Major,' she said, 'Mrs Major!'

'He was upset,' said her husband judiciously.

She snorted. Then, after a silence: 'So, it was all my fault.'

'He didn't say so.'

'I thought that was what he was saying. He behaves like a brute and then says it is my fault.'

'It was no one's fault,' said Major Gale, patting her vaguely on shoulders and back as they stumbled back home.

They reached the gate, and entered the garden, which was now musical with birds.

'A lovely morning,' remarked Major Gale.

'Next time you get an assistant,' she said finally, 'get people of our kind. These might be savages, the way they behave.'

And that was the last word she would ever say on the subject.

JEAN STAFFORD

A Summer Day

He wore hot blue serge knickerbockers and a striped green shirt, but he had no shoes and he had no hat and the only things in his pants pockets were a handkerchief that was dirty now, and a white pencil from the Matchless Lumber Company, and a card with Mr Wilkins' name printed on it and his own, Jim Littlefield, written on below the printing, and a little aspirin box. In the aspirin box were two of his teeth and the scab from his vaccination. He had come on the train barefoot all the way from Missouri to Oklahoma, because his grandmother had died and Mr Wilkins, the preacher, had said it would be nice out here with other Indian boys and girls. Mr Wilkins had put him on the through train and given the nigger man in the coach half a dollar to keep an eye on him, explaining that he was an orphan and only eight years old. Now he stood on the crinkled cinders beside the tracks and saw the train moving away like a fast little fly, and although Mr Wilkins had promised on his word of honour, there was no one to meet him.

There was no one anywhere. He looked in the windows of the yellow depot, where there was nothing but a fat stove and a bench and a tarnished spittoon and a small office where a telegraph machine nervously ticked to itself. A freshly painted handcar stood on a side track near the water tower, looking as if no one were ever going to get into it again. There wasn't a sound, there wasn't even a dog or a bee, and there was nothing to look at except the bare blue sky and, across the tracks, a field of stubble that stretched as far as year after next beyond a rusty barbed-wire fence. Right by the door of the depot, there was an oblong piece of tin, which, shining in the sun, looked cool, although, of course, Jim knew it would be hot enough to bite your foot. It looked cool because it made him think of how the rain water used to shine in the washtubs in Grandma's back yard. On washday, when he had drawn buckets of it for her, it would sometimes splash over on his feet with a wonderful sound and a wonderful feeling. After the washing was on the line, she would black the stove and scrub the kitchen floor, and then she would take her ease, drinking a drink of blood-red sassafras as she sat rocking on the porch, shaded with wisteria. At times like that, on a hot summer day, she used to smell as cool as the underside of a leaf.

There was nothing cool here, so far as you could see. The paint on the depot was so bright you could read the newspaper by it in the dark. Jim could not see any trees save one, way yonder in the stubble field, and it looked poor and lean. In Missouri, there were big trees, as shady as a parasol. He remembered how he had sat on the cement steps of the mortuary parlour in the shade of the acacias, crying for his grandmother, whom he had seen in her cat-grey coffin. Mr Wilkins had lipped some snuff and consoled him, talking through his nose, which looked like an unripe strawberry. 'I don't want to be no orphan,' Jim had cried, thinking of the asylum out by the fairground, where the kids wore grey cotton uniforms and came to town once a week on the trolley car to go to the library. Many of them wore glasses and some of them were lame. Mr Wilkins had said, 'Landagoshen, Jim boy, didn't I say you were going to be Uncle Sam's boy? Uncle Sam don't fool with orphans, he only takes care of *citizens*.' On the train, a fat man had asked him what he was going to be when he grew up and Jim had said, 'An aborigine.' The man had laughed until he'd had to wipe his round face with a blue bandanna, and the little girl who was with him had said crossly, 'What's funny, Daddy? What did the child say?' It had been cool before that, when he and Mr Wilkins were waiting under the tall maple trees that grew beside the depot in Missouri and Mr Marvin Dannenbaum's old white horse was drinking water out of the moss-lined trough. And just behind them, on Linden Street, Miss Bessie Ryder had been out in her yard picking a little mess of red raspberries for her breakfast. The dew would have still been on them when she doused them good with cream. Over the front of her little house there was a lattice where English ivy grew and her well was surrounded by periwinkle.

But Jim could not remember any of that coolness when he went out of the shade of the maples into the coach. Mrs Wilkins had put up a lunch for him; when he ate it later, he found a dead ant on one of the peanut-butter sandwiches and the Baby Ruth had run all over the knobby apple. His nose had felt swollen and he'd got a headache and the green seat was as scratchy as a brush when he lay down and put his cheek on it. The train had smelled like the Fourth of July, like punk and lady crackers, and when it stopped in little towns, its rest was uneasy, for it throbbed and jerked and hissed like an old dog too feeble to get out of the sun. Once, the nigger man had taken him into the baggage car to look at some kind of big, expensive collie in a cage, muzzled and glaring fiercely through the screen; there were trunks and boxes of every shape, including one large, round one that the nigger man said held nothing but one enormous cheese from Michigan. When Jim got back to his seat, the fat man with the little girl had bought a box lunch that was put on the train at Sedalia, and Jim had watched them eat fried chicken and mustard greens and beet pickles and pone. The next time the train stopped, the nigger man had collected the plates and the silverware and had taken them into the station.

Jim had made the train wheels say 'Uncle Sam, Uncle Sam', and then he hadn't been able to make them stop, even when he was half asleep. Mr Wilkins had said that Uncle Sam wasn't one of your fair-weather friends that would let a Cherokee down when all his kin were dead. It was a blessing to be an Indian, the preacher had said, and Mrs Wilkins had said, 'It surely is, Jim boy. I'd give anything to be an Indian, just anything you can name.' She had been stringing wax beans when she'd said that, and the ham hock she would cook with them had already been simmering on the back of the stove. Jim had wanted to ask her why she would like to be an Indian, but she'd seemed to have her mind on the beans, so he'd said nothing and stroked the turkey wing she used for brushing the stove.

It was hot enough to make a boy sick here in this cinder place, and Jim did not know what he would do if someone did not come. He could not walk barefoot all the way back to Missouri; he would get lost if he did not follow the tracks, and if he did follow them and a train came when he was drowsy, he might get scooped up by the cowcatcher and be hurled to kingdom come. He sat on his heels and waited, feeling the grey clinkers pressing into his feet, listening to the noontime sleep. Heat waves trembled between him and the depot and for a long time there was no sound save for the anxious telegraph machine, which was saying something important, although no one would heed. Perhaps it was about him—Jim! It could be a telegram from Mr Wilkins saying for them to send him back. The preacher might have found a relation that Jim could live with. The boy saw, suddenly, the tall, white colonnade of a rich man's house by the Missouri River; he had gone there often to take the brown bread and the chilli sauce Grandma used to make, and the yellow-haired lady at the back door of the big house had always said, 'Don't you want to rest a spell, Jimmy, here where it's cool?' He would sit on a bench at the long table and pet the mother cat who slept on the windowsill and the lady would say, 'You like my old puss-in-boots, don't you? Maybe you'd best come and live with me and her, seeing that she's already got your tongue.' Sometimes this lady wore a lace boudoir cap with a blue silk bow on the front, and once she had given him a button with a pin that said, 'LET'S CRACK THE VOLSTEAD ACT'. The stubborn stutter of the machine could be a message from her, or maybe it was from Miss Bessie Ryder, who once had told his fortune with cards in a little room with pictures of Napoleon everywhere; the English ivy growing just outside made patterns on Napoleon's face, and in the little silver pitcher in the shape of Napoleon's head there was a blue anemone. Or it could be the Wilkinses themselves sending for him to come and live in the attic room, where there was the old cradle their baby had died in and a pink quilt on the bed with six-pointed stars.

Jim cried, catching his tears with his gentle tongue. Then, a long way off, a bell began to ring slowly and sweetly, and when it stopped, he heard an automobile coming with its bumptious cutout open. He went on crying, but in a different way, and his stomach thumped with excitement, for he knew it would be the people from the school, and suddenly he could not bear to have them find him. He ran the length of the depot and then ran back again, and then he hopped on one foot to the door and hopped on the piece of tin. He screamed with the awful, surprising pain. He sat down and seized his burned foot with both hands, and through his sobs he said, 'Oh, hell on you, oh Judas Priest!' He heard the car stop and the doors slam and he heard a lady say, 'Wait a minute. Oh, it's all right.' Jim shut his eyes as feet munched the cinders, closer and closer to him.

'Don't touch me!' he shrieked, not opening his eyes, and there was a silence like the silence after the district nurse in Missouri had looked down his throat. They did not touch him, so he stopped crying, and the lady said, 'Why, the train must have come *long ago*! I will positively give that stationmaster a piece of my mind.'

Jim opened his eyes. There was a big man, with very black hair, which fell into his face, wearing a spotted tan suit and a ring with a turquoise the size of a quarter. The woman had gold earrings and gold teeth, which she showed in a mechanical smile, and she wore a blue silk dress with white embroidery on the bertha. They both smelled of medicine. The man touched Jim on the arm where he had been vaccinated; baffled by everything in the world, he cried wildly. The woman bent down and said, 'Well, well, well, there, there, there.' Jim was half suffocated by the smell of medicine and of her buttery black hair. The man and woman looked at each other, and Jim's skin prickled because he knew they were wondering why he had not brought anything. Mr Wilkins had said you didn't need to, not even shoes.

'Well, honey,' said the lady, taking his hand, 'we've come a long way all by our lonesome, haven't we?'

'A *mighty* long way,' said the man, laughing heartily to make a joke of it. He took Jim's other hand and made him stand up, and then they started down the cinder path and around the corner of the depot to a tall, black touring car, which said on the door: 'DEPARTMENT OF THE INTERIOR INDIAN SERVICE'. In the back seat there were two huge empty demijohns and a brand-new hoe.

'Hop in front, sonny,' said the man. The black leather seat scorched Jim's legs, and he put his hand over his eyes to shut out the dazzle of the windshield.

'No shoes,' said the woman, getting in beside him.

'Already noted,' said the man. He got in, too, and his fat thigh was dampish at Jim's elbow.

Jim worried about the telegraph machine. Would it go on until someone came to listen to it or would it stop after a while like a telephone? It must be about him, because he was the only one who had got off the train here, and it must be from someone saying to send him back, because there was nothing else it could be about. His heart went as fast as a bobbin being filled and he wanted to throw up and to hide and to cram a million grapes into his mouth and to chase a scared girl with a garter snake, all at once. He thought of screaming bloody murder so that they would let him get out of the car, but they might just whip him for that, whip him with an inner tube or beat him over the head with the new hoe. But he wouldn't stay at the school! If there was no other way, he would ride home on a freight car, like a hobo, and sleep in the belfry of the church under the crazy bell. He would escape tonight, he told himself, and he pressed his hand on his heart to make it quiet down.

From the other side of the depot, you could see the town. A wide street went straight through the level middle of it, and it had the same kind of stores and houses and lamp-posts that any other town had. The trees looked like leftovers, and the peaked brown dogs slinked behind the trash cans in an ornery way. The man started the car, and as they drove up the main street, Jim could tell that the men sitting on the kerb were Indians, for they had long pigtails and closed-up faces. They sat in a crouch, with their big heads hanging forward and their flat-fingered hands motionless between their knees. The women who were not fat were as lean and spry as katydids, and all of them walked up and down the main street with baskets full of roasting ears on one arm and babies on the other. The wooden cupola on the red brick courthouse was painted yellow-green and in the yard men lay with their hats over their eyes or sat limply on the iron benches under the runty trees, whose leaves were grey with dust or lice. A few children with ice-cream cones skulked in the doorways, like abused cats. Everyone looked ailing.

The man from the school gestured with the hand that wore the heavy turquoise, and he said, 'Son, this is your ancestors' town. This here is the capital of the Cherokee nation.'

'You aren't forgetting the water, are you, Billings?' said the woman in a distracted way, and when the man said he was not, she said to Jim, 'Do you know what "Cherokee" means?'

'No,' said Jim.

The woman looked over his head at the man. 'Goodness knows, we earn our bread. What can you do with Indians if they don't know they're Indians?'

'I always knew I was an Indian,' said the man.

'And so did I,' said the woman. 'Always.'

Jim sat, in this terrible heat and terrible lack of privacy, between their mature bodies and dared not even change the position of his legs, lest he hit the gearshift. He felt that they were both looking at him as if a rash were coming out on his face and he wished they would hurry and get to the school, so that he could start escaping. At the thought of running away after the sun was down and the animals and robbers started creeping in the dark, his heart started up again, like an engine with no one in charge.

The car stopped at a drugstore, and the man got out and heaved the demijohns onto the sidewalk. In the window of the store was a vast pink foot with two corn plasters and a bunion plaster. Next door was an empty building and on its window lights were pasted signs for J. M. Barclay's Carnival Show and for Copenhagen snuff and for Clabber Girl baking powder. The carnival sign was torn and faded, the way such signs always are, and the leg of a red-haired bareback rider was tattered shabbily. How hot a carnival would be, with the smell of dung and popcorn! Even a Ferris wheel on a day like this would be no fun. Awful as it was here, where the sun made a sound on the roof of the car, it would be even worse to be stuck in the highest seat of a Ferris wheel when something went wrong below. A boy would die of the heat and the fear and the sickness as he looked down at the distant ground, littered with disintegrated popcorn balls.

The lady beside Jim took a handkerchief out of her white linen purse, and as she wiped the sweat away from her upper lip, he caught a delicate fragrance that made him think of the yellow-haired lady in Missouri and he said, 'I want to write a letter as soon as I get there.'

'Well, we'll see,' the woman said. 'Who do you want to write to?' But the man came back, so Jim did not have to answer. The man staggered, with his stomach pushed out, under the weight of the demijohn, and as he put it in the back seat, he said savagely, 'I wish one of those fellers in Washington would have to do this a couple, three times. Then maybe the Department would get down to brass tacks about that septic tank.'

'The Department!' ejaculated the woman bitterly.

The man brought the other jug of water, and they drove off again, coming presently to a highway that stretched out long and white, and as shining as the piece of tin at the depot. They passed an old farm wagon with a rocking chair in the back, in which a woman smaller and more withered than Jim's grandmother sat, smoking a corncob pipe. Three dark little children were sitting at her feet, lined up along one edge of the wagon with their chins on the sideboard, and they stared hard at the Indian Service car. The one in the middle waved timidly and then hid his head in his shoulder, like a bird, and giggled.

'Creeks!' cried the woman angrily. 'Everywhere we see Creeks these days! What will become of the Cherokees?'

'Ask the boy what his blood is,' said the man.

'Well, Jim,' said the woman, 'did you hear what Mr Standing-Deer said?'

'What?' said Jim and turned convulsively to look at the man with that peculiar name.

'Do you remember your mother and father?' said the woman.

'No, they were dead.'

'How did they die?'

'I don't know. Of the ague, maybe.'

'He says they may have died of the ague,' said the woman to Mr Standing-Deer, as if he were deaf. 'I haven't heard that word "ague" for years. Probably he means flu. Do you think perhaps this archaism is an index to the culture pattern from which he comes?'

Mr Standing-Deer made a doglike sound in his throat. 'Ask me another,' he said. 'I don't care about his speech at this stage of the game—it's the blood I'm talking about.'

'Were Mama and Daddy both Indians?' ask the woman kindly.

'I don't care!' Jim said. He had meant to say 'I don't know', but he could not change it afterward, because he commenced to cry again so hard that the woman patted his shoulder and did not ask him any more questions. She told him that her name was Miss Hornet and that she had been born in Chickasha and that she was the little boys' dormitory matron and that Mr Standing-Deer was the boys' counsellor. She said she was sure Jim would like it at the school. 'Uncle Sam takes care of us all just as well as he can, so we should be polite to him and not let him see that we are homesick,' she said, and Jim, thinking of his getaway this night, said softly, 'Yes'm, Mr Wilkins already told me.'

After a time they turned into a drive, at the end of which was a big, white gate. Beyond it lay terraced lawns, where trees grew beside a group of buildings. It was hushed here, too. In spots, the grass was yellow, and the water in the ditch beyond the gate was slow. There was a gravelly space for kids to play in, but there were no kids there. There were a slide and some swings and a teeter-totter, but they looked as deserted as bones, and over the whole place there hung a tight feeling, as if a twister were coming. Once, when a twister had come at home, all the windows in Mr Dannenbaum's house had been blown out, and it had taken the dinner off some old folks' table, and when Jim and his grandmother went out to look, there was the gravy bowl sitting on top of a fence post without a drop gone out of it.

Jim meant to be meek and mild until the sun went down, so that they would not suspect, and when Mr Standing-Deer got out to open the gate, he said quietly to Miss Hornet, 'Are the children all asleep now?'

'Yes, we are all asleep now,' she said. 'Some of us aren't feeling any too well these hot days.' Jim stole an anxious glance at her to see if she were sick with something catching, but he could tell nothing from her smooth brown face.

The buildings were big and were made of dark stone, and because the shades were down in most of the windows, they looked cool, and Jim thought comfortably of how he would spend this little time before nightfall and of all the cool things there would be inside—a drink of water and some potted ferns and cold white busts of Abraham Lincoln and George Washington and rubber treads on the stairs, like those in the public school back in Missouri. Mr Standing-Deer stopped the car by one of the smaller buildings, whose walls were covered with trumpet creeper. There had been trumpet creeper at Grandma's, too, growing over the backhouse, and a silly little girl named Lady had thought the blossoms were really trumpets and said the fairies could hear her playing 'The Battle Hymn of the Republic' on them. She was the girl who had said she had found a worm in a chocolate bar and a tack in a cracker. With Lady, Jim used to float nasturtium leaves on the rain water in the tubs, and then they would eat them as they sat in the string hammock under the shade of the sycamores.

It was true that there were ferns in the hall of the small building, and Jim looked at them greedily, though they were pale and juiceless-looking and grew out of a sagging wicker-covered box. To the left of the door was an office, and in it, behind a desk, sat a big Indian woman who was lacing the fingers of one hand with a rubber band. She was wearing a man's white shirt and a necktie with an opal stickpin, and around her fat waist she wore a broad beaded belt. Her hair was braided around her head, and right at the top there was a trumpet flower, looking perfectly natural, as if it grew there.

'Is this the new boy?' she said to Miss Hornet.

'Who else would it be, pray tell?' said Miss Hornet crossly.

'My name is Miss Dreadfulwater,' said the woman at the desk in an awful, roaring voice, and then she laughed and grabbed Jim's hand and shouted, 'And you'd better watch your step or I'll dreadfulwater *you*.'

Jim shivered and turned his eyes away from this crazy woman, and he heard his distant voice say, 'Did you get Mr Wilkins' telegram?'

'Telegram?' boomed Miss Dreadfulwater, and laughed uproariously. 'Oh, sure, we got his telegram. Telegram and long-distance telephone call. Didn't you come in a de-luxe Pullman drawing-room? And didn't Uncle Sam his own self meet you in the company limousine? Why, yes, sir, Mr Wilkins, and Uncle Sam and Honest Harold in Washington, and all of us here have just been thinking about hardly anything else but Jim Littlefield.'

Mr Standing-Deer said wearily, 'For Christ's sake, Sally, turn on the soft music. The kid's dead beat.'

'I'm dead beat, too, Mr Lying-Moose and Miss Yellow-Jacket, and I say it's too much. It's too much, I say. There are six more down in this dormitory alone, and that leaves, altogether, eight well ones. And the well ones are half dead on their feet at that, the poor little old buzzards.'

There was something wrong with Miss Dreadfulwater that Jim could not quite understand. He would have said she was drunk if she hadn't been a woman and a sort of teacher. She took a card out of the desk and asked him how old he was and if he had been vaccinated and what his parents' names were. He wanted a drink of water, or wanted at least to go and smell the ferns, but he dared not ask and stood before the desk feeling that he was already sick with whatever it was the others were sick with. Mr Standing-Deer took a gun out of his coat pocket and put it on the desk and then he went down the hall, saying over his shoulder, 'I guess they're all too sick to try and fly the coop for a while.'

'How old was your mother when she died?' said Miss Dread-fulwater.

'Eighteen and a half,' said Jim.

'How do you know?' she said.

'Grandma told me. Besides, I knew.'

'You *knew*? You remember your mother?'

'Yes,' said Jim. 'She was a Bolshevik.'

Miss Dreadfulwater put down her Eversharp and looked straight into his eyes. 'Are you crazy with the heat or am I?' she said.

He rather liked her, after all, and so he smiled until Miss Hornet said, 'Hurry along, Sally, I haven't got all day.'

'OK, OK, Queenie. I just wanted to straighten out this about the Bolshevik.'

'Oh, do it later,' said Miss Hornet. 'You know he's just making up a story. They all do when they first come.'

Miss Dreadfulwater asked some more questions—whether his tonsils were out, who Mr Wilkins was, whether Jim thought he was a full-blood or a half-breed or what. She finished finally and put the card back in the drawer, and then Miss Hornet said to Jim, 'What would you like to do now? You're free to do whatever you like till suppertime. It's perfectly clear that you have no unpacking to do.'

'Did he come just like this?' said Miss Dreadfulwater, astonished. 'Really?'

Miss Hornet ignored her and said, 'What would you like to do?'

'I don't know,' Jim said.

'Of course you do,' she said sharply. 'Do you want to play on the slide? Or the swings? None of the other children are out, but I should think a boy of eight could find plenty of ways to amuse himself.'

'I can,' he said. 'I'll go outside.'

'He ought to go to bed,' said Miss Dreadfulwater. 'You ought to put him to bed right now if you don't want him to come down with it.'

'Be still, Sally,' said Miss Hornet. 'You run along now, Jim.'

Although Jim was terribly thirsty, he did not stop to look for a drinking fountain or even to glance at the ferns. The composition floor was cool to his feet, but when he went out the door the heat came at him like a slapping hand. He did not mind it, because he would soon escape. The word 'escape' itself refreshed him and he said it twice under his breath as he walked across the lawn.

In back of the building, there was a good-sized tree and a boy was sitting in the shade of it. He wore a green visor, and he was reading a book and chewing gum like sixty.

Jim walked up to him and said, 'Do you know where any water is?'

The boy took off the visor, and Jim saw that his eyes were bright red. They were so startling that he could not help staring. The boy said, 'The water's poisonous. There's an epidemic here.'

Jim connected the poisonous water and the sickness in the dormitory with the boy's red eyes, and he was motionless with fear. The boy put his gum on his lower lip and clamped it there with his upper teeth, which were striped with grey and were finely notched, like a bread knife. 'One died,' he said, and laughed and rolled over on his stomach.

At the edge of the lawn beyond all the buildings, Jim saw a line of trees, the sort that follow a riverbank, and he thought that when it got dark, that was where he would go. But he was afraid, and even though it was hot and still here and he was thirsty, he did not want the day to end soon, and he said to the ugly, laughing boy, 'Isn't there any good water at all?'

'There is,' said the boy, sitting up again and putting his visor on, 'but not for Indians. I'm going to run away.' He popped his gum twice and then he pulled it out of his mouth for a full foot and swung it gently, like a skipping rope.

Jim said, 'When?'

'When my plans are laid,' said the boy, showing all his strange teeth in a smile that was not the least friendly. 'You know whose hangout is over there past the trees?'

'No, whose?'

'Clyde Barrow's,' whispered the boy. 'Not long ago, they came and smoked him out with tommy guns. That's where I'm going when I leave here.'

For the first time, Jim noticed the boy's clothes. He wore blue denim trousers and a blue shirt to match, and instead of a belt, he wore a bright-red sash, about the colour of his eyes. It was certainly not anything Jim had ever seen any other boy wear, and he said, pointing to it, 'Is that a flag or something?'

'It's the red sash,' replied the boy. 'It's a penalty. You aren't supposed to be talking to me when I have it on.' He gave Jim a nasty, secret smile and took his gum out of his mouth and rolled it between his thumb and forefinger. 'What's your name, anyway?' he asked.

'Jim Littlefield.'

'That's not Indian. My name is Rock Forward Mankiller. My father's name is Son-of-the-Man-Who-Looked-Like-a-Bunch-of-Rags-Thrown-Down. It's not that long in Navajo.'

'Navajo?' asked Jim.

'Hell, yés. I'm not no Cherokee,' said the boy.

'What did you do to make them put the red sash on you?' Jim asked, wishing to know, yet not wanting to hear.

'Wouldn't you like to know?' said Rock Forward and started to chew his gum again. Jim sat down in the shade beside him and looked at his burned foot. There was no blister, but it was red and the skin felt drawn. His head ached and his throat was sore, and he wanted to lie down on his stomach and go to sleep, but he dared not, lest he be sleeping when the night came. He felt again the burden of the waiting silence; once a fool blue jay started to raise the roof in Clyde Barrow's woods and a couple of times he heard a cow moo, but the rest of the time there was only this hot stillness in which the red-eyed boy stared at him calmly.

'What do they do if you escape and they catch you?' Jim asked, trembling and giving himself away.

'Standing-Deer comes after you with his six-gun, and then you get the red sash,' said Rock Forward, eyeing him closely. 'You can't get far unless you lay your plans. I know what you're thinking about, Littlefield. All new kids do. I'm wise to it.' He giggled and stretched his arms out wide, and once again he showed his sickening teeth.

The desire to sleep was so strong that Jim was not even angry with Rock Forward, and he swayed to and fro, half dozing, longing to lie full length on a bed and dimly to hear the sounds the awake people made through a half-open door. Little, bright-coloured memories came to him pleasantly, like the smallest valentines. The reason he knew that his mother had been a Bolshevik was that she'd had a pair of crimson satin slippers, which Grandma had kept in a drawer, along with her best crocheted pot holders and an album of picture postal cards from Gettysburg. The lovely shoes were made of satin and the heels were covered with rhinestones. The shiny cloth, roughened in places, was the colour of Rock Forward's eyes and of his sash. Jim said, 'No kidding, why do you have to wear the red sash?'

'I stole Standing-Deer's gun, if you want to know, and I said, "To hell with Uncle Sam." '

Jim heard what the boy said but he paid no mind, and he said, not to the boy or to anyone, 'I'll wait till tomorrow. I'm too sleepy now.'

Nor did Rock Forward pay any heed to Jim. Instead, he said, turning his head away and talking in the direction of the outlaw's hangout, 'If I get sick with the epidemic and die, I'll kill them all. Standing-Deer first and Dreadfulwater second and Hornet third. I'll burn the whole place up and I'll spit everywhere.'

'Do you have a father?' said Jim, scarcely able to get the words out.

'Of course I have a father,' said Rock Forward in a sudden rage. 'Didn't I just tell you his name? Didn't you know he was in jail for killing a well-known attorney in Del Rio, Texas? If he knew I was here, he'd kill them all. He'd take this red sash and tear it to smithereens. I'm no orphan and I'm not a Cherokee like the rest of you either, and when I get out of here, Standing-Deer had just better watch out. He'd just better watch his p's and q's when I get a six-gun of my own.' Passionately, he tore off his visor and bent it double, cracking it smack down the middle of the isinglass, and then, without another word, he went running off in the direction of the line of trees, the ends of the red sash flapping at his side.

Jim was too sleepy to care about anything now—now that he had decided to wait until tomorrow. He did not even care that it was hot. He lay down on the sickly grass, and for a while he watched a lonesome leaf-cutter bee easing a little piece of plantain to its hole. He hoped they would not wake him up and make him walk into the dormitory; he hoped that Mr Standing-Deer would come and carry him, and he could see himself with his head resting on that massive shoulder in the spotted coat. He saw himself growing smaller and smaller and lying in a bureau drawer, like Kayo in the funny papers. He rustled in his sleep, moving away from the sharp heels of the red shoes, and something as soft and deep and safe as fur held him in a still joy.

Nadine Gordimer

Six Feet of the Country

My wife and I are not real farmers—not even Lerice, really. We bought our place, ten miles out of Johannesburg on one of the main roads, to change something in ourselves, I suppose; you seem to rattle about so much within a marriage like ours. You long to hear nothing but a deep satisfying silence when you sound a marriage. The farm hasn't managed that for us, of course, but it has done other things, unexpected, illogical. Lerice, who I thought would retire there in Chekhovian sadness for a month or two, and then leave the place to the servants while she tried yet again to get a part she wanted and become the actress she would like to be, has sunk into the business of running the farm with all the serious intensity with which she once imbued the shadows in a playwright's mind. I should have given it up long ago it if had not been for her. Her hands, once small and plain and well-kept—she was not the sort of actress who wears red paint and diamond rings—are hard as a dog's pads.

I, of course, am there only in the evenings and at weekends. I am a partner in a travel agency which is flourishing—needs to be, as I tell Lerice, in order to carry the farm. Still, though I know we can't afford it, and though the sweetish smell of the fowls Lerice breeds sickens me, so that I avoid going past their runs, the farm is beautiful in a way I had almost forgotten—especially on a Sunday morning when I get up and go out into the paddock and see not the palm trees and fishpond and imitation-stone bird bath of the suburbs but white ducks on the dam, the lucerne field brilliant as window-dresser's grass, and the little, stocky, mean-eyed bull, lustful but bored, having his face tenderly licked by one of his ladies. Lerice comes out with her hair uncombed, in her hand a stick dripping with cattle dip. She will stand and look dreamily for a moment, the way she would pretend to look sometimes in those plays. 'They'll mate tomorrow,' she will say. 'This is their second day. Look how she loves him, my little Napoleon.' So that when people come to see us on Sunday afternoon, I am likely to hear myself saying as I pour out the drinks, 'When I drive back home from the city every day past those rows of suburban houses, I wonder how the devil we ever did stand it . . . Would you care to look around?' And there I am, taking some pretty girl and her young husband stumbling down to our riverbank, the girl catching her stockings on the mealie-stooks and stepping over cow turds humming with jewel-green flies while she says, '. . . the *tensions* of the damned city. And you're near enough to get into town to a show, too! I think it's wonderful. Why, you've got it both ways!'

And for a moment I accept the triumph as if I *had* managed it—the impossibility that I've been trying for all my life: just as if the truth was that you could get it 'both ways', instead of finding yourself with not even one way or the other but a third, one you had not provided for at all.

But even in our saner moments, when I find Lerice's earthy enthusiasms just as irritating as I once found her histrionical ones, and she finds what she calls my 'jealousy' of her capacity for enthusiasm as big a proof of my inadequacy for her as a mate as ever it was, we do believe that we have at least honestly escaped those tensions peculiar to the city about which our visitors speak. When Johannesburg people speak of 'tension', they don't mean hurrying people in crowded streets, the struggle for money, or the general competitive character of city life. They mean the guns under the white men's pillows and the burglar bars on the white men's windows. They mean those strange moments on city pavements when a black man won't stand aside for a white man.

Out in the country, even ten miles out, life is better than that. In the country, there is a lingering remnant of the pre-transitional stage; our relationship with the blacks is almost feudal. Wrong, I suppose, obsolete, but more comfortable all around. We have no burglar bars, no gun. Lerice's farm boys have their wives and their piccanins living with them on the land. They brew their sour beer without the fear of police raids. In fact, we've always rather prided ourselves that the poor devils have nothing much to fear, being with us; Lerice even keeps an eye on their children, with all the competence of a woman who has never had a child of her own, and she certainly doctors them all—children and adults—like babies whenever they happen to be sick.

It was because of this that we were not particularly startled one

173

night last winter when the boy Albert came knocking at our window long after we had gone to bed. I wasn't in our bed but sleeping in the little dressing-room-cum-linen-room next door, because Lerice had annoyed me and I didn't want to find myself softening towards her simply because of the sweet smell of the talcum powder on her flesh after her bath. She came and woke me up. 'Albert says one of the boys is very sick,' she said. 'I think you'd better go down and see. He wouldn't get us up at this hour for nothing.'

'What time is it?'

'What does it matter?' Lerice is maddeningly logical.

I got up awkwardly as she watched me—how is it I always feel a fool when I have deserted her bed? After all, I know from the way she never looks at me when she talks to me at breakfast next day that she is hurt and humiliated at my not wanting her—and I went out, clumsy with sleep.

'Which of the boys is it?' I asked Albert as we followed the dance of my torch.

'He's too sick. Very sick,' he said.

'But who? Franz?' I remember Franz had had a bad cough for the past week.

Albert did not answer; he had given me the path, and was walking along beside me in the tall dead grass. When the light of the torch caught his face, I saw that he looked acutely embarrassed. 'What's this all about?' I said.

He lowered his head under the glance of the light. 'It's not me, baas. I don't know. Petrus he send me.'

Irritated, I hurried him along to the huts. And there, on Petrus's iron bedstead, with its brick stilts, was a young man, dead. On his forehead there was still a light, cold sweat; his body was warm. The boys stood around as they do in the kitchen when it is discovered that someone has broken a dish—uncooperative, silent. Somebody's wife hung about in the shadows, her hands wrung together under her apron.

I had not seen a dead man since the war. This was very different. I felt like the others—extraneous, useless. 'What was the matter?' I asked.

The woman patted at her chest and shook her head to indicate the painful impossibility of breathing.

He must have died of pneumonia.

I turned to Petrus. 'Who was this boy? What was he doing here?' The light of a candle on the floor showed that Petrus was weeping. He followed me out the door.

When we were outside, in the dark, I waited for him to speak. But he didn't. 'Now, come on, Petrus, you must tell me who this boy was. Was he a friend of yours?'

'He's my brother, baas. He came from Rhodesia to look for work.'

The story startled Lerice and me a little. The young boy had walked down from Rhodesia to look for work in Johannesburg, had caught a chill from sleeping out along the way, and had lain ill in his brother Petrus's hut since his arrival three days before. Our boys had been frightened to ask us for help for him because we had never been intended ever to know of his presence. Rhodesian natives are barred from entering the Union unless they have a permit; the young man was an illegal immigrant. No doubt our boys had managed the whole thing successfully several times before; a number of relatives must have walked the seven or eight hundred miles from poverty to the paradise of zoot suits, police raids, and black slum townships that is their *Egoli*, City of Gold—the African name for Johannesburg. It was merely a matter of getting such a man to lie low on our farm until a job could be found with someone who would be glad to take the risk of prosecution for employing an illegal immigrant in exchange for the services of someone as yet untainted by the city.

Well, this was one who would never get up again.

'You would think they would have felt they could tell *us*,' said Lerice next morning. 'Once the man was ill. You would have thought at least—' When she is getting intense over something, she has a way of standing in the middle of a room as people do when they are shortly to leave on a journey, looking searchingly about her at the most familiar objects as if she had never seen them before. I had noticed that in Petrus's presence in the kitchen, earlier, she had had the air of being almost offended with him, almost hurt.

In any case, I really haven't the time or inclination any more to go into everything in our life that I know Lerice, from those alarmed and pressing eyes of hers, would like us to go into. She is the kind of woman who doesn't mind if she looks plain, or odd; I don't suppose she would even care if she knew how strange she looks when her whole face is out of proportion with urgent uncertainty. I said, 'Now I'm the one who'll have to do all the dirty work, I suppose.'

She was still staring at me, trying me out with those eyes—wasting her time, if she only knew.

'I'll have to notify the health authorities,' I said calmly. 'They can't just cart him off and bury him. After all, we don't really know what he died of.'

She simply stood there, as if she had given up—simply ceased to see me at all.

I don't know when I've been so irritated. 'It might have been something contagious,' I said. 'God knows.' There was no answer.

I am not enamoured of holding conversations with myself. I went out to shout to one of the boys to open the garage and get the car ready for my morning drive to town.

As I had expected, it turned out to be quite a business. I had to notify the police as well as the health authorities, and answer a lot of tedious questions: How was it I was ignorant of the boy's presence? If I did not supervise my native quarters, how did I know that that sort of thing didn't go on all the time? And when I flared up and told them that so long as my natives did their work, I didn't think it my right or concern to poke my nose into their private lives, I got from the coarse, dull-witted police sergeant one of those looks that come not from any thinking process going on in the brain but from that faculty common to all who are possessed by the master-race theory—a look of insanely inane certainty. He grinned at me with a mixture of scorn and delight at my stupidity.

Then I had to explain to Petrus why the health authorities had to take away the body for a post-mortem—and, in fact, what a post-mortem was. When I telephoned the health department some days later to find out the result, I was told that the cause of death was, as we had thought, pneumonia, and that the body had been suitably disposed of. I went out to where Petrus was mixing a mash for the fowls and told him that it was all right, there would be no trouble; his brother had died from that pain in his chest. Petrus put down the paraffin tin and said, 'When can we go to fetch him, baas?'

'To fetch him?'

'Will the baas please ask them when we must come?'

I went back inside and called Lerice, all over the house. She came down the stairs from the spare bedrooms, and I said, '*Now* what am I going to do? When I told Petrus, he just asked calmly when they could go and fetch the body. They think they're going to bury him themselves.'

'Well, go back and tell him,' said Lerice. 'You must tell him. Why didn't you tell him then?'

When I found Petrus again, he looked up politely. 'Look, Petrus,' I said. 'You can't go to fetch your brother. They've done it already—they've *buried* him, you understand?'

'Where?' he said slowly, dully, as if he thought that perhaps he was getting this wrong.

'You see, he was a stranger. They knew he wasn't from here, and they didn't know he had some of his people here so they thought they must bury him.' It was difficult to make a pauper's grave sound like a privilege.

'Please, baas, the baas must ask them.' But he did not mean that he wanted to know the burial place. He simply ignored the incomprehensible machinery I told him had set to work on his dead brother; he wanted the brother back.

'But, Petrus,' I said, 'how can I? Your brother is buried already. I can't ask them now.'

'Oh, baas!' he said. He stood with his bran-smeared hands uncurled at his sides, one corner of his mouth twitching.

'Good God, Petrus, they won't listen to me! They can't, anyway. I'm sorry, but I can't do it. You understand?'

He just kept on looking at me, out of his knowledge that white men have everything, can do anything; if they don't, it is because they won't.

And then, at dinner, Lerice started. 'You could at least phone,' she said.

'Christ, what d'you think I am? Am I supposed to bring the dead back to life?'

But I could not exaggerate my way out of this ridiculous responsibility that had been thrust on me. 'Phone them up,' she went on. 'And at least you'll be able to tell him you've done it and they've explained that it's impossible.'

She disappeared somewhere into the kitchen quarters after coffee. A little later she came back to tell me, 'The old father's coming down from Rhodesia to be at the funeral. He's got a permit and he's already on his way.'

Unfortunately, it was not impossible to get the body back. The authorities said that it was somewhat irregular, but that since the hygiene conditions had been fulfilled, they could not refuse permission for exhumation. I found out that, with the undertaker's charges, it would cost twenty pounds. Ah, I thought, that settles it. On five pounds a month, Petrus won't have twenty pounds—and just as well, since it couldn't do the dead any good. Certainly I should not offer it to him myself. Twenty pounds—or anything else within reason, for that matter—I would have spent without grudging it on doctors or medicines that might have helped the boy when he was alive. Once he was dead, I had no intention of encouraging Petrus to throw away, on a gesture, more than he spent to clothe his whole family in a year.

When I told him, in the kitchen that night, he said, 'Twenty pounds?'

I said, 'Yes, that's right, twenty pounds.'

For a moment, I had the feeling, from the look on his face, that he was calculating. But when he spoke again I thought I must have imagined it. 'We must pay twenty pounds!' he said in the faraway voice in which a person speaks of something so unattainable it does not bear thinking about.

'All right, Petrus,' I said, and went back to the living-room.

The next morning before I went to town, Petrus asked to see me. 'Please, baas,' he said, awkwardly, handing me a bundle of notes. They're so seldom on the giving rather than the receiving side, poor devils, they don't really know how to hand money to a white man. There it was, the twenty pounds, in ones and halves, some creased and folded until they were soft as dirty rags, others smooth and fairly new—Franz's money, I suppose, and Albert's, and Dora the cook's, and Jacob the gardener's, and God knows who else's besides, from all the farms and small holdings round about. I took it in irritation more than in astonishment, really—irritation at the waste, the uselessness of this sacrifice by people so poor. Just like the poor everywhere, I thought, who stint themselves the decencies of life in order to ensure themselves the decencies of death. So incomprehensible to people like Lerice and me, who regard life as something to be spent extravagantly and, if we think about death at all, regard it as the final bankruptcy.

* * *

The farm hands don't work on Saturday afternoon anyway, so it was a good day for the funeral. Petrus and his father had borrowed our donkey-cart to fetch the coffin from the city, where, Petrus told Lerice on their return, everything was 'nice'—the coffin waiting for them, already sealed up to save them from what must have been a rather unpleasant sight after two weeks' interment. (It had taken all that time for the authorities and the undertaker to make the final arrangements for moving the body.) All morning, the coffin lay in Petrus's hut, awaiting the trip to the little old burial ground, just outside the eastern boundary of our farm, that was a relic of the days when this was a real farming district rather than a fashionable rural estate. It was pure chance that I happened to be down there near the fence when the procession came past; once again Lerice had forgotten her promise to me and had made the house uninhabitable on a Saturday afternoon. I had come home and been infuriated to find her in a pair of filthy old slacks and with her hair uncombed since the night before, having all the varnish scraped from the living-room floor, if you please. So I had taken my No 8 iron and gone off to practise my approach shots. In my annoyance, I had forgotten about the funeral, and was reminded only when I saw the procession coming up the path along the outside of the fence towards me; from where I was standing, you can see the graves quite clearly, and that day the sun glinted on bits of broken pottery, a lopsided homemade cross, and jam-jars brown with rainwater and dead flowers.

I felt a little awkward, and did not know whether to go on hitting my golf ball or stop at least until the whole gathering was decently past. The donkey-cart creaks and screeches with every revolution of the wheels, and it came along in a slow, halting fashion somehow peculiarly suited to the two donkeys who drew it, their little potbellies rubbed and rough, their heads sunk between the shafts, and their ears flattened back with an air submissive and downcast; peculiarly suited, too, to the group of men and women who came along slowly behind. The patient ass. Watching, I thought, you can see now why the creature became a Biblical symbol. Then the procession drew level with me and stopped, so I had to put down my club. The coffin was taken down off the cart—it was a shiny, yellow-varnished wood, like cheap furniture—and the donkeys twitched their ears against the flies. Petrus, Franz, Albert, and the old father from Rhodesia hoisted it on their shoulders and the procession moved on, on foot. It was really a very awkward moment. I stood there rather foolishly at the fence, quite still, and slowly they filed past, not looking up, the four men bent beneath the shiny wooden box, and the straggling troop of mourners. All of them were servants or neighbours' servants whom I knew as casual easygoing gossipers about our lands or kitchen. I heard the old man's breathing.

I had just bent to pick up my club again when there was a sort of jar in the flowing solemnity of their processional mood; I felt it at once, like a wave of heat along the air, or one of those sudden currents of cold catching at your legs in a placid stream. The old man's voice was muttering something; the people had stopped, confused, and they bumped into one another, some pressing to go on, others hissing them to be still. I could see that they were embarrassed, but they could not ignore the voice; it was much the way that the mumblings of a prophet, though not clear at first, arrest the mind. The corner of the coffin the old man carried was sagging at an angle; he seemed to be trying to get out from under the weight of it. Now Petrus expostulated with him.

The little boy who had been left to watch the donkeys dropped the reins and ran to see. I don't know why—unless it was for the same reason people crowd around someone who has fainted in a cinema—but I parted the wires of the fence and went through, after him.

Petrus lifted his eyes to me—to anybody—with distress and horror. The old man from Rhodesia had let go of the coffin entirely, and the three others, unable to support it on their own, had laid it on the ground, in the pathway. Already there was a film of dust lightly wavering up its shiny sides. I did not understand what the old man was saying; I hesitated to interfere. But now the whole seething group turned on my silence. The old man himself came over to me, with his hands outspread and shaking, and spoke directly to me, saying something that I could tell from the tone, without understanding the words, was shocking and extraordinary.

'What is it, Petrus? What's wrong?' I appealed.

Petrus threw up his hands, bowed his head in a series of hysterical shakes, then thrust his face up at me suddenly. 'He says, "My son was not so heavy." '

Silence. I could hear the old man breathing; he kept his mouth a little open, as old people do. 'My son was young and thin,' he said at last, in English.

Again silence. Then babble broke out. The old man thundered against everybody; his teeth were yellowed and few, and he had one of those fine, grizzled, sweeping moustaches one doesn't often see nowadays, which must have been grown in emulation of early Empire-builders. It seemed to frame all his utterances with a special validity. He shocked the assembly; they thought he was mad, but they had to listen to him. With his own hands he began to prise the lid off the coffin and three of the men came forward to help him. Then he sat down on the ground; very old, very weak, and unable to speak, he merely lifted a trembling hand towards what was there. He abdicated, he handed it over to them; he was no good any more.

They crowded round to look (and so did I), and now they forgot the nature of this surprise and the occasion of grief to which it belonged, and for a few minutes were carried up in the astonishment of the surprise itself. They gasped and flared noisily with excitement. I even noticed the little boy who had held the donkeys jumping up and down, almost weeping with rage because the backs of the grownups crowded him out of his view.

In the coffin was someone no one had seen before: a heavily built, rather light-skinned native with a neatly stitched scar on his forehead—perhaps from a blow in a brawl that had also dealt him some other, slower-working injury that had killed him.

I wrangled with the authorities for a week over that body. I had the feeling that they were shocked, in a laconic fashion, by their own mistake, but that in the confusion of their anonymous dead they were helpless to put it right. They said to me, 'We are trying to find out,' and 'We are still making inquiries.' It was as if at any moment they might conduct me into their mortuary and say, 'There! Lift up the sheets; look for him—your poultry boy's brother. There are so many black faces—surely one will do?'

And every evening when I got home, Petrus was waiting in the kitchen. 'Well, they're trying. They're still looking. The baas is seeing to it for you, Petrus,' I would tell him. 'God, half the time I should be in the office I'm driving around the back end of the town chasing after this affair,' I added aside, to Lerice, one night.

She and Petrus both kept their eyes turned on me as I spoke, and, oddly, for those moments they looked exactly alike, though it sounds impossible: my wife, with her high, white forehead and her attenuated Englishwoman's body, and the poultry boy, with his horny bare feet below khaki trousers tied at the knee with string and the peculiar rankness of his nervous sweat coming from his skin.

'What makes you so indignant, so determined about this now?' said Lerice suddenly.

I stared at her. 'It's a matter of principle. Why should they get away with a swindle? It's time these officials had a jolt from someone who'll bother to take the trouble.'

She said, 'Oh.' And as Petrus slowly opened the kitchen door to leave, sensing that the talk had gone beyond him, she turned away, too.

I continued to pass on assurances to Petrus every evening, but although what I said was the same and the voice in which I said it was the same, every evening it sounded weaker. At last, it became clear that we would never get Petrus's brother back, because nobody really knew where he was. Somewhere in a graveyard as uniform as a housing scheme, somewhere under a number that didn't belong to him, or in the medical school, perhaps, laboriously reduced to layers of muscle and strings of nerve? Goodness knows. He had no identity in this world anyway.

It was only then, and in a voice of shame, that Petrus asked me to try and get the money back.

'From the way he asks, you'd think he was robbing his dead brother,' I said to Lerice later. But as I've said, Lerice had got so intense about this business that she couldn't even appreciate a little ironic smile.

I tried to get the money; Lerice tried. We both telephoned and wrote and argued, but nothing came of it. It appeared that the main expense had been the undertaker, and after all he had done his job. So the whole thing was a complete waste, even more of a waste for the poor devils than I had thought it would be.

The old man from Rhodesia was about Lerice's father's size, so she gave him one of her father's old suits, and he went back home rather better off, for the winter, than he had come.

Grace Paley

The Loudest Voice

There is a certain place where dumb-waiters boom, doors slam, dishes crash; every window is a mother's mouth bidding the street shut up, go skate somewhere else, come home. My voice is the loudest.

There, my own mother is still as full of breathing as me and the grocer stands up to speak to her. 'Mrs Abramowitz,' he says, 'people should not be afraid of their children.'

'Ah, Mr Bialik,' my mother replies, 'if you say to her or her father "Ssh," they say, "In the grave it will be quiet." '

'From Coney Island to the cemetery,' says my papa. 'It's the same subway; it's the same fare.'

I am right next to the pickle barrel. My pinky is making tiny whirlpools in the brine. I stop a moment to announce: 'Campbell's Tomato Soup. Campbell's Vegetable Beef Soup. Campbell's S-c-otch Broth . . .'

'Be quiet,' the grocer says, 'the labels are coming off.'

'Please, Shirley, be a little quiet,' my mother begs me.

In that place the whole street groans: Be quiet! Be quiet! but steals from the happy chorus of my inside self not a tittle or a jot.

There, too, but just around the corner, is a red brick building that has been old for many years. Every morning the children stand before it in double lines which must be straight. They are not insulted. They are waiting anyway.

I am usually among them. I am, in fact, the first, since I begin with 'A'.

One cold morning the monitor tapped me on the shoulder. 'Go to Room 409, Shirley Abramowitz,' he said. I did as I was told. I went in a hurry up a down staircase to Room 409, which contained sixth-graders. I had to wait at the desk without wiggling until Mr Hilton, their teacher, had time to speak.

After five minutes he said, 'Shirley?'

'What?' I whispered.

He said, 'My! My! Shirley Abramowitz! They told me you have a particularly loud, clear voice and read with lots of expression. Could that be true?'

'Oh yes,' I whispered.

'In that case, don't be silly; I might very well be your teacher someday. Speak up, speak up.'

'Yes,' I shouted.

'More like it,' he said. 'Now, Shirley, can you put a ribbon in your hair or a bobby pin? It's too messy.'

'Yes!' I bawled.

'Now, now, calm down.' He turned to the class. 'Children, not a sound. Open at page 39. Read till 52. When you finish, start again.' He looked me over once more. 'Now, Shirley, you know, I suppose, that Christmas is coming. We are preparing a beautiful play. Most of the parts have been given out. But I still need a child with a strong voice, lots of stamina. Do you know what stamina is? You do? Smart kid. You know, I heard you read "The Lord is my shepherd" in Assembly yesterday. I was very impressed. Wonderful delivery. Mrs Jordan, your teacher, speaks highly of you. Now listen to me, Shirley Abramowitz, if you want to take the part and be in the play, repeat after me, "I swear to work harder than I ever did before." '

I looked to heaven and said at once, 'Oh, I swear.' I kissed my pinky and looked at God.

'That is an actor's life, my dear,' he explained. 'Like a soldier's, never tardy or disobedient to his general, the director. Everything,' he said, 'absolutely everything will depend on you.'

That afternoon, all over the building, children scraped and scrubbed the turkeys and the sheaves of corn off the schoolroom windows. Goodbye Thanksgiving. The next morning a monitor brought red paper and green paper from the office. We made new shapes and hung them on the walls and glued them to the doors.

The teachers became happier and happier. Their heads were ringing like the bells of childhood. My best friend Evie was prone to evil, but she did not get a single demerit for whispering. We learned 'Hóly Night' without an error. 'How wonderful!' said Miss Glacé, the student teacher. 'To think that some of you don't even speak the language!' We learned 'Deck the Halls' and 'Hark! The Herald Angels'. . . . They weren't ashamed and we weren't embarrassed.

Oh, but when my mother heard about it all, she said to my father:

184

'Misha, you don't know what's going on there. Cramer is the head of the Tickets Committee.'

'Who?' asked my father. 'Cramer? Oh yes, an active woman.'

'Active? Active has to have a reason. Listen,' she said sadly, 'I'm surprised to see my neighbours making tra-la-la for Christmas.'

My father couldn't think of what to say to that. Then he decided: 'You're in America! Clara, you wanted to come here. In Palestine the Arabs would be eating you alive. Europe you had pogroms. Argentina is full of Indians. Here you got Christmas. . . . Some joke, ha?'

'Very funny, Misha. What is becoming of you? If we came to a new country a long time ago to run away from tyrants, and instead we fall into a creeping pogrom, that our children learn a lot of lies, so what's the joke? Ach, Misha, your idealism is going away.'

'So is your sense of humour.'

'That I never had, but idealism you had a lot of.'

'I'm the same Misha Abramovitch, I didn't change an iota. Ask anyone.'

'Only ask me,' says my mama, may she rest in peace. 'I got the answer.'

Meanwhile the neighbours had to think of what to say too.

Marty's father said: 'You know, he has a very important part, my boy.'

'Mine also,' said Mr Sauerfeld.

'Not my boy!' said Mrs Klieg. 'I said to him no. The answer is no. When I say no! I mean no!'

The rabbi's wife said, 'It's disgusting!' But no one listened to her. Under the narrow sky of God's great wisdom she wore a strawberry-blond wig.

Every day was noisy and full of experience. I was Right-hand Man. Mr Hilton said: 'How could I get along without you, Shirley?'

He said: 'Your mother and father ought to get down on their knees every night and thank God for giving them a child like you.'

He also said: 'You're absolutely a pleasure to work with, my dear, dear child.'

Sometimes he said: 'For God's sakes, what did I do with the script? Shirley! Shirley! Find it.'

Then I answered quietly: 'Here it is, Mr Hilton.'

Once in a while, when he was very tired, he would cry out:

'Shirley, I'm just tired of screaming at those kids. Will you tell Ira Pushkov not to come in till Lester points to that star the second time?'

Then I roared: 'Ira Pushkov, what's the matter with you? Dope! Mr Hilton told you five times already, don't come in till Lester points to that star the second time.'

'Ach, Clàra,' my father asked, 'what does she do there till six o'clock she can't even put the plates on the table?'

'Christmas,' said my mother coldly.

'Ho! Ho!' my father said. 'Christmas. What's the harm? After all, history teaches everyone. We learn from reading this is a holiday from pagan times also, candles, lights, even Chanukah. So we learn it's not altogether Christian. So if they think it's a private holiday, they're only ignorant, not patriotic. What belongs to history, belongs to all men. You want to go back to the Middle Ages? Is it better to shave your head with a secondhand razor? Does it hurt Shirley to learn to speak up? It does not. So maybe someday she won't live between the kitchen and the shop. She's not a fool.'

I thank you, Papa, for your kindness. It is true about me to this day. I am foolish but I am not a fool.

That night my father kissed me and said with great interest in my career, 'Shirley, tomorrow's your big day. Congrats.'

'Save it,' my mother said. Then she shut all the windows in order to prevent tonsillitis.

In the morning it snowed. On the street corner a tree had been decorated for us by a kind city administration. In order to miss its chilly shadow our neighbours walked three blocks east to buy a loaf of bread. The butcher pulled down black window shades to keep the coloured lights from shining on his chickens. Oh, not me. On the way to school, with both my hands I tossed it a kiss of tolerance. Poor thing, it was a stranger in Egypt.

I walked straight into the auditorium past the staring children. 'Go ahead, Shirley!' said the monitors. Four boys, big for their age, had already started work as propmen and stagehands.

Mr Hilton was very nervous. He was not even happy. Whatever he started to say ended in a sideward look of sadness. He sat slumped in the middle of the first row and asked me to help Miss Glacé. I did this, although she thought my voice too resonant and said, 'Show-off!'

Parents began to arrive long before we were ready. They wanted to make a good impression. From among the yards of drapes I peeked out at the audience. I saw my embarrassed mother.

Ira, Lester, and Meyer were pasted to their beards by Miss Glacé. She almost forgot to thread the star on its wire, but I reminded her. I coughed a few times to clear my throat. Miss Glacé looked around and saw that everyone was in costume and on line waiting to play his part. She whispered, 'All right . . .' Then:

Jackie Sauerfeld, the prettiest boy in first grade, parted the curtains with his skinny elbow and in a high voice sang out:

> 'Parents dear
> We are here
> To make a Christmas play in time.
> It we give
> In narrative
> And illustrate with pantomime.'

He disappeared.

My voice burst immediately from the wings to the great shock of Ira, Lester, and Meyer, who were waiting for it but were surprised all the same.

'I remember, I remember, the house where I was born . . .'

Miss Glacé yanked the curtain open and there it was, the house—an old hayloft, where Celia Kornbluh lay in the straw with Cindy Lou, her favourite doll. Ira, Lester, and Meyer moved slowly from the wings towards her, sometimes pointing to a moving star and sometimes ahead to Cindy Lou.

It was a long story and it was a sad story. I carefully pronounced all the words about my lonesome childhood, while little Eddie Braunstein wandered upstage and down with his shepherd's stick, looking for sheep. I brought up lonesomeness again, and not being understood at all except by some women everybody hated. Eddie was too small for that and Marty Groff took his place, wearing his father's prayer shawl. I announced twelve friends, and half the boys in the fourth grade gathered round Marty, who stood on an orange crate while my voice harangued. Sorrowful and loud, I declaimed about love and God and Man, but because of the terrible deceit of Abie Stock we came suddenly to a famous moment. Marty, whose remembering tongue I was, waited at the foot of the cross. He stared desperately at the audience. I groaned, 'My God, my God, why hast thou forsaken me?' The soldiers who were sheiks grabbed poor Marty to pin him up to die, but he wrenched free, turned again to the audience, and spread his arms aloft to show despair and the end. I murmured at the top of my voice, 'The rest is silence, but as everyone in this room, in this city—in this world—now knows, I shall have life eternal.'

That night Mrs Kornbluh visited our kitchen for a glass of tea. 'How's the virgin?' asked my father with a look of concern.

'For a man with a daughter, you got a fresh mouth, Abramovitch.'

'Here,' said my father kindly, 'have some lemon, it'll sweeten your disposition.'

They debated a little in Yiddish, then fell in a puddle of Russian and Polish. What I understood next was my father, who said, 'Still and all, it was certainly a beautiful affair, you have to admit, introducing us to the beliefs of a different culture.'

'Well, yes,' said Mrs Kornbluh. 'The only thing . . . you know Charlie Turner—that cute boy in Celia's class—a couple others? They got very small parts or no part at all. In very bad taste, it seemed to me. After all, it's their religion.'

'Ach,' explained my mother, 'what could Mr Hilton do? They got very small voices; after all, why should they holler? The English language they know from the beginning by heart. They're blond like angels. You think it's so important they should get in the play? Christmas . . . the whole piece of goods . . . they own it.'

I listened and listened until I couldn't listen any more. Too sleepy, I climbed out of bed and kneeled. I made a little church of my hands and said, 'Hear, O Israel . . .' Then I called out in Yiddish, 'Please, good night, good night. Ssh.' My father said, 'Ssh yourself,' and slammed the kitchen door.

I was happy. I fell asleep at once. I had prayed for everybody: my talking family, cousins far away, passers-by, and all the lonesome Christians. I expected to be heard. My voice was certainly the loudest.

JEAN RHYS

Let Them Call It Jazz

One bright Sunday morning in July I have trouble with my Notting Hill landlord because he ask for a month's rent in advance. He tell me this after I live there since winter, settling up every week without fail. I have no job at the time, and if I give the money he want there's not much left. So I refuse. The man drunk already at that early hour, and he abuse me—all talk, he can't frighten me. But his wife is a bad one—now she walk in my room and say she must have cash. When I tell her no, she give my suitcase one kick and it burst open. My best dress fall out, then she laugh and give another kick. She say month in advance is usual, and if I can't pay find somewhere else.

Don't talk to me about London. Plenty people there have heart like stone. Any complaint—the answer is 'prove it'. But if nobody see and bear witness for me, how to prove anything? So I pack up and leave. I think better not have dealings with that woman. She too cunning, and Satan don't lie worse.

I walk about till a place nearby is open where I can have coffee and a sandwich. There I start talking to a man at my table. He talk to me already, I know him, but I don't know his name. After a while he ask, 'What's the matter? Anything wrong?' and when I tell him my trouble he say I can use an empty flat he own till I have time to look around.

This man is not at all like most English people. He see very quick, and he decide very quick. English people take long time to decide—you three-quarter dead before they make up their mind about you. Too besides, he speak very matter of fact, as if it's nothing. He speak as if he realize well what it is to live like I do—that's why I accept and go.

He tell me somebody occupy the flat till last week, so I find everything all right, and he tell me how to get there—three-quarters of an hour from Victoria Station, up a steep hill, turn left, and I can't mistake the house. He give me the keys and an envelope with a telephone number on the back. Underneath is written 'After 6 p.m. ask for Mr Sims'.

In the train that evening I think myself lucky, for to walk about London on a Sunday with nowhere to go—that take the heart out of you.

I find the place and the bedroom of the downstairs flat is nicely furnished—two looking glass, wardrobe, chest of drawers, sheets, everything. It smell of jasmine scent, but it smell strong of damp too.

I open the door opposite and there's a table, a couple chairs, a gas stove and a cupboard, but this room so big it look empty. When I pull the blind up I notice the paper peeling off and mushrooms growing on the walls—you never see such a thing.

The bathroom the same, all the taps rusty. I leave the two other rooms and make up the bed. Then I listen, but I can't hear one sound. Nobody come in, nobody go out of that house, I lie awake for a long time, then I decide not to stay and in the morning I start to get ready quickly before I change my mind. I want to wear my best dress, but it's a funny thing—when I take up that dress and remember how my landlady kick it I cry. I cry and I can't stop. When I stop I feel tired to my bones, tired like old woman. I don't want to move again—I have to force myself. But in the end I get out in the passage and there's a postcard for me. 'Stay as long as you like. I'll be seeing you soon—Friday probably. Not to worry.' It isn't signed, but I don't feel so sad and I think, 'All right, I wait here till he come. Perhaps he know of a job for me.'

Nobody else live in the house but a couple on the top floor—quiet people and they don't trouble me. I have no word to say against them.

First time I meet the lady she's opening the front door and she give me a very inquisitive look. But next time she smile a bit and I smile back—once she talk to me. She tell me the house very old, hundred and fifty year old, and she and her husband live there since long time. 'Valuable property,' she says, 'it could have been saved, but nothing done of course.' Then she tells me that as to the present owner—if he is the owner—well he have to deal with local authorities and she believe they make difficulties. 'These people are determined to pull down all the lovely old houses—it's shameful.'

So I agree that many things shameful. But what to do? What to do? I say it have an elegant shape, it make the other houses in the street look cheap trash, and she seem pleased. That's true too. The house sad and out of place, especially at night. But it have style. The second floor shut up, and as for my flat, I go in the two empty rooms once, but never again.

Underneath was the cellar, full of old boards and broken-up furniture—I see a big rat there one day. It was no place to be alone in I tell you, and I get the habit of buying a bottle of wine most evenings, for I don't like whisky and the rum here no good. It don't even *taste* like rum. You wonder what they do to it.

After I drink a glass or two I can sing and when I sing all the misery goes from my heart. Sometimes I make up songs but next morning I forget them, so other times I sing the old ones like *Tantalizin'* or *Don't Trouble Me Now*.

I think I go but I don't go. Instead I wait for the evening and the wine and that's all. Everywhere else I live—well, it doesn't matter to me, but this house is different—empty and no noise and full of shadows, so that sometimes you ask yourself what make all those shadows in an empty room.

I eat in the kitchen, then I clean up everything and have a bath for coolness. Afterwards I lean my elbows on the windowsill and look at the garden. Red and blue flowers mix up with the weeds and there are five–six apple trees. But the fruit drop and lie in the grass, so sour nobody want it. At the back, near the wall, is a bigger tree—this garden certainly take up a lot of room, perhaps that's why they want to pull the place down.

Not much rain all the summer, but not much sunshine either. More of a glare. The grass get brown and dry, the weeds grow tall, the leaves on the trees hang down. Only the red flowers—the poppies—stand up to that light, everything else look weary.

I don't trouble about money, but what with wine and shillings for the slot-meters, it go quickly; so I don't waste much on food. In the evening I walk outside—not by the apple trees but near the street—it's not so lonely.

There's no wall here and I can see the woman next door looking at me over the hedge. At first I say good evening, but she turn away her head, so afterwards I don't speak. A man is often with her, he wear a straw hat with a black ribbon and goldrim spectacles. His suit hang on him like it's too big. He's the husband it seems and he stare at me worse than his wife—he stare as if I'm wild animal let loose. Once I laugh in his face because why these people have to be like that? I don't bother them. In the end I get that I don't even give them one single glance. I have plenty other things to worry about.

To show you how I felt. I don't remember exactly. But I believe it's the second Saturday after I come that when I'm at the window just before I go for my wine I feel somebody's hand on my shoulder and it's Mr Sims. He must walk very quiet because I don't know a thing till he touch me.

He says hullo, then he tells me I've got terrible thin, do I ever eat. I say of course I eat but he goes on that it doesn't suit me at all to be so thin and he'll buy some food in the village. (That's the way he talk. There's no village here. You don't get away from London so quick.)

It don't seem to me he look very well himself, but I just say bring a drink instead, as I am not hungry.

He come back with three bottles—vermouth, gin and red wine. Then he ask if the little devil who was here last smash all the glasses and I tell him she smash some, I find the pieces. But not all. 'You fight with her, eh?'

He laugh, and he don't answer. He pour out the drinks then he says, 'Now, you eat up those sandwiches.'

Some men when they are there you don't worry so much. These sort of men you do all they tell you blindfold beccause they can take the trouble from your heart and make you think you're safe. It's nothing they say or do. It's a feeling they can give you. So I don't talk with him seriously—I don't want to spoil that evening. But I ask about the house and why it's so empty and he says:

'Has the old trout upstairs been gossiping?'

I tell him, 'She suppose they make difficulties for you.'

'It was a damn bad buy,' he says and talks about selling the lease or something. I don't listen much.

We were standing by the window then and the sun low. No more glare. He puts his hand over my eyes. 'Too big—much too big for your face,' he says and kisses me like you kiss a baby. When he takes his hand away I see he's looking out at the garden and he says this—'It gets you. My God it does.'

I know very well it's not me he means, so I ask him, 'Why sell it then? If you like it, keep it.'

'Sell what?' he says. 'I'm not talking about this damned house.'

I ask what he's talking about. 'Money,' he says. 'Money. That's what I'm talking about. Ways of making it.'

'I don't think so much of money. It don't like me and what do I care?' I was joking, but he turns around, his face quite pale and he tells me I'm a fool. He tells me I'll get pushed around all my life and die like a dog, only worse because they'd finish off a dog, but they'll let me live till I'm a caricature of myself. That's what he say, 'Caricature of yourself.' He say I'll curse the day I was born and everything and everybody in this bloody world before I'm done.

I tell him, 'No I'll never feel like that,' and he smiles, if you can call it a smile, and says he's glad I'm content with my lot. 'I'm disappointed in you, Selina. I thought you had more spirit.'

'If I contented that's all right,' I answer him. 'I don't see very many looking contented over here.' We're standing staring at each other when the doorbell rings. 'That's a friend of mine,' he says. 'I'll let him in.'

As to the friend, he's all dressed up in stripe pants and a black jacket and he's carrying a brief-case. Very ordinary looking but with a soft kind of voice.

'Maurice, this is Selina Davis,' says Mr Sims, and Maurice smiles very kind but it don't mean much, then he looks at his watch and says they ought to be getting along.

At the door Mr Sims tells me he'll see me next week and I answer straight out, 'I won't be here next week because I want a job and I won't get one in this place.'

'Just what I'm going to talk about. Give it a week longer, Selina.'

I say, 'Perhaps I stay a few more days. Then I go. Perhaps I go before.'

'Oh no you won't go,' he says.

They walk to the gates quickly and drive off in a yellow car. Then I feel eyes on me and it's the woman and her husband in the next door garden watching. The man make some remark and she look at me so hateful, so hating I shut the front door quick.

I don't want more wine. I want to go to bed early because I must think. I must think about money. It's true I don't care for it. Even when somebody steal my savings—this happen soon after I get to the Notting Hill house—I forget it soon. About thirty pounds they steal. I keep it roll up in a pair of stockings, but I go to the drawer one day, and no money. In the end I have to tell the police. They ask me exact sum and I say I don't count it lately, about thirty pounds. 'You don't know how much?' they say. 'When did you count it last? Do you remember? Was it before you move or after?'

I get confuse, and I keep saying, 'I don't remember,' though I remember well I see it two days before. They don't believe me and when a policeman come to the house I hear the landlady tell him, 'She certainly had no money when she came here. She wasn't able to pay a month's rent in advance for her room though it's a rule in this house.' 'These people terrible liars,' she say and I think 'it's you a terrible liar, because when I come you tell me weekly or monthly as you like.' It's from that time she don't speak to me and perhaps it's she take it. All I know is I never see one penny of my savings again, all I know is they pretend I never have any, but as it's gone, no use to cry about it. Then my mind goes to my father, for my father is a white man and I think a lot about him. If I could see him only once, for I too small to remember when he was there. My mother is fair coloured woman, fairer than I am they say, and she don't stay long with me either. She have a chance to go to Venezuela when I three–four year old and she never come back. She send money instead. It's my grandmother take care of me. She's quite dark and what we call 'country-cookie' but she's the best I know.

She save up all the money my mother send, she don't keep one penny for herself—that's how I get to England. I was a bit late in going to school regular, getting on for twelve years, but I can sew very beautiful, excellent—so I think I get a good job—in London perhaps.

However here they tell me all this fine handsewing take too long. Waste of time—too slow. They want somebody to work quick and to hell with the small stitches. Altogether it don't look so good for me, I must say, and I wish I could see my father. I have his name—Davis. But my grandmother tell me, 'Every word that comes out of that man's mouth a damn lie. He is certainly first class liar, though no class otherwise.' So perhaps I have not even his real name.

Last thing I see before I put the light out is the postcard on the dressing table. 'Not to worry.'

Not to worry! Next day is Sunday, and it's on the Monday the people next door complain about me to the police. That evening the woman is by the hedge, and when I pass her she says in very sweet quiet voice, '*Must* you stay? *Can't* you go?' I don't answer. I walk out in the street to get rid of her. But she run inside her house to the window, she can still see me. Then I start to sing, so she can understand I'm not afraid of her. The husband call out: 'If you don't stop that noise I'll send for the police.' I answer them quite short. I say, 'You go to hell and take your wife with you.' And I sing louder.

The police come pretty quick—two of them. Maybe they just round the corner. All I can say about police, and how they behave is I think it all depends who they dealing with. Of my own free will I don't want to mix up with police. No.

One man says, you can't cause this disturbance here. But the other asks a lot of questions. What is my name? Am I tenant of a flat in No. 17? How long have I lived there? Last address and so on. I get vexed the way he speak and I tell him, 'I come here because somebody steal my savings. Why you don't look for my money instead of bawling at me? I work hard for my money. All-you don't do one single thing to find it.'

'What's she talking about?' the first one says, and the other one tells me, 'You can't make that noise here. Get along home. You've been drinking.'

I see that woman looking at me and smiling, and other people at their windows, and I'm so angry I bawl at them too. I say, 'I have absolute and perfect right to be in the street same as anybody else, and I have absolute and perfect right to ask the police why they don't even look for my money when it disappear. It's because a dam' English thief take it you don't look,' I say. The end of all this is that I have to go before a magistrate, and he fine me five pounds for drunk and disorderly, and he give me two weeks to pay.

When I get back from the court I walk up and down the kitchen, up and down, waiting for six o'clock because I have no five pounds left, and I don't know what to do. I telephone at six and a woman answers me very short and sharp, then Mr Sims comes along and he don't sound too pleased either when I tell him what happen. 'Oh Lord!' he says, and I say I'm sorry. 'Well don't panic,' he says, 'I'll pay the fine. But look, I don't think . . .' Then he breaks off and talk to some other person in the room. He goes on, 'Perhaps better not stay at No. 17. I think I can arrange something else. I'll call for you Wednesday—Saturday latest. Now behave till then.' And he hang up before I can answer that I don't want to wait till Wednesday, much less Saturday. I want to get out of that house double quick and with no delay. First I think I ring back, then I think better not as he sound so vex.

I get ready, but Wednesday he don't come, and Saturday he don't come. All the week I stay in the flat. Only once I go out and arrange for bread, milk and eggs to be left at the door, and seems to me I meet up with a lot of policemen. They don't look at me, but they see me all right. I don't want to drink—I'm all the time listening, listening and thinking, how can I leave before I know if my fine is paid? I tell myself the police let me know, that's certain. But I don't trust them. What they care? The answer is Nothing. Nobody care. One afternoon I knock at the old lady's flat upstairs, because I get the idea she give me good advice. I can hear her moving about and talking, but she don't answer and I never try again.

Nearly two weeks pass like that, then I telephone. It's the woman speaking and she say, 'Mr Sims is not in London at present.' I ask, 'When will he be back—it's urgent,' and she hang up. I'm not surprised. Not at all, I knew that would happen. All the same I feel heavy like lead. Near the phone box is a chemist's shop, so I ask him for something to make me sleep, the day is bad enough, but to lie awake all night—Ah no! He gives me a little bottle marked '*One or two tablets only*' and I take three when I go to bed because more and more I think that sleeping is better than no matter what else. However, I lie there, eyes wide open as usual, so I take three more. Next thing I know the room is full of sunlight, so it must be late afternoon, but the lamp is still on. My head turn around and I can't think well at all. At first I ask myself how I get to the place. Then it comes to me, but in pictures—like the landlady kicking my dress, and when I take my ticket at Victoria Station, and Mr Sims telling me to eat the sandwiches, but I can't remember everything clear, and I feel very giddy and sick. I take in the milk and eggs at the door, go in the kitchen, and try to eat but the food hard to swallow.

It's when I'm putting the things away that I see the bottles—pushed back on the lowest shelf in the cupboard.

There's a lot of drink left, and I'm glad I tell you. Because I can't bear the way I feel. Not any more. I mix a gin and vermouth and I drink it quick, then I mix another and drink it slow by the window. The garden looks different, like I never see it before. I know quite well what I must do, but it's late now—tomorrow I have one more drink, of wine this time, and then a song comes in my head, I sing it and I dance it, and more I sing, more I am sure this is the best tune that has ever come to me in all my life.

The sunset light from the window is gold colour. My shoes sound loud on the boards. So I take them off, my stockings too and go on dancing but the room feel shut in, I can't breathe, and I go outside still singing. Maybe I dance a bit too. I forget all about that woman till I hear her saying, 'Henry, look at this.' I turn around and I see her at the window. 'Oh yes, I wanted to speak with you,' I say, 'Why bring the police and get me in bad trouble? Tell me that.'

'And you tell me what you're doing here at all,' she says. 'This is a respectable neighbourhood.'

Then the man come along. 'Now young woman, take yourself off. You ought to be ashamed of this behaviour.'

'It's disgraceful,' he says, talking to his wife, but loud so I can hear, and she speaks loud too—for once. 'At least the other tarts that crook installed here were *white* girls,' she says.

'You a dam' fouti liar,' I say. 'Plenty of those girls in your country already. Numberless as the sands on the shore. You don't need me for that.'

'You're not a howling success at it certainly.' Her voice sweet sugar again. 'And you won't be seeing much more of your friend Mr Sims. He's in trouble too. Try somewhere else. Find somebody else. If you can, of course.' When she say that my arm moves of itself. I pick up a stone and bam! through the window. Not the one they are standing at but the next, which is of coloured glass, green and purple and yellow.

I never see a woman look so surprise. Her mouth fall open she so full of surprise. I start to laugh, louder and louder—I laugh like my grandmother, with my hands on my hips and my head back. (When she laugh like that you can hear her to the end of our street.) At last I say, 'Well, I'm sorry. An accident. I get it fixed tomorrow early.' 'That glass is irreplaceable,' the man says. 'Irreplaceable.' 'Good thing,' I say, 'those colours look like they sea-sick to me. I buy you a better windowglass.'

He shake his fist at me. 'You won't be let off with a fine this time,' he says. Then they draw the curtains, I call out at them. 'You run away. Always you run away. Ever since I come here you hunt me down because I don't answer back. It's you shameless.' I try to sing 'Don't trouble me now'.

> Don't trouble me now
> You without honour.
> Don't walk in my footstep
> You without shame.

But my voice don't sound right, so I get back indoors and drink one more glass of wine—still wanting to laugh, and still thinking of my grandmother for that is one of her songs.

It's about a man whose doudou give him the go-by when she find somebody rich and he sail away to Panama. Plenty people die there of fever when they make that Panama canal so long ago. But he don't die. He come back with dollars and the girl meet him on the jetty, all dressed up and smiling. Then he sing to her, 'You without honour, you without shame'. It sound good in Martinique patois too: 'Sans honte.'

Afterwards I ask myself, 'Why I do that? It's not like me. But if they treat you wrong over and over again the hour strike when you burst out that's what.'

Too besides, Mr Sims can't tell me now I have no spirit. I don't care, I sleep quickly and I'm glad I break the woman's ugly window. But as to my own song it go *right* away and it never come back. A pity.

Next morning the doorbell ringing wake me up. The people upstairs don't come down, and the bell keeps on like fury self. So I go to look, and there is a policeman and a policewoman outside. As soon as I open the door the woman put her foot in it. She wear sandals and thick stockings and I never see a foot so big or so bad. It look like it want to mash up the whole world. Then she come in after the foot, and her face not so pretty either. The policeman tell me my fine is not paid and people make serious complaints about me, so they're taking me back to the magistrate. He show me a paper and I look at it, but I don't read it. The woman push me in the bedroom, and tell me to get dress quickly, but I just stare at her, because I think perhaps I wake up soon. Then I ask her what I must wear. She say she suppose I had some clothes on yesterday. Or not? 'What's it matter, wear anything,' she says. But I find clean underclothes and stockings and my shoes with high heels and I comb my hair. I start to file my nails, because I think they too long for magistrate's court but she get angry. 'Are you coming quietly or aren't you?' she says. So I go with them and we get in a car outside.

I wait for a long time in a room full of policemen. They come in, they go out, they telephone, they talk in low voices. Then it's my turn, and first thing I notice in the court room is a man with frowning black eyebrows. He sit below the magistrate, he dressed in black and he is so handsome I can't take my eyes off him. When he see that he frowns worse than before.

First comes a policeman to testify I cause disturbance, and then comes the old gentleman from next door. He repeat that bit about nothing but the truth so help me God. Then he says I make dreadful noise at night and use abominable language, and dance in obscene fashion. He says when they try to shut the curtains because his wife so terrify of me, I throw stones and break a valuable stain-glass window. He say his wife get serious injury if she'd been hit, and as it is she in terrible nervous condition and the doctor is with her. I think, 'Believe me, if I aim at your wife I hit your wife—that's certain.' 'There was no provocation,' he says. 'None at all.' Then another lady from across the street says this is true. She heard no provocation whatsoever, and she swear that they shut the curtains but I go on insulting them and using filthy language and she saw all this and heard it.

The magistrate is a little gentleman with a quiet voice, but I'm very suspicious of these quiet voices now. He ask me why I don't pay any fine, and I say because I haven't the money. I get the idea they want to find out all about Mr Sims—they listen so very attentive. But they'll find out nothing from me. He ask how long I have the flat and I say I don't remember. I know they want to trip me up like they trip me up about my savings so I won't answer. At last he ask if I have anything to say as I can't be allowed to go on being a nuisance. I think, 'I'm nuisance to you because I have no money that's all.' I want to speak up and tell him how they steal all my savings, so when my landlord asks for month's rent I haven't got it to give. I want to tell him the woman next door provoke me since long time and call me bad names but she have a soft sugar voice and nobody hear—that's why I broke her window, but I'm ready to buy another after all. I want to say all I do is sing in that old garden, and I want to say this in decent quiet voice. But I hear myself talking loud and I see my hands wave in the air. Too besides it's no use, they won't believe me, so I don't finish. I stop, and I feel the tears on my face. 'Prove it.' That's all they will say. They whisper, they whisper. They nod, they nod.

Next thing I'm in a car again with a different policewoman, dressed very smart. Not in uniform. I ask her where she's taking me and she says 'Holloway' just that 'Holloway'.

I catch hold of her hand because I'm afraid. But she takes it away. Cold and smooth her hand slide away and her face is china face—smooth like a doll and I think, 'This is the last time I ask anything from anybody. So help me God.'

The car come up to a black castle and little mean streets are all round it. A lorry was blocking up the castle gates. When it get by we pass through and I am in jail. First I stand in a line with others who are waiting to give up handbags and all belongings to a woman behind bars like in a post office. The girl in front bring out a nice compact, look like gold to me, lipstick to match and a wallet full of notes. The woman keep the money, but she give back the powder and lipstick and she half-smile. I have two pounds seven shillings and sixpence in pennies. She take my purse, then she throw me my compact (which is cheap) my comb and my handkerchief like everything in my bag is dirty. So I think, 'Here too, here too.' But I tell myself, 'Girl, what you expect, eh? They all like that. All.'

Some of what happen afterwards I forget, or perhaps better not remember. Seems to me they start by trying to frighten you. But they don't succeed with me for I don't care for nothing now, it's as if my heart hard like a rock and I can't feel.

Then I'm standing at the top of a staircase with a lot of women and girls. As we are going down I notice the railing very low on one side, very easy to jump, and a long way below there's the grey stone passage like it's waiting for you.

As I'm thinking this a uniform woman step up alongside quick and grab my arm. She say, 'Oh no you don't.'

I was just noticing the railing very low that's all—but what's the use of saying so.

Another long line waits for the doctor. It move forward slowly and my legs terrible tired. The girl in front is very young and she cry and cry. 'I'm scared,' she keeps saying. She's lucky in a way—as for me I never will cry again. It all dry up and hard in me now. That, and a lot besides. In the end I tell her to stop, because she doing just what these people want her to do.

She stop crying and start a long story, but while she is speaking her voice get very far away, and I find I can't see her face clear at all.

Then I'm in a chair, and one of those uniform women is pushing my head down between my knees, but let her push—everything go away from me just the same.

They put me in the hospital because the doctor say I'm sick. I have cell by myself and it's all right except I don't sleep. The things they say you mind I don't mind.

When they clang the door on me I think, 'You shut me in, but you shut all those other dam' devils *out*. They can't reach me now.'

At first it bothers me when they keep on looking at me all through the night. They open a little window in the doorway to do this. But I get used to it and get used to the night chemise they give me. It very thick, and to my mind it not very clean either—but what's that matter to me? Only the food I can't swallow—especially the porridge. The woman ask me sarcastic, 'Hunger striking?' But afterwards I can leave most of it, and she don't say nothing.

One day a nice girl comes around with books and she give me two, but I don't want to read so much. Beside one is about a murder, and the other is about a ghost and I don't think it's at all like those books tell you.

There is nothing I want now. It's no use. If they leave me in peace and quiet that's all I ask. The window is barred but not small, so I can see a little thin tree through the bars, and I like watching it.

After a week they tell me I'm better and I can go out with the others for exercise. We walk round and round one of the yards in that castle—it is fine weather and the sky is a kind of pale blue, but the yard is a terrible sad place. The sunlight fall down and die there. I get tired walking in high heels and I'm glad when that's over.

We can talk, and one day an old woman come up and ask me for dog-ends. I don't understand, and she start muttering at me like she very vexed. Another woman tell me she mean cigarette ends, so I say I don't smoke. But the old woman still look angry, and when we're going in she give me one push and I nearly fall down. I'm glad to get away from these people, and hear the door clang and take my shoes off.

Sometimes I think, 'I'm here because I wanted to sing' and I have to laugh. But there's a small looking glass in my cell and I see myself and I'm like somebody else. Like some strange new person. Mr Sims tell me I too thin, but what he say now to this person in the looking glass? So I don't laugh again.

Usually I don't think at all. Everything and everybody seem small and far away, that is the only trouble.

Twice the doctor come to see me. He don't say much and I don't say anything, because a uniform woman is always there. She looks like she thinking, 'Now the lies start.' So I prefer not to speak. Then

I'm sure they can't trip me up. Perhaps I there still, or in a worse place. But one day this happen.

We were walking round and round in the yard and I hear a woman singing—the voice come from high up, from one of the small barred windows. At first I don't believe it. Why should anybody sing here? Nobody wants to sing in jail, nobody want to do anything. There's no reason, and you have no hope. I think I must be asleep, dreaming, but I'm awake all right and I see all the others are listening too. A nurse is with us that afternoon, not a policewoman. She stop and look up at the window.

It's a smoky kind of voice, and a bit rough sometimes, as if those old dark walls theyselves are complaining, because they see too much misery—too much. But it don't fall down and die in the courtyard; seems to me it could jump the gates of the jail easy and travel far, and nobody could stop it. I don't hear the words—only the music. She sing one verse and she begin another, then she break off sudden. Everybody starts walking again, and nobody says one word. But as we go in I ask the woman in front who was singing. 'That's the Holloway song,' she says. 'Don't you know it yet? She was singing from the punishment cells, and she tell the girls cheerio and never say die.' Then I have to go one way to the hospital block and she goes another so we don't speak again.

When I'm back in my cell I can't just wait for bed. I walk up and down and I think, 'One day I hear that song on trumpets and these walls will fall and rest.' I want to get out so bad I could hammer on the door, for I know now that anything can happen, and I don't want to stay lock up here and miss it.

Then I'm hungry. I eat everything they bring and in the morning I'm still so hungry I eat the porridge. Next time the doctor come he tells me I seem much better. Then I say a little of what really happen in that house. Not much. Very careful.

He look at me hard and kind of surprised. At the door he shake his finger and says, 'Now don't let me see you here again.'

That evening the woman tells me I'm going, but she's so upset about it I don't ask questions. Very early, before it's light she bangs the door open and shouts at me to hurry up. As we're going along the passages I see the girl who gave me the books. She's in a row with others doing exercises. Up Down, Up Down, Up. We pass quite close and I notice she's looking very pale and tired. It's crazy, it's all crazy. This up down business and everything else too. When they give me my money I remember I leave my compact in the cell, so I ask if I can go back for it. You should see that policewoman's face as she shoo me on.

There's no car, there's a van and you can't see through the windows. The third time it stop I get out with one other, a young girl, and it's the same magistrates' court as before.

The two of us wait in a small room, nobody else there, and after a while the girl say, 'What the hell are they doing? I don't want to spend all day here.' She go to the bell and she keep her finger press on it. When I look at her she say, 'Well, what are they *for*?' That girl's face is hard like a board—she could change faces with many and you wouldn't know the difference. But she get results certainly. A policeman comes in, all smiling, and we go in the court. The same magistrate, the same frowning man sits below, and when I hear my fine is paid I want to ask who paid it, but he yells at me, 'Silence.'

I think I will never understand the half of what happen, but they tell me I can go, and I understand that. The magistrate ask if I'm leaving the neighbourhood and I say yes, then I'm out in the streets again, and it's the same fine weather, same feeling I'm dreaming.

When I get to the house I see two men talking in the garden. The front door and the door of the flat are both open. I go in, and the bedroom is empty, nothing but the glare streaming inside because they take the Venetian blinds away. As I'm wondering where my suitcase is, and the clothes I leave in the wardrobe, there's a knock and it's the old lady from upstairs carrying my case packed, and my coat is over her arm. She says she sees me come in. 'I kept your things for you.' I start to thank her but she turn her back and walk away. They like that here, and better not expect too much. Too besides, I bet they tell her I'm terrible person.

I go in the kitchen, but when I see they are cutting down the big tree at the back I don't stay to watch.

At the station I'm waiting for the train and a woman asks if I feel well. 'You look so tired,' she says. 'Have you come a long way?' I want to answer, 'I come so far I lose myself on that journey.' But I tell her, 'Yes, I am quite well. But I can't stand the heat.' She says she can't stand it either, and we talk about the weather till the train come in.

I'm not frightened of them any more—after all what else can they do? I know what to say and everything go like a clock works.

I get a room near Victoria where the landlady accept one pound in advance, and next day I find a job in the kitchen of a private hotel close by. But I don't stay there long. I hear of another job going in a big store—altering ladies' dresses and I get that. I lie and tell them I work in very expensive New York shop. I speak bold and smooth faced, and they never check up on me. I make a friend there—Clarice—very light coloured, very smart, she have a lot to do with the customers and she laugh at some of them behind their backs. But I say it's not their fault if the dress don't fit. Special dress for one person only—that's very expensive in London. So it's take in, or let out all the time. Clarice have two rooms not far from the store. She furnish herself gradual and she gives parties sometimes Saturday nights. It's there I start whistling the Holloway Song. A man comes up to me and says, 'Let's hear that again.' So I whistle it again (I never sing now) and he tells me 'Not bad'. Clarice have an old piano somebody give her to store and he plays the tune, jazzing it up. I say, 'No, not like that,' but everybody else say the way he do it is first class. Well I think no more of this till I get a letter from him telling me he has sold the song and as I was quite a help he encloses five pounds with thanks.

I read the letter and I could cry. For after all, that song was all I had. I don't belong nowhere really, and I haven't money to buy my way to belonging. I don't want to either.

But when that girl sing, she sing to me and she sing for me. I was there because I was *meant* to be there. It was *meant* I should hear it—this I *know*.

Now I've let them play it wrong, and it will go from me like all the other songs—like everything. Nothing left for me at all.

But then I tell myself all this is foolishness. Even if they played it on trumpets, even if they played it just right, like I wanted—no walls would fall so soon. 'So let them call it jazz,' I think, and let them play it wrong. That won't make no difference to the song I heard.

I buy myself a dusty pink dress with the money.

FLANNERY O'CONNOR

Revelation

The doctor's waiting room, which was very small, was almost full when the Turpins entered and Mrs Turpin, who was very large, made it look even smaller by her presence. She stood looming at the head of the magazine table set in the centre of it, a living demonstration that the room was inadequate and ridiculous. Her little bright black eyes took in all the patients as she sized up the seating situation. There was one vacant chair and a place on the sofa occupied by a blond child in a dirty blue romper who should have been told to move over and make room for the lady. He was five or six, but Mrs Turpin saw at once that no one was going to tell him to move over. He was slumped down in the seat, his arms idle at his sides and his eyes idle in his head; his nose ran unchecked.

Mrs Turpin put a firm hand on Claud's shoulder and said in a voice that included anyone who wanted to listen, 'Claud, you sit in that chair there,' and gave him a push down into the vacant one. Claud was florid and bald and sturdy, somewhat shorter than Mrs Turpin, but he sat down as if he were accustomed to doing what she told him to.

Mrs Turpin remained standing. The only man in the room besides Claud was a lean stringy old fellow with a rusty hand spread out on each knee, whose eyes were closed as if he were asleep or dead or pretending to be so as not to get up and offer her his seat. Her gaze settled agreeably on a well-dressed grey-haired lady whose eyes met hers and whose expression said: if that child belonged to me, he would have some manners and move over— there's plenty of room there for you and him too.

Claud looked up with a sigh and made as if to rise.

'Sit down,' Mrs Turpin said. 'You know you're not supposed to stand on that leg. He has an ulcer on his leg,' she explained.

Claud lifted his foot onto the magazine table and rolled his trouser leg up to reveal a purple swelling on a plump marble-white calf.

'My!' the pleasant lady said. 'How did you do that?'

'A cow kicked him,' Mrs Turpin said.

'Goodness!' said the lady.

Claud rolled his trouser leg down.

'Maybe the little boy would move over,' the lady suggested, but the child did not stir.

'Somebody will be leaving in a minute,' Mrs Turpin said. She could not understand why a doctor—with as much money as they made charging five dollars a day to just stick their head in the hospital door and look at you—couldn't afford a decent-sized waiting room. This one was hardly bigger than a garage. The table was cluttered with limp-looking magazines and at one end of it there was a big green glass ash tray full of cigarette butts and cotton wads with little blood spots on them. If she had had anything to do with the running of the place, that would have been emptied every so often. There were no chairs against the wall at the head of the room. It had a rectangular-shaped panel in it that permitted a view of the office where the nurse came and went and the secretary listened to the radio. A plastic fern in a gold pot sat in the opening and trailed its fronds down almost to the floor. The radio was softly playing gospel music.

Just then the inner door opened and a nurse with the highest stack of yellow hair Mrs Turpin had ever seen put her face in the crack and called for the next patient. The woman sitting beside Claud grasped the two arms of her chair and hoisted herself up; she pulled her dress free from her legs and lumbered through the door where the nurse had disappeared.

Mrs Turpin eased into the vacant chair, which held her tight as a corset. 'I wish I could reduce,' she said, and rolled her eyes and gave a comic sigh.

'Oh, *you* aren't fat,' the stylish lady said.

'Ooooo I am too,' Mrs Turpin said. 'Claud he eats all he wants to and never weighs over one hundred and seventy-five pounds, but me I just look at something good to eat and I gain some weight,' and her stomach and shoulders shook with laughter. 'You can eat all you want to, can't you, Claud?' she asked, turning to him.

Claud only grinned.

'Well, as long as you have such a good disposition,' the stylish lady said, 'I don't think it makes a bit of difference what size you are. You just can't beat a good disposition.'

Next to her was a fat girl of eighteen or nineteen, scowling into a thick blue book which Mrs Turpin saw was entitled *Human Development*. The girl raised her head and directed her scowl at Mrs Turpin as if she did not like her looks. She appeared annoyed that anyone should speak while she tried to read. The poor girl's face was blue with acne and Mrs Turpin thought how pitiful it was to have a face like that at that age. She gave the girl a friendly smile but the girl scowled the harder. Mrs Turpin herself was fat but she had always had good skin, and, though she was forty-seven years old, there was not a wrinkle in her face except around her eyes from laughing too much.

Next to the ugly girl was the child, still in exactly the same position, and next to him was a thin leathery old woman in a cotton print dress. She and Claud had three sacks of chicken feed in their pump house that was in the same print. She had seen from the first that the child belonged with the old woman. She could tell by the way they sat—kind of vacant and white-trashy, as if they would sit there until Doomsday if nobody called and told them to get up. And at right angles but next to the well-dressed pleasant lady was a lank-faced woman who was certainly the child's mother. She had on a yellow sweat shirt and wine-coloured slacks, both gritty-looking, and the rims of her lips were stained with snuff. Her dirty yellow hair was tied behind with a little piece of red paper ribbon. Worse than niggers any day, Mrs Turpin thought.

The gospel hymn playing was, 'When I looked up and He looked down,' and Mrs Turpin, who knew it, supplied the last line mentally, 'And wona these days I know I'll we-eara crown.'

Without appearing to, Mrs Turpin always noticed people's feet. The well-dressed lady had on red and grey suede shoes to match her dress. Mrs Turpin had on her good black patent leather pumps. The ugly girl had on Girl Scout shoes and heavy socks. The old woman had on tennis shoes and the white-trashy mother had on what appeared to be bedroom slippers, black straw with gold braid threaded through them—exactly what you would have expected her to have on.

Sometimes at night when she couldn't go to sleep, Mrs Turpin would occupy herself with the question of who she would have chosen to be if she couldn't have been herself. If Jesus had said to her before he made her, 'There's only two places available for you. You can either be a nigger or white-trash,' what would she have said?

'Please, Jesus, please,' she would have said, 'just let me wait until there's another place available,' and he would have said, 'No, you have to go right now and I have only those two places so make up your mind.' She would have wiggled and squirmed and begged and pleaded but it would have been no use and finally she would have said, 'All right, make me a nigger then—but that don't mean a trashy one.' And he would have made her a neat clean respectable Negro woman, herself but black.

Next to the child's mother was a red-headed youngish woman, reading one of the magazines and working a piece of chewing gum, hell for leather, as Claud would say. Mrs Turpin could not see the woman's feet. She was not white-trash, just common. Sometimes Mrs Turpin occupied herself at night naming the classes of people. On the bottom of the heap were most coloured people, not the kind she would have been if she had been one, but most of them; then next to them—not above, just away from—were the white-trash; then above them were the home-owners, and above them the home-and-land owners, to which she and Claud belonged. Above she and Claud were people with a lot of money and much bigger houses and much more land. But here the complexity of it would begin to bear in on her, for some of the people with a lot of money were common and ought to be below she and Claud and some of the people who had good blood had lost their money and had to rent and then there were coloured people who owned their homes and land as well. There was a coloured dentist in town who had two red Lincolns and a swimming pool and a farm with registered white-face cattle on it. Usually by the time she had fallen asleep all the classes of people were moiling and roiling around in her head, and she would dream they were all crammed in together in a box car, being ridden off to be put in a gas oven.

'That's a beautiful clock,' she said and nodded to her right. It was a big wall clock, the face encased in a brass sunburst.

'Yes, it's very pretty,' the stylish lady said agreeably. 'And right on the dot too,' she added, glancing at her watch.

The ugly girl beside her cast an eye upward at the clock, smirked, then looked directly at Mrs Turpin and smirked again. Then she returned her eyes to her book. She was obviously the lady's daughter because, although they didn't look anything alike as to disposition, they both had the same shape of face and the same blue eyes. On the lady they sparkled pleasantly but in the girl's seared face they appeared alternately to smoulder and to blaze.

What if Jesus had said, 'All right, you can be white-trash or a nigger or ugly'!

Mrs Turpin felt an awful pity for the girl, though she thought it was one thing to be ugly and another to act ugly.

The woman with the snuff-stained lips turned around in her chair and looked up at the clock. Then she turned back and appeared to look a little to the side of Mrs Turpin. There was a cast in one of her eyes. 'You want to know wher you can get you one of themther clocks?' she asked in a loud voice.

'No, I already have a nice clock,' Mrs Turpin said. Once somebody like her got a leg in the conversation, she would be all over it.

'You can get you one with green stamps,' the woman said. 'That's most likely wher he got hisn. Save you up enough, you can get you most anythang. I got me some joo'ry.'

Ought to have got you a wash rag and some soap, Mrs Turpin thought.

'I get contour sheets with mine,' the pleasant lady said.

The daughter slammed her book shut. She looked straight in front of her, directly through Mrs Turpin and on through the yellow curtain and the plate glass window which made the wall behind her. The girl's eyes seemed lit all of a sudden with a peculiar light, an unnatural light like night road signs give. Mrs Turpin turned her head to see if there was anything going on outside that she should see, but she could not see anything. Figures passing cast only a pale shadow through the curtain. There was no reason the girl should single her out for her ugly looks.

'Miss Finley,' the nurse said, cracking the door. The gum-chewing woman got up and passed in front of her and Claud and went into the office. She had on red high-heeled shoes.

Directly across the table, the ugly girl's eyes were fixed on Mrs Turpin as if she had some very special reason for disliking her.

'This is wonderful weather, isn't it?' the girl's mother said.

'It's good weather for cotton if you can get the niggers to pick it,' Mrs Turpin said, 'but niggers don't want to pick cotton any more. You can't get the white folks to pick it and now you can't get the niggers—because they got to be right up there with the white folks.'

'They gonna *try* anyways,' the white-trash woman said, leaning forward.

'Do you have one of those cotton-picking machines?' the pleasant lady asked.

'No,' Mrs Turpin said, 'they leave half the cotton in the field. We don't have much cotton anyway. If you want to make it farming now, you have to have a little of everything. We got a couple of acres of cotton and a few hogs and chickens and just enough white-face that Claud can look after them himself.'

'One thang I don't want,' the white-trash woman said, wiping her mouth with the back of her hand. 'Hogs. Nasty stinking things, a-gruntin and a-rootin all over the place.'

Mrs Turpin gave her the merest edge of her attention. 'Our hogs are not dirty and they don't stink,' she said. 'They're cleaner than some children I've seen. Their feet never touch the ground. We have a pig-parlour—that's where you raise them on concrete,' she explained to the pleasant lady, 'and Claud scoots them down with the hose every afternoon and washes off the floor.' Cleaner by far than that child right there, she thought. Poor nasty little thing. He had not moved except to put the thumb of his dirty hand into his mouth.

The woman turned her face away from Mrs Turpin. 'I know I wouldn't scoot down no hog with no hose,' she said to the wall.

You wouldn't have no hog to scoot down, Mrs Turpin said to herself.

'A-gruntin and a-rootin and a-groanin,' the woman muttered.

'We got a little of everything,' Mrs Turpin said to the pleasant lady. 'It's no use in having more than you can handle yourself with help like it is. We found enough niggers to pick our cotton this year but Claud he has to go after them and take them home again in the evening. They can't walk that half a mile. No they can't. I tell you,' she said and laughed merrily, 'I sure am tired of buttering up niggers, but you got to love em if you want em to work for you. When they come in the morning, I run out and I say, "Hi yawl this morning?" and when Claud drives them off to the field I just wave to beat the band and they just wave back.' And she waved her hand rapidly to illustrate.

'Like you read out of the same book,' the lady said, showing she understood perfectly.

'Child, yes,' Mrs Turpin said. 'And when they come in from the field, I run out with a bucket of icewater. That's the way it's going to be from now on,' she said. 'You may as well face it.'

'One thang I know,' the white-trash woman said. 'Two thangs I ain't going to do: love no niggers or scoot down no hog with no hose.' And she let out a bark of contempt.

The look that Mrs Turpin and the pleasant lady exchanged indicated they both understood that you had to *have* certain things before you could *know* certain things. But every time Mrs Turpin exchanged a look with the lady, she was aware that the ugly girl's peculiar eyes were still on her, and she had trouble bringing her attention back to the conversation.

'When you got something,' she said, 'you got to look after it.' And when you ain't got a thing but breath and britches, she added to herself, you can afford to come to town every morning and just sit on the Court House coping and spit.

A grotesque revolving shadow passed across the curtain behind her and was thrown palely on the opposite wall. Then a bicycle clattered down against the outside of the building. The door opened and a coloured boy glided in with a tray from the drug store. It had two large red and white paper cups on it with tops on them. He was a tall, very black boy in discoloured white pants and a green nylon shirt. He was chewing gum slowly, as if to music. He set the tray down in the office opening next to the fern and stuck his head through to look for the secretary. She was not in there. He rested his arms on the ledge and waited, his narrow bottom stuck out, swaying slowly to the left and right. He raised a hand over his head and scratched the base of his skull.

'You see that button there, boy?' Mrs Turpin said. 'You can punch that and she'll come. She's probably in the back somewhere.'

'Is thas right?' the boy said agreeably, as if he had never seen the button before. He leaned to the right and put his finger on it. 'She sometime out,' he said and twisted around to face his audience, his elbows behind him on the counter. The nurse appeared and he twisted back again. She handed him a dollar and he rooted in his pocket and made the change and counted it out to her. She gave him fifteen cents for a tip and he went out with the empty tray. The heavy door swung to slowly and closed at length with the sound of suction. For a moment no one spoke.

'They ought to send all them niggers back to Africa,' the white-trash woman said. 'That's wher they come from in the first place.'

'Oh, I couldn't do without my good coloured friends,' the pleasant lady said.

'There's a heap of things worse than a nigger,' Mrs Turpin agreed. 'It's all kinds of them just like it's all kinds of us.'

'Yes, and it takes all kinds to make the world go round,' the lady said in her musical voice.

As she said it, the raw-complexioned girl snapped her teeth together. Her lower lip turned downwards and inside out, revealing the pale pink inside of her mouth. After a second it rolled back up. It was the ugliest face Mrs Turpin had ever seen anyone make and for a moment she was certain that the girl had made it at her. She was looking at her as if she had known and disliked her all her life—all of Mrs Turpin's life, it seemed too, not just all the girl's life. Why, girl, I don't even know you, Mrs Turpin said silently.

She forced her attention back to the discussion. 'It wouldn't be practical to send them back to Africa,' she said. 'They wouldn't want to go. They got it too good here.'

'Wouldn't be what they wanted—if I had anythang to do with it,' the woman said.

'It wouldn't be a way in the world you could get all the niggers back over there,' Mrs Turpin said. 'They'd be hiding out and lying down and turning sick on you and wailing and hollering and raring and pitching. It wouldn't be a way in the world to get them over there.'

'They got over here,' the trashy woman said. 'Get back like they got over.'

'It wasn't so many of them then,' Mrs Turpin explained.

The woman looked at Mrs Turpin as if here was an idiot indeed but Mrs Turpin was not bothered by the look, considering where it came from.

'Nooo,' she said, 'they're going to stay here where they can go to New York and marry white folks and improve their colour. That's what they all want to do, every one of them, improve their colour.'

'You know what comes of that, don't you?' Claud asked.

'No, Claud, what?' Mrs Turpin said.

Claud's eyes twinkled. 'White-faced niggers,' he said with never a smile.

Everybody in the office laughed except the white-trash and the ugly girl. The girl gripped the book in her lap with white fingers. The trashy woman looked around her from face to face as if she thought they were all idiots. The old woman in the feed sack dress continued to gaze expressionless across the floor at the high-top shoes of the man opposite her, the one who had been pretending to be asleep when the Turpins came in. He was laughing heartily, his hands still spread out on his knees. The child had fallen to the side and was lying now almost face down in the old woman's lap.

While they recovered from their laughter, the nasal chorus on the radio kept the room from silence.

> 'You go to blank blank
> And I'll go to mine
> But we'll all blank along
> To-geth-ther,
> And all along the blank
> We'll hep eachother out
> Smile-ling in any kind of
> Weath-ther!'

Mrs Turpin didn't catch every word but she caught enough to agree with the spirit of the song and it turned her thoughts sober. To help anybody out that needed it was her philosophy of life. She never spared herself when she found somebody in need, whether they were white or black, trash or decent. And of all she had to be thankful for, she was most thankful that this was so. If Jesus had said, 'You can be high society and have all the money you want and be thin and svelte-like, but you can't be a good woman with it,' she would have had to say, 'Well don't make me that then. Make me a good woman and it don't matter what else, how fat or how ugly or how poor!' Her heart rose. He had not made her a nigger or white-trash or ugly! He had made her herself and given her a little of everything. Jesus, thank you! she said. Thank you thank you thank you! Whenever she counted her blessings she felt as buoyant as if she weighed one hundred and twenty-five pounds instead of one hundred and eighty.

'What's wrong with your little boy?' the pleasant lady asked the white-trashy woman.

'He has a ulcer,' the woman said proudly. 'He ain't give me a minute's peace since he was born. Him and her are just alike,' she said, nodding at the old woman, who was running her leathery fingers through the child's pale hair. 'Look like I can't get nothing down them two but Co' Cola and candy.'

That's all you try to get down em, Mrs Turpin said to herself.

Too lazy to light the fire. There was nothing you could tell her about people like them that she didn't know already. And it was not just that they didn't have anything. Because if you gave them everything, in two weeks it would all be broken or filthy or they would have chopped it up for lightwood. She knew all this from her own experience. Help them you must, but help them you couldn't.

All at once the ugly girl turned her lips inside out again. Her eyes were fixed like two drills on Mrs Turpin. This time there was no mistaking that there was something urgent behind them.

Girl, Mrs Turpin exclaimed silently, I haven't done a thing to you! The girl might be confusing her with somebody else. There was no need to sit by and let herself be intimidated. 'You must be in college,' she said boldly, looking directly at the girl. 'I see you reading a book there.'

The girl continued to stare and pointedly did not answer.

Her mother blushed at this rudeness. 'The lady asked you a question, Mary Grace,' she said under her breath.

'I have ears,' Mary Grace said.

The poor mother blushed again. 'Mary Grace goes to Wellesley College,' she explained. She twisted one of the buttons on her dress. 'In Massachusetts,' she added with a grimace. 'And in the summer she just keeps right on studying. Just reads all the time, a real book worm. She's done real well at Wellesley; she's taking English and Math and History and Psychology and Social Studies,' she rattled on, 'and I think it's too much. I think she ought to get out and have fun.'

The girl looked as if she would like to hurl them all through the plate glass window.

'Way up north,' Mrs Turpin murmured and thought, well, it hasn't done much for her manners.

'I'd almost rather to have him sick,' the white-trash woman said, wrenching the attention back to herself. 'He's so mean when he ain't. Look like some children just take natural to meanness. It's some gets bad when they get sick but he was the opposite. Took sick and turned good. He don't give me no trouble now. It's me waitin to see the doctor,' she said.

If I was going to send anybody back to Africa, Mrs Turpin thought, it would be your kind, woman. 'Yes, indeed,' she said aloud, but looking up at the ceiling, 'it's a heap of things worse than a nigger.' And dirtier than a hog, she added to herself.

'I think people with bad dispositions are more to be pitied than anyone on earth,' the pleasant lady said in a voice that was decidedly thin.

'I thank the Lord he has blessed me with a good one,' Mrs Turpin said. 'The day has never dawned that I couldn't find something to laugh at.'

'Not since she married me anyways,' Claud said with a comical straight face.

Everybody laughed except the girl and the white-trash.

Mrs Turpin's stomach shook. 'He's such a caution,' she said, 'that I can't help but laugh at him.'

The girl made a loud ugly noise through her teeth.

Her mother's mouth grew thin and tight. 'I think the worst thing in the world,' she said, 'is an ungrateful person. To have everything and not appreciate it. I know a girl,' she said, 'who has parents who would give her anything, a little brother who loves her dearly, who is getting a good education, who wears the best clothes, but who can never say a kind word to anyone, who never smiles, who just criticizes and complains all day long.'

'Is she too old to paddle?' Claud asked.

The girl's face was almost purple.

'Yes,' the lady said, 'I'm afraid there's nothing to do but leave her to her folly. Some day she'll wake up and it'll be too late.'

'It never hurt anyone to smile,' Mrs Turpin said. 'It just makes you feel better all over.'

'Of course,' the lady said sadly, 'but there are just some people you can't tell anything to. They can't take criticism.'

'If it's one thing I am,' Mrs Turpin said with feeling, 'it's grateful. When I think who all I could have been besides myself and what all I got, a little of everything, and a good disposition besides, I just feel like shouting, "Thank you, Jesus, for making everything the way it is!" It could have been different!' For one thing, somebody else could have got Claud. At the thought of this, she was flooded with gratitude and a terrible pang of joy ran through her. 'Oh thank you, Jesus, Jesus, thank you!' she cried aloud.

The book struck her directly over her left eye. It struck almost at the same instant that she realized the girl was about to hurl it. Before she could utter a sound, the raw face came crashing across the table toward her, howling. The girl's fingers sank like clamps into the soft flesh of her neck. She heard the mother cry out and

Claud shout, 'Whoa!' There was an instant when she was certain that she was about to be in an earthquake.

All at once her vision narrowed and she saw everything as if it were happening in a small room far away, or as if she were looking at it through the wrong end of a telescope. Claud's face crumpled and fell out of sight. The nurse ran in, then out, then in again. Then the gangling figure of the doctor rushed out of the inner door. Magazines flew this way and that as the table turned over. The girl fell with a thud and Mrs Turpin's vision suddenly reversed itself and she saw everything large instead of small. The eyes of the white-trashy woman were staring hugely at the floor. There the girl, held down on one side by the nurse and on the other by her mother, was wrenching and turning in their grasp. The doctor was kneeling astride her, trying to hold her arm down. He managed after a second to sink a long needle into it.

Mrs Turpin felt entirely hollow except for her heart which swung from side to side as if it were agitated in a great empty drum of flesh.

'Somebody that's not busy call for the ambulance,' the doctor said in the off-hand voice young doctors adopt for terrible occasions.

Mrs Turpin could not have moved a finger. The old man who had been sitting next to her skipped nimbly into the office and made the call, for the secretary still seemed to be gone.

'Claud!' Mrs Turpin called.

He was not in his chair. She knew she must jump up and find him but she felt like someone trying to catch a train in a dream, when everything moves in slow motion and the faster you try to run the slower you go.

'Here I am,' a suffocated voice, very unlike Claud's, said.

He was doubled up in the corner on the floor, pale as paper, holding his leg. She wanted to get up and go to him but she could not move. Instead, her gaze was drawn slowly downward to the churning face on the floor, which she could see over the doctor's shoulder.

The girl's eyes stopped rolling and focused on her. They seemed a much lighter blue than before, as if a door that had been tightly closed behind them was now open to admit light and air.

Mrs Turpin's head cleared and her power of motion returned. She leaned forward until she was looking directly into the fierce brilliant eyes. There was no doubt in her mind that the girl did know her, knew her in some intense and personal way, beyond time and place and condition. 'What you got to say to me?' she asked hoarsely and held her breath, waiting, as for a revelation.

The girl raised her head. Her gaze locked with Mrs Turpin's. 'Go back to hell where you came from, you old wart hog,' she whispered. Her voice was low but clear. Her eyes burned for a moment as if she saw with pleasure that her message had struck its target.

Mrs Turpin sank back in her chair.

After a moment the girl's eyes closed and she turned her head wearily to the side.

The doctor rose and handed the nurse the empty syringe. He leaned over and put both hands for a moment on the mother's shoulders, which were shaking. She was sitting on the floor, her lips pressed together, holding Mary Grace's hand in her lap. The girl's fingers were gripped like a baby's around her thumb. 'Go on to the hospital,' he said. 'I'll call and make the arrangements.'

'Now let's see that neck,' he said in a jovial voice to Mrs Turpin. He began to inspect her neck with his first two fingers. Two little moon-shaped lines like pink fish bones were indented over her windpipe. There was the beginning of an angry red swelling above her eye. His fingers passed over this also.

'Lea' me be,' she said thickly and shook him off. 'See about Claud. She kicked him.'

'I'll see about him in a minute,' he said and felt her pulse. He was a thin grey-haired man, given to pleasantries. 'Go home and have yourself a vacation the rest of the day,' he said and patted her on the shoulder.

Quit your pattin me, Mrs Turpin growled to herself.

'And put an ice pack over that eye,' he said. Then he went and squatted down beside Claud and looked at his leg. After a moment he pulled him up and Claud limped after him into the office.

Until the ambulance came, the only sounds in the room were the tremulous moans of the girl's mother, who continued to sit on the floor. The white-trash woman did not take her eyes off the girl. Mrs Turpin looked straight ahead at nothing. Presently the ambulance drew up, a long dark shadow, behind the curtain. The attendants came in and set the stretcher down beside the girl and lifted her expertly onto it and carried her out. The nurse helped the mother gather up her things. The shadow of the ambulance moved silently away and the nurse came back in the office.

'That ther girl is going to be a lunatic, ain't she?' the white-trash woman asked the nurse, but the nurse kept on to the back and never answered her.

'Yes, she's going to be a lunatic,' the white-trash woman said to the rest of them.

'Po' critter,' the old woman murmured. The child's face was still in her lap. His eyes looked idly out over her knees. He had not moved during the disturbance except to draw one leg up under him.

'I thank Gawd,' the white-trash woman said fervently, 'I ain't a lunatic.'

Claud came limping out and the Turpins went home.

As their pick-up truck turned into their own dirt road and made the crest of the hill, Mrs Turpin gripped the window ledge and looked out suspiciously. The land sloped gracefully down through a field dotted with lavender weeds and at the start of the rise their small yellow frame house, with its little flower beds spread out around it like a fancy apron, sat primly in its accustomed place between two giant hickory trees. She would not have been startled to see a burnt wound between two blackened chimneys.

Neither of them felt like eating so they put on their house clothes and lowered the shade in the bedroom and lay down, Claud with his leg on a pillow and herself with a damp washcloth over her eye. The instant she was flat on her back, the image of a razor-backed hog with warts on its face and horns coming out behind its ears snorted into her head. She moaned, a low quiet moan.

'I am not,' she said tearfully, 'a wart hog. From hell.' But the denial had no force. The girl's eyes and her words, even the tone of her voice, low but clear, directed only to her, brooked no repudiation. She had been singled out for the message, though there was trash in the room to whom it might justly have been applied. The full force of this fact struck her only now. There was a woman there who was neglecting her own child but she had been overlooked. The message had been given to Ruby Turpin, a respectable, hardworking, church-going woman. The tears dried. Her eyes began to burn instead with wrath.

She rose on her elbow and the washcloth fell into her hand. Claud was lying on his back, snoring. She wanted to tell him what the girl had said. At the same time, she did not wish to put the image of herself as a wart hog from hell into his mind.

'Hey, Claud,' she muttered and pushed his shoulder.

Claud opened one pale baby blue eye.

She looked into it warily. He did not think about anything. He just went his way.

'Wha, whasit?' he said and closed the eye again.

'Nothing,' she said. 'Does your leg pain you?'

'Hurts like hell,' Claud said.

'It'll quit terreckly,' she said and lay back down. In a moment Claud was snoring again. For the rest of the afternoon they lay there. Claud slept. She scowled at the ceiling. Occasionally she raised her fist and made a small stabbing motion over her chest as if she was defending her innocence to invisible guests who were like the comforters of Job, reasonable-seeming but wrong.

About five-thirty Claud stirred. 'Got to go after those niggers,' he sighed, not moving.

She was looking straight up as if there were unintelligible handwriting on the ceiling. The protuberance over her eye had turned a greenish-blue. 'Listen here,' she said.

'What?'

'Kiss me.'

Claud leaned over and kissed her loudly on the mouth. He pinched her side and their hands interlocked. Her expression of ferocious concentration did not change. Claud got up, groaning and growling, and limped off. She continued to study the ceiling.

She did not get up until she heard the pick-up truck coming back with the Negroes. Then she rose and thrust her feet in her brown oxfords, which she did not bother to lace, and stumped out onto the back porch and got her red plastic bucket. She emptied a tray of ice cubes into it and filled it half full of water and went out into the back yard. Every afternoon after Claud brought the hands in, one of the boys helped him put out hay and the rest waited in the back of the truck until he was ready to take them home. The truck was parked in the shade under one of the hickory trees.

'Hi yawl this evening?' Mrs Turpin asked grimly, appearing with the bucket and the dipper. There were three women and a boy in the truck.

'Us doin nicely,' the oldest woman said. 'Hi you doin?' and her gaze stuck immediately on the dark lump on Mrs Turpin's forehead. 'You done fell down, ain't you?' she asked in a solicitous voice. The old woman was dark and almost toothless. She had on an old felt hat of Claud's set back on her head. The other two women were younger and lighter and they both had new bright green sun hats. One of them had hers on her head; the other had taken hers off and the boy was grinning beneath it.

Mrs Turpin set the bucket down on the floor of the truck. 'Yawl hep yourselves,' she said. She looked around to make sure Claud had gone. 'No. I didn't fall down,' she said, folding her arms. 'It was something worse than that.'

'Ain't nothing bad happen to you!' the old woman said. She said it as if they all knew that Mrs Turpin was protected in some special way by Divine Providence. 'You just had you a little fall.'

'We were in town at the doctor's office for where the cow kicked Mr Turpin,' Mrs Turpin said in a flat tone that indicated they could leave off their foolishness. 'And there was this girl there. A big fat girl with her face all broke out. I could look at that girl and tell she was peculiar but I couldn't tell how. And me and her mama were just talking and going along and all of a sudden WHAM! She throws this big book she was reading at me and . . .'

'Naw!' the old woman cried out.

'And then she jumps over the table and commences to choke me.'

'Naw!' they all exclaimed, 'Naw!'

'Hi come she do that?' the old woman asked. 'What ail her?'

Mrs Turpin only glared in front of her.

'Somethin ail her,' the old woman said.

'They carried her off in an ambulance,' Mrs Turpin continued, 'but before she went she was rolling on the floor and they were trying to hold her down to give her a shot and she said something to me.' She paused. 'You know what she said to me?'

'What she say?' they asked.

'She said,' Mrs Turpin began, and stopped, her face very dark and heavy. The sun was getting whiter and whiter, blanching the sky overhead so that the leaves of the hickory tree were black in the face of it. She could not bring forth the words. 'Something real ugly,' she muttered.

'She sho shouldn't said nothin ugly to you,' the old woman said. 'You so sweet. You the sweetest lady I know.'

'She pretty too,' the one with the hat on said.

'And stout,' the other one said. 'I never knowed no sweeter white lady.'

'That's the truth befo' Jesus,' the old woman said. 'Amen! You des as sweet and pretty as you can be.'

Mrs Turpin knew just exactly how much Negro flattery was worth and it added to her rage. 'She said,' she began again and finished this time with a fierce rush of breath, 'that I was an old wart hog from hell.'

There was an astounded silence.

'Where she at?' the youngest woman cried in piercing voice.

'Lemme see her. I'll kill her!'

'I'll kill her with you!' the other one cried.

'She b'long in the 'sylum,' the old woman said emphatically. 'You the sweetest white lady I know.'

'She pretty too,' the other two said. 'Stout as she can be and sweet. Jesus satisfied with her!'

'Deed he is,' the old woman declared.

Idiots! Mrs Turpin growled to herself. You could never say anything intelligent to a nigger. You could talk at them but not with them. 'Yawl ain't drunk your water,' she said shortly. 'Leave the bucket in the truck when you're finished with it. I got more to do than just stand around and pass the time of day,' and she moved off and into the house.

She stood for a moment in the middle of the kitchen. The dark protuberance over her eye looked like a miniature tornado cloud which might any moment sweep across the horizon of her brow. Her lower lip protruded dangerously. She squared her massive shoulders. Then she marched into the front of the house and out the side door and started down the road to the pig parlour. She had the look of a woman going single-handed, weaponless, into battle.

The sun was a deep yellow now like a harvest moon and was riding westward very fast over the far tree line as if it meant to reach the hogs before she did. The road was rutted and she kicked several good-sized stones out of her path as she strode along. The pig parlour was on a little knoll at the end of a lane that ran off from the side of the barn. It was a square of concrete as large as a small room, with a board fence about four feet high around it. The concrete floor sloped slightly so that the hog wash could drain off into a trench where it was carried to the field for fertilizer. Claud was standing on the outside, on the edge of the concrete, hanging onto the top board, hosing down the floor inside. The hose was connected to the faucet of a water trough nearby.

Mrs Turpin climbed up beside him and glowered down at the hogs inside. There were seven long-snouted bristly shoats in it—tan with liver-coloured spots—and an old sow a few weeks off from farrowing. She was lying on her side grunting. The shoats were running about shaking themselves like idiot children, their little slit pig eyes searching the floor for anything left. She had read that pigs were the most intelligent animal. She doubted it. They were supposed to be smarter than dogs. There had even been a pig astronaut. He had performed his assignment perfectly but died of a heart attack afterwards because they left him in his electric suit, sitting upright throughout his examination when naturally a hog should be on all fours.

A-gruntin and a-rootin and a-groanin.

'Gimme that hose,' she said, yanking it away from Claud. 'Go on and carry them niggers home and then get off that leg.'

'You look like you might have swallowed a mad dog,' Claud observed, but he got down and limped off. He paid no attention to her humours.

Until he was out of earshot, Mrs Turpin stood on the side of the pen, holding the hose and pointing the stream of water at the hind quarters of any shoat that looked as if it might try to lie down. When he had had time to get over the hill, she turned her head slightly and her wrathful eyes scanned the path. He was nowhere in sight. She turned back again and seemed to gather herself up. Her shoulders rose and she drew in her breath.

'What do you send me a message like that for?' she said in a low fierce voice, barely above a whisper but with the force of a shout in its concentrated fury. 'How am I a hog and me both? How am I saved and from hell too?' Her free fist was knotted and with the other she gripped the hose, blindly pointing the stream of water in and out of the eye of the old sow whose outraged squeal she did not hear.

The pig parlour commanded a view of the back pasture where their twenty beef cows were gathered around the hay-bales Claud and the boy had put out. The freshly cut pasture sloped down to the highway. Across it was their cotton field and beyond that a dark green dusty wood which they owned as well. The sun was behind the wood, very red, looking over the paling of trees like a farmer inspecting his own hogs.

'Why me?' she rumbled. 'It's no trash around here, black or white, that I haven't given to. And break my back to the bone every day working. And do for the church.'

She appeared to be the right size woman to command the arena before her. 'How am I a hog?' she demanded. 'Exactly how am I like them?' and she jabbed the stream of water at the shoats. 'There was plenty of trash there. It didn't have to be me.

'If you like trash better, go get yourself some trash then,' she railed. 'You could have made me trash. Or a nigger. If trash is what you wanted why didn't you make me trash?' She shook her fist with the hose in it and a watery snake appeared momentarily in the air. 'I could quit working and take it easy and be filthy,' she growled. 'Lounge about the sidewalks all day drinking root beer. Dip snuff and spit in every puddle and have it all over my face. I could be nasty.

'Or you could have made me a nigger. It's too late for me to be a nigger,' she said with deep sarcasm, 'but I could act like one. Lay down in the middle of the road and stop traffic. Roll on the ground.'

In the deepening light everything was taking on a mysterious hue. The pasture was growing a peculiar glassy green and the streak of highway had turned lavender. She braced herself for a final assault and this time her voice rolled out over the pasture. 'Go on,' she yelled, 'call me a hog! Call me a hog again. From hell. Call me a wart hog from hell. Put that bottom rail on top. There'll still be a top and bottom!'

A garbled echo returned to her.

A final surge of fury shook her and she roared, 'Who do you think you are?'

The colour of everything, field and crimson sky, burned for a moment with a transparent intensity. The question carried over the pasture and across the highway and the cotton field and returned to her clearly like an answer from beyond the wood.

She opened her mouth but no sound came out of it.

A tiny truck, Claud's, appeared on the highway, heading rapidly out of sight. Its gears scraped thinly. It looked like a child's toy. At any moment a bigger truck might smash into it and scatter Claud's and the niggers' brains all over the road.

Mrs Turpin stood there, her gaze fixed on the highway, all her muscles rigid, until in five or six minutes the truck reappeared, returning. She waited until it had had time to turn into their own road. Then like a monumental statue coming to life, she bent her head slowly and gazed, as if through the very heart of mystery, down into the pig parlour at the hogs. They had settled all in one corner around the old sow who was grunting softly. A red glow suffused them. They appeared to pant with a secret life.

Until the sun slipped finally behind the tree line, Mrs Turpin remained there with her gaze bent to them as if she were absorbing some abysmal life-giving knowledge. At last she lifted her head. There was only a purple streak in the sky, cutting through a field of crimson and leading, like an extension of the highway, into the descending dusk. She raised her hands from the side of the pen in a gesture hieratic and profound. A visionary light settled in her eyes. She saw the streak as a vast swinging bridge extending upward from the earth through a field of living fire. Upon it a vast horde of souls were rumbling toward heaven. There were whole companies of white-trash, clean for the first time in their lives, and bands of black niggers in white robes, and battalions of freaks and lunatics shouting and clapping and leaping like frogs. And bringing up the end of the procession was a tribe of people whom she recognized at once as those who, like herself and Claud, had always had a little of everything and the God-given wit to use it right. She leaned forward to observe them closer. They were marching behind the others with great dignity, accountable as they had always been for good order and common sense and respectable behaviour. They alone were on key. Yet she could see by their shocked and altered faces that even their virtues were being burned away. She lowered her hands and gripped the rail of the hog pen, her eyes small but fixed unblinkingly on what lay ahead. In a moment the vision faded but she remained where she was, immobile.

At length she got down and turned off the faucet and made her slow way on the darkening path to the house. In the woods around her the invisible cricket choruses had struck up, but what she heard were the voices of the souls climbing upward into the starry field and shouting hallelujah.

Elizabeth Taylor

Mr Wharton

The furnished flat in a London suburb fell vacant on a Monday and
Hilda Provis, having collected the key from the agents in the High
Street, walked down the hill towards Number Twenty. It was
half-past eleven in the morning and early summer. In the quiet
road, houses—some quite large—stood in dusty gardens full of
may trees and laburnums, past blossoming. There had been no rain
for a fortnight and, in the gutters and under garden walls, drifts of
powdery dead petals and seeds had collected. The air had a dry,
polleny smell.

It was a strange land to Hilda, and a great adventure. She was to
be here for a week, to see her daughter settled into the flat; had
quite insisted on coming, had been obliged to insist; for Pat had
thought she could manage very well on her own, had begged her
mother not to put herself to so much trouble, coming so far—from
the country near Nottingham, in fact. There was no need, she had
written. But Hilda desperately maintained that there was.

When Pat first went to work in London, living there in a hostel,
Hilda, left alone and nervous at night, moved to her sister's,
thinking that anything was better than seeming to hear burglars all
the time; but she and her brother-in-law did not get on well
together, and she longed for a home of her own and to have her
daughter back. It was with a joyful excitement that she descended
the hill this morning and pushed open the heavy gate of Number
Twenty.

It was a tall house with a flight of steps to the front door and
below them a basement area. The garden was neglected, growing
only ferns and the grass between the broken tiles of the path. The
lawn at the back was a lower level—in fact, the house was found to
be built on a hillside. Down below, beyond the roofs of other
houses, was London itself—grey, but for one or two bone-white
church spires, sudden glitterings from windows or weather vanes
struck by the sun, and one green dome floating in haze.

Hilda stood by the side door with the key in her hand and looked down at the view. It is a panorama, she thought; that really is the word for it. She could imagine it at night—dazzling it would be. She had never seen anything like it. Life teemed down there—traffic strove to disentangle itself, Pat pounded her typewriter; but to Hilda it was a lulled and dormant city, under its nearly midday haze, nothing doing, nothing stirring. She could not imagine anything happening beneath those pigeon-coloured roofs going down, street after street, lower and lower into the smoky mist.

After the brilliant out-of-doors, she was hit by cold dismay when she unlocked the door and stepped inside—such darkness, such an unfriendly smell of other people's belongings. The flat was clean, but not up to Hilda's standards. She went from the hall into a kitchen. The previous tenants had left remains—a little flour in a bin, some sugar in a jar, a worn-out dish-cloth and a piece of dirty soap. She disposed of these before taking off her hat. A spider sat in the sink and she swilled it down the drain.

The living-room window looked into the area. She opened it and let in the sound of footsteps on the pavement above. Furniture was either black and in the Jacobean style, or Indian with trellis-work and brass. So many twisted chair-legs needing a polish. A green stain had been allowed to spread from bath taps to plug, but Hilda knew a way of removing it. The bedroom was full of sunshine, for the smeared windows looked out over the lawn at the back and at the panorama beyond it. It smelt of sun-warmed carpet and cushion dust. She opened the windows, and then the drawers of the chest. They were lined with old paper and there were oddments left behind in most of them—curtain-rings, safety pins, a strip of beading which she could see had fallen off the wardrobe. This she could glue on again, though it was not her duty to do so. Of the two beds, she thought Pat would prefer the one by the window.

In the afternoon, she went shopping. The street where the shops were climbed steeply towards the heath and, turning corners, looking down side streets, she was sometimes surprised by a sudden openness and glimpsed from different sides the city below.

Everything she bought added to her pleasure and excitement. She was reminded of being a bride again. It seemed a long time since she had planned a meal or chosen a piece of fish or done anything on her own. Knowing no one in the shops, she felt shy; but her loneliness was wonderful to her and her slow pace, as she sauntered along, was tuned to it.

The leisurely afternoon was very pleasant. Babies lay awake under the canopies of their perambulators, staring sternly upwards, making purling sounds like doves, or fidgeted, turning their wrists impatiently, arching their backs and thrusting limbs out into the sunshine. Hilda peeped at each one, stooped to look under the canopies, and blew kisses. If she had been childless herself, she thought she must have looked in another direction. As it was, she just felt momentarily wistful; it was nothing distressing. The young mothers all paused for her, quite patient while they shared their marvels.

Everything glittered in the fine air of this high suburb. A warm rubbery puff of air flowed out from the Underground station at the crossroads; and out of it, too, in a couple of hours, Pat would hasten—on a tide of rush-hour workers, gradually thinning themselves out in different directions, she down the hill under the trees to Number Twenty.

Outside a greengrocer's, on the wide pavement, was a stall of bedding plants and, although her basket was full, Hilda stopped to buy a pot of bright red double daisies. ('Chubby' daisies, Pat had called them when she was a little girl.) She was tired, for she had scoured the bath, and polished all the curly furniture, and was not used to doing so much. At her sister's, she was inclined to indispositions and began most days with a health bulletin which was taken in silence—discourteously, she thought. They were selfish people—her sister and brother-in-law—she had long ago decided; too much wrapped up in themselves, in the manner of childless people.

The front door of Number Twenty was open, and there were sounds of life. A toddler with wide-apart legs, napkins dropping, came on to the steps, then an arm swooped after him and lifted him back out of sight. I could get to know them, Hilda thought. I could keep an ear open for the baby while they went for a stroll in the evening. She even chose a pub in which they—whoever they were—could sit and have a quiet drink. She had noticed a nice one on her walk home from the shops; it had a horse's trough outside and a chestnut tree—like a country pub.

The flat was cool and smelt better now. She had discovered that other people's belongings were more interesting than her own—which by now were so familiar as to be invisible. She had innovated, improvised with the material to hand and was pleased with the effect. Unpacking her basket, stacking food on bare shelves, she remembered her first home, her first shopping—such a young bride she had been that she had thought of it as running the errands, until the moving truth had dawned on her that she herself must choose, and pay for, and bring home. Again, after all those years, she had a feeling of being watched, of not being entirely spontaneous. Methodically, she put the food away, washed some lettuce, found a saucer for the pot of daisies and began to lay the table for supper. 'Hilda's managing well,' she seemed to hear a voice say. It was as if she were doing everything for the first time.

The evening began to go slowly. She wandered about, waiting for Pat, putting finishing touches, glancing at the clock, straightening pictures ('Too awful,' she thought—heathery moorlands, a rosy glow on the Alps), turning the chipped side of a vase to the wall.

She would have liked to unpack the big suitcase which had arrived from the hostel, but she had done this for her daughter before, and been told that she was interfering.

She sat down in the living-room, and stared out of the window, waiting for Pat's legs to appear above the area. She was by now quite nervous with anticipation, and felt that the girl would never come.

As long-awaited people come in the end as a surprise, so Pat did.

'Hello, dear,' Hilda said, almost shyly, when she had hurried to open the door.

'My *feet*!' Pat said, flopping into a chair, dropping gloves and parcels on the floor. She kicked off her shoes and stared down at her large, bare, mottled feet. Her heaviness—of bone and features— suggested sculpture. 'Seated Woman' she might have been, glumly motionless.

'Did you have a bad day?' Hilda asked timidly.

'Oh, I had a bad day all right,' Pat said, as if this went without saying. She leaned back now—almost 'Reclining Woman'—and shook a lock of hair off her forehead. 'That man!' She yawned and her eyes watered. Even looking at her made Hilda feel weary. The man was Mr Wharton, Pat's employer—a big Masonic Golfer, as she described him. He had a habit of returning from lunch at half-past three and then would dictate letters at a great rate to make up for lost time, and Pat, trying at the end of the day to keep up, was worn out, she said, by the time she left to join the rush-hour traffic.

Mr Wharton was a very real person to Hilda, who had never seen him.

'Inconsiderate,' she said, made quite indignant by Pat's long plaint.

'Comes back reeking—face the colour of those daisies.'

'Disgusting,' Hilda murmured, following Pat's glance. 'I bought them this afternoon. "Chubby daisies," you used to call them.'

'Did I?' Pat was not so much in love with herself as a child as her mother was and Hilda always found this indifference strange. 'Expense accounts,' Pat went on, and blew out her lips in contempt. 'Eat and drink themselves stupid, and then go home and tell their wives what a hard day they've had. Well, it all looks very nice,' she said at last, glancing round. 'Even my cardigan smells of his bloody cigars.' She sniffed at her sleeve with distaste. 'You literally can't see across the office.'

A huge man, like a bison, Hilda visualized. She felt great respect for her daughter, cooped up in that blue haze with such a character—managing him, too, with her icy reminders, her appearance at other times of praying for patience, her eyes closed, her pencil tapping her teeth. Hilda could see it all from her descriptions—Pat giving him one of her looks and saying briskly '*Do* you mind,' when he stood too close to her. It was not a question.

Mother and daughter had changed places, Hilda sometimes thought. She felt a young girl in the shade of Pat's knowledge of the world. Yet once she herself had worked for her living—serving in a milliner's shop, full of anxieties, trying to oblige, so afraid of displeasing and being dismissed. To earn one's livelihood is a precarious affair, and even Pat would say, 'Well, if I can hold down a job like that for all these years . . .' She held it down firmly, her clever eyes on those who might try to snatch it from her; but she made it sound a desperate business.

'Well, it's nice not to be in that perishing hostel,' she said. Hilda glowed with pleasure when they sat down at the table and Pat began to eat, as if she were quite content to be where she was. 'Canteens!' she said. 'The Lord preserve me from them. Tinned pilchards. Cottage pie. Never again.'

Hilda had been worried for years about the food, especially as she had heard about working girls in London going without lunch—window-shopping or having their hair done instead. It will all be different now, she thought, watching Pat's knife and fork slashing criss-cross at the food which, though not commented on, seemed to be approved. I can't at her age, Hilda thought, tell her not to talk with her mouth full—for all the time the knife and fork were shredding and spearing and popping things into her mouth, Pat was describing Mr Wharton's private life. Hilda found it all trivial and uninteresting. She did not care enough to try to visualize Mr Wharton gardening on Saturday, playing golf on Sundays and going to cocktail parties, of which there seemed to be so many in the Green Belt where he lived. She saw him more clearly in his smoke-filled office.

'I met his wife once,' Pat said. 'She came to call for him and they went out to lunch. Very dowdy. I'll give you a hand,' she added, and stirred slightly as Hilda began to stack up plates.

'No, you sit still. Make the most of it while I'm here.' But Hilda had begun to believe that she would never go. She would make herself so useful.

'I wish I had your figure,' Pat said, watching her mother moving neatly about the room. She said it in a grudging voice, as if Hilda had meanly kept something for herself which she, Pat, would have liked to possess. It was not and had not been the pattern of their lives for this to happen.

Hilda blushed with guilty pleasure. There was something so sedentary about her daughter—not only because of her office job, for as a child she had sat about all the time, reading comics, chewing her handkerchief, twisting her braided hair, very often just lethargically sulking. At this moment, she was slumped back in her chair, eating a banana, the skin of it hanging down in strips over her hand.

'I might bring Mavis Willis back tomorrow evening,' she said. 'She's thinking of sharing the flat with me. Let her have a look round and make up her mind.' She got up and went to the area window and looked meditatively up at the railings.

'Quiet here, isn't it?' she said. She stayed there for a long time, just gazing out of the window, and Hilda, clearing the table, wondered what she was thinking.

Mavis Willis was a young woman of much refinement, and Hilda, watching her eat her supper daintily, was taken by her manners. A rather old-fashioned type of girl, Hilda thought. If she had been asked to, she could not have chosen anyone more suitable to share the flat with her daughter. This one would not lead her into bad company or have wild parties; but Hilda had not been asked, and it was a disappointment to her that the question had not arisen.

When Mavis had been shown round the flat before supper, something in her manner had surprised Hilda; there was a sense of effort she could not define. The girl had gushed without showing much interest, had given the bathroom the briefest glance and not opened the cupboard where she would be hanging her clothes—the first thing any normal young woman would do.

Now, at supper, she gushed in the same way about Hilda's cooking. Pat's compulsive grumbling about Mr Wharton was resumed, and Mavis joined in. She referred to him as 'H.W.'—which sounded more officey, Hilda decided, listening humbly.

'One of these days, you'll find yourself out of a job,' she told Pat, who had repeated one of her tarter rebukes to her employer—'I gave him one of my looks and I said to him, "That'll be the day," I said. "When you get back before three o'clock. We'll hang the flags out *that* day," I said to him.'

Mavis took off her spectacles and began to polish them on a clean handkerchief she had kept tucked in her cuff. She looked down her shiny nose, smiling a little. Her face was pale and glistened unhealthily, and she reminded Hilda of the languid, indoors young women who had sat all day—long days then—in the milliner's workroom, stitching buckram and straw and flowers, hardly moving, sadly cooped up in the stuffy room. She, in the shop itself, had seemed as free as air.

Mavis put back her spectacles and rearranged her hair, and at once she appeared less secretive. She insisted on helping Hilda to wash the dishes, while Pat spent the time looking for cigarettes and then for her lighter.

'I hope Pat won't leave all the work to you, if you come,' Hilda said.

'Oh, she won't.' Mavis wiped a glass and held it up to the light. 'Once we're on our own, she'll be enthusiastic. You know, she'll feel it's more hers and want to take a pride in it. Of course, it's been wonderful for her, having you to settle her in and get it looking so nice. Simply wonderful. You must have done marvels.' She looked vaguely round the kitchen.

'Well, it was in rather a pickle,' Hilda said warmly. 'All I hope is you won't just live on tinned food.'

'You can rest assured we won't.'

'I'm afraid Pat hasn't been brought up to be very domesticated. I did try, but I ended up doing things myself, because it was quicker.'

'Well, it always happens. I know I'd be the same.'

Pat, through the doorway, in the living-room, was looking for an ashtray. She moved clumsily about, knocked into something and swore. Hilda and Mavis glanced at one another and smiled, as if over a child's head.

'What did you think of her?' Pat asked, as soon as she got back from walking with Mavis to the Tube station.

'A nice girl. I thought slightly enigmatic,' said Hilda, who took a pride in finding the right word.

'Well, she's decided to move in next Monday. I said I thought you'd be going back at the weekend.'

'I might stay and clear up on Monday morning. Leave you a little supper, her first night,' Hilda said, and pretended she did not hear a resigned intake of breath from Pat.

That girl Mavis, Hilda was thinking—perhaps she's no intention of coming; perhaps she's wasting Pat's time. Yet she sensed something arranged between them, something she could not understand. She used the word 'duplicity' in her mind.

They began to get ready for bed, and when Pat, stout in her dressing-gown, came from the bathroom into the bedroom, she found the room in darkness and her mother peeping through the curtains of the french windows. 'What are you doing, mother?' she asked, switching on the light.

As guilty as a little girl caught out of bed, Hilda made for hers. 'I really love London,' she said. 'All that panorama, at night, and yet it's so quiet. I sat out there this afternoon for a bit, and it was so peaceful, like being in the country. It's been like a lovely holiday here.'

'It's been good of you to come,' Pat said, in a cautious voice.

When she had switched the light off, her mother turned on her side, put her hands under her cheek, and with faint purring, puffing sounds, fell lightly asleep. Pat lay on her back like a figure on a tomb, and presently began to snore.

*　　*　　*

On Hilda's last day, it set in wet, and she could not go into the garden again. She went out shopping in the rain, said good-bye to the shop-assistants she had made friends of, and thought how extraordinary it was that the little High Street had become so familiar in such a short time. The view was obscured by mist. But the holiday feeling persisted and at twelve o'clock she entered the saloon bar of the little pub by the water trough and bought herself a glass of sherry. She had never been alone into a bar before, and was gratified that no one seemed surprised to see her do so. The barmaid was warmly chatty, the landlord courteous; an old man by the fire did not even raise his head. A stale beery smell pervaded the room, as if everything—the heavy curtains, the varnished furniture, even perhaps the old man by the fire—was gently fermenting.

'So cosy,' said Hilda.

'A day like this,' the barmaid agreed, scalloping a damp cloth along the bar.

'A fire's nice.'

'It makes a difference. You live hereabouts?'

Hilda told her about Pat and the flat, and Mavis Willis.

'Nice to have a mother,' the barmaid said.

'I think she appreciates it. But I've enjoyed myself. It's made a lovely break. I'd like a bottle of sherry to take away, if you please. I'll leave it as a surprise for the girls—warm them up when they come in wet from work.'

'Well,' said the barmaid, wrapping the bottle in a swirl of pink paper, 'let's hope we see you when you're in these parts again.'

'Good-morning, madam. Thank you,' the landlord added and Hilda, with her heavy shopping basket, stepped out into the rain. How very pleasant, she was thinking, rather muzzily, as she walked down the hill. The only pity was not having made friends with the people on the first floor. Glimpses of the toddler she had had from time to time, heard his little footsteps running overhead; but had not had a word with his mother. That had been a disappointment.

She made herself a cup of tea when she had hung up her wet coat. The flat was so dark that afternoon that she had to switch on the lights. The rain seemed to keep her company, as a coal fire does the very lonely—the sound of it falling softly into the ferns in the garden, or with a sharp, ringing noise on the dustbin lids outside the door. She could hear the splashing of cars going by on the road above the window, changing gear to take the hill.

Although she felt sad, packing her case, she cheered up when she was putting the finishing touches to the supper table, leaving the sherry on a tray with a note and two glasses. She watered the double daisy and added a reminder about it to her note. At three o'clock, she put on her still damp coat and was ready to go to the station. She locked the door and hid the key under the dustbin as they had arranged and, feeling melancholy, in tune with the afternoon, walked with head bowed, carrying her heavy suitcase up the hill to the Underground station.

At four o'clock the rain suddenly stopped. Already on her way back to Nottingham in the train, Hilda watched the watery sunshine on the fields and the slate roofs drying. She reminded herself that she was always sad on train journeys. It's a sensation of fantasy, she decided, having searched for and found the word.

The sunshine was short-lived. The dark purple clouds soon gathered over again and in London, crowds surging towards stations, queueing for buses, were soaked. The pavements steamed in the hissing rain, and taxis were unobtainable, although commissionaires under huge umbrellas stood at kerbs, whistling shrilly and vainly whenever one appeared in the distance.

In a positive deluge, Pat and Mr Wharton drove up to Number Twenty. He, too, had an umbrella, and held it carefully over her as they went down the garden path and round the side of the house.

'Excusez-moi,' she said, stooping to get the key from under the dustbin.

'Could be a nice view on a nice day,' he said.

'Could be,' she agreed, putting the key in the door.

ALICE MUNRO

The Time of Death

Afterwards the mother, Leona Parry, lay on the couch, with a quilt around her, and the women kept putting more wood on the fire although the kitchen was very hot, and no one turned the light on. Leona drank some tea and refused to eat, and talked, beginning like this, in a voice that was ragged and insistent but not yet hysterical: I wasn't hardly out of the house, I wasn't out of the house twenty minutes—

(Three-quarters of an hour at the least, Allie McGee thought, but she did not say so, not at the time. But she remembered, because there were three serials on the radio she was trying to listen to, she listened to every day, and she couldn't get half of them; Leona was there in her kitchen going on about Patricia. Leona was sewing this cowgirl outfit for Patricia on Allie's machine; she raced the machine and she pulled the thread straight out to break it instead of pulling it back though Allie had told her don't do that please it's liable to break the needle. Patricia was supposed to have the outfit for that night when she sang at a concert up the valley; she was singing Western pieces. Patricia sang with the Maitland Valley Entertainers, who went all over the country playing at concerts and dances. Patricia was introduced as the Little Sweetheart of Maitland Valley, the Baby Blonde, the Pint-Size Kiddie with the Great Big Voice. She did have a big voice, almost alarming in so frail a child. Leona had started her singing in public when she was three years old.

Never was ascared once, Leona said, leaning forward with a jerky pressure on the pedal, it just comes natural to her to perform. Her kimono fallen open revealed her lean chest, her wilted breasts with their large blue veins sloping into the grey-pink night-gown. She don't care, it could be the King of England watching her, she'd get up and sing, and when she was through singing she'd sit down, that's just the way she is. She's even got a good name for a singer, Patricia Parry, doesn't that sound like you just heard it announced

235

over the air? Another thing is natural blonde hair. I have to do it up in rags every night of her life, but that real blonde is a lot scarcer than natural curly. It don't get dark, either, there's that strain of natural blondes in my family that don't get dark. My cousin I told you about, that won the Miss St Catharines of 1936, she was one, and my aunt that died—)

Allie McGee did not say, and Leona caught her breath and plunged on: Twenty minutes. And that last thing I said to her as I went out the door was, you keep an eye on the kids! She's nine years old, isn't she? I'm just going to run acrost the road to sew up this outfit, you keep an eye on the kids. And I went out the door and down the steps and down to the end of the garden and just as I took the hook off the gate something stopped me, I thought, *something's wrong!* What's wrong, I said to myself. I stood there and I looked back at the garden and all I could see was the cornstalks standing and the cabbages there frozen, we never got them in this year, and I looked up and down the road and all I could see was Mundy's old hound laying out in front of their place, no cars comin' one way or the other and the yards all empty, it was cold I guess and no kids playin' out— And I thought, My Lord, maybe I got my days mixed up and this isn't Saturday morning, it's some special day I forgot about— Then I thought all it was was the snow coming I could feel in the air, and you know how cold it was, the puddles in the road was all turned to ice and splintered up—but it didn't snow, did it, it hasn't snowed yet— And I run acrost the road then over to McGee's and up the front steps and Allie says, Leona, what's the matter with you, you look so white, she says—

Allie McGee heard this too and said nothing, because it was not a time for any sort of accuracy. Leona's voice had gone higher and higher as she talked and any time now she might break off and begin to scream: Don't let that kid come near me, don't let me see her, just don't let her come near me.

And the women in the kitchen would crowd around the couch, their big bodies indistinct in the half-light, their faces looming pale and heavy, hung with the ritual masks of mourning and compassion. Now lay down, they would say, in the stately tones of ritual soothing. Lay down, Leona, she ain't here, it's all right.

And the girl from the Salvation Army would say, in her gentle unchanging voice, You must forgive her, Mrs Parry, she is only a child. Sometimes the Salvation Army girl would say: It is God's

236

will, we do not understand. The other woman from the Salvation Army, who was older, with an oily, sallow face and an almost masculine voice, said: In the garden of heaven the children bloom like flowers. God needed another flower and he took your child. Sister, you should thank him and be glad.

The other women listened uneasily while these spoke; their faces at such words took on a look of embarrassed childish solemnity. They made tea and set out on the table the pies and fruitcake and scones that people had sent, and they themselves had made. Nobody ate anything because Leona would not eat. Many of the women cried, but not the two from the Army. Allie McGee cried. She was stout, placid-faced, big-breasted; she had no children. Leona drew up her knees under the quilt and rocked herself back and forth as she wept, and threw her head down and then back (showing, as some of them noticed with a feeling of shame, the dirty lines on her neck). Then she grew quiet and said with something like surprise: I nursed him till he was ten months old. He was so good, too, you never would of known you had him in the house. I always said, that's the best one I ever had.

In the dark overheated kitchen the women felt the dignity of this sorrow in their maternal flesh, they were humble before this unwashed, unliked and desolate Leona. When the men came in—the father, a cousin, a neighbour, bringing a load of wood or asking shamefacedly for something to eat—they were at once aware of something that shut them out, that reproved them. They went out and said to the other men, Yeah, they're still at it. And the father who was getting a little drunk, and belligerent, because he felt that something was expected of him and he was not equal to it, it was not fair, said, Yeah, that won't do Benny any good, they can bawl their eyes out.

George and Irene had been playing their cut-out game, cutting things out of the catalogue. They had this family they had cut out of the catalogue, the mother and father and the kids and they cut out clothes for them. Patricia watched them cutting and she said, Look at the way you kids cut out! Lookit all the white around the edges! How are you going to make those clothes stay on, she said, you didn't even cut any foldover things. She took the scissors and she cut very neatly, not leaving any white around the edges; her pale shrewd little face was bent to one side; her lips bitten together. She did things the way a grown-up does; she did not pretend things. She did not play at being a singer, though she was going to be a singer when she grew up, maybe in the movies or maybe on the radio. She liked to look at movie magazines and magazines with pictures of clothes and rooms in them; she liked to look in the windows of some of the houses uptown.

Benny was trying to climb up on the couch. He grabbed at the catalogue and Irene hit his hand. He began to whimper. Patricia picked him up competently and carried him to the window. She stood him on a chair looking out, saying to him, Bow-wow, Benny, see bow-wow— It was Mundy's dog, getting up and shaking himself and going off down the road.

Bow-wow, said Benny interrogatively, putting his hands flat and leaning against the window to see where the dog went. Benny was eighteen months old and the only words he knew how to say were Bow-wow and Bram. Bram was for the scissors-man who came along the road sometimes; Brandon was his name. Benny remembered him, and ran out to meet him when he came. Other little kids only thirteen, fourteen months old knew more words than Benny, and could do more things, like waving bye-bye and clapping hands, and most of them were cuter to look at. Benny was long and thin and bony and his face was like his father's—pale, mute, unexpectant; all it needed was a soiled peaked cap. But he was good; he would stand for hours just looking out a window saying Bow-wow, bow-wow, now in a low questioning tone, now crooningly, stroking his hands down the window-pane. He liked you to pick him up and hold him, long as he was, just like a little baby; he would lie looking up and smiling, with a little timidity or misgiving. Patricia knew he was stupid; she hated stupid things. He was the only stupid thing she did not hate. She would go and wipe his nose, expertly and impersonally, she would try to get him to talk, repeating words after her, she would put her face down to his, saying anxiously, Hi, Benny, *Hi*, and he would look at her and smile in his slow dubious way. That gave her this feeling, a kind of sad tired feeling, and she would go away and leave him, she would go and look at a movie magazine.

She had had a cup of tea and part of a sugar-bun for breakfast; now she was hungry. She rummaged around among the dirty dishes and puddles of milk and porridge on the kitchen table; she picked up a bun, but it was sopping with milk and she threw it down again.

This place stinks, she said. Irene and George paid no attention. She kicked at a crust of porridge that had dried on the linoleum. Lookit that, she said. Lookit *that*! What's it always a mess around here for? She walked around kicking at things perfunctorily. Then she got the scrub-pail from under the sink and a dipper, and she began to dip water from the reservoir of the stove.

I'm going to clean this place up, she said. It never gets cleaned up like other places. The first thing I'm going to do I'm going to scrub the floor and you kids have to help me—

She put the pail on the stove.

That water is hot to start with, Irene said.

It's not hot enough. It's got to be good and boiling hot. I seen Mrs McGee scrub *her* floor.

They stayed at Mrs McGee's all night. They had been over there since the ambulance came. They saw Leona and Mrs McGee and the other neighbours start to pull off Benny's clothes and it looked like parts of his skin were coming away too, and Benny was making a noise not like crying, but more a noise like they had heard a dog making after its hind parts were run over, but worse, and louder— But Mrs McGee saw them; she cried, Go away, go away from here! Go over to my place, she cried. After that the ambulance had come and taken Benny away to the hospital, and Mrs McGee came over and told them that Benny was going to the hospital for a while and they were going to stay at her place. She gave them bread and peanut butter and bread and strawberry jam.

The bed they slept in had a feather tick and smooth ironed sheets; the blankets were pale and fluffy and smelled faintly of mothballs. On top of everything else was a Star-of-Bethlehem quilt; they knew it was called that because when they were getting ready for bed Patricia said, My, what a beautiful quilt! and Mrs McGee looking surprised and rather distracted said, Oh, yes, that's a Star-of-Bethlehem.

Patricia was very polite in Mrs McGee's house. It was not as nice as some of the houses uptown but it was covered on the outside with imitation brick and inside it had an imitation fireplace, as well as a fern in a basket; it was not like the other houses along the highway. Mr McGee did not work in the mill like the other men, but in a store.

George and Irene were so shy and alarmed in this house that they could not answer when they were spoken to.

They all woke up very early; they lay on their backs, uneasy between the fresh sheets, and they watched the room getting light. This room had mauve silk curtains and Venetian blinds and mauve and yellow roses on the wallpaper; it was the guest room. Patricia said, We slept in the guest room.

I have to go, George said.

I'll show you where the bathroom is, Patricia said. It's down the hall.

But George wouldn't go down there to the bathroom. He didn't like it. Patricia tried to make him but he wouldn't.

See if there is a pot under the bed, Irene said.

They got a bathroom here they haven't got any pots, Patricia said angrily. What would they have a stinking old pot for?

George said stolidly that he wouldn't go down there.

Patricia got up and tip-toed to the dresser and got a big vase. When George had gone she opened the window very carefully with hardly any noise and emptied the vase and dried it out with Irene's underpants.

Now, she said, you kids shut up and lay still. Don't talk out loud just whisper.

George whispered, Is Benny still in the hospital?

Yes he is, said Patricia shortly.

Is he going to die?

I told you a hundred times, no.

Is he?

No! Just his skin got burnt, he didn't get burnt inside. He isn't going to die of a little bit of burnt skin is he? Don't talk so loud.

Irene began to twist her head into the pillow.

What's the matter with you? Patricia said.

He cried awful, Irene said, her face in the pillow.

Well it hurt, that's why he cried. When they got him to the hospital they gave him some stuff that made it stop hurting.

How do you know? George said.

I know.

They were quiet for a while and then Patricia said, I never in my life heard of anybody that died of a burnt skin. Your whole skin could be burnt off it wouldn't matter you could just grow another. Irene stop crying or I'll hit you.

Patricia lay still, looking up at the ceiling, her sharp profile white against the mauve silk curtains of Mrs McGee's guestroom.

For breakfast they had grapefruit, which they did not remember having tasted before, and cornflakes and toast and jam. Patricia watched George and Irene and snapped at them, Say please! Say thank-you! She said to Mr and Mrs McGee, What a cold day, I wouldn't be surprised if it snowed today would you?

But they did not answer. Mrs McGee's face was swollen. After breakfast she said, Don't get up, children, listen to me. Your little brother—

Irene began to cry and that started George crying too; he said sobbingly, triumphantly to Patricia. He did so die, he did so! Patricia did not answer. *It's her fault*, George sobbed, and Mrs McGee said, Oh, no, oh, no! But Patricia sat still, with her face wary and polite. She did not say anything until the crying had died down a bit and Mrs McGee got up sighing and began to clear the table. Then Patricia offered to help with the dishes.

Mrs McGee took them downtown to buy them all new shoes for the funeral. Patricia was not going to the funeral because Leona said she never wanted to see her again as long as she lived, but she was to get new shoes too; it would have been unkind to leave her out. Mrs McGee took them into the store and sat them down and explained the situation to the man who owned it; they stood together nodding and whispering gravely. The man told them to take off their shoes and socks. George and Irene took theirs off and stuck out their feet, with the black dirt-caked toenails. Patricia whispered to Mrs McGee that she had to go to the bathroom and Mrs McGee told her where it was, at the back of the store, and she went out there and took off her shoes and socks. She got her feet as clean as she could with cold water and paper towels. When she came back she heard Mrs McGee was saying softly to the storeman, You should of seen the bedsheets I had them on. Patricia walked past them not letting on she heard.

Irene and George got oxfords and Patricia got a pair she chose herself, with a strap across. She looked at them in the low mirror. She walked back and forth looking at them until Mrs McGee said, Patricia never mind about shoes now! Would you believe it? she said in that same soft voice to the store-man as they walked out of the store.

After the funeral was over they went home. The women had cleaned up the house and put Benny's things away. Their father had got sick from so much beer in the back shed after the funeral and he stayed away from the house. Their mother had been put to bed. She stayed there for three days and their father's sister looked after the house.

Leona said they were not to let Patricia come near her room. Don't let her come up here, she cried, I don't want to see her, I haven't forgot my baby boy. But Patricia did not try to go upstairs. She paid no attention to any of this; she looked at movie magazines and did her hair up in rags. If someone cried she did not notice; with her it was as if nothing had happened.

The man who was the manager of the Maitland Valley Entertainers came to see Leona. He told her they were doing the programme for a big concert and barn-dance over at Rockland, and he wanted Patricia to sing in it, if it wasn't too soon after what happened and all. Leona said she would have to think about it. She got out of bed and went downstairs. Patricia was sitting on the couch with one of her magazines. She kept her head down.

That's a fine head of hair you got there, Leona said. I see you been doing it up your ownself. Get me the brush and comb!

To her sister-in-law she said, What's life? You gotta go on.

She went downtown and bought some sheet music, two songs: May the Circle Be Unbroken, and It Is No Secret, What God Can Do. She had Patricia learn them, and Patricia sang these two songs at the concert in Rockland. People in the audience started whispering, because they had heard about Benny, it had been in the paper. They pointed out Leona, who was dressed up and sitting on the platform, and she had her head down, she was crying. Some people in the audience cried too. Patricia did not cry.

In the first week of November (and the snow had not come, the snow had not come yet) the scissors-man with his cart came walking along beside the highway. The children were playing out in the yards and they heard him coming; when he was still far down the road they heard his unintelligible chant, mournful and shrill, and so strange that you would think, if you did not know it was the scissors-man, that there was a madman loose in the world. He wore the same stained brown overcoat, with the hem hanging ragged, and the same crownless felt hat; he came up the road, calling like this and the children ran into the houses to get knives and scissors, or they ran out in the road calling excitedly,

Old Brandon, old Brandon (for that was his name).

Then in the Parry's yard Patricia began to scream: I hate that old scissors-man! I hate him! she screamed. I hate that old scissors-man, I hate him! She screamed, standing stockstill in the yard with her face looking so wizened and white. The shrill shaking cries brought Leona running out, and the neighbours; they pulled her into the house, still screaming. They could not get her to say what was the matter; they thought she must be having some kind of fit. Her eyes were screwed up tight and her mouth wide open; her tiny pointed teeth were almost transparent, and faintly rotten at the edges; they made her look like a ferret, a wretched little animal insane with rage or fear. They tried shaking her, slapping her, throwing cold water on her face; at last they got her to swallow a big dose of soothing-syrup with a lot of whisky in it, and they put her to bed.

That is a prize kid of Leona's, the neighbours said to each other as they went home. That *singer*, they said, because now things were back to normal and they disliked Leona as much as before. They laughed gloomily and said, Yeah, that future movie-star. Out in the yard yelling, you'd think she'd gone off her head.

There was this house, and the other wooden houses that had never been painted, with their steep patched roofs and their narrow, slanting porches, the wood-smoke coming out of their chimneys and dim children's faces pressed against their windows. Behind them there was the strip of earth, ploughed in some places, run to grass in others, full of stones, and behind this the pine trees, not very tall. In front were the yards, the dead gardens, the grey highway running out from town. The snow came, falling slowly, evenly, between the highway and the houses and the pine trees, falling in big flakes at first and then in smaller and smaller flakes that did not melt on the hard furrows, the rock of the earth.

ALICE WALKER

Everyday Use

for your grandmama

I will wait for her in the yard that Maggie and I made so clean and wavy yesterday afternoon. A yard like this is more comfortable than most people know. It is not just a yard. It is like an extended living-room. When the hard clay is swept clean as a floor and the fine sand around the edges lined with tiny, irregular grooves, anyone can come and sit and look up into the elm tree and wait for the breezes that never come inside the house.

Maggie will be nervous until after her sister goes: she will stand hopelessly in corners, homely and ashamed of the burn scars down her arms and legs, eyeing her sister with a mixture of envy and awe. She thinks her sister has held life always in the palm of one hand, that 'no' is a word the world never learned to say to her.

You've no doubt seen those TV shows where the child who has 'made it' is confronted, as a surprise, by her own mother and father, tottering in weakly from backstage. (A pleasant surprise, of course: What would they do if parent and child came on the show only to curse out and insult each other?) On TV mother and child embrace and smile into each other's faces. Sometimes the mother and father weep, the child wraps them in her arms and leans across the table to tell how she would not have made it without their help. I have seen these programmes.

Sometimes I dream a dream in which Dee and I are suddenly brought together on a TV programme of this sort. Out of a dark and soft-seated limousine I am ushered into a bright room filled with many people. There I meet a smiling, grey, sporty man like Johnny Carson who shakes my hand and tells me what a fine girl I have. Then we are on the stage and Dee is embracing me with tears in her eyes. She pins on my dress a large orchid, even though she has told me once that she thinks orchids are tacky flowers.

In real life I am a large, big-boned woman with rough, man-working hands. In the winter I wear flannel night-gowns to bed and overalls during the day. I can kill and clean a hog as mercilessly as a man. My fat keeps me hot in zero weather. I can work outside all day, breaking ice to get water for washing; I can eat pork liver cooked over the open fire minutes after it comes steaming from the hog. One winter I knocked a bull calf straight in the brain between the eyes with a sledge hammer and had the meat hung up to chill before nightfall. But of course all this does not show on television. I am the way my daughter would want me to be: a hundred pounds lighter, my skin like an uncooked barley pancake. My hair glistens in the hot bright lights. Johnny Carson has much to do to keep up with my quick and witty tongue.

But that is a mistake. I know even before I wake up. Who ever knew a Johnson with a quick tongue? Who can even imagine me looking a strange white man in the eye? It seems to me I have talked to them always with one foot raised in flight, with my head turned in whichever way is farthest from them. Dee, though. She would always look anyone in the eye. Hesitation was no part of her nature.

'How do I look, Mama?' Maggie says, showing just enough of her thin body enveloped in pink skirt and red blouse for me to know she's there, almost hidden by the door.

'Come out into the yard,' I say.

Have you ever seen a lame animal, perhaps a dog run over by some careless person rich enough to own a car, sidle up to someone who is ignorant enough to be kind to him? That is the way my Maggie walks. She has been like this, chin on chest, eyes on ground, feet in shuffle, ever since the fire that burned the other house to the ground.

Dee is lighter than Maggie, with nicer hair and a fuller figure. She's a woman now, though sometimes I forget. How long ago was it that the other house burned? Ten, twelve years? Sometimes I can still hear the flames and feel Maggie's arms sticking to me, her hair smoking and her dress falling off her in little black papery flakes. Her eyes seemed stretched open, blazed open by the flames reflected in them. And Dee. I see her standing off under the sweet gum tree she used to dig gum out of; a look of concentration on her face as she watched the last dingy grey board of the house fall in toward

245

the red-hot brick chimney. Why don't you do a dance around the ashes? I'd wanted to ask her. She had hated the house that much.

I used to think she hated Maggie, too. But that was before we raised the money, the church and me, to send her to Augusta to school. She used to read to us without pity; forcing words, lies, other folks' habits, whole lives upon us two, sitting trapped and ignorant underneath her voice. She washed us in a river of make-believe, burned us with a lot of knowledge we didn't necessarily need to know. Pressed us to her with the serious way she read, to shove us away at just the moment, like dimwits, we seemed about to understand.

Dee wanted nice things. A yellow organdie dress to wear to her graduation from high school; black pumps to match a green suit she'd made from an old suit somebody gave me. She was determined to stare down any disaster in her efforts. Her eyelids would not flicker for minutes at a time. Often I fought off the temptation to shake her. At sixteen she had a style of her own: and knew what style was.

I never had an education myself. After second grade the school was closed down. Don't ask me why: in 1927 coloured asked fewer questions than they do now. Sometimes Maggie reads to me. She stumbles along good-naturedly but can't see well. She knows she is not bright. Like good looks and money, quickness passed her by. She will marry John Thomas (who has mossy teeth in an earnest face) and then I'll be free to sit here and I guess just sing church songs to myself. Although I never was a good singer. Never could carry a tune. I was always better at a man's job. I used to love to milk till I was hooked in the side in '49. Cows are soothing and slow and don't bother you, unless you try to milk them the wrong way.

I have deliberately turned my back on the house. It is three rooms, just like the one that burned, except the roof is tin; they don't make shingle roofs any more. There are no real windows, just some holes cut in the sides, like the portholes in a ship, but not round and not square, with rawhide holding the shutters up on the outside. This house is in a pasture, too, like the other one. No doubt when Dee sees it she will want to tear it down. She wrote me once that no matter where we 'choose' to live, she will manage to come see us. But she will never bring her friends. Maggie and I thought about this and Maggie asked me, 'Mama, when did Dee ever *have* any friends?'

She had a few. Furtive boys in pink shirts hanging about on washday after school. Nervous girls who never laughed. Impressed with her they worshipped the well-turned phrase, the cute shape, the scalding humour that erupted like bubbles in lye. She read to them.

When she was courting Jimmy T she didn't have much time to pay to us, but turned all her faultfinding power on him. He *flew* to marry a cheap city girl from a family of ignorant flashy people. She hardly had time to recompose herself.

When she comes I will meet—but there they are!

Maggie attempts to make a dash for the house, in her shuffling way, but I stay her with my hand. 'Come back here,' I say. And she stops and tries to dig a well in the sand with her toe.

It is hard to see them clearly through the strong sun. But even the first glimpse of leg out of the car tells me it is Dee. Her feet were always neat-looking, as if God himself had shaped them with a certain style. From the other side of the car comes a short, stocky man. Hair is all over his head a foot long and hanging from his chin like a kinky mule tail. I hear Maggie suck in her breath. 'Uhnnnh', is what it sounds like. Like when you see the wriggling end of a snake just in front of your foot on the road. 'Uhnnnh.'

Dee next. A dress down to the ground, in this hot weather. A dress so loud it hurts my eyes. There are yellows and oranges enough to throw back the light of the sun. I feel my whole face warming from the heat waves it throws out. Earrings gold, too, and hanging down to her shoulders. Bracelets dangling and making noises when she moves her arm up to shake the folds of the dress out of her armpits. The dress is loose and flows, and as she walks closer, I like it. I hear Maggie go 'Uhnnnh' again. It is her sister's hair. It stands straight up like the wool on a sheep. It is black as night and around the edges are two long pigtails that rope about like small lizards disappearing behind her ears.

'Wa-su-zo-Tean-o!' she says, coming on in that gliding way the dress makes her move. The short stocky fellow with the hair to his navel is all grinning and he follows up with 'Asalamalakim, my mother and sister!' He moves to hug Maggie but she falls back, right up against the back of my chair. I feel her trembling there and when I look up I see the perspiration falling off her chin.

'Don't get up,' says Dee. Since I am stout it takes something of a push. You can see me trying to move a second or two before I make it. She turns, showing white heels through her sandals, and goes back to the car. Out she peeks next with a Polaroid. She stoops down quickly and lines up picture after picture of me sitting there in front of the house with Maggie cowering behind me. She never takes a shot without making sure the house is included. When a cow comes nibbling around the edge of the yard she snaps it and me and Maggie *and* the house. Then she puts the Polaroid in the back seat of the car, and comes up and kisses me on the forehead.

Meanwhile Asalamalakim is going through motions with Maggie's hand. Maggie's hand is as limp as a fish, and probably as cold, despite the sweat, and she keeps trying to pull it back. It looks like Asalamalakim wants to shake hands but wants to do it fancy. Or maybe he don't know how people shake hands. Anyhow, he soon gives up on Maggie.

'Well,' I say. 'Dee.'

'No, Mama,' she says. 'Not "Dee," Wangero Leewanika Kemanjo!'

'What happened to "Dee"?' I wanted to know.

'She's dead,' Wangero said. 'I couldn't bear it any longer, being named after the people who oppress me.'

'You know as well as me you was named after your aunt Dicie,' I said. Dicie is my sister. She named Dee. We called her 'Big Dee' after Dee was born.

'But who was *she* named after?' asked Wangero.

'I guess after Grandma Dee,' I said.

'And who was she named after?' asked Wangero.

'Her mother,' I said, and saw Wangero was getting tired. 'That's about as far back as I can trace it,' I said. Though, in fact, I probably could have carried it back beyond the Civil War through the branches.

'Well,' said Asalamalakim, 'there you are.'

'Uhnnnh,' I heard Maggie say.

'There I was not,' I said, 'before "Dicie" cropped up in our family, so why should I try to trace it that far back?'

He just stood there grinning, looking down on me like somebody inspecting a Model A car. Every once in a while he and Wangero sent eye signals over my head.

'How do you pronounce this name?' I asked.

'You don't have to call me by it if you don't want to,' said Wangero.

'Why shouldn't I?' I asked. 'If that's what you want us to call you, we'll call you.'

'I know it might sound awkward at first,' said Wangero.

'I'll get used to it,' I said. 'Ream it out again.'

Well, soon we got the name out of the way. Asalamalakim had a name twice as long and three times as hard. After I tripped over it two or three times he told me to just call him Hakim-a-barber. I wanted to ask him was he a barber, but I didn't really think he was, so I didn't ask.

'You must belong to those beef-cattle peoples down the road,' I said. They said 'Asalamalakim' when they met you, too, but they didn't shake hands. Always too busy: feeding the cattle, fixing the fences, putting up salt-lick shelters, throwing down hay. When the white folks poisoned some of the herd the men stayed up all night with rifles in their hands. I walked a mile and a half just to see the sight.

Hakim-a-barber said, 'I accept some of their doctrines, but farming and raising cattle is not my style.' (They didn't tell me, and I didn't ask, whether Wangero (Dee) had really gone and married him.)

We sat down to eat and right away he said he didn't eat collards and pork was unclean. Wangero, though, went on through the chitlins and corn bread, the greens and everything else. She talked a blue streak over the sweet potatoes. Everything delighted her. Even the fact that we still used the benches her daddy made for the table when we couldn't afford to buy chairs.

'Oh, Mama!' she cried. Then turned to Hakim-a-barber. 'I never knew how lovely these benches are. You can feel the rump prints,' she said, running her hands underneath her and along the bench. Then she gave a sigh and her hand closed over Grandma Dee's butter dish. 'That's it!' she said. 'I knew there was something I wanted to ask you if I could have.' She jumped up from the table and went over in the corner where the churn stood, the milk in it clabber by now. She looked at the churn and looked at it.

'This churn top is what I need,' she said. 'Didn't Uncle Buddy whittle it out of a tree you all used to have?'

'Yes,' I said.

'Uh huh,' she said happily. 'And I want the dasher, too.'

'Uncle Buddy whittle that, too?' asked the barber.

Dee (Wangero) looked up at me.

'Aunt Dee's first husband whittled the dash,' said Maggie so low you almost couldn't hear her. 'His name was Henry, but they called him Stash.'

'Maggie's brain is like an elephant's,' Wangero said, laughing. 'I can use the churn top as a centrepiece for the alcove table,' she said, sliding a plate over the churn, 'and I'll think of something artistic to do with the dasher.'

When she finished wrapping the dasher the handle stuck out. I took it for a moment in my hands. You didn't even have to look close to see where hands pushing the dasher up and down to make butter had left a kind of sink in the wood. In fact, there were a lot of small sinks; you could see where thumbs and fingers had sunk into the wood. It was beautiful light yellow wood, from a tree that grew in the yard where Big Dee and Stash had lived.

After dinner Dee (Wangero) went to the trunk at the foot of my bed and started rifling through it. Maggie hung back in the kitchen over the dishpan. Out came Wangero with two quilts. They had been pieced by Grandma Dee and then Big Dee and me had hung them on the quilt frames on the front porch and quilted them. One was in the Lone Star pattern. The other was Walk Around the Mountain. In both of them were scraps of dresses Grandma Dee had worn fifty and more years ago. Bits and pieces of Grandpa Jarrell's Paisley shirts. And one teeny faded blue piece, about the size of a penny matchbox, that was from Great Grandpa Ezra's uniform that he wore in the Civil War.

'Mama,' Wangero said sweet as a bird. 'Can I have these old quilts?'

I heard something fall in the kitchen, and a minute later the kitchen door slammed.

'Why don't you take one or two of the others?' I asked. 'These old things was just done by me and Big Dee from some tops your grandma pieced before she died.'

'No,' said Wangero. 'I don't want those. They are stitched around the borders by machine.'

'That'll make them last better,' I said.

'That's not the point,' said Wangero. 'These are all pieces of dresses Grandma used to wear. She did all this stitching by hand.

Imagine!' She held the quilts securely in her arms, stroking them.

'Some of the pieces, like those lavender ones, come from old clothes her mother handed down to her,' I said, moving up to touch the quilts. Dee (Wangero) moved back just enough so that I couldn't reach the quilts. They already belonged to her.

'Imagine!' she breathed again, clutching them closely to her bosom.

'The truth is,' I said, 'I promised to give them quilts to Maggie, for when she marries John Thomas.'

She gasped like a bee had stung her.

'Maggie can't appreciate these quilts!' she said. 'She'd probably be backward enough to put them to everyday use.'

'I reckon she would,' I said. 'God knows I been saving 'em for long enough with nobody using 'em. I hope she will!' I didn't want to bring up how I had offered Dee (Wangero) a quilt when she went away to college. Then she had told me they were old-fashioned, out of style.

'But they're *priceless*!' she was saying now, furiously; for she has a temper. 'Maggie would put them on the bed and in five years they'd be in rags. Less than that!'

'She can always make some more,' I said. 'Maggie knows how to quilt.'

Dee (Wangero) looked at me with hatred. 'You just will not understand. The point is these quilts, *these* quilts!'

'Well,' I said, stumped. 'What would *you* do with them?'

'Hang them,' she said. As if that was the only thing you *could* do with quilts.

Maggie by now was standing in the door. I could almost hear the sound her feet made as they scraped over each other.

'She can have them, Mama,' she said, like somebody used to never winning anything, or having anything reserved for her. 'I can 'member Grandma Dee without the quilts.'

I looked at her hard. She had filled her bottom lip with checker-berry snuff and it gave her face a kind of dopey, hangdog look. It was Grandma Dee and Big Dee who taught her how to quilt herself. She stood there with her scarred hands hidden in the folds of her skirt. She looked at her sister with something like fear but she wasn't mad at her. This was Maggie's portion. This was the way she knew God to work.

When I looked at her like that something hit me in the top of my head and ran down to the soles of my feet. Just like when I'm in church and the spirit of God touches me and I get happy and shout. I did something I never had done before: hugged Maggie to me, then dragged her on into the room, snatched the quilts out of Miss Wangero's hands and dumped them into Maggie's lap. Maggie just sat there on my bed with her mouth open.

'Take one or two of the others,' I said to Dee.

But she turned without a word and went out to Hakim-a-barber.

'You just don't understand,' she said, as Maggie and I came out to the car.

'What don't I understand?' I wanted to know.

'Your heritage,' she said. And then she turned to Maggie, kissed her, and said, 'You ought to try to make something of yourself, too, Maggie. It's really a new day for us. But from the way you and Mama still live you'd never know it.'

She put on some sunglasses that hid everything above the tip of her nose and her chin.

Maggie smiled; maybe at the sunglasses. But a real smile, not scared. After we watched the car dust settle I asked Maggie to bring me a dip of snuff. And then the two of us sat there just enjoying, until it was time to go in the house and go to bed.

ELIZABETH JANE HOWARD

Child's Play

'Walking out on her in the middle of the night! I'm not easily shocked, but that shocks me!'

His conversation, she thought, was full of exceptions he made to his own rules. 'They've only been married a few weeks—it's just a tiff.'

'I dare say.' He stretched out a sunburned muscular arm, reached for a ginger-nut and popped it whole into his mouth. Speaking through it, he went on: 'But he's got his own way out of it, hasn't he? It's he who's off to Scotland, spoiling her holiday and leaving her on her own. Poor little thing! She's only eighteen—only a child!'

'Shirley won't be on her own: she's coming down to us just the same.'

He said nothing for a moment, swilled back the rest of his chestnut-coloured tea, wiped his moustache with a huge, navy handkerchief, and thrusting it back into his breeches pocket pronounced, 'Well! It may sound funny to you, but *I* don't like the idea of *my* daughter being mucked about. It annoys me, that's all. Gets my goat.'

There was silence in the kitchen while Kate Ewbank did not retort, 'She's my daughter too, isn't she? How do you know she's being mucked about?' or simply, 'You don't say!' Years of not airing them had cramped and damped her responses into this kind of thing which she would not sink to out loud.

The stable clock struck five and Brian Ewbank got to his feet, collecting his old tweed jacket from the back of his chair. Then, stooping slightly to see himself in it, he combed his thick, wavy grey hair in front of the small mirror that hung by the sink. 'You'll be fetching her from the station, then?'

'I will.'

The Ewbanks lived in what had been the coachman's cottage near a large Victorian stable block built round three sides of a courtyard. It had been designed to serve the huge neo-gothic house that was now a girls' boarding school set in vast, semi-derelict grounds of parkland and wooded drives. At five-thirty on summer term-time evenings he took a flock of girls, chiefly called Sarah and Caroline, on bulging, grass-fed ponies for a ride. They called him Brian behind his back, but he was really Captain Ewbank, and they held interminable conferences about whether his marriage was happy, or a tragic failure.

The moment Kate was alone, Marty, the tortoise-shell cat, slammed through the cat door with a mouse in her jaws. She tossed it under a chair, mentioned it several times in a high-pitched voice until she had forced Kate to meet her glassy, insolent gaze, and then began to crunch it up like a club sandwich. She liked Kate, in a limited way, to share her triumphs. In ten seconds the mouse was gone, she had drunk a saucer of milk and was polishing her spotless paws. She kept herself in a gleaming state of perpetual readiness—like a fire engine.

When she had cleared the tea, Kate went up to make the bed in Shirley's old room, in case she would rather sleep there than in the twin beds pushed together to make a double in the spare room. She also moved the jar of marigolds and pinks. She wanted Shirley to feel welcome. After that, she could not think at all what else she ought to do, and stood motionless, wondering what it could possibly be. But then, as sometimes nowadays, a moment after she had stopped physically moving and was still, despair engulfed her, as dense, as sudden and palpable as stepping into a rain-cloud or a fog. Senses of futility and failure fused; then the pall receded, leaving her with a feeling of weakness and mediocrity.

Percy was calling from his room, which was downstairs by the front door. Whenever she thought of him, she had to pull herself together. 'You still have your health,' she told herself. Apart from a touch of arthritis, migraines that irregularly punctured her attempts to face up to things, and these freakish sweats—hot flushes by name and as amusing to those unencumbered by them as piles or gout—she had little to complain about, whereas poor old Percy . . .

He had somehow got wind of the fact that she was going out in the car; must have heard Brian mentioning the station, although goodness knows he was deaf enough when he felt like it. By the time she got to him, he had levered himself to his feet with one hand perilously heavy on the corner of his loaded card-table. He had always borne a marked resemblance to Boris Karloff, and since his—fortunately mild—stroke now looked astonishingly like that actor in the role of Frankenstein's Monster. He'd got his speech painfully back, but he kept it to a minimum.

'I'm only going to fetch Shirley from the station, Father.'

'Shoes,' he said, his hopeful smile undimmed. 'Outdoor shoes.' He pointed with his stick to where his black shoes—as sleek and polished as a pair of police cars—were parked beneath his wardrobe. But his gesture with the stick involved further weight upon the card-table; it tipped, and its formidable coverage fell and rolled all over the floor as he lurched involuntarily on to his bed in a sitting position.

'Whoops-a-daisy,' he said, smiling again to show he was all right, and stuck one of his dreadful old feet with its Walt Disney ogre's toenails almost into her face as she knelt recovering his travelling clock, his pills, his spilled water-carafe, his spectacles, his address book that he kept up to date by crossing off his friends as they died, his saucer that he'd used for grape pips, a couple of chessmen he'd been mending and a plastic heart-shaped box in which he kept alternate rows of false teeth at night.

'Percy, dear, there isn't time: I'll be late. I won't be long.'

His lower lip trembled ponderously, like a baby's, working up to a scene; he withdrew his foot, and then, with a look so cunning that it was pathetic, shot the other one out at her.

'Oh—all *right* then,' she said, and fetched his socks.

In the tack room, Eunice, the stable-girl, was applying mascara to the double pair of false eyelashes that were her second most salient feature. Brian knew that she had heard him come in, but he also knew what he thought she liked. Coming up behind her, he put a large hand over each heavily confined breast, and squeezed them like someone tooting a horn. She squealed.

'Bry—*yern*!'

'I'll be a bit late tonight. Mind you wait.'

She did not answer, but he knew she would.

In the train from Manchester to London, Shirley decided over and over again that her marriage was a total, utter, flop. It must be, if in just over eight weeks they could have a row like that. After he had gone off ('Please yourself!')—what a filthy, *stupid*, *childish* thing to say!—she had never cried so much before in her life; in fact she couldn't believe he'd only been gone twenty minutes, as she discovered he had when she went to wash her face and happened to look at her watch. She'd cleared up the kitchen with meticulous care, wasn't going to let him put her in the wrong about a wife's mess in the flat, but she'd thrown away the sausage rolls so that he wouldn't have anything to eat when he came back—serve him right. But he hadn't *come* back. Instead, when she was frantic with waiting and wanting to tell him what she thought of him, he'd rung to say he was staying the night with friends. She'd been icy on the telephone, but the moment she'd rung off, she'd burst into tears again. Then, like a fool, she'd waited to see him in the morning, but he still didn't come back, and she'd missed the express and had to catch a slow train. It was a failure all right.

By the time she'd changed stations in London and caught the four-twenty from Charing Cross, her whole life with him had begun to seem faintly unreal. She hated the flat, she hated Manchester—she didn't know a single person there, she missed the country, she hated the housework and the awful, endless business of shopping for boring petty things, getting food ready and clearing it up. None of it had turned out at all as she had imagined. Beforehand, she'd thought of being married as candlelit dinners, friends dropping in, using all the presents, setting the table as perfectly as she did her face, moving in the television world (Douglas was a cameraman), Douglas's friends admiring her, envying him, sometimes even making him a little jealous . . . they'd bring her flowers and chocs and ask her advice about their girl-friends. None of this had happened at all. Instead, he'd come back at awful hours—never the same time—fagged out, only talking about his work and a whole lot of people she never met; when she wasn't bored, she was lonely. She missed her friends and her life at home and Dad who'd always been so decent to her . . .

As they changed into their riding clothes, Sarah Hughenden said to Caroline Polsden-Lacey, 'I tell you one thing. He's got the most super heavenly sweat.'

'Who?'

'Brian—stupid. He smells of smoked salmon.'

'How do you know?'

'I sort of fell up against him.'

'Sarah! You really *are*!'

It took Kate nearly half an hour to get her father dressed and into the car. In spite of her telling him it was a hot day, he wore a vest, flannel shirt, thick Norfolk jacket, his burberry and a cashmere muffler she'd given him last Christmas. He also took his pocket book of British birds in case a British bird got near enough—and stayed still long enough—for him to identify it. It was indeed hot. The wild roses were blanched by the heat; buttercups glittered in the rich grass, the chestnut trees lining the unkempt drive had leaves that were already shabby from drought, and the Herefords clumped together under them in a miasma of flies. Without glancing at him, Kate could feel the intensity with which her father was looking out of the car window; she was unhappily divided between going slowly to give him the maximum enjoyment, and not being late for Shirley, who would anyway not be pleased at his making a third in the car. It was extraordinary, she felt, how much of life consisted of having to displease somebody.

As Shirley walked down the platform, she could see her mother standing at the barrier, dressed, as usual, in a faded flowered cotton skirt, a blue tee-shirt and sandals, her dark glasses pushed up over her fringe. From the distance, she looked like a dowdy, rather arty girl. At least, Shirley thought, I've stopped her wearing trousers—she really wasn't the shape for them.

They kissed, rather awkwardly; neither was sure what degree of warmth was appropriate to the occasion. Kate said quickly,

'I'm terribly sorry, but I simply had to bring Percy.'

'Surely you didn't *have* to.'

'You know how he feels about going out in the car. How are you?' She looked at her daughter's incredibly pretty, apparently unravaged face, turning sulky now at the news about her grandfather.

'I'm all right,' stony, snubbing, walking ahead of her mother in silence to the car.

Percy was dragging a dusty fruit-drop from his overcoat pocket. He had recently taken to eating them with the cellophane wrappers still on, and enjoyed being asked why he did so, so that he could say he always ate his sweet papers. He longed to confound people by turning out always to have done something that surprised them. He popped the sweet in just as they got into the car, but when neither of them asked him, he took the sweet out again, dropped it on the floor and ground his foot on it as though it was a cigarette.

'Here's Shirley,' said Kate, pretending not to notice.

'So I see. Had a good term?'

'She hasn't been to school, Father. She's been in Manchester, with Douglas.'

He crunched his dentures and didn't answer. Kate thought he was sulking because he'd got something wrong, but really he was peeved because he hadn't embarrassed Shirley with his pretended memory lapse (he knew she wasn't at school, and who on earth was Douglas?).

'How's my father?'

'He's fine. He's taking the evening ride.'

'What's the new stable-girl like?'

'I've hardly seen her. She's called Eunice.'

'Is she attractive?'

Kate paused before replying evenly: 'Oh yes, I should think she's quite attractive.' It had recently begun to amaze her that in all these years, Shirley had never noticed anything . . .

'. . . and I'm not a child! Why should he suddenly spoil all our plans just because he wants to work on his wretched film! If he can't be bothered even to think what I might feel, why on earth did he ever want to marry me?' She was sitting cross-legged on the floor of her room, having a post-cry cigarette, and looking, Kate thought, very childish indeed.

'Perhaps he *had* to do the job?' she suggested—very gently, but not gently enough.

'Whenever I try to tell you anything, you always take the other person's side! You *always* do!'

'I didn't mean it to sound like that: I'm only trying to understand. I can't believe he simply wanted to hurt your feelings.'

'He doesn't care about my feelings. All he cares about is his bloody film unit. He never stops thinking and talking about them.'

'Could you have gone to Scotland with him?'

'He never said so. Anyway, I've told him it's not my idea of a holiday to sit about cooped up in some ghastly hotel while he's out on an oil rig or something. He told me he'd got three days' leave, and he promised to come home. He *promised* me.' She thrust her knuckles under her firm little chin and glared into space. After a minute, she said:

'The truth is, it's got to be all or nothing for me. I'm jealous of his work.' She looked at her mother with something like triumph. 'That's what it is! I expect him to put me first, and he doesn't, and it makes me jealous!'

The discovery seemed actually to relieve her. After it, she became much easier to reason with: allowed Kate to discuss with her the possibility of getting some sort of part-time job, admitted that Douglas had said something about standing in for a friend whose wife was having a baby, and even volunteered that she could be terrible when she didn't get her own way. She was of an age, Kate thought, when self-recrimination seemed to be unaccompanied by pain. 'I know I've got a hot temper!' She was simply very young for a situation into which her appearance had trapped her so early; an only and childish child, which Kate, in her turn, had to admit meant that she was to some degree spoiled, although with Brian as a father, how could she have prevented it? He had always defended her, backed her up whatever she did . . .

'Where's the most beautiful girl in the world?'

He was standing at the bottom of the staircase, and Kate, in the kitchen doorway, watched her as she stood at the top—dressed now in her old jeans and a sleeveless green angora jerkin: she posed for a moment, and then hurled herself down—hair flying, eyes shining—into his arms. He gave a great laugh, and held her at arm's length.

'Let's look at you, *Mrs* Thornton: let's have a look.'

'I'm fine, Daddy.' But Kate could hear that little touch of the gallant waif—knew that those dog-violet eyes were gazing at her father with the expression of quivering self-reliance that he would find irresistible. Was she play-acting, or was it real? Certainly their relationship was like the way fathers and daughters went on in bad films: even in these few weeks she had forgotten how much and how quickly it exasperated her.

'Mrs Thornton!' He had picked up her left hand now, and was contemplating the gold wedding-ring quizzically. 'To think I should live to see the day! I tell you one thing. I'm jealous of Mr Thornton.'

'You needn't be. Oh—you smell—*nice*!'

Kate was conscious of a small, but regular, hammer thudding

from somewhere inside her as she became miserably transfixed.

'And what, may I ask, does this call itself?' He caressed the fluffy green jerkin that seemed to be fastened only in one place just below her breasts, so that the sides flew out to reveal the slender rib cage, tiny waist and concave upper belly.

'Really, Daddy—you are impossible! Your own daughter!' Some luxuriant head-tossing, and his hairy wrists picked from the sides of her jeans.

'How do you get your hair to shine like that!'

'My herbal rinse.' Demure now, walking towards her, ahead of him, into the kitchen.

('How dare you behave like this!—In front of your wife! Behind your husband's back!') She needed two voices to scream it, but her body felt like some roaring conduit of surging blood, with a trap-door slammed shut in the bottom of her throat. As they approached her, she began fiddling unsteadily with the strawberries in the colander before her.

'Oh—strawberries! How fabulous!' Kate recognized the stringing-along-with-Mummy tone that so often came after what had gone before.

'Don't bother your mother now, she's busy, and I'm going to take you for a drink at the Woodman.' His hole-in-one technique, she called that.

'Oh—great! Let's ride, Dad: we can ride through the wood and up the lane.'

A few minutes later, they were gone. There had been a few last moments of 'Sure you don't want any help?' 'Sure you don't mind?' followed by 'We'll be back at half past on the dot—promise,' and then they were off. She was left alone in silence—except for the cold tap dripping and the distant, velvety gabble of Percy's radio.

She discovered that things were taking on a dirty, speckled appearance, and she fumbled in her bag to find the orange pills encased in foil that helped to prevent migraine. Cafergot had to be crunched up to work quickly, and she washed down the cheap, stale chocolate taste with a glass of tap water. She wanted a cigarette, but that would be fatal. What she must do was to sit quite still, and relax, but that only made it more difficult to stop what she had just been thinking. After trying for a bit, it seemed reasonable—even mild—simply to dislike them, compared with what she felt about herself.

They came back to supper in high spirits with half a bottle of gin. She didn't dare have a drink, but he made Shirley and himself a couple of John Collins with a tin of grapefruit juice and soda. Supper was cold, so it didn't matter when they had it, and she did Percy's tray while they finished their drinks. Brian was in his entertaining, expansive mood; taking off the little girls he taught to ride: 'Oh—Cuptain Ewbunk!' He was a good mimic—could do all the various off-white upper-class vowel sounds; could indicate the braces on their teeth, their stiff little pigtails below their hard velvet hats. He finished with a telling imitation of a fat and frightened girl being taught to jump. The sports mistress had many times told Kate how popular he was with the girls. And, of course, someone at the pub had thought Shirley was his girl-friend: Shirley thought that madly funny. She ate like a school-girl—three helpings of new potatoes and home-cooked tongue. 'It's so marvellous not cooking. I'm simply not the domesticated type, I've decided.' It wasn't until she returned from taking Percy his strawberries that she heard Brian say casually,

'There's no need for you to go back on Tuesday. Stay and help me knock some sense into that new pony. He's not safe for the children and he's not up to my weight.'

And Shirley, seeing her mother, said automatically: 'Oh—I couldn't. I'll have to go back.'

'Why not? If you stay a little extra, you might also knock some sense into that husband of yours.'

Kate said: 'Brian! Of course she must go back.'

'I don't see that. He shouldn't go flouncing off—out all night—that's no way to treat any woman—let alone your wife. Do him good to worry about her for a change.'

Kate turned to her daughter: 'Shirley, you don't really feel that you can—'

But Shirley, pouring cream on to her strawberries, said quickly: 'I was talking to Dad in the pub about it. I thought it would be interesting to know what another man thought, you know—'

'Damn right! Well, I think the sooner he learns that life doesn't entirely revolve round his blasted television the better. I mean, he'd made a plan with Shirley, and he ought to have stuck to it, that's what he ought to have done. I mean, she's never going to know where she is, is she? One minute he makes a promise—the next minute he breaks it. That's no way to treat *any* girl—let alone *my* girl. Well?' Magnanimity was momentarily extended to her: 'What do you think?'

She took a long breath trying to control her anger at his outrageous attitude and said coldly, 'I think you should mind your own business.'

Before she had finished speaking, the telephone rang, and Shirley, glad of the escape, ran to answer it. A second later, she was back: 'It's Douglas, I'm going to take it upstairs. Will you put the receiver back for me?'

When she had done so, and returned to the kitchen determined to stop the irresponsible mischief he was making, Kate found him on his feet, cramming hunting flask, pipe and tobacco into his pockets; his face suffused, set sullen, avoiding her eye.

'I'm off. Forgot to fetch that liniment from the vet. The grey's been knocking herself. Forgot it earlier.'

'Don't bother to tell me a pack of—'

'Tell her not to wait up. I've promised her a ride in the morning.'

'Brian, listen to me. Don't you dare interfere any more with her marriage. It's not fair: it's very wrong.' It sounded weak as she said it, and he seized the advantage.

'*I'm* not interfering. She asked me what I thought, and I told her. That's natural, isn't it? She's only a child. And why should my opinion be any more interfering than yours? Tell me that.'

'You know perfectly well why it is. And she's no longer a child. She's a married woman.'

'I *don't* know. And I don't care. I do—not—care a bugger—what do you think—about anything at all.'

He went, shutting, nearly slamming, the kitchen door behind him.

The telephone conversation seemed to be going on for ever. She supposed drearily that it must be a good sign they were talking at such length: she was sure Douglas cared. Poor boy, he was only twenty-two, had his way to make, and although he was reputed to be clever, cleverness was not particularly helpful when it came to making a marriage work—especially with someone as self-willed as Shirley. Could they, she and Brian, as parents, have stopped her marrying so young? If they had been united about it and had wanted to, she supposed they might just have—have made her wait longer, anyhow. But they were not united, and for different reasons neither of them had seen fit even to try. Brian had always thought that Shirley should have whatever she wanted, and she . . . she was ashamed of her reason—it wasn't even a reason really, just a hope, forlorn as it had turned out, that Brian would be—easier, a bit nicer to her, if Shirley simply wasn't there.

Her head felt as though someone had bruised something inside it rather badly, but she decided not to take any more of the migraine drug. When she had finished clearing supper, she noticed Shirley's cigarettes, and took one for something to do.

She heard Shirley ring off, and minutes later she strolled into the kitchen, cool, expressionless, clearly pleased with herself.

'Where's Dad?'

'He's gone out—said don't wait up.'

'I wouldn't dream of going to bed yet. Whew! It's hot!' She sat on the corner of the table, kicked off her shoes and put her bare feet on the arm of her father's chair. Her toenails were painted a pale, pearly pink.

'Well—is everything better now?'

'Douglas? Oh—fine. He's coming down tomorrow.'

'Shirley, I am glad. How has he managed to get away?'

'Oh—some change in the shooting schedule—I didn't bother. The point is, I've won!'

Kate looked at her. 'How do you mean?'

She repeated impatiently, 'I've won! He wanted me to go back—to meet him at the flat, but I told him come down here or else.' She leaned across the table to take a cigarette.

'I took one, I hope you don't mind.'

'Feel free. Got a light?'

Kate struck a match and held it out, watching her daughter's face as she bent her head, cigarette poised in the wide Cupid's-bow mouth, heavy lashes lowered over the violet eyes, calmly intent upon her first puff.

'But he'll have to go back again on Monday night, won't he? It hardly seems worth it for such a little time.'

'He thinks it's worth it. Any case, he had no choice. Daddy was quite right. He'll think twice before he ever walks out on me again. I haven't even told him I'll go back with him for sure.'

'Shirley! You can't behave like this! You're just *playing* at being married! You can't be so—'

'I can! I can! I'm perfectly serious. He wants far more from me than I want from him. He's more turned on than I am. Let him sweat.'

There was a brutal pause, then she added with some feeling: 'I *hate* being alone. I *hate* that flat. I *loathe* being tied down. Daddy said I could stay as long as I like.'

Then, perhaps aware of some fractional discomfort from her mother's silence, she rose from the table and began looking for her shoes.

'Where's he gone to at this time of night?'

'To put some liniment on a horse.'

'In the stables?'

Kate hesitated only a moment: 'I expect in the stables.'

After she had gone, Kate remained completely still: why had she done it? But she refused to consider why—simply sat at the table and followed Shirley: down the garden path to the gate, along the drive to the archway; she might pause there to see if there was a light in the stables, but there would be no light since none was needed. Would she go on, as Kate had done that first time, long ago, because there had been an urgent telephone message? It had been autumn then, and dark, but some instinct had driven her to the stables door, undone at the latch and ajar. The horses had shifted softly in their straw; moonlight, like a shaft of lemonade, had lain across the little empty coal-grate in the tack room and the place had the affectionate, sweet smell of warm horses and hay. She had stood there wondering (where could he have gone?), when, with shocking suddenness, and from just above her head, had come a high-pitched, explosively ugly and frightening laugh. Dead silence: she had heard her own heart beating . . . then a man's inaudible protest and heavy, sibilant, thrashing commotion. They were in the hay-loft; she had turned to see the ladder set squarely to its open trap. The laughter had begun moaning and she had fled. Since that first time, she had returned once or twice when he had hired new girls, but only enough to feed her reason, to keep her fearful hatred sane, because she had known that if there was no reason for feeling as she did, she must be mad.

She had done nothing. Shirley had been determined to go—she had simply not prevented her.

She became aware of Percy calling. He might have been calling for some time; for once she had forgotten him, and she hurried, with a feeling of shame, to his room. She had got him undressed and into bed before his supper, but had not even fetched his supper tray, let alone settled him for the night.

He gave her his gentle lop-sided smile as she came in; he had been sticking things into his scrap-book and seemed not to have noticed the time. As soon as he saw her, he began hunting through the back pages.

'You haven't eaten your strawberries!'

He gave her a reproachful look. 'Too many stones.' He was still searching in his book. 'Here! Found Douglas. Douglas and Shirley marriage.' It was the wedding picture cut out of the local paper. 'Douglas,' he explained again, in case she wasn't sure.

'Yes,' she agreed. She helped him out of bed to the lavatory, and got his pillows right for the night. His sheets seemed always to be covered with toast crumbs. She filled up his water-carafe, opened his window and put the box for his false teeth handy. When he was in bed again, she bent to kiss his cold, papery-dry forehead and he closed his eyes as though for a benediction. She picked up the supper tray and was turning to go when he suddenly thrust a screwed-up piece of paper at her, pushing it into her hand as though he was stopping up a chink.

'For you. To read.'

'All right, Father dear.' He sometimes wrote lists of what he needed: glue, fruit-drops, aspirin—that kind of thing.

'Read later.'

'Yes. I will.'

In the kitchen, Shirley stood heating something on the stove. She must have heard her mother come in, but neither turned round nor spoke.

Kate said: 'You're back.' She had begun to feel afraid.

'So it would seem.' Hostility was naked. She poured the contents of the saucepan into a mug and turned off the heat. 'Why did you let me go to the stables? You knew what was going on, didn't you? What made you do that?'

Kate tried to say something, but she was not a liar, and could not.

'I suppose you thought it would turn me against him, and make me sorry for you! Well it hasn't. I suppose you thought that as you don't enjoy screwing, you'd put me off it! It's him I'm sorry for—having to go to those lengths. I despise you—more completely than I've ever despised anyone in my life! Letting me go out there was just typical of how horrible you really are. Drab, and smug and self-righteous. Underneath it—you're just nasty. Nobody could love you—not a single person in the world!' Her hand holding the milk was shaking, but she didn't spill any—just walked out of the room, shutting the kitchen door behind her.

Kate stood, heart hammering, listening to the steps going away from her to the bedroom above. She put up her hand, to hold her face together, and the piece of screwed-up paper fell on to the table. When she smoothed it out the note, written large and quavering with a black felt pen, read: 'Thank you, my Darling, for the Lovely Outing in your Motor Car. Today.'

She read it for a long time. The message, with its drops of grateful love, made a slow, unsteady course, until eventually, in the end, it reached her.

Muriel Spark

The First Year of My Life

I was born on the first day of the second month of the last year of the First World War, a Friday. Testimony abounds that during the first year of my life I never smiled. I was known as the baby whom nothing and no one could make smile. Everyone who knew me then has told me so. They tried very hard, singing and bouncing me up and down, jumping around, pulling faces. Many times I was told this later by my family and their friends; but, anyway, I knew it at the time.

You will shortly be hearing of that new school of psychology, or maybe you have heard of it already, which, after long and far-adventuring research and experimenting, has established that all of the young of the human species are omniscient. Babies, in their waking hours, know everything that is going on everywhere in the world; they can tune in to any conversation they choose, switch on to any scene. We have all experienced this power. It is only after the first year that it was brainwashed out of us; for it is demanded of us by our immediate environment that we grow to be of use to it in a practical way. Gradually, our know-all brain-cells are blacked out, although traces remain in some individuals in the form of E.S.P., and in the adults of some primitive tribes.

It is not a new theory. Poets and philosophers, as usual, have been there first. But scientific proof is now ready and to hand. Perhaps the final touches are being put to the new manifesto in some cell at Harvard University. Any day now it will be given to the world, and the world will be convinced.

Let me therefore get my word in first, because I feel pretty sure, now, about the authenticity of my remembrance of things past. My autobiography, as I very well perceived at the time, started in the very worst year that the world had ever seen so far. Apart from being born bedridden and toothless, unable to raise myself on the pillow or utter anything but farmyard squawks or police-siren wails, my bladder and my bowels totally out of control, I was further depressed by the curious behaviour of the two-legged mammals around me. There were those black-dressed people, females of the species to which I appeared to belong, saying they had lost their sons. I slept a great deal. Let them go and find their sons. It was like the special pin for my nappies which my mother or some other hoverer dedicated to my care was always losing. These careless women in black lost their husbands and their brothers. Then they came to visit my mother and clucked and crowed over my cradle. I was not amused.

'Babies never really smile till they're three months old,' said my mother. 'They're not *supposed* to smile till they're three months old.'

My brother, aged six, marched up and down with a toy rifle over his shoulder.

> The grand old Duke of York
> He had ten thousand men;
> He marched them up to the top of the hill
> And he marched them down again.
>
> And when they were up, they were up.
> And when they were down, they were down.
> And when they were neither down nor up
> They were neither up nor down.

'Just listen to him!'

'Look at him with his rifle!'

I was about ten days old when Russia stopped fighting. I tuned in to the Czar, a prisoner, with the rest of his family, since evidently the country had put him off his throne and there had been a revolution not long before I was born. Everyone was talking about it. I tuned in to the Czar. 'Nothing would ever induce me to sign the treaty of Brest-Litovsk,' he said to his wife. Anyway, nobody had asked him to.

At this point I was sleeping twenty hours a day to get my strength up. And from what I discerned in the other four hours of the day I knew I was going to need it. The Western Front on my frequency was sheer blood, mud, dismembered bodies, blistering crashes, hectic flashes of light in the night skies, explosions, total terror. Since it was plain I had been born into a bad moment in the history of the world, the future bothered me, unable as I was to raise my head from the pillow and as yet only twenty inches long. 'I truly wish I were a fox or a bird,' D. H. Lawrence was writing to somebody. Dreary old creeping Jesus. I fell asleep.

Red sheets of flame shot across the sky. It was 21 March, the fiftieth day of my life, and the German Spring Offensive had started before my morning feed. Infinite slaughter. I scowled at the scene, and made an effort to kick out. But the attempt was feeble. Furious, and impatient for some strength, I wailed for my feed. After which I stopped wailing but continued to scowl.

> The grand old Duke of York
> He had ten thousand men . . .

They rocked the cradle. I never heard a sillier song. Over in Berlin and Vienna the people were starving, freezing, striking, rioting and yelling in the streets. In London everyone was bustling to work and muttering that it was time the whole damn business was over.

The big people around me bared their teeth; that meant a smile, it meant they were pleased or amused. They spoke of ration cards for meat and sugar and butter.

'Where will it all end?'

I went to sleep. I woke and tuned in to Bernard Shaw who was telling someone to shut up. I switched over to Joseph Conrad who, strangely enough, was saying precisely the same thing. I still didn't think it worth a smile, although it was expected of me any day now. I got on to Turkey. Women draped in black huddled and chattered in their harems; yak-yak-yak. This was boring, so I came back to home base.

In and out came and went the women in British black. My mother's brother, dressed in his uniform, came coughing. He had been poison-gassed in the trenches. '*Tout le monde à la bataille!*' declaimed Marshal Foch the old swine. He was now Commander-in-Chief of the Allied Forces. My uncle coughed from deep within his lungs, never to recover but destined to return to the Front. His brass buttons gleamed in the firelight. I weighed twelve pounds by now; I stretched and kicked for exercise, seeing that I had a lifetime before me, coping with this crowd. I took six feeds a day and kept most of them down by the time the *Vindictive* was sunk in Ostend harbour, on which day I kicked with special vigour in my bath.

In France the conscripted soldiers leap-frogged over the dead on the advance and littered the fields with limbs and hands, or drowned in the mud. The strongest men on all fronts were dead before I was born. Now the sentries used bodies for barricades and the fighting men were unhealthy from the start. I checked my toes and my fingers, knowing I was going to need them. *The Playboy of the Western World* was playing at the Court Theatre in London, but occasionally I beamed over to the House of Commons which made me drop off gently to sleep. Generally, I preferred the Western Front where one got the true state of affairs. It was essential to know the worst, blood and explosions and all, for one had to be prepared, as the boy scouts said. Virginia Woolf yawned and reached for her diary. Really, I preferred the Western Front.

In the fifth month of my life I could raise my head from my pillow and hold it up. I could grasp the objects that were held out to me. Some of these things rattled and squawked. I gnawed on them to get my teeth started. 'She hasn't smiled yet?' said the dreary old aunties. My mother, on the defensive, said I was probably one of those late smilers. On my wavelength Pablo Picasso was getting married and early in that month of July the Silver Wedding of King George V and Queen Mary was celebrated in joyous pomp at St Paul's Cathedral. They drove through the streets of London with their children. Twenty-five years of domestic happiness. A lot of fuss and ceremonial handing over of swords went on at the Guildhall where the King and Queen received a cheque for £53,000 to dispose of for charity as they thought fit. *Tout le monde à la bataille!* Income tax in England had reached six shillings in the pound. Everyone was talking about the Silver Wedding; yak-yak-yak, and ten days later the Czar and his family, now in Siberia, were invited to descend to a little room in the basement. Crack, crack, went the guns; screams and blood all over the place, and that was the end of the Romanoffs. I flexed my muscles. 'A fine healthy baby,' said the doctor; which gave me much satisfaction.

Tout le monde à la bataille! That included my gassed uncle. My health had improved to the point where I was able to crawl in my playpen. Bertrand Russell was still cheerily in prison for writing something seditious about pacifism. Tuning in as usual to the Front Lines it looked as if the Germans were winning all the battles yet losing the war. And so it was. The upper-income people were upset about the income tax at six shillings to the pound. But all women over thirty got the vote. 'It seems a long time to wait,' said one of my drab old aunts, aged twenty-two. The speeches in the House of Commons always sent me to sleep which was why I missed, at the actual time, a certain oration by Mr Asquith following the armistice on 11 November. Mr Asquith was a greatly esteemed former prime minister later to be an Earl, and had been ousted by Mr Lloyd George. I clearly heard Asquith, in private, refer to Lloyd George as 'that damned Welsh goat'.

The armistice was signed and I was awake for that. I pulled myself on to my feet with the aid of the bars of my cot. My teeth were coming through very nicely in my opinion, and well worth all the trouble I was put to in bringing them forth. I weighed twenty pounds. On all the world's fighting fronts the men killed in action or dead of wounds numbered 8,538,315 and the warriors wounded and maimed were 21,219,452. With these figures in mind I sat up in my high chair and banged my spoon on the table. One of my mother's black-draped friends recited:

> I have a rendezvous with Death
> At some disputed barricade,
> When spring comes back with rustling shade
> And apple blossoms fill the air—
> I have a rendezvous with Death.

Most of the poets, they said, had been killed. The poetry made them dab their eyes with clean white handkerchiefs.

Next February on my first birthday, there was a birthday-cake with one candle. Lots of children and their elders. The war had been over two months and twenty-one days. 'Why doesn't she smile?' My brother was to blow out the candle. The elders were talking about the war and the political situation. Lloyd George and Asquith. Asquith and Lloyd George. I remembered recently having switched on to Mr Asquith at a private party where he had been drinking a lot. He was playing cards and when he came to cut the cards he tried to cut a large box of matches by mistake. On another occasion I had seen him putting his arm around a lady's shoulder in a Daimler motor car, and generally behaving towards her in a very friendly fashion. Strangely enough she said, 'If you don't stop this nonsense immediately I'll order the chauffeur to stop and I'll get out.' Mr Asquith replied, 'And pray, what reason will you give?' Well anyway it was my feeding time.

The guests arrived for my birthday. It was so sad, said one of the black widows, so sad about Wilfred Owen who was killed so late in the war, and she quoted from a poem of his:

> What passing bells for these who die as cattle?
> Only the monstrous anger of the guns.

The children were squealing and toddling around. One was sick and another wet the floor and stood with his legs apart gaping at the puddle. All was mopped up. I banged my spoon on the table of my high chair.

> But I've a rendezvous with Death
> At midnight in some flaming town;
> When spring trips north again this year,
> And I to my pledged word am true,
> I shall not fail that rendezvous.

More parents and children arrived. One stout man who was warming his behind at the fire, said, 'I always think those words of Asquith's after the armistice were so apt . . .'

They brought the cake close to my high chair for me to see, with the candle shining and flickering above the pink icing. 'A pity she never smiles.'

'She'll smile in time,' my mother said, obviously upset.

'What Asquith told the House of Commons just after the war,' said that stout gentleman with his backside to the fire, '—so apt, what Asquith said. He said that the war has cleansed and purged the world, by God! I recall his actual words: "All things have become new. In this great cleansing and purging it has been the privilege of our country to play her part . . ." '

That did it. I broke into a decided smile and everyone noticed it, convinced that it was provoked by the fact that my brother had blown out the candle on the cake. 'She smiled!' my mother exclaimed. And everyone was clucking away about how I was smiling. For good measure I crowed like a demented raven. 'My baby's smiling!' said my mother.

'It was the candle on her cake,' they said.

The cake be damned. Since that time I have grown to smile quite naturally, like any other healthy and house-trained person, but when I really mean a smile, deeply felt from the core, then to all intents and purposes it comes in response to the words uttered in the House of Commons after the First World War by the distinguished, the immaculately dressed and the late Mr Asquith.

RUTH PRAWER JHABVALA

How I Became a Holy Mother

On my 23rd birthday when I was fed up with London and all the rest of it—boyfriends, marriages (two), jobs (modelling), best friends that are suddenly your best enemies—I had this letter from my girl friend Sophie who was finding peace in an ashram in South India:

> '. . . oh Katie you wouldn't know me I'm such a changed person. I get up at 5—*a.m.*!!! I am an absolute vegetarian let alone no meat no eggs either and am making fabulous progress with my meditation. I have a special mantra of my own that Swamiji gave me at a special ceremony and I say it over and over in my mind. The sky here is blue all day long and I sit by the sea and watch the waves and have good thoughts . . .'

But by the time I got there Sophie had left—under a cloud, it seemed, though when I asked what she had done, they wouldn't tell me but only pursed their lips and looked sorrowful. I didn't stay long in that place. I didn't like the bitchy atmosphere, and that Swamiji was a big fraud, anyone could see that. I couldn't understand how a girl as sharp as Sophie had ever let herself be fooled by such a type. But I suppose if you want to be fooled you are. I found that out in some of the other ashrams I went to. There were some quite intelligent people in all of them but the way they just shut their eyes to certain things, it was incredible. It is not my rôle in life to criticize others so I kept quiet and went on to the next place. I went to quite a few of them. These ashrams are a cheap way to live in India and there is always company and it isn't bad for a few days provided you don't get involved in their power politics. I was amazed to come across quite a few people I had known over the years and would never have expected to meet here. It is a shock when you see someone you had last met on the beach at St Tropez

274

now all dressed up in a saffron robe and meditating in some very dusty ashram in Madhya Pradesh. But really I could see their point because they were all as tired as I was of everything we had been doing and this certainly was different.

I enjoyed myself going from one ashram to the other and travelling all over India. Trains and buses are very crowded—I went third class, I had to be careful with my savings—but Indians can tell when you want to be left alone. They are very sensitive that way. I looked out of the window and thought my thoughts. After a time I became quite calm and rested. I hadn't brought too much stuff with me, but bit by bit I discarded most of that too till I had only a few things left that I could easily carry myself. I didn't even mind when my watch was pinched off me one night in a railway rest-room (so-called). I felt myself to be a changed person. Once, at the beginning of my travels, there was a man sitting next to me on a bus who said he was an astrologer. He was a very sensitive and philosophical person—and I must say I was impressed by how many such one meets in India, quite ordinary people travelling third class. After we had been talking for a time and he had told me the future of India for the next 40 years, suddenly out of the blue he said to me 'Madam, you have a very sad soul.' It was true. I thought about it for days afterwards and cried a bit to myself. I did feel sad inside myself and heavy like with a stone. But as time went on and I kept going round India—the sky always blue like Sophie had said, and lots of rivers and fields as well as desert—just quietly travelling and looking, I stopped feeling like that. Now I was as a matter of fact quite light inside as if that stone had gone.

Then I stopped travelling and stayed in this one place instead. I liked it better than any of the other ashrams for several reasons. One of them was that the scenery was very picturesque. This cannot be said of all ashrams as many of them seem to be in sort of dust bowls, or in the dirtier parts of very dirty holy cities or even cities that aren't holy at all but just dirty. But this ashram was built on the slope of a mountain, and behind it there were all the other mountains stretching right up to the snow-capped peaks of the Himalayas; and on the other side it ran down to the river which I will not say can have been very clean (with all those pilgrims dipping in it) but certainly looked clean from up above and not only clean but as clear and green as the sky was clear and blue. Also along the bank of the river there were many little pink temples with pink cones and they certainly made a pretty scene. Inside the ashram also the atmosphere was good which again cannot be said of all of them, far from it. But the reason the atmosphere was good here was because of the head of this ashram who was called Master. They are always called something like that—if not Swamiji then Maharaj-ji or Babaji or Maharishiji or Guruji; but this one was just called plain Master, in English.

He was full of pep and go. Early in the morning he would say 'Well what shall we do today!' and then plan some treat like all of us going for a swim in the river with a picnic lunch to follow. He didn't want anyone to have a dull moment or to fall into a depression which I suppose many there were apt to do, left to their own devices. In some ways he reminded me of those big business types that sometimes (in other days!) took me out to dinner. They too had that kind of superhuman energy and seemed to be stronger than other people. I forgot to say that Master was a big burly man, and as he didn't wear all that many clothes—usually only a loincloth—you could see just how big and burly he was. His head was large too and it was completely shaven so that it looked even larger. He wasn't ugly, not at all. Or perhaps if he was one forgot about it very soon because of all that dynamism.

As I said, the ashram was built on the slope of a mountain. I don't think it was planned at all but had just grown: there was one little room next to the other and the Meditation Hall and the dining hall and Master's quarters—whatever was needed was added and it all ran higgledy-piggledy down the mountain. I had one of the little rooms to myself and made myself very snug in there. The only furniture provided by the ashram was one string bed, but I bought a handloom rug from the Lepers Rehabilitation Centre and I also put up some pictures, like a Tibetan Mandala which was very colourful. Everyone liked my room and wanted to come and spend time there, but I was a bit cagey about that as I needed my privacy. I always had lots to do, like writing letters or washing my hair and I was also learning to play the flute. So I was quite happy and independent and didn't really need company though there was plenty of it, if and when needed.

There were Master's Indian disciples who were all learning to be swamis. They wanted to renounce the world and had shaved their heads and wore an orange sort of toga thing. When they were ready, Master was going to make them into full swamis. Most of these junior swamis were very young—just boys, some of them—but even those that weren't all that young were certainly so at heart. Sometimes they reminded me of a lot of school kids, they were so full of tricks and fun. But I think basically they were very serious—they couldn't not be, considering how they were renouncing and were supposed to be studying all sorts of very difficult things. The one I liked the best was called Vishwa. I liked him not only because he was the best looking, which he undoubtedly was, but I felt he had a lot going for him. Others said so too—in fact, they all said that Vishwa was the most advanced and was next in line for full initiation. I always let him come and talk to me in my room whenever he wanted to, and we had some interesting conversations.

Then there were Master's foreign disciples. They weren't so different from the other Europeans and Americans I had met in other ashrams except that the atmosphere here was so much better and that made them better too. They didn't have to fight with each other over Master's favours—I'm afraid that was very much the scene in some of the other ashrams which were like harems, the way they were all vying for the favour of their guru. But Master never encouraged that sort of relationship, and although of course many of them did have very strong attachments to him, he managed to keep them all healthy. And that's really saying something because, like in all the other ashrams, many of them were not healthy people; through no fault of their own quite often, they had just had a bad time and were trying to get over it.

Once Master said to me 'What about you, Katie?' This was when I was alone with him in his room. He had called me in for some dictation—we were all given little jobs to do for him from time to time, to keep us busy and happy I suppose. Just let me say a few words about his room and get it over with. It was *awful*. It had linoleum on the floor of the nastiest pattern, and green strip lighting, and the walls were painted green too and had been decorated with calendars and pictures of what were supposed to be gods and saints but might as well have been Bombay film stars, they were so fat and gaudy. Master and all the junior swamis were terribly proud of this room. Whenever he acquired anything new—like some plastic flowers in a hideous vase—he would call everyone to admire and was so pleased and complacent that really it was not possible to say anything except 'Yes very nice.'

When he said 'What about you, Katie?' I knew at once what he meant. That was another thing about him—he would suddenly come out with something as if there had already been a long talk between you on this subject. So when he asked me that, it was like the end of a conversation, and all I had to do was think for a moment and then I said 'I'm okay.' Because that was what he had asked: was I okay? Did I want anything, any help or anything? And I didn't. I really was okay now. I hadn't always been but I got so travelling around on my own and then being in this nice place here with him.

This was before the Countess came. Once she was there, everything was rather different. For weeks before her arrival people started talking about her: she was an important figure there, and no wonder since she was very rich and did a lot for the ashram and for Master when he went abroad on his lecture tours. I wondered what she was like. When I asked Vishwa about her, he said 'She is a great spiritual lady.'

We were both sitting outside my room. There was a little open space round which several other rooms were grouped. One of these—the biggest, at the corner—was being got ready for the Countess. It was the one that was always kept for her. People were vigorously sweeping in there and scrubbing the floor with soap and water.

'She is rich and from very aristocratic family,' Vishwa said, 'but when she met Master she was ready to give up everything.' He pointed to the room which was being scrubbed: 'This is where she stays. And see—not even a bed—she sleeps on the floor like a holy person. Oh Katie, when someone like me gives up the world, what is there? It is not such a great thing. But when *she* does it—' His face glowed. He had very bright eyes and a lovely complexion. He always looked very pure, owing no doubt to the very pure life he led.

Of course I got more and more curious about her, but when she came I was disappointed. I had expected her to be very special, but the only special thing about her was that I should meet her *here*. Otherwise she was a type I had often come across at posh parties and in the salons where I used to model. And the way she walked towards me and said 'Welcome!'—she might as well have been walking across a carpet in a salon. She had a full-blown, middle-aged figure (she must have been in her fifties) but very thin legs on which she took long strides with her toes turned out. She gave me a deep searching look—and that too I was used to from someone like her because very worldly people always do that: to find out who you are and how usable. But in her case now I suppose it was to search down into my soul and see what that was like.

I don't know what her conclusion was, but I must have passed because she was always kind to me and even asked for my company quite often. Perhaps this was partly because we lived across from each other and she suffered from insomnia and needed someone to talk to at night. I'm a sound sleeper myself and wasn't always very keen when she came to wake me. But she would nag me till I got up. 'Come on, Katie, be a sport,' she would say. She used many English expressions like that: she spoke English very fluently though with a funny accent. I heard her speak to the French and Italian and German people in the ashram very fluently in their languages too. I don't know what nationality she herself was—a sort of mixture I think—but of course people like her have been everywhere, not to mention their assorted governesses when young.

She always made me come into her room. She said mine was too *luxurious*, she didn't feel right in it as she had given up all that. Hers certainly wasn't luxurious. Like Vishwa had said, there wasn't a stick of furniture in it and she slept on the floor on a mat. As the electricity supply in the ashram was very fitful, we usually sat by candlelight. It was queer sitting like that with her on the floor with a stub of candle between us. I didn't have to do much talking as she did it all. She used her arms a lot, in sweeping gestures, and I can still see them weaving around there by candlelight as if she was doing a dance with them; and her eyes which were big and baby-blue were stretched wide open in wonder at everything she was telling me. Her life was like a fairy tale, she said. She gave me all the details though I can't recall them as I kept dropping off to sleep (naturally at two in the morning). From time to time she'd stop and say sharply 'Are you asleep, Katie,' and then she would poke me till I said no I wasn't. She told me how she first met Master at a lecture he had come to give in Paris. At the end of the lecture she went up to him—she said she had to elbow her way through a crowd of women all trying to get near him—and simply bowed down at his feet. No words spoken. There had been no need. It had been predestined.

She was also very fond of Vishwa. It seemed all three of them—i.e. her, Master, and Vishwa—had been closely related to each other in several previous incarnations. I think they had been either her sons or her husbands or fathers, I can't remember which exactly but it was very close so it was no wonder she felt about them the way she did. She had big plans for Vishwa. He was to go abroad and be a spiritual leader. She and Master often talked about it, and it was fascinating listening to them, but there was one thing I couldn't understand and that was why did it have to be Vishwa and not Master who was to be a spiritual leader in the West? I'd have thought Master himself had terrific qualifications for it.

Once I asked them. We were sitting in Master's room and the two of them were talking about Vishwa's future. When I asked 'What about Master?' she gave a dramatic laugh and pointed at him like she was accusing him: 'Ask him! Why don't you ask him!'

He gave a guilty smile and shifted around a bit on his throne. I say throne—it really was that: he received everyone in this room so a sort of dais had been fixed up at one end and a deer-skin spread on it for him to sit on; loving disciples had painted an arched back to the dais and decorated it with stars and symbols stuck on in silver paper (hideous!).

When she saw him smile like that, she really got exasperated. 'If you knew, Katie,' she said, 'how I have argued with him, how I have fought, how I have begged and pleaded on my *knees*. But he is as stubborn as—as—'

'A mule,' he kindly helped her out.

'Forgive me,' she said (because you can't call your guru names, that just isn't done!); though next moment she had worked herself up again: 'Do you know,' she asked me, 'how many people were waiting for him at the airport last time he went to New York? Do you know how many came to his lectures? That they had to be turned away from the *door* till we took a bigger hall! And not to speak of those who came to enrol for the special 3-week Meditation-via-Contemplation course.'

'She is right,' he said. 'They are very kind to me.'

'Kind! They want him—need him—are crazy with love and devotion—'

'It's all true,' he said. 'But the trouble is, you see, I'm a very, very lazy person.' And as he said this, he gave a big yawn and stretched himself to prove how lazy he was: but he didn't look it—on the contrary, when he stretched like that, pushing out his big chest, he looked like he was humming with energy.

That evening he asked me to go for a stroll with him. We walked by the river which was very busy with people dipping in it for religious reasons. The temples were also busy—whenever we passed one, they seemed to be bursting in there with hymns, and cymbals, and little bells.

Master said: 'It is true that everyone is very kind to me in the West. Oh they make a big fuss when I come. They have even made a song for me—it goes—wait, let me see—'

He stopped still and several people took the opportunity to come up to ask for his blessing. There were many other holy men walking about but somehow Master stood out. Some of the holy men also came up to be blessed by him.

'Yes it goes: "*He's here! Our Master ji is here Jai jai Master! Jai jai He!*" They stand waiting for me at the airport, and when I come out of the customs they burst into song. They carry big banners and also have drums and flutes. What a noise they make! Some of them begin to dance there and then on the spot, they are so happy. And everyone stares and looks at me, all the respectable people at the airport, and they wonder "Now who is this ruffian?" '

He had to stop again because a shopkeeper came running out of his stall to crouch at Master's feet. He was the grocer—everyone knew he used false weights—as well as the local moneylender and the biggest rogue in town, but when Master blessed him I could see tears come in his eyes, he felt so good.

'A car has been bought for my use,' Master said when we walked on again. 'Also a lease has been taken on a beautiful residence in New Hampshire. Now they wish to buy an aeroplane to enable me to fly from coast to coast.' He sighed. 'She is right to be angry with me. But what am I to do? I stand in the middle of Times Square or Piccadilly, London, and I look up and there are all the beautiful beautiful buildings stretching so high up into heaven: yes I look at them but it is not them I see at all, Katie! Not them at all!'

He looked up and I with him, and I understood that what he saw in Times Square and Piccadilly was what we saw now—all those mountains growing higher and higher above the river, and some of them so high that you couldn't make out whether it was them, with snow on top or the sky with clouds in it.

Before the Countess' arrival, everything had been very easy-going. We usually did our meditation, but if we happened to miss out, it never mattered too much. Also there was a lot of sitting around gossiping or trips to the bazaar for eats. But the Countess put us on a stricter régime. Now we all had a time-table to follow, and there were gongs and bells going off all day to remind us. This started at 5 a.m. when it was meditation time, followed by purificatory bathing time, and study time, and discussion time, and hymn time, and so on till lights-out time. Throughout the day disciples could be seen making their way up or down the mountain-side as they passed from one group activity to the other. If there was any delay in the schedule, the Countess got impatient and clapped her hands and chivied people along. The way she herself clambered up and down the mountain was just simply amazing for someone her age. Sometimes she went right to the top of the ashram where there was a pink plaster pillar inscribed with Golden Rules for Golden Living (a sort of Indian Ten Commandments): from here she could look all round, survey her domain as it were. When she wanted to summon everyone, she climbed up there with a pair of cymbals and how she beat them together! Boom! Bang! She must have had military blood in her veins, probably German.

She had drawn up a very strict time-table for Vishwa to cover every aspect of his education. He had to learn all sorts of things; not only English and a bit of French and German, but also how to use a knife and fork and even how to address people by their proper titles in case ambassadors and big church people and such were drawn into the movement as was fully expected. Because I'd been a model, I was put in charge of his deportment. I was supposed to teach him how to walk and sit nicely. He had to come to my room for lessons in the afternoons, and it was quite fun though I really didn't know what to teach him. As far as I was concerned, he was more graceful than anyone I'd ever seen. I loved the way he sat on the floor with his legs tucked under him; he could sit like that without moving for hours and hours. Or he might lie full length on the floor with his head supported on one hand and his ascetic's robe falling in folds around him so that he looked like a piece of sculpture you might see in a museum. I forgot to say that the Countess had decided he wasn't to shave his hair any more like the other junior swamis but was to grow it and have long curls. It wasn't long yet but it was certainly curly and framed his face very prettily.

After the first few days we gave up having lessons and just talked and spent our time together. He sat on the rug and I on the bed. He told me the story of his life and I told him mine. But his was much better than mine. His father had been the station master at some very small junction, and the family lived in a little railway house near enough the tracks to run and put the signals up or down as required. Vishwa had plenty of brothers and sisters to play with, and friends at the little school he went to at the other end of town; but quite often he felt like not being with anyone. He would set off to school with his copies and pencils like everyone else, but half way he would change his mind and take another turning that led out of town into some open fields. Here he would lie down under a tree and look at patches of sky through the leaves of the tree, and the leaves moving ever so gently if there was a breeze or some birds shook their wings in there. He would stay all day and in the evening go home and not tell anyone. His mother was a religious person who regularly visited the temple and sometimes he went with her but he never felt anything special. Then Master came to town and gave a lecture in a tent that was put up for him on the Parade Ground. Vishwa went with his mother to hear him, again not expecting anything special, but the moment he saw Master something very peculiar happened: he couldn't quite describe it, but he said it was like when there is a wedding on a dark night and the fireworks start and there are those that shoot up into the sky and then burst into a huge white fountain of light scattering sparks all over so that you are blinded and dazzled with it. It was like that, Vishwa said. Then he just went away with Master. His family were sad at first to lose him, but they were proud too like all families are when one of them renounces the world to become a holy man.

Those were good afternoons we had, and we usually took the precaution of locking the door so no one could interrupt us. If we heard the Countess coming—one good thing about her, you could always *hear* her a mile off, she never moved an inch without shouting instructions to someone—the moment we heard her we'd jump up and unlock the door and fling it wide open: so when she looked in, she could see us having our lesson—Vishwa walking up and down with a book on his head, or sitting like on a dais to give a lecture and me showing him what to do with his hands.

When I told him the story of *my* life, we both cried. Especially when I told him about my first marriage when I was only 16 and Danny just 20. He was a bass player in a group and he was really good and would have got somewhere if he hadn't freaked out. It was terrible seeing him do that, and the way he treated me after those first six months we had together which were out of this world. I never had anything like that with anyone ever again, though I got involved with many people afterwards. Everything just got worse and worse till I reached an all-time low with my second marriage which was to a company director (so-called, though don't ask me what sort of company) and a very smooth operator indeed besides being a sadist. Vishwa couldn't stand it when I came to that part of my story. He begged me not to go on, he put his hands over his ears. We weren't in my room that time but on top of the ashram by the Pillar of the Golden Rules. The view from here was fantastic, and it was so high up that you felt you might as well be in heaven, especially at this hour of the evening when the sky was turning all sorts of colours though mostly gold from the sun setting in it. Everything I was telling Vishwa seemed very far away. I can't say it was as if it had never happened, but it seemed like it had happened in someone else's life. There were tears on Vishwa's lashes, and I couldn't help myself, I had to kiss them away. After which we kissed properly. His mouth was as soft as a flower and his breath as sweet; of course he had never tasted meat nor eaten anything except the purest food such as a lamb might eat.

The door of my room was not the only one that was locked during those hot afternoons. Quite a few of the foreign disciples locked theirs for purposes I never cared to enquire into. At first I used to pretend to myself they were sleeping, and afterwards I didn't care what they were doing. I mean, even if they weren't sleeping, I felt there was something just as good and innocent about what they actually *were* doing. And after a while—when we had told each other the story of our respective lives and had run out of conversation—Vishwa and I began to do it too. This was about the time when preparations were going on for his final Renunciation and Initiation ceremony. It's considered the most important day in the life of a junior swami, when he ceases to be junior and becomes a senior or proper swami. It's a very solemn ceremony. A funeral pyre is lit and his junior robe and his caste thread are burned on it. All this is symbolic—it means he's dead to the world but resurrected to the spiritual life. In Vishwa's case, his resurrection was a bit different from the usual. He wasn't fitted out in the standard senior swami outfit—which is a piece of orange cloth and a begging bowl—but instead the Countess dressed him up in the clothes he was to wear in the West. She had herself designed a white silk robe for him, together with accessories like beads, sandals, the deer-skin he was to sit on, and an embroidered shawl.

Getting all this ready meant many trips to the bazaar, and often she made Vishwa and me go with her. She swept through the bazaar the same way she did through the ashram, and the shopkeepers leaned eagerly out of their stalls to offer their salaams which she returned or not as they happened to be standing in her books. She was pretty strict with all of them—but most of all with the tailor whose job it was to stitch Vishwa's new silk robes. We spent hours in his little shop while Vishwa had to stand there and be fitted. The tailor crouched at his feet, stitching and restitching the hem to the Countess' instructions. She and I would stand back and look at Vishwa with our heads to one side while the tailor waited anxiously for her verdict. Ten to one she would say 'No! Again!'

But once she said not to the tailor but to me 'Vishwa stands very well now. He has a good pose.'

'Not bad,' I said, continuing to look critically at Vishwa and in such a way that he had a job not to laugh.

What she said next however killed all desire for laughter: 'I think we could end the deportment lessons now,' and then she shouted at the tailor: 'What is this! What are you doing! What sort of monkey-work do you call that!'

I managed to persuade her that I hadn't finished with Vishwa yet and there were still a few tricks of the trade I had to teach him. But I knew it was a short reprieve and that soon our lessons would have to end. Also plans were now afoot for Vishwa's departure. He was to go with the Countess when she returned to Europe in a few weeks' time; and she was already very busy corresponding with her contacts in various places, and all sorts of lectures and meetings were being arranged. But that wasn't the only thing worrying me: what was even worse was the change I felt taking place in Vishwa himself, especially after his Renunciation and Initiation ceremony. I think he was getting quite impressed with himself. The Countess made a point of treating him as if he were a guru already, and she bowed to him the same way she did to Master. And of course whatever she did everyone else followed suit, specially the foreign disciples. I might just say that they're always keen on things like that—I mean, bowing down and touching feet—I don't know what kick they get out of it but they do, the Countess along with the rest.

Most of them do it very clumsily—not like Indians who are *born* to it—so sometimes you feel like laughing when you look at them. But they're always very solemn about it and afterwards, when they stumble up again, there's a sort of holy glow on their faces. Vishwa looked down at them with a benign expression and he also got into the habit of blessing them the way Master did.

Now I stayed alone in the afternoons, feeling very miserable, specially when I thought of what was going on in some of the other rooms and how happy people were in there. After a few days of this I couldn't stand being on my own and started wandering around looking for company. But the only person up and doing at that time of day was the Countess who I didn't particularly want to be with. So I went and sat in Master's room where the door was always open in case any of us needed him any time. Like everybody else, he was often asleep that time of afternoon but it didn't matter. Just being in his presence was good. I sat on one of the green plastic benches that were ranged round his room and looked at him sleeping which he did sitting upright on his throne. Quite suddenly he would open his eyes and look straight at me and say 'Ah Katie' as if he'd known all along that I was sitting there.

One day there was an awful commotion outside. Master woke up as the Countess came in with two foreign disciples, a boy and a girl, who stood hanging their heads while she told us what she had caught them doing. They were two very young disciples; I think the boy didn't even have to shave yet. One couldn't imagine them doing anything really evil, and Master didn't seem to think so. He just told them to go away and have their afternoon rest. But because the Countess was very upset he tried to comfort her which he did by telling about his early life in the world when he was a married man. It had been an arranged marriage of course, and his wife had been very young, just out of school. Being married for them had been like a game, specially the cooking and housekeeping part which she had enjoyed very much. Every Sunday she had dressed up in a spangled sari and high-heeled shoes and he had escorted her on the bus to the cinema where they stood in a queue for the one-rupee seats. He had loved her more than he had ever loved anyone or anything in all his life and had not thought it possible to love so much. But it only lasted two years at the end of which time she died of a miscarriage. He left his home then and wandered about for many years, doing all sorts of different jobs. He worked as a motor mechanic, and a salesman for medical supplies, and had even been in films for a while on the distribution side. But not finding rest anywhere, he finally decided to give up the world. He explained to us that it had been the only logical thing to do. Having learned during his two years of marriage how happy it was possible for a human being to be, he was never again satisfied to settle for anything less; but also seeing how it couldn't last on a worldly plane, he had decided to look for it elsewhere and help other people to do so with him.

I liked what he said, but I don't think the Countess took much of it in. She was more in her own thoughts. She was silent and gloomy which was *very* unusual for her. When she woke me that night for her midnight confessions, she seemed quite a different person: and now she didn't talk about her fairy-tale life or her wonderful plans for the future but on the contrary about all the terrible things she had suffered in the past. She went right back to the time she was in her teens and had eloped with and married an old man, a friend of her father's, and from there on it was all just one long terrible story of bad marriages and unhappy love affairs and other sufferings that I wished I didn't have to listen to. But I couldn't leave her in the state she was in. She was crying and sobbing and lying face down on the ground. It was eerie in that bare cell of hers with the one piece of candle flickering in the wind which was very strong, and the rain beating down like fists on the tin roof.

The monsoon had started, and when you looked up now, there weren't any mountains left, only clouds hanging down very heavily; and when you looked down, the river was also heavy and full. Every day there were stories of pilgrims drowning in it, and one night it washed over one bank and swept away a little colony of huts that the lepers had built for themselves. Now they no longer sat sunning themselves on the bridge but were carted away to the infectious diseases hospital. The rains came gushing down the mountain right into the ashram so that we were all wading ankle-deep in mud and water. Many rooms were flooded and their occupants had to move into other people's rooms resulting in personality clashes. Everyone bore grudges and took sides so that it became rather like the other ashrams I had visited and not liked.

The person who changed the most was the Countess. Although she was still dashing up and down the mountain, it was no longer to get the place in running order. Now she tucked up her skirts to wade from room to room to peer through chinks and see what people were up to. She didn't trust anyone but appointed herself as a one-man spying organization. She even suspected Master and me! At least me—she asked me what I went to his room for in the afternoon and sniffed at my reply in a way I didn't care for. After that one awful outburst she had, she didn't call me at night any more but she was certainly after me during the day.

She guarded Vishwa like a dragon. She wouldn't even let me pass his room, and if she saw me going anywhere in that direction, she'd come running to tell me to take the other way round. I wasn't invited any more to accompany them to the bazaar but only she and Vishwa set off, with her holding a big black umbrella over them both. If they happened to pass me on the way, she would tilt the umbrella so he wouldn't be able to see me. Not that this was necessary as he never seemed to see me anyway. His eyes were always lowered and the expression on his face very serious. He had stopped joking around with the junior swamis, which I suppose was only fitting now he was a senior swami as well as about to become a spiritual leader. The Countess had fixed up a throne for him at the end of Master's room so he wouldn't have to sit on the floor and the benches along with the rest of us. When we all got together in there, Master would be at one end on his throne and Vishwa at the other on his. At Master's end there was always lots going on—everyone laughing and Master making jokes and having his fun—but Vishwa just sat very straight in the lotus pose and never looked at anyone or spoke, and only when the Countess pushed people to go and touch his feet, he'd raise a hand to bless them.

With the rains came flies and mosquitoes, and people began to fall sick with all sorts of mysterious fevers. The Countess—who was terrified of germs and had had herself pumped full of every kind of injection before coming to India—was now in a great hurry to be off with Vishwa. But before they could leave, he too came down with one of those fevers. She took him at once into her own room and kept him isolated in there with everything shut tight. She wouldn't let any of us near him. But I peeped in through the chinks, not caring whether she saw me or not. I even pleaded with her to let me come in, and once she let me but only to look at him from the door while she stood guard by his pillow. His eyes were shut and he was breathing heavily and moaning in an awful way. The Countess said I could go now, but instead I rushed up to Vishwa's bed. She tried to get between us but I pushed her out of the way and got down by the bed and held him where he lay moaning with his eyes shut. The Countess shrieked and pulled at me to get me away. I was shrieking too. We must have sounded and looked like a couple of madwomen. Vishwa opened his eyes and when he saw me there and moreover found that he was in my arms, *he* began to shriek too, as if he was frightened of me and that perhaps I was the very person he was having those terrible fever dreams about that made him groan.

It may have been this accidental shock treatment but that night Vishwa's fever came down and he began to get better. Master announced that there was going to be a Yagna or prayer-meet to give thanks for Vishwa's recovery. It was to be a really big show. Hordes of helpers came up from the town, all eager to take part in this event so as to benefit from the spiritual virtue it was expected to generate. The Meditation Hall was repainted salmon pink and the huge holy OM sign at one end of it was lit up all round with coloured bulbs that flashed on and off. Everyone worked with a will, and apparently good was already beginning to be generated because the rains stopped, the mud lanes in the ashram dried up, and the river flowed back into its banks. The disciples stopped quarrelling which may have been partly due to the fact that everyone could move back into their own rooms.

The Countess and Vishwa kept going down into the town to finish off with the tailors and embroiderers. They also went to the printer who was making large posters to be sent abroad to advertise Vishwa's arrival. The Countess often asked me to go with them: she was really a good-natured person and did not want me to feel left out. Especially now that she was sure there wasn't a dangerous situation working up between me and Vishwa. There she was right. I wasn't in the least interested in him and felt that the less I saw of him the better. I couldn't forget the way he had shrieked that night in the Countess' room as if I was something impure and dreadful. But on the contrary to me it seemed that it had been *he* who was impure and dreadful with his fever dreams. I didn't even like to think what went on in them.

The Great Yagna began and it really was great. The Meditation Hall was packed and was terribly hot not only with all the people there but also because of the sacrificial flames that sizzled as more and more clarified butter was poured on them amid incantations.

Everyone was smiling and singing and sweating. Master was terrific—he was right by the fire stark naked except for the tiniest bit of loincloth. His chest glistened with oil and seemed to reflect the flames leaping about. Sometimes he jumped up on his throne and waved his arms to make everyone join in louder; and when they did, he got so happy he did a little jig standing up there. Vishwa was on the other side of the Hall also on a throne. He was half reclining in his spotless white robe; he did not seem to feel the heat at all but lay there as if made out of cool marble. He reminded me of the god Shiva resting on top of his snowy mountain. The Countess sat near him, and I saw how she tried to talk to him once or twice but he took no notice of her. After a while she got up and went out which was not surprising for it really was not her scene, all that noise and singing and the neon lights and decorations.

It went on all night. No one seemed to get tired—they just got more and more worked up and the singing got louder and the fire hotter. Other people too began to do little jigs like Master's. I left the Hall and walked around by myself. It was a fantastic night, the sky sprinkled all over with stars and a moon like a melon. When I passed the Countess' door, she called me in. She was lying on her mat on the floor and said she had a migraine. No wonder, with all that noise. I liked it myself but I knew that, though she was very much attracted to Eastern religions, her taste in music was more for the Western classical type (she loved string quartets and had had a long *affaire* with a cellist). She confessed to me that she was very anxious to leave now and get Vishwa started on his career. I think she would have liked to confess more things, but I had to get on. I made my way uphill past all the different buildings till I had reached the top of the ashram and the Pillar of the Golden Rules. Here I stood and looked down.

I saw the doors of the Meditation Hall open and Master and Vishwa come out. They were lit up by the lights from the Hall. Master was big and black and naked except for his triangle of orange cloth, and Vishwa was shining in white. I saw Master raise his arm and point it up, up to the top of the ashram. The two of them reminded me of a painting I've seen of I think it was an angel pointing out a path to a pilgrim. And like a pilgrim Vishwa began to climb up the path that Master had shown him. I stood by the Pillar of the Golden Rules and waited for him. When he got to me, we didn't have to speak one word. He was like a charged dynamo; I'd never known him like that. It was more like it might have been with Master instead of Vishwa. The drums and hymns down in the Meditation Hall also reached their crescendo just then. Of course Vishwa was too taken up with what he was doing to notice anything going on round him, so it was only me that saw the Countess come uphill. She was walking quite slowly and I suppose I could have warned Vishwa in time but it seemed a pity to interrupt him, so I just let her come on up and find us.

Master finally settled everything to everyone's satisfaction. He said Vishwa and I were to be a couple, and whereas Vishwa was to be the Guru, I was to embody the Mother principle (which is also very important). Once she caught on to the idea, the Countess rather liked it. She designed an outfit for me too—a sort of flowing white silk robe, really quite becoming. You might have seen posters of Vishwa and me together, both of us in these white robes, his hair black and curly, mine blonde and straight. I suppose we do make a good couple—anyway, people seem to like us and to get something out of us. We do our best. It's not very hard; mostly we just have to sit there and radiate. The results are quite satisfactory—I mean the effect we seem to have on people who need it. The person who really has to work hard is the Countess because she has to look after all the business and organizational end. We have a strenuous tour programme. Sometimes it's like being on a one-night stand and doing your turn and then packing up in a hurry to get to the next one. Some of the places we stay in aren't too good—motels where you have to pay in advance in case you flit—and when she is very tired, the Countess wrings her hands and says 'My God, what am I doing here?' It must be strange for her who's been used to all the grand hotels everywhere, but of course really she likes it. It's her life's fulfilment. But for Vishwa and me it's just a job we do, and all the time we want to be somewhere else and are thinking of that other place. I often remember what Master told me, what happened to him when he looked up in Times Square and Piccadilly, and it's beginning to happen to me too. I seem to *see* those mountains and the river and temples; and then I long to be there.

JOYCE CAROL OATES

Small Avalanches

I kept bothering my mother for a dime, so she gave me a dime, and I went down our lane and took the shortcut to the highway, and down to the gas station. My uncle Winfield ran the gas station. There were two machines in the garage and I had to decide between them: the pop machine and the candy bar machine. No, there were three machines, but the other one sold cigarettes and I didn't care about that.

It took me a few minutes to make up my mind, then I bought a bottle of Pepsi-Cola.

Sometimes a man came to unlock the machines and take out the coins, and if I happened to be there it was interesting—the way the machines could be changed so fast if you just had the right key to open them. This man drove up in a white truck with a licence plate from Kansas, a different colour from our licence plates, and he unlocked the machines and took out the money and loaded the machines up again. When we were younger we liked to hang around and watch. There was something strange about it, how the look of the machines could be changed so fast, the fronts swinging open, the insides showing, just because a man with the right keys drove up.

I went out front where my uncle was working on a car. He was under the car, lying on a thing made out of wood that had rollers on it so that he could roll himself under the car; I could just see his feet. He had on big heavy shoes that were all greasy. I asked him if my cousin Georgia was home—they lived about two miles away and I could walk—and he said no, she was baby-sitting in Stratton for three days. I already knew this but I hoped the people might have changed their minds.

'Is that man coming today to take out the money?'

My uncle didn't hear me. I was sucking at the Pepsi-Cola and running my tongue around the rim of the bottle. I always loved the taste of pop, the first two or three swallows. Then I would feel a little filled up and would have to drink it slowly. Sometimes I even poured the last of it out, but not so that anyone saw me.

'That man who takes care of the machines, is he coming today?'

'Who? No. Sometime next week.'

My uncle pushed himself out from under the car. He was my mother's brother, a few years older than my mother. He had bushy brown hair and his face was dirty. 'Did you call Georgia last night?'

'No. Ma wouldn't let me.'

'Well, somebody was on the line because Betty wanted to check on her and the goddam line was busy all night. So Betty wanted to drive in, all the way to Stratton, drive six miles when probably nothing's wrong. You didn't call her, huh?'

'No.'

'This morning Betty called her and gave her hell and she tried to say she hadn't been talking all night, that the telephone lines must have gotten mixed up. Georgia is a goddam little liar and if I catch her fooling around. . . .'

He was walking away, into the garage. In the back pocket of his overalls was a dirty rag, stuffed there. He always yanked it out and wiped his face with it, not looking at it, even if it was dirty. I watched to see if he would do this and he did.

I almost laughed at this, and at how Georgia got away with murder. I had a good idea who was talking to her on the telephone.

The pop made my tongue tingle, a strong acid-sweet taste that almost hurt. I sat down and looked out at the road. This was in the middle of Colorado, on the road that goes through, east and west. It was a hot day. I drank one, two, three, four small swallows of pop. I pressed the bottle against my knees because I was hot. I tried to balance the bottle on one knee and it fell right over; I watched the pop trickle out onto the concrete.

I was too lazy to move my feet, so my bare toes got wet.

Somebody came along the road in a pickup truck, Mr Watkins, and he tapped on the horn to say hello to me and my uncle. He was on his way to Stratton. I thought, *Damn it, I could have hitched a ride with him*. I don't know why I bothered to think this because I had to get home pretty soon, anyway, my mother would kill me if I went to town without telling her. Georgia and I did that once, back just after school let out in June, we went down the road a ways and hitched a ride with some guy in a beat-up car we thought looked familiar, but when he stopped to let us in we didn't know him and it was too late. But nothing happened, he was all right. We walked all the way back home again because we were scared to hitch another ride. My parents didn't find out, or Georgia's, but we didn't try it again.

I followed my uncle into the gas station. The building was made of ordinary wood, painted white a few years ago but starting to peel. It was just one room. The floor was concrete, all stained with grease and cracked. I knew the whole place by heart: the ceiling planks, the black rubber things hanging on the wall, looped over big rusty spikes, the Cat's Paw ad that I liked, and the other ads for beer and cigarettes on shiny pieces of cardboard that stood up. To see those things you wouldn't guess how they came all flat, and you could unfold them and fix them yourself, like fancy things for under the Christmas tree. Inside the candy machine, behind the little windows, the candy bars stood up on display: *Milky Way, O Henry, Junior Mints, Mallow Cup, Three Musketeers, Hershey*. I liked them all. Sometimes *Milky Way* was my favourite, other times I only bought *Mallow Cup* for weeks in a row, trying to get enough of the cardboard letters to spell out *Mallow Cup*. One letter came with each candy bar, and if you spelled out the whole name you could send away for a prize. But the letter 'w' was hard to find. There were lots of 'l's, it was rotten luck to open the wrapper up and see another 'l' when you already had ten of them.

'Could I borrow a nickel?' I asked my uncle.

'I don't have any change.'

Like hell, I thought. My uncle was always stingy.

I pressed the 'return coin' knob but nothing came out. I pulled the knob out under *Mallow Cup* but nothing came out.

'Nancy, don't fool around with that thing, okay?'

'I don't have anything to do.'

'Yeah, well, your mother can find something for you to do.'

'She can do it herself.'

'You want me to tell her that?'

'Go right ahead.'

'Hey, did your father find out any more about that guy in Polo?'

'What guy?'

'Oh, I don't know, some guy who got into a fight and was arrested—he was in the Navy with your father, I don't remember his name.'

'I don't know.'

My uncle yawned. I followed him back outside and he stretched his arms and yawned. It was very hot. You could see the fake water puddles on the highway that were so mysterious and always moved back when you approached them. They could hypnotize you. Across from the garage was the mailbox on a post and then just scrub-land, nothing to look at, pasture land and big rocky hills.

I thought about going to check to see if my uncle had any mail, but I knew there wouldn't be anything inside. We only got a booklet in the mail that morning, some information about how to make money selling jewellery door-to-door that I had written away for, but now I didn't care about. 'Georgia has all the luck,' I said. 'I could use a few dollars myself.'

'Yeah,' my uncle said. He wasn't listening.

I looked at myself in the outside mirror of the car he was fixing. I don't know what kind of car it was, I never memorized the makes like the boys did. It was a dark maroon colour with big heavy fenders and a bumper that had little bits of rust in it, like sparks. The running board had old, dried mud packed down inside its ruts. It was covered with black rubber, a mat. My hair was blown-looking. It was a big heavy mane of hair the colour everybody called dishwater blond. My baby pictures showed that it used to be light blond.

'I wish I could get a job like Georgia,' I said.

'Georgia's a year older than you.'

'Oh hell. . . .'

I was thirteen but I was Georgia's size, all over, and I was smarter. We looked alike. We both had long bushy flyaway hair that frizzed up when the air was wet, but kept curls in very well when we set it, like for church. I forgot about my hair and leaned closer to the mirror to look at my face. I made my lips shape a little circle, noticing how wrinkled they got. They could wrinkle up into a small space. I poked the tip of my tongue out.

There was the noise of something on gravel, and I looked around to see a man driving in. Out by the highway my uncle just had gravel, then around the gas pumps he had concrete. This man's car was white, a colour you don't see much, and his licence plate was from Kansas.

He told my uncle to fill up the gas tank and he got out of the car, stretching his arms.

He looked at me and smiled. 'Hi,' he said.

'Hi.'

He said something to my uncle about how hot it was, and my uncle said it wasn't too bad. Because that's the way he is—always contradicting you. My mother hates him for this. But then he said, 'You read about the dry spell coming up?—right into September?' My uncle meant the ranch bureau thing but the man didn't know what he was talking about. He meant the 'Bureau News & Forecast'. This made me mad, that my uncle was so stupid, thinking that a man from out of state and probably from a city would know about that, or give a damn. It made me mad. I saw my pop bottle where it fell and I decided to go home, not to bother putting it in the case where you were supposed to.

I walked along on the edge of the road, on the pavement, because there were stones and prickles and weeds with bugs in them off the side that I didn't like to walk in barefoot. I felt hot and mad about something. A yawn started in me, and I felt it coming up like a little bubble of gas from the pop. There was my cousin Georgia in town, and all she had to do was watch a little girl who wore thick glasses and was sort of strange, but very nice and quiet and no trouble, and she'd get two dollars. I thought angrily that if anybody came along I'd put out my thumb and hitch a ride to Stratton, and the hell with my mother.

Then I did hear a car coming but I just got over to the side and waited for him to pass. I felt stubborn and wouldn't look around to see who it was, but then the car didn't pass and I looked over my shoulder—it was the man in the white car, who had stopped for gas. He was driving very slow. I got farther off the road and waited for him to pass. But he leaned over to this side and said out the open window, 'You want a ride home? Get in.'

'No, that's okay,' I said.

'Come on, I'll drive you home. No trouble.'

'No, it's okay. I'm almost home,' I said.

I was embarrassed and didn't want to look at him. People didn't do this, a grown-up man in a car wouldn't bother to do this. Either you hitched for a ride or you didn't, and if you didn't, people would never slow down to ask you. This guy is crazy, I thought. I felt very strange. I tried to look over into the field but there wasn't anything to look at, not even any cattle, just land and scrubby trees and a barbed-wire fence half falling down.

'Your feet will get all sore, walking like that,' the man said.

'I'm okay.'

'Hey, watch out for the snake!'

There wasn't any snake and I made a noise like a laugh to show that I knew it was a joke but didn't think it was very funny.

'Aren't there rattlesnakes around here? Rattlers?'

'Oh I don't know,' I said.

He was still driving right alongside me, very slow. You are not used to seeing a car slowed-down like that, it seems very strange. I tried not to look at the man. But there was nothing else to look at, just the country and the road and the mountains in the distance and some clouds.

'That man at the gas station was mad, he picked up the bottle you left.'

I tried to keep my lips pursed shut, but they were dry and came open again. I wondered if my teeth were too big in front.

'How come you walked away so fast? That wasn't friendly,' the man said. 'You forgot your pop bottle and the man back there said somebody could drive over it and get a flat tire, he was a little mad.'

'He's my uncle,' I said.

'What?'

He couldn't hear or was pretending he couldn't hear, so I had to turn toward him. He was all-right-looking, he was smiling. 'He's my uncle,' I said.

'Oh, is he? You don't look anything like *him*. Is your home nearby?'

'Up ahead.' I was embarrassed and started to laugh, I don't know why.

'I don't see any house there.'

'You can't see it from here,' I said, laughing.

'What's so funny? My face? You know, when you smile you're a very pretty girl. You should smile all the time. . . .' He was paying so much attention to me it made me laugh. 'Yes, that's a fact. Why are you blushing?'

I blushed fast, like my mother; we both hated to blush and hated people to tease us. But I couldn't get mad.

'I'm worried about your feet and the rattlers around here. Aren't there rattlers around here?'

'Oh I don't know.'

'Where I come from there are streets and sidewalks and no snakes, of course, but it isn't interesting. It isn't dangerous. I think I'd like to live here, even with the snakes—this is very beautiful, hard country, isn't it? Do you like the mountains way over there? Or don't you notice them?'

I didn't pay any attention to where he was pointing, I looked at him and saw that he was smiling. He was my father's age but he wasn't stern like my father, who had a line between his eyebrows like a knife-cut, from frowning. This man was wearing a shirt, a regular white shirt, out in the country. His hair was dampened and combed back from his forehead; it was damp right now, as if he had just combed it.

'Yes, I'd like to take a walk out here and get some exercise,' he said. His voice sounded very cheerful. 'Snakes or no snakes! You turned me down for a free ride so maybe I'll join you in a walk.'

That really made me laugh: *join you in a walk*.

'Hey, what's so funny?' he said, laughing himself.

People didn't talk like that, but I didn't say anything. He parked the car on the shoulder of the road and got out and I heard him drop the car keys in his pocket. He was scratching at his jaw. 'Well, excellent! This is excellent, healthy, divine country air! Do you like living out here?'

I shook my head, no.

'You wouldn't want to give all this up for a city, would you?'

'Sure. Any day.'

I was walking fast to keep ahead of him, I couldn't help but giggle, I was so embarrassed—this man in a white shirt was really walking out on the highway, he was really going to leave his car parked like that! You never saw a car parked on the road around here, unless it was by the creek, fishermen's cars, or unless it was a wreck. All this made my face get hotter.

He walked fast to catch up with me. I could hear coins and things jingling in his pockets.

'You never told me your name,' he said. 'That isn't friendly.'

'It's Nancy.'

'Nancy what?'

'Oh I don't know,' I laughed.

'Nancy I Don't Know?' he said.

I didn't get this. He was smiling hard. He was shorter than my father and now that he was out in the bright sun I could see he was older. His face wasn't tanned, and his mouth kept going into a soft smile. Men like my father and my uncles and other men never bothered to smile like that at me, they never bothered to look at me

at all. Some men did, once in a while, in Stratton, strangers waiting
for Greyhound buses to Denver or Kansas City, but they weren't
friendly like this, they didn't keep on smiling for so long.

When I came to the path I said, 'Well, good-bye, I'm going to cut
over this way. This is a shortcut.'

'A shortcut where?'

'Oh I don't know,' I said, embarrassed.

'To your house, Nancy?'

'Yeah. No, it's to our lane, our lane is half a mile long.'

'Is it? That's very long. . . .'

He came closer. 'Well, good-bye,' I said.

'That's a long lane, isn't it?—it must get blocked up with snow in
the winter, doesn't it? You people get a lot of snow out here—'

'Yeah.'

'So your house must be way back there . . . ?' he said, pointing.
He was smiling. When he stood straight like this, looking over my
head, he was more like the other men. But then he looked down at
me and smiled again, so friendly. I waved good-bye and jumped over
the ditch and climbed the fence, clumsy as hell just when somebody
was watching me, wouldn't you know it. Some barbed wire caught
at my shorts and the man said, 'Let me get that loose—' but I jerked
away and jumped down again. I waved good-bye again and started
up the path. But the man said something and when I looked back he
was climbing over the fence himself. I was so surprised that I just
stood there.

'I like shortcuts and secret paths,' he said. 'I'll walk a little way
with you.'

'What do you—' I started to say. I stopped smiling because
something was wrong. I looked around and there was just the path
behind me that the kids always took, and some boulders and old
dried-up manure from cattle, and some scrubby bushes. At the top
of the hill was the big tree that had been struck by lightning so many
times. I was looking at all this and couldn't figure out why I was
looking at it.

'You're a brave little girl to go around barefoot,' the man said,
right next to me. 'Or are your feet tough on the bottom?'

I didn't know what he was talking about because I was worried;
then I heard his question and said vaguely, 'I'm all right,' and
started to walk faster. I felt a tingling all through me like the
tingling from the Pepsi-Cola in my mouth.

'Do you always walk so fast?' the man laughed.

'Oh I don't know.'

'Is that all you can say? Nancy I-Don't-Know! That's a funny name—is it foreign?'

This made me start to laugh again. I was walking fast, then I began to run a few steps. Right away I was out of breath. That was strange—I was out of breath right away.

'Hey, Nancy, where are you going?' the man cried.

But I kept running, not fast. I ran a few steps and looked back and there he was, smiling and panting, and I happened to see his foot come down on a loose rock. I knew what would happen—the rock rolled off sideways and he almost fell, and I laughed. He glanced up at me with a surprised grin. 'This path is a booby trap, huh? Nancy has all sorts of little traps and tricks for me, huh?'

I didn't know what he was talking about. I ran up the side of the hill, careful not to step on the manure or anything sharp, and I was still out of breath but my legs felt good. They felt as if they wanted to run a long distance. 'You're going off the path,' he said, pretending to be mad. 'Hey. That's against the rules. Is that another trick?'

I giggled but couldn't think of any answer.

'Did you make this path up by yourself?' the man asked. But he was breathing hard from the hill. He stared at me, climbing up, with his hands pushing on his knees as if to help him climb. 'Little Nancy, you're like a wild colt or a deer, you're so graceful—is this your own private secret path? Or do other people use it?'

'Oh, my brother and some other kids, when they're around,' I said vaguely. I was walking backward up the hill now, so that I could look down at him. The top of his hair was thin, you could see the scalp. The very top of his forehead seemed to have two bumps, not big ones, but as if the bone went out a little, and this part was a bright pink, sunburned, but the rest of his face and his scalp were white.

He stepped on another loose rock, and the rock and some stones and mud came loose. He fell hard onto his knee. 'Jesus!' he said. The way he stayed down like that looked funny. I had to press my hand over my mouth. When he looked up at me his smile was different. He got up, pushing himself up with his hands, grunting, and then he wiped his hands on his trousers. The dust showed on them. He looked funny.

'Is my face amusing? Is it a good joke?'

I didn't mean to laugh, but now I couldn't stop. I pressed my hand over my mouth hard.

He stared at me. 'What do you see in my face, Nancy? What do you see—anything? Do you see my soul, do you see *me*, is that what you're laughing at?' He took a fast step toward me, but I jumped back. It was like a game. 'Come on, Nancy, slow down, just slow down,' he said. 'Come on, Nancy. . . .'

I didn't know what he was talking about, I just had to laugh at his face. It was so tense and strange; it was so *important*.

I noticed a big rock higher up, and I went around behind it and pushed it loose—it rolled right down toward him and he had to scramble to get out of the way. 'Hey! Jesus!' he yelled. The rock came loose with some other things and a mud chunk got him in the leg.

I laughed so hard my stomach started to ache.

He laughed too, but a little different from before.

'This is a little trial for me, isn't it?' he said. 'A little preliminary contest. Is that how the game goes? Is that your game, Nancy?'

I ran higher up the hill, off to the side where it was steeper. Little rocks and things came loose and rolled back down. My breath was coming so fast it made me wonder if something was wrong. Down behind me the man was following, stooped over, looking at me, and his hand was pressed against the front of his shirt. I could see his hand moving up and down because he was breathing so hard. I could even see his tongue moving around the edge of his dried-out lips. . . . I started to get afraid, and then the tingling came back into me, beginning in my tongue and going out through my whole body, and I couldn't help giggling.

He said something that sounded like, '—won't be laughing—' but I couldn't hear the rest of it. My hair was all wet in back where it would be a job for me to unsnarl it with the hairbrush. The man came closer, stumbling, and just for a joke I kicked out at him, to scare him—and he jerked backward and tried to grab onto a branch of a bush, but it slipped through his fingers and he lost his balance and fell. He grunted. He fell so hard that he just lay there for a minute. I wanted to say I was sorry, or ask him if he was all right, but I just stood there grinning.

He got up again; the fleshy part of his hand was bleeding. But he didn't seem to notice it and I turned and ran up the rest of the hill, going almost straight up the last part, my legs were so strong and felt so good. Right at the top I paused, just balanced there, and a gust of wind would have pushed me over—but I was all right. I laughed aloud, my legs felt so springy and strong.

I looked down over the side where he was crawling, down on his hands and knees again. 'You better go back to Kansas! Back home to Kansas!' I laughed. He stared up at me and I waited for him to smile again but he didn't. His face was very pale. He was staring at me but he seemed to be seeing something else, his eyes were very serious and strange. I could see his belt creasing his-stomach, the bulge of his white shirt. He pressed his hand against his chest again. 'Better go home, go home, get in your damn old car and go home,' I sang, making a song of it. He looked so serious, staring up at me. I pretended to kick at him again and he flinched, his eyes going small.

'Don't leave me—' he whimpered.

'Oh go on,' I said.

'Don't leave—I'm sick—I think I—'

His face seemed to shrivel. He was drawing in his breath very slowly, carefully, as if checking to see how much it hurt, and I waited for this to turn into another joke. Then I got tired of waiting and just rested back on my heels. My smile got smaller and smaller, like his.

'Good-bye, I'm going,' I said, waving. I turned and he said something—it was like a cry—but I didn't want to bother going back. The tingling in me was almost noisy.

I walked over to the other side, and slid back down to the path and went along the path to our lane. I was very hot. I knew my face was flushed and red. 'Damn old nut,' I said. But I had to laugh at the way he had looked, the way he kept scrambling up the hill and was just crouched there at the end, on his hands and knees. He looked so funny, bent over and clutching at his chest, pretending to have a heart attack or maybe having one, a little one, for all I knew. This will teach you a lesson, I thought.

By the time I got home my face had dried off a little, but my hair was like a haystack. I stopped by the old car parked in the lane, just a junker on blocks, and looked in the outside rear-view mirror—the mirror was all twisted around because people looked in it all the time. I tried to fix my hair by rubbing my hands down hard against it, but no luck. 'Oh damn,' I said aloud, and went up the steps to the back, and remembered not to let the screen door slam so my mother wouldn't holler at me.

She was in the kitchen ironing, just sprinkling some clothes on the ironing board. She used a pop bottle painted blue and fitted out with a sprinkler top made of rubber, that I fixed for her at grade school a long time ago for a Christmas present; she shook the bottle over the clothes and stared at me. 'Where have you been? I told you to come right back.'

'I did come right back.'

'You're all dirty, you look like hell. What happened to you?'

'Oh I don't know,' I said. 'Nothing.'

She threw something at me—it was my brother's shirt—and I caught it and pressed it against my hot face.

'You get busy and finish these,' my mother said. 'It must be ninety-five in here and I'm fed up. And you do a good job, I'm really fed up. Are you listening, Nancy? Where the hell is your mind?'

I liked the way the damp shirt felt on my face. 'Oh I don't know,' I said.

Anita Desai

Private Tuition by Mr Bose

Mr Bose gave his private tuition out on the balcony, in the evenings, in the belief that, since it faced south, the river Hooghly would send it a wavering breeze or two to drift over the rooftops, through the washing and the few pots of *tulsi* and marigold that his wife had placed precariously on the balcony rail, to cool him, fan him, soothe him. But there was no breeze: it was hot, the air hung upon them like a damp towel, gagging him and, speaking through this gag, he tiredly intoned the Sanskrit verses that should, he felt, have been roared out on a hill-top at sunrise.

'*Aum. Usa va asvasya medhyasya sirah . . .*'

It came out, of course, a mumble. Asked to translate, his pupil, too, scowled as he had done, thrust his fist through his hair and mumbled:

'Aum is the dawn and the head of a horse . . .'

Mr Bose protested in a low wail. 'What horse, my boy? What horse?'

The boy rolled his eyes sullenly. 'I don't know, sir, it doesn't say.'

Mr Bose looked at him in disbelief. He was the son of a Brahmin priest who himself instructed him in the Mahabharata all morning, turning him over to Mr Bose only in the evening when he set out to officiate at weddings, *puja* and other functions for which he was so much in demand on account of his stately bearing, his calm and inscrutable face and his sensuous voice that so suited the Sanskrit language in which he, almost always, discoursed. And this was his son—this Pritam with his red-veined eyes and oiled locks, his stumbling fingers and shuffling feet that betrayed his secret life, its scruffiness, its gutters and drains full of resentment and destruction. Mr Bose suddenly remembered how he had seen him, from the window of a bus that had come to a standstill on the street due to a fist fight between the conductor and a passenger, Pritam slipping up the stairs, through the door, into a neon-lit bar off Park Street.

'The sacrificial horse,' Mr Bose explained with forced patience.

304

'Have you heard of Asvamedha, Pritam, the royal horse that was let loose to run through the kingdom before it returned to the capital and was sacrificed by the king?'

The boy gave him a look of such malice that Mr Bose bit the end of his moustache and fell silent, shuffling through the pages. 'Read on, then,' he mumbled and listened, for a while, as Pritam blundered heavily through the Sanskrit verses that rolled off his father's experienced tongue, and even Mr Bose's shy one, with such rich felicity. When he could not bear it any longer, he turned his head, slightly, just enough to be able to look out of the corner of his eye through the open door, down the unlit passage at the end of which, in the small, dimly lit kitchen, his wife sat kneading dough for bread, their child at her side. Her head was bowed so that some of her hair had freed itself of the long steel pins he hated so much and hung about her pale, narrow face. The red border of her sari was the only stripe of colour in that smoky scene. The child beside her had his back turned to the door so that Mr Bose could see his little brown buttocks under the short white shirt, squashed firmly down upon the woven mat. Mr Bose wondered what it was that kept him so quiet—perhaps his mother had given him a lump of dough to mould into some thick and satisfying shape. Both of them seemed bound together and held down in some deeply absorbing act from which he was excluded. He would have liked to break in and join them.

Pritam stopped reading, maliciously staring at Mr Bose whose lips were wavering into a smile beneath the ragged moustache. The woman, disturbed by the break in the recitation on the balcony, looked up, past the child, down the passage and into Mr Bose's face. Mr Bose's moustache lifted up like a pair of wings and, beneath them, his smile lifted up and out with almost a laugh of tenderness and delight. Beginning to laugh herself, she quickly turned, pulled down the corners of her mouth with mock sternness, trying to recall him to the path of duty, and picking up a lump of sticky dough, handed it back to the child, softly urging him to be quiet and let his father finish the lesson.

Pritam, the scabby, oil-slick son of a Brahmin priest, coughed theatrically—a cough imitating that of a favourite screen actor, surely, it was so false and over-done and suggestive. Mr Bose swung around in dismay, crying 'Why have you stopped? Go on, go on.'

'You weren't listening, sir.'

Many words, many questions leapt to Mr Bose's lips, ready to pounce on this miserable boy whom he could hardly bear to see sitting beneath his wife's holy *tulsi* plant that she tended with prayers, water-can and oil-lamp every evening. Then, growing conscious of the way his moustache was agitating upon his upper lip, he said only, 'Read.'

'*Ahar va asvam purustan mahima nvajagata . . .*'

Across the road someone turned on a radio and a song filled with a pleasant, lilting *weltschmerz* twirled and sank, twirled and rose from that balcony to this. Pritam raised his voice, grinding through the Sanskrit consonants like some dying, diseased tram-car. From the kitchen only a murmur and the soft thumping of the dough in the pan could be heard—sounds as soft and comfortable as sleepy pigeons'. Mr Bose longed passionately to listen to them, catch every faintest nuance of them, but to do this he would have to smash the radio, hurl the Brahmin's son down the iron stairs . . . He curled up his hands on his knees and drew his feet together under him, horrified at this welling up of violence inside him, under his pale pink bush-shirt, inside his thin, ridiculously heaving chest. As often as Mr Bose longed to alter the entire direction of the world's revolution, as often as he longed to break the world apart into two halves and shake out of them—what? Festival fireworks, a woman's soft hair, blood-stained feathers?—he would shudder and pale at the thought of his indiscretion, his violence, this secret force that now and then threatened, clamoured, so that he had quickly to still it, squash it. After all, he must continue with his private tuitions: that was what was important. The baby had to have his first pair of shoes and soon he would be needing oranges, biscuits, plastic toys. 'Read,' said Mr Bose, a little less sternly, a little more sadly.

But, 'It is seven, I can go home now,' said Pritam triumphantly, throwing his father's thick yellow Mahabharata into his bag, knocking the bag shut with one fist and preparing to fly. Where did he fly to? Mr Bose wondered if it would be the neon-lit bar off Park Street. Then, seeing the boy disappear down the black stairs—the bulb had fused again—he felt it didn't matter, didn't matter one bit since it left him alone to turn, plunge down the passage and fling himself at the doorposts of the kitchen, there to stand and gaze down at his wife, now rolling out *purees* with an exquisite, back-and-forth rolling motion of her hands, and his son, trying now to make a spoon stand on one end.

She only glanced at him, pretended not to care, pursed her lips to keep from giggling, flipped the *puree* over and rolled it finer and flatter still. He wanted so much to touch her hair, the strand that lay over her shoulder in a black loop, and did not know how to—she was so busy. 'Your hair is coming loose,' he said.

'Go, go,' she warned, 'I hear the next one coming.'

So did he, he heard the soft patting of sandals on the worn steps outside, so all he did was bend and touch the small curls of hair on his son's neck. They were so soft, they seemed hardly human and quite frightened him. When he took his hand away he felt the wisps might have come off onto his fingers and he rubbed the tips together wonderingly. The child let fall the spoon, with a magnificent ring, onto a brass dish and started at this discovery of percussion.

The light on the balcony was dimmed as his next pupil came to stand in the doorway. Quickly he pulled himself away from the doorpost and walked back to his station, tense with unspoken words and unexpressed emotion. He had quite forgotten that his next pupil, this Wednesday, was to be Upneet. Rather Pritam again than this once-a-week typhoon, Upneet of the flowered sari, ruby earrings and shaming laughter. Under this Upneet's gaze such ordinary functions of a tutor's life as sitting down at a table, sharpening a pencil and opening a book to the correct page became matters of farce, disaster and hilarity. His very bones sprang out of joint. He did not know where to look—everywhere were Upneet's flowers, Upneet's giggles. Immediately, at the very sight of the tip of her sandal peeping out beneath the flowered hem of her sari, he was a man broken to pieces, flung this way and that, rattling. Rattling.

Throwing away the Sanskrit books, bringing out volumes of Bengali poetry, opening to a poem by Jibanandan Das, he wondered ferociously: Why did she come? What use had she for Bengali poetry? Why did she come from that house across the road where the loud radio rollicked, to sit on his balcony, in view of his shy wife, making him read poetry to her? It was intolerable. Intolerable, all of it—except, only, for the seventy-five rupees paid at the end of the month. Oranges, he thought grimly, and milk, medicines, clothes. And he read to her:

> 'Her hair was the dark night of Vidisha,
> Her face the sculpture of Svarasti . . .'

307

Quite steadily he read, his tongue tamed and enthralled by the rhythm of the verse he had loved (copied on a sheet of blue paper, he had sent it to his wife one day when speech proved inadequate).

' "Where have you been so long?" she asked,
Lifting her bird's-nest eyes,
Banalata Sen of Natore.'

Pat-pat-pat. No, it was not the rhythm of the verse, he realized, but the tapping of her foot, green-sandalled, red-nailed, swinging and swinging to lift the hem of her sari up and up. His eyes slid off the book, watched the flowered hem swing out and up, out and up as the green-sandalled foot peeped out, then in, peeped out, then in. For a while his tongue ran on of its own volition:

'All birds come home, and all rivers,
Life's ledger is closed . . .'

But he could not continue—it was the foot, the sandal that carried on the rhythm exactly as if he were still reciting. Even the radio stopped its rollicking and, as a peremptory voice began to enumerate the day's disasters and achievements all over the world, Mr Bose heard more vigorous sounds from his kitchen as well. There too the lulling pigeon sounds had been crisply turned off and what he heard were bangs and rattles among the kitchen pots, a kettledrum of commands, he thought. The baby, letting out a wail of surprise, paused, heard the nervous commotion continue and intensify and launched himself on a series of wails.

Mr Bose looked up, aghast. He could not understand how these two halves of the difficult world that he had been holding so carefully together, sealing them with reams of poetry, reams of Sanskrit, had split apart into dissonance. He stared at his pupil's face, creamy, feline, satirical, and was forced to complete the poem in a stutter:

'Only darkness remains, to sit facing
Banalata Sen of Natore.'

But the darkness was filled with hideous sounds of business and anger and command. The radio news commentator barked, the baby wailed, the kitchen pots clashed. He even heard his wife's voice raised, angrily, at the child, like a threatening stick. Glancing again at his pupil whom he feared so much, he saw precisely that lift of the eyebrows and that twist of a smile that disjointed him, rattled him.

'Er—please read,' he tried to correct, to straighten that twist of eyebrows and lips. 'Please read.'

'But you have read it to me already,' she laughed, mocking him with her eyes and laugh.

'The next poem,' he cried, 'read the next poem,' and turned the page with fingers as clumsy as toes.

'It is much better when you read to me,' she complained impertinently, but read, keeping time to the rhythm with that restless foot which he watched as though it were a snake-charmer's pipe, swaying. He could hear her voice no more than the snake could the pipe's—it was drowned out by the baby's wails, swelling into roars of self-pity and indignation in this suddenly hard-edged world.

Mr Bose threw a piteous, begging look over his shoulder at the kitchen. Catching his eye, his wife glowered at him, tossed the hair out of her face and cried, 'Be quiet, be quiet, can't you see how busy your father is?' Red-eared, he turned to find Upneet looking curiously down the passage at this scene of domestic anarchy, and said, 'I'm sorry, sorry—please read.'

'I have read!' she exclaimed. 'Didn't you hear me?'

'So much noise—I'm sorry,' he gasped and rose to hurry down the passage and hiss, pressing his hands to his head as he did so, 'Keep him quiet, can't you? Just for half an hour!'

'He is hungry,' his wife said, as if she could do nothing about that.

'Feed him then,' he begged.

'It isn't time,' she said angrily.

'Never mind. Feed him, feed him.'

'Why? So that you can read poetry to that girl in peace?'

'Shh!' he hissed, shocked, alarmed that Upneet would hear. His chest filled with the injustice of it. But this was no time for pleas or reason. He gave another desperate look at the child who lay crouched on the kitchen floor, rolling with misery. When he turned to go back to his pupil who was watching them interestedly, he heard his wife snatch up the child and tell him, 'Have your food then, have it and eat it—don't you see how angry your father is?'

He spent the remaining half-hour with Upneet trying to distract her from observation of his domestic life. Why should it interest her? he thought angrily. She came here to study, not to mock, not to

309

make trouble. He was her tutor, not her clown! Sternly, he gave her dictation but she was so hopeless—she learnt no Bengali at her convent school, found it hard even to form the letters of the Bengali alphabet—that he was left speechless. He crossed out her errors with his red pencil—grateful to be able to cancel out, so effectively, some of the ugliness of his life—till there was hardly a word left uncrossed and, looking up to see her reaction, found her far less perturbed than he. In fact, she looked quite mischievously pleased. Three months of Bengali lessons to end in this! She was as triumphant as he was horrified. He let fall the red pencil with a discouraged gesture. So, in complete discord, the lesson broke apart, they all broke apart and for a while Mr Bose was alone on the balcony, clutching at the rails, thinking that these bars of cooled iron were all that were left for him to hold. Inside all was a conflict of shame and despair, in garbled grammar.

But, gradually, the grammar rearranged itself according to rule, corrected itself. The composition into quiet made quite clear the exhaustion of the child, asleep or nearly so. The sounds of dinner being prepared were calm, decorative even. Once more the radio was tuned to music, sympathetically sad. When his wife called him in to eat, he turned to go with his shoulders beaten, sagging, an attitude repeated by his moustache.

'He is asleep,' she said, glancing at him with a rather ashamed face, conciliatory.

He nodded and sat down before his brass tray. She straightened it nervously, waved a hand over it as if to drive away a fly he could not see, and turned to the fire to fry hot *purees* for him, one by one, turning quickly to heap them on his tray so fast that he begged her to stop.

'Eat more,' she coaxed. 'One more'—as though the extra *puree* were a peace offering following her rebellion of half an hour ago.

He took it with reluctant fingers but his moustache began to quiver on his lip as if beginning to wake up. 'And you?' he asked. 'Won't you eat now?'

About her mouth, too, some quivers began to rise and move. She pursed her lips, nodded and began to fill her tray, piling up the *purees* in a low stack.

'One more,' he told her, 'just one more,' he teased, and they laughed.

ELSPETH DAVIE

The Time-Keeper

It was taken as a matter of course that at one time or other during
the summer he would be showing people around his city. Renwick
was a hospitable man and for certain weeks it was a duty to be
available to visitors. The beauty of the place was written on its
skyline in a sharp, black script of spires, chimneys and turrets and in
the flowing line of a long crag and hill. It was written up in books.
He had shelves devoted to its history and its architecture. It was
written on anti-litter slogans with the stern injunction that this was
a beautiful city and it had better be kept that way.

Sometimes the people he took on were those wished on him for
an hour or two, friends of friends, or persons he'd met by chance
passing through on their way north. They were all sightseers of a
sort and the first sight they wanted to see, particularly if they were
foreigners, was himself. Well, he was on the spot, of course. Yes, he
had to admit he probably *was* a sight and even worth looking at in a
very superficial way. At certain times he put on his advocate's
garb—a highly stylized get-up, dark, narrow and formal. A bowler
hat went with the suit and an umbrella which—because of the
windiness of the city—often remained unrolled. He was never
solemn about the business. He was the first to point out that it was
traditional wear—a kind of fancy dress or disguise. 'And there are
plenty of them about these days,' he would say. 'We ourselves are
falling behind in the game. Look at all the people either dressing the
part or the opposite of the part!' But there was no need of excuse.
Visitors enjoyed him in his dress and were disappointed to discover
he seldom wore it when the Court was not sitting. Sometimes
however they were lucky. And he had a face that went with the
garb—a rather masked face, long and grave with hair well plastered
down over a neat skull, as though to show what an extreme of
flatness could be achieved in comparison with the dashing wig
which he might later put on.

Renwick's hospitality didn't mean that he was always a patient man. There was a good deal of exasperation and sharpness in his character, and he shared with many of his fellow citizens a highly argumentative and sceptical turn of mind. He developed it and was valued for it. That hint of the suspicious Scot in his make-up was well hidden. The impatience was not so well in check. It boiled up silently at dullness. It occasionally exploded at stupidity. As time went on, he had even begun to be impatient with those visitors who insisted on taking a purely romantic view of the city. It was not after all made up only of interesting old stones, nor were the people going about their business on top of these stones particularly romantic. Certainly not. They were a commonsense, very businesslike lot and more to be compared to down-to-earth scene-shifters doing their jobs against a theatrical background.

This was made clear to an American couple one afternoon, as they stood with him in one of the oldest graveyards of the city. There was a great deal to see and a lot to hear about. Renwick had given them something of the turbulent history of the place and listed the succession of famous people who had been buried here. They in their turn exclaimed about the ancient monuments and walls. They touched the moss-covered dates on headstones. It was getting late. The three or four still left in the place were slowly making their way out. In the distance a blonde girl was moving around the dark church between black and white tombstones. But Renwick's couple were all for lingering in the place until the sun went down. Renwick felt a sudden flare of impatience rise inside him. He directed them to look up and out of the place. From where they stood they could see, rising on all sides, the backs of houses and churches, and beyond that a glimpse of the bridge which carried a busy street over a chasm. Cars and buses crossed it. People went striding past. 'But look up there,' he said pointing. 'We are rather an energetic crowd. You can see we're in a hurry. You're not going to find your ordinary citizen of the place sitting around staring at old stones for long. I believe you might find it hard enough to get him to stop and talk for any length of time unless there was very good reason for it. For better or worse—that is our character!'

The Americans didn't deny this. They had already attempted to detain people on the bridge. They had sensed the bracing air. Now, polite but silent, they stared down at an angel whose round and rather sulky face was crowned by a neat green crewcut of moss and backed by frilly wings sprouting behind his ears. Cautiously they mentioned the old ghosts of the place.

'But just behind you,' came the brisk voice, 'there, in that wall, there are still lived-in houses. Look at that window for instance.' It was true that in the actual ancient wall of the place they were looking into the room of a house. Sitting in the open window was an old man being shaved by someone standing behind. At first they saw only a hand holding his chin, the other hand drawing a razor along his cheek. But while they watched the job was done. The head of the old man and his middle-aged daughter emerged from the window. It was close enough to get a clear sight of them—keen, unsmiling, both staring straight down with eyes which were shrewd but without much curiosity as though they had seen decades of tourists standing just below them there on that particular spot in the churchyard.

'You see there are more than just angels around us,' said Renwick tersely. 'There are also ordinary, busy folk getting on with their own jobs.'

The young couple looked for a moment as though they might question the business and even the ordinariness, but had thought better of it, especially as they had seen Renwick look openly at his wrist.

Renwick counted himself a polite man. Lately, however, he had given in to this habit, common to persons of consequence in the city, of glancing at his watch—and often while people were actually talking to him. He believed that he was indicating in the politest possible way that he was a very busy man, that even in summer his time was limited. But as the habit grew, not only visitors but even friends began to see the wrist shoot out, no longer surreptitiously but very openly. Those who still hung around after that had only themselves to blame. And as well as the watch he was very well up in the tactics of the engagement diary. 'Well, certainly not tomorrow, nor the day after. This week's out in fact. Next week? Full up, I'm afraid. No, I have a space here. I think I can *just* about manage to fit you in.' Acquaintances might sound grateful, but they felt squeezed and sometimes throttled as they watched him writing them into the minimal space between appointments.

Just as Renwick was both proud and yet irritated by the romantic reputation of the city, so he felt about the supernatural history of the place. He was good-natured about disguises, masks of all kinds.

He understood the hidden. But the guise of the supernatural he didn't care for. He had lost count of the number of times he was asked about the witches and warlocks of the city, mediaeval apparitions hidden down closes, the eighteenth-century ghosts of the New Town. Grudgingly he pointed to deserted windows where heads had looked out and stairs where persons without their heads had walked down. Reluctantly he led willing visitors to the district where the Major had made his pact, pointed out infamous tenements and doorways blasted with the Devil's curse. 'And now you'll want to see the spot where the gallows stood—and you'll not mind if I leave you there. I have to keep an eye on my time. The fact is I have a good deal of business to attend to between now and supper.'

Friends dated his concern with time back to a year when his post brought new responsibilities. Others pointed out that business was all a matter of choice, and that the time-obsession was common to most middle-aged men once they'd begun to feel it making up on them. 'And worse things can happen to a man than keeping to a tight schedule,' remarked a colleague as they discussed others in the profession. 'We've had a good few suicides by his age, and quite a tearing of the silk. There was McInnes letting it all rip and making off for the South Seas. And Webster? Wasn't it the stage he'd always yearned for, never the Bar? Yes, retired now, white hair to the shoulders—happy enough they say, and no guile in the man at all. Still, meeting him late on summer nights in loopy hats with orange feathers gave some people more of a turn than seeing the Devil himself.' Other names came up. They decided it was nothing more than a little touchiness about time—Renwick was doing well enough.

By midsummer a stream of holiday-makers were on the streets. Renwick would become impatient—or was it envious?—at the idea of an endless enjoyment of leisure. How could they wander for days and weeks, sometimes for months? From early spring, when the first few aimless visitors arrived, he would begin to take note of the city clocks. Not that he hadn't known them all his life—the clocks under church spires, the clocks on schools and hospitals and hotel towers. He'd seen brand-new time-pieces erected in his day and had attended the unveilings of memorial clocks. But now he counted them as allies in the summer game, to give him backing when the wristwatch methods had no result. It was his habit, then, to stare about him for the nearest clock—if it was old, so much the better. Having alerted visitors to its history, it was an easy step to exclaim at the time of day, to excuse himself and make off with all possible speed to the next appointment.

During one summer Renwick had several visitors of his own for a short time. He enjoyed their stay. They knew the city well. It was not always necessary to accompany them, but he had the pleasure of their talk in the evening. Later, however, he was asked if he would help a friend out with four visitors who had been staying in the city and, with little warning, were to land on him for twelve hours. The friend had to be out of town on the evening of that day. Could Renwick possibly take them round for half an hour or so? Yes, he could do that. When the time came, they turned out to be two middle-aged couples from the south who had not set foot in the city before this visit. But they had read the necessary books. They were well primed with history and they knew legends about every door and windowframe. They had expected smoky sunsets and they got them. They knew that on certain nights there might be a moon directly above the floodlit castle. The moon was in the prescribed spot the first night they arrived. They did not mind bad weather. They said that gloom and darkness suited the place. They liked the mist and even the chill haar that could swirl up out of the sea after a warm day. They were amiable, and they had an equal and unqualified love for all the figures in the city's past.

That evening Renwick had taken them down into one of the closes of the Lawnmarket, and they were now standing in a large court enclosed by tenement walls. There were a few people besides themselves in the place; a group of youths with bottles bulging at their hips, a fair-haired girl holding a guide-book and three small children who had raced in after a ball and out again. It was getting late and a few small yellow lights were appearing high up on the surrounding walls.

'If only we could get in there and see some of those weird old rooms,' said one of the wives, staring up.

'And speak to one or two of the old folk,' her husband added. 'There'll be ones up there with many a tale to tell of the old days.'

'Many a tale?' Renwick straightened his shoulders. He directed a rather chilly smile over the heads of the group. 'No doubt there might be tales—and ones not so very different from our own. Of course those particular rooms you're looking at have all been re-done. They are expensive places, very well equipped, I should imagine, with all the latest gadgets. You'll find quite young, very well set-up people living there, I believe. You'll get your dank walls, poor drains, black corners in a good many other places if you care to look. But not up there!'

They had been with him now for half an hour. Renwick had begun to check the various times on their watches with his own, and murmuring 'I will just make sure,' had walked down the few steps at the far end of the court and out to where, overlooking street and gardens, he could see the large, lit clock at the east end of the city.

'I must be off in five minutes,' he said, when he came back, '. . . letters to attend to . . . a paper to prepare.' They asked if he could give them an idea what they should look at the following morning. Briefly he outlined a plan and described the things they should see. They asked if they would meet him again. He explained that in a couple of days he might or might not meet them, depending on his work. 'Do you work all through the holidays?' someone innocently asked. Renwick made a non-committal gesture to the sky. At the same time he noticed that the fair-haired girl, who'd been wandering about for some time between their group and the shadowy end of the court, had come forward and now stood with them directly under the lamp. Stunning. Not nowadays a word he was in the habit of using. But what other word for this particular kind of fairness? Straight white-blonde hair, fair eyebrows against brown skin, and eyes so pale they had scarcely more colour than water. A Scandinavian—the intonation was plain in a few words she spoke to one of the women, but she was also that idealized version which, along with its opposite, each country holds of another part of the world—strikingly tall, strong and fair, and no doubt outspoken. Renwick waited for her to speak. She lifted her arm with the back of her wrist towards him. She tapped her watch.

'You have given us your minutes. Exactly five. Your time is up,' she said. The others laughed. Renwick smiled. So she had seen his clock-watching, heard his work programme, had simply stopped in passing for a laugh. But attention was now turned her way. They were asking questions. And it appeared that in her country the light was different. The sun, they gathered, was very bright, the darkness more intense. Different, she made it plain, though not of course better. They took it in, unblinking, while they stared. It seemed they got the message on light in a single flash and with no trouble at all. The girl left the place soon afterwards, and to Renwick it seemed that his two couples were slowly merged together again, and he with them—all welded into the state called middle-age. No amount of good sense, no bracing talk of God-sent wisdom or hard-won experience, and least, least of all the beauties of maturity, were ever going to mend this matter. There they were. Some light had left them.

One way or another, this was to occupy him a good deal during the next day. It was not just that at some stage of life the optimistic beam had been replaced by a smaller light, but that from the start even his awareness of actual physical light had been limited. It was hard for him to imagine variations—how some lights sharpened every object and its shadow for miles around, while others made a featureless flatness of the same scene. He tried to imagine those regions of the world made barren to the bone by sun, and others soaked by the same sun to make ground and water prosper from one good year to the next. He thought with relief of white corn-fields nearer home and remembered with a shock of hope streams so transparent you could see the fish, leaves and stones shining in their depths.

The phone drilled at his skull. 'Tomorrow evening—would it be possible for half an hour, if you can manage to spare the time?' Both couples were leaving the next morning. Yes, it would be just possible to fit it in. They would meet at the bottom of the street leading from Palace to Castle. They would walk slowly up. Another voice joined the first in thanking him.

'The weather has been disappointing for you today,' said Renwick as he waited for the moment to put the phone down.

'No, this is how we like it,' came the reply. 'Clear, sharp, with a touch of frost.' This might pass, with those who knew him, as a rough description of himself. Or not so rough. Exact perhaps—though some might put the complimentary touch, others a hatching of black lines. Renwick said he was glad to hear it and replaced the receiver thoughtfully.

The next evening was overcast with a slight wind which sent the black and white clouds slowly across the sky. They were waiting for him eagerly. 'A disappointing evening,' he said, as if to test them again. On the contrary they were enthusiastic. This was the city at its best, at its most characteristic. Renwick saved his disappointment for himself. They walked slowly up, going in and out of closes, through doors and arches. They saw the sea through openings and climbed halfway up stairways worn into deep curves. Renwick led the way through the darker wynds. He answered questions. Apart from that he said little. The street grew steep, crossed a main road and went on up until it opened out to the broad space in front of the church of St Giles with the Law Courts behind. It was growing dark, and from this rise where they were standing they could see down almost the whole length of the street illumined by blue street lights. It was a favourite viewing point for tourist buses and their guides, and there were still a few about. People were roaming around the precincts of the Courts and going to and from the church.

Renwick looked round and stared pointedly at the large, lit clock of the Tolbooth, big as a harvest moon. Further down the street were smaller clocks. Automatically following his eyes, the others stared too. They got the message. Time was important even to citizens of an historic city. Things must move on. Turning back again, Renwick saw the blonde girl a few steps away. She had been looking at the church. Now she was making a beeline for his group. So he had been watched again, scrutinized no doubt as an exhibit of the place, one worth remembering perhaps, but remembered with a good deal more amusement than respect. She had reached the group now and stood waiting until the couples wandered off to make the most of their last minutes of sight-seeing. Then she remarked: 'You have very few angels inside. I have seen the churches. Some of them are very beautiful and very bare.'

'You're absolutely right,' said Renwick. He lectured her gently on the reasons for it. 'Any angels we do have are mostly outside,' he added, 'hidden away in cemeteries.'

And if it came to angels, it was true enough the blue light had given her own face a marbly shine, her hair a touch of green. But her eyes had neither the exalted nor the downcast look of churchyard angels. They were too direct, too challenging for an angel's eyes. She was not the kind to be hidden away. He was going on to an explanation of the spot where they were standing when something struck him. He stopped in mid-sentence. 'I am not a guide,' said Renwick.

'Well, I think you are,' said the young woman. 'You keep them all together. You keep the time. That is important—how you keep the time. Clocks are important, very important indeed. Clocks are—how do you say?—they are very much up your street.' Saying this, she made a quick survey of the street from top to bottom as he had done some minutes before. Her performance managed, miraculously, to be both amiable and derisive. She made way genially for the others when they came back, and after some talk with them, went off again.

There was nothing to take him out the following evening. Nobody demanded his time. Yet the next night after supper, he was out trudging up the High Street again. The place was still crowded and he made his way around groups at corners and through lines of people who were spread out across the width of the street. This time he felt the need to look about him with the eye of a stranger. Many times he stopped to stare at familiar things, and once in a while, as if from the corner of his eye, managed to catch some object by surprise. It was a warm night. Far above him he saw rows of elbows upon windowsills and shadowy heads staring down, and above the heads a rocky outline of roofs and steep, black gable walls blocking the night sky. Sometimes he turned back for a closer look at the scrolls on archways, or to search for some small stone head over a door. He had become a tourist among tourists, staring at persons and buildings—critical, admiring, sometimes bored, sometimes amazed at what he saw. He grew tired. His own feet looked strange to him as he stepped on and off the kerb or dodged the slippery stones on uneven bits of pavement. He plodded on. His face confronted him, unawares, in dark shop windows, and different from the conscious face in the bedroom mirror. This person looked distraught, looked lonely, battered even, and hardly to be distinguished from some of the down-and-outs who wandered in and out of nearby pubs.

Renwick had come a long way. The Castle was now in view and it was giving all of them the full treatment. He had seen this often enough—illumined stone and black battlements against a sky still red with sunset. To crown all, a huge, white supermoon breaking through clouds. Renwick found himself in the midst of a large group, all turned that way, all staring as if at a high stage. They were a long time staring. Suddenly, as if at a warning buzz in the brain, Renwick resumed citizenship. He was proud yet impatient of the wide eyes around him. He glanced at his watch, heard his own voice repeat familiar words:

'Yes, that's often how it is—very dramatic, very spectacular. Illumined? Yes, very often. The full moon? Yes, don't ask me how—it *seems* often to be full and very well placed, though more romantically speaking than astronomically I would say. You must remember though—we are not only a romantic city. Far from it. Yes, yes, of course there's stuff coming down, but have you seen the new things going up—the business side of things. In other words, we are a *busy* people. Time moves on, you see. It moves on here as in every other place.' He looked a man of some consequence, a very busy man with a full timetable to get through. They made way for him. He wished them goodnight, passed on.

He was alone now and walking in a quiet side street. The moon and the red sky were behind, the illumination blocked out by high office buildings. He was making for home. Once he stopped in passing for a word with an acquaintance, until they reminded one another of the time and quickly separated. Five persons made up on him and passed, talking animatedly, and Renwick recognized the cadence of this tongue. The blonde girl was walking with three others and a young man. The man was native to the city. The rest, he noted, were all tall, all fair, all dressed with a flair and colour that stood out even in the dark street. If this was the northern myth it was coming over in style. The girl gave him a wave as they went by. 'A fine night,' said Renwick.

'Yes,' the girl called back. 'And how about your moon tonight? Have you looked yet? Has it turned into a clock for you?' He heard her answering the young man, heard her say in a voice—low, but audible to touchy ears: 'No, no, not moonstruck. He is a time-keeper. The man is clock-mad!' She made some remark to the others in her own language. They laughed, looked back over their shoulders and gave him a friendly wave. All five went on their way, noiseless, in rubber soles, and disappeared round the next corner.

But Renwick's shoes were loud on the paving-stones, the foot-steps rang in his ears like a metronome. But what were they counting out? Minutes or stones? He stared round once, then turned his back again. This moon had looked cold and white as a snowball. Yet his moonlit ears burned as he walked on.

Mamasita

Mamasita goes out after dark to chase the drunks with a stick. And
they stumble up the lighted broken steps of the Men's Social Care
Centre while the cops laugh at Mamasita. Mamasita hairy and
black, drooped red melons in her shirt. Oh Billy Babo you is the
plague of your mother, Oh she screams, I will beeet you . . . And she
herds them in. To the showers and the tin cups and the hard horned
hands of the cops. She squeeze their nuts, they say Oh mama no.
She slap, slap, they say Oh yes mama. Mamasita remembers her
daddy, falling up and down steps in the Bowery, poison exhale of
his breath, gagging and raging his young drunk curses and she a
small fat swab in a corner. How the closet, hunker, press, oh press
close, where she sat for hours when he forgot where he put her.
How she look up, weepy snot, and him big hands reaching down.
How the bottles smell. Dark, thick-edged, and the feet drag on
another step. Brothers drunk and flashy, young flashy drunks, cut
each other up for bangles oh press close. Mamasita long time ago
fat and pregnant gets her jaw broke up. But she feel big now, she is
big. Till the drunks, the old ones, tell their whimpers in the dark.
Their soft mousy sex, such whisper. Bony crouch on newspaper,
cornered swabs. Got nothin get nothin. Mamasita hard as nails.
They crouch, pick their crabbed groins there by the lamps. Mamasita, oh she goes out with her stick. She likes the ones so gone they
don't attack, they don't defend. She feel that soft swab, snivelling
girl in her gut, oh she want to kill her. And the frowzy stumblers
with their faces cut, with their dank dumb eyes and weighted lids,
they look up at Mamasita. Their guts rolled up in tiny balls. Long
time ago they roll up their guts, what they got. Got to get somethin
mama. Mama. Mamasita with her sausage smell and big stick
pouring down. Something ground up, rolled in offal, wrapped in a
slick spiced skin. Eat it, eat it up. The pigs roll in their pissed pants
up into the light. Because that's how she wants them, that's what
she wants.

ANGELA CARTER

Peter and the Wolf

At length the grandeur of the mountains becomes monotonous; with familiarity, the landscape ceases to provoke awe and wonder. Above a certain line, no trees grow. Shadows of clouds move across the bare alps as freely as the clouds themselves move across the sky. All is vast, barren, unprofitable, unkind.

A girl from a village on the lower slopes left her widowed mother to marry a man who lived up in the empty places. Soon she was pregnant. In October, there was a severe storm. The old woman knew her daughter was near her time and waited for a message but none arrived. After the storm passed off, the old woman went up to see for herself, taking her grown son with her because she was afraid.

From a long way off, they saw no smoke rising from the chimney. Solitude swelled around them. The open door banged backwards and forwards on its hinges. Solitude engulfed them. There were traces of wolf-dung on the floor so they knew wolves had been in the house but had left the corpse of the young mother alone although of her baby nothing was left except some mess that showed it had been born. Nor was there a trace of the son-in-law but a gnawed foot in a boot.

They wrapped the dead body in a quilt and took it home with them. Now it was late. The howling of the wolves excoriated the approaching silence of the night.

Then winter came with icy blasts, when everyone stays indoors and stokes the fire. The old woman's son married the blacksmith's daughter and she moved in with them. The snow melted and it was spring. By the next Christmas, there was a bouncing grandson. Time passed. More children came.

The summer that the eldest grandson, Peter, reached the age of seven, he was old enough to go up the mountain with his father, as the men did every year, to feed the goats on the young grass. There Peter sat in the clean, new sunlight, plaiting straw for baskets, contented as could be until he saw the thing he had been taught most to fear advancing silently along the lee of an outcrop of rock. Then another wolf, following the first one.

If they had not been the first wolves he had ever seen, the boy would not have looked at them so closely, their plush, grey pelts, of which the hairs are tipped with white, giving them a ghostly look, as if their edges were disappearing; their sprightly, plumey tails; their sharp, inquiring masks that reflect an intelligence which, however acute, is not our way of dealing with the world.

Because Peter did not turn and run but, instead, looked, he saw that the third one was a prodigy, a marvel, a naked one, going on all fours, as they did, but hairless as regards the body although it had a brown mane around its head like a pony.

He was so fascinated by the sight of this bald wolf that he would have lost his flock, perhaps himself been eaten and certainly been beaten to the bone for negligence had not the goats themselves raised their heads, snuffed danger and run off, bleating and whinnying, so that the men came, firing guns, making hullabaloo, scaring the wolves away.

His father was too angry to listen to what Peter said. He cuffed Peter round the head and sent him home in disgrace. His mother was feeding this year's baby. His grandmother sat at the table, shelling peas into a pot.

'There was a little girl with the wolves, granny,' said Peter. Why was he so sure it had been a little girl? Perhaps because her hair was so long, so long and lively. 'A little girl about my age, from her size,' he said.

His grandmother threw a flat pod out of the door so the chickens could peck it up.

'I saw a little girl with the wolves,' he said.

His grandmother tipped water into the pot, heaved up from the table and suspended the pot of peas on the hook over the fire. There wasn't time, that night, but, next morning, very early, she herself took the boy up the mountain.

'Tell your father what you told me.'

They went to look at the wolves' tracks. On a bit of dampish ground they found a print, not like that of a dog's pad, much less like that of a child's footprint, yet Peter worried and puzzled over it until he made sense of it.

'She was running on all fours with her arse stuck up in the air . . .

therefore . . . she'd put all her weight on the ball of her foot, wouldn't she? And splay out her toes, see . . . like that.'

He went barefoot in summer, like all the village children; he inserted the ball of his own foot in the print, to show his father what kind of mark it would make if he, too, always ran on all fours.

'No use for a heel, if you run that way. So she doesn't leave a heelprint. Stands to reason.'

His father nodded a slow acknowledgement of Peter's powers of deduction.

They soon found her. She was asleep. Her spine had grown so supple she could curl into a perfect C. She woke up when she heard them and ran, but somebody caught her with a sliding noose at the end of a rope; the noose over her head jerked tight so that she fell to the ground with her eyes popping and rolling. A big, grey, angry bitch appeared out of nowhere but Peter's father blasted it to bits with his shotgun. The girl would have choked if the old woman hadn't taken her head on her lap and pulled the knot loose. The girl bit the grandmother's hand.

The girl scratched, fought and bit until the men tied her wrists and ankles together with twine and slung her from a pole to carry her back to the village. Then she went limp. She didn't scream or shout, she didn't seem to be able to, she made only a few dull, guttural sounds in the back of her throat, and, though she did not seem to know how to cry, water trickled out of the corners of her eyes.

How burned she was by the weather! Bright brown all over; and how filthy she was! Caked and mired with mud and dirt. And every inch of her chestnut hide was scored and scabbed with dozens of scars of sharp abrasions of rock and thorn. Her hair dragged on the ground as they carried her along; it was stuck with burrs and you could not see what colour it might be, it was so dirty. She was dreadfully verminous. She stank. She was so thin that all her ribs stuck out. The fine, plump, potato-fed boy was far bigger than she, although she was a year or so older.

Solemn with curiosity, he trotted behind her. Granny stumped alongside with her bitten hand wrapped up in her apron. When they dumped the girl on the earth floor of her grandmother's house, the boy secretly poked at her left buttock with his forefinger, out of curiosity, to see what she felt like. She felt warm but hard as wood. She did not so much as twitch when he touched her. She had given up the struggle; she lay trussed on the floor and pretended to be dead.

Granny's house had the one large room which, in winter, they shared with the goats. As soon as it caught a whiff of her, the big tabby mouser let out a hiss like a pricked balloon and bounded up the ladder that went to the hayloft above. Soup smoked on the fire and the table was laid. It was now about supper-time but still quite light; night comes late on the summer mountain.

'Untie her,' said the grandmother.

Her son wasn't willing at first but the old woman would not be denied, so he got the breadknife and cut the rope round the girl's ankles. All she did was kick a bit but, when he cut the rope round her wrists, it was as if he had let a fiend loose. The onlookers ran out of the door, the rest of the family ran for the ladder to the hayloft but granny and Peter both made for the door, to pull it to and shoot the bolt, so that she could not get out.

The trapped one knocked round the room. Bang—over went the table. Crash, tinkle—the supper dishes smashed. Bang, crash, tinkle—the dresser fell forward in a hard white hail of broken crockery. Over went the meal barrel and she coughed, she sneezed like a child sneezes, no different, and then she bounced around on fear-stiffened legs in a white cloud until the flour settled on everything like a magic powder that made everything strange.

She started to make little rushes, now here, now there, snapping and yelping and tossing her bewildered head.

She never rose up on two legs; she crouched, all the time, on her hands and tiptoes, yet it was not quite like crouching, for you could see how all fours came naturally to her as though she had made a different pact with gravity than we have, and you could see, too, how strong the muscles in her thighs had grown on the mountain, how taut the twanging arches of her feet, and that indeed, she only used her heels when she sat back on her haunches. She growled; now and then she coughed out those intolerable, thick grunts of distress. All you could see of her rolling eyes were the whites, which were the bluish, glaring white of snow.

Several times, her bowels opened, apparently involuntarily, and soon the kitchen smelled like a privy yet even her excrement was different to ours, the refuse of raw, strange, unguessable, wicked feeding, shit of a wolf.

Oh, horror!

She bumped into the hearth, knocked over the pan hanging from the hook and the spilled contents put out the fire. Hot soup scalded her forelegs. Shock of pain. Squatting on her hindquarters, holding the hurt paw dangling piteously before her from its wrist, she howled, she howled, she howled, high, sobbing arcs that seemed to pierce the roof.

Even the old woman, who had contracted with herself to love the child of her dead daughter, was frightened when she heard the girl howl.

Peter's heart gave a hop, a skip, so that he had a sensation of falling; he was not conscious of his own fear because he could not take his eyes off the sight of the crevice of her girl child's sex, that was perfectly visible to him as she sat there square on the base of her spine. The night was now as dark as, at this season, it would go—which is to say, not very dark; a white thread of moon hung in the blond sky at the top of the chimney so that it was neither dark nor light indoors yet the boy could see her intimacy clearly, as if by its own phosphoresence. It exercised an absolute fascination upon him. Everything. He could see everything.

Her lips opened up as she howled so that she offered him, without her own intention or volition, a view of a set of Chinese boxes of whorled flesh that seemed to open one upon another into herself, drawing him into an inner, secret place in which destination perpetually receded before him, his first, devastating, vertiginous intimation of infinity, as if, in the luminous, ambiguous dusk of the night/not-night of the northern uplands, she showed him the gnawed fruit of the tree of knowledge, although she herself did not know what 'knowledge' was.

She howled.

And went on howling until, from the mountain, first singly, then in a complex polyphony, answered at last voices in the same language.

She continued to howl, though now with a less tragic resonance.

Soon it was impossible for the occupants of the house to deny to themselves that the wolves were descending on the village in a pack.

Then she was consoled, sank down, laid her head on her forepaws so that her hair trailed in the cooling soup and so closed up her forbidden book without the least notion she had ever opened it or that it was banned. The household gun hung on a nail over the fireplace where Peter's father had put it when he came in but when the man set his foot on the top rung of the ladder in order to come down for his weapon, the girl jumped up, snarling and showing her long, yellow canines.

The howling outside was now mixed with the agitated dismay of the domestic beasts. All the other villagers were well locked up at home.

The wolves were at the door.

The boy took hold of his grandmother's uninjured hand. First the old woman would not budge but he gave her a good tug and she came to herself. The girl raised her head suspiciously but let them by. The boy pushed his grandmother up the ladder in front of him and drew it up behind them. He was full of nervous dread. He would have given anything to turn back, so that he might have run, shouting a warning, when he first caught sight of the wolves, and never seen her.

The door shook as the wolves outside jumped up at it and the screws that held the socket of the bolt to the frame cracked, squeaked and started to give. The girl jumped up, at that, and began to make excited little sallies back and forth in front of the door. The screws tore out of the frame quite soon. The pack tumbled over one another to get inside.

Dissonance. Terror. The clamour within the house was that of all the winds of winter trapped in a box. That which they feared most, outside, was now indoors with them. The baby in the hayloft whimpered and its mother crushed it to her breast as if the wolves might snatch this one away, too; but the rescue party had arrived only in order to collect their fosterling.

They left behind a riotous stench in the house, and white tracks of flour everywhere. The broken door creaked backwards and forwards on its hinges. Black sticks of dead wood from the extinguished fire scattered the floor.

Peter thought the old woman would cry, now, but she seemed unmoved. When all was safe, they came down the ladder one by one and, as if released from a spell of silence, all burst into excited speech at once except for the mute old woman and the boy. Although it was well past midnight, the daughter-in-law went to the well for water to scrub the wild smell out of the house. The broken things were cleared up and thrown away. Peter's father nailed the table and the dresser back together. The neighbours came out of their houses, full of amazement; the wolves had not taken so much as a chicken from the hen-coops, not snatched even a single egg.

People brought beer into the starlight, and schnapps made from potatoes, and snacks, because the excitement had made them hungry. That terrible night ended up in one big party but the grandmother would eat or drink nothing and went to bed as soon as her house was clean.

Next day, she went to the graveyard and sat for a while beside her daughter's grave but she did not pray. Then she came home and started chopping cabbage for the evening meal but had to leave off because her bitten hand was festering.

That winter, during the leisure imposed by the snow, after his grandmother's death, Peter asked the village priest to teach him to read the Bible. The priest gladly complied; Peter was the first of his flock who had ever expressed any interest in literacy.

Now the boy became amazingly pious, so much so that his family were startled and impressed. The younger children teased him and called him 'Saint Peter' but that did not stop him sneaking off to church to pray whenever he had a spare moment. In Lent, he fasted to the bone. On Good Friday, he lashed himself. It was as if he blamed himself for the death of the old lady, as if he believed he had brought into the house the fatal infection that had taken her out of it. He was consumed by an imperious passion for atonement. Each night, he pored over his book by the flimsy candlelight, looking for a clue to grace, until his mother shooed him off to sleep.

But, as if to spite the four angels he nightly invoked to protect his bed, the nightmare regularly disordered his sleeps. He tossed and turned on the rustling straw pallet he shared with two little ones. He grew up haggard.

Delighted with Peter's precocious intelligence, the priest started to teach him Latin; Peter visited the priest as his duties with the herd permitted. When he was fourteen, the priest told his parents that Peter should now go to the seminary in the town in the valley where the boy would learn to become a priest himself. Rich in sons, they spared one to God, since he had become a stranger to them. After the goats came down from the high pasture for the winter, Peter set off. It was October.

At the end of his first day's travel, he reached a river that flowed from the mountain into the valley. The nights were already chilly; he lit himself a fire, prayed, ate the bread and cheese his mother had packed for him and slept as well as he could. In spite of his eagerness to plunge into the white world of penance and devotion that awaited him, he was anxious and troubled for reasons he could not explain to himself.

In the first light, the light that no more than clarifies darkness like egg shells dropped in cloudy liquid, he went down to the river to drink and to wash his face. It was so still he could have been the one thing living.

Her forearms, her loins and her legs were thick with hair and the hair on her head hung round her face in such a way that you could hardly make out her features. She crouched on the other side of the river. She was lapping up water so full of mauve light that it looked as if she were drinking up the dawn as fast as it appeared yet all the same the air grew pale while he was looking at her.

Solitude and silence; all still. -- ...

She could never have acknowledged that the reflection beneath her in the river was that of herself. She did not know she had a face; she had never known she had a face and so her face itself was the mirror of a different kind of consciousness than ours is, just as her nakedness, without innocence or display, was that of our first parents, before the Fall, and if she was hairy as Magdalen in the wilderness, she need never fear to lose her soul since she had never got one.

Language crumbled into dust under the weight of her speechlessness.

A pair of cubs rolled out of the bushes, cuffing one another. She did not pay them any heed.

The boy began to tremble and shake. His skin strangely prickled. He felt he had been made of snow and now might melt. He mumbled something, or sobbed.

She cocked her head at the vague, river-washed sound and the cubs heard it too, left off tumbling and ran to burrow their scared heads in her side. But she decided, after a moment, there was no danger and lowered her muzzle again, to the surface of the water that took hold of her hair and spread it out around her head.

When she finished her drink, she backed a few paces, shaking her wet pelt. The little cubs fastened their mouths on her dangling breasts.

Peter could not help it, he burst out crying. He had not cried since his grandmother's funeral. Tears rolled down his face and splashed on the grass. He blundered forward a few steps into the river with his arms held open, intending to cross over to the other side to join her, impelled by the access of an almost visionary ecstasy to see her so complete, so private. But his cousin took fright at the sudden movement, wrenched her teats away from the cubs and ran off. The squeaking cubs scampered behind. She ran on hands and feet as if that were the only way to run, towards the high ground, into the bright maze of the uncompleted dawn.

When the boy recovered himself, he dried his tears on his sleeve, took off his soaked boots and dried his feet and legs on the tail of his shirt. Then he ate something from his pack, he scarcely knew what, and continued on the way to the town; but what would he do at the seminary, now? Now he knew there was nothing to be afraid of.

He pissed against a tree and, for the first time in his life, took a good, long, unembarrassed look at his prick. He laughed out loud. Had he truly thought this sturdily sprouting young fellow would lie still under a surplice?

He experienced the vertigo of freedom.

He carried his boots slung over his shoulder by the laces. They seemed a great burden. He debated with himself whether or not to throw them away but, when he came to a road, he put them on, although they were still damp, because bare feet can't cope with hard roads.

The birds woke up and sang. The cool, rational sun surprised him; morning had broken on his exhilaration and the mountain now lay behind him. He looked over his shoulder and saw how, with distance, the mountain began to acquire a flat, two-dimensional look. It was already turning into a picture of itself, into the postcard hastily bought as a souvenir of childhood at a railway station or a border post, the newspaper cutting, the snapshot he would show in strange towns, strange cities, other countries he could not, at this moment, imagine, whose names he did not yet know: 'That was where I spent my childhood. Imagine!'

He turned and stared at the mountain for a long time. He had lived in it for fourteen years but he had never seen it before as it might look to someone who had not known it as almost part of the self. The simplicity of the mountain, its magnificence. Its indifference. As he said goodbye to it, he saw it turn into so much scenery, into the wonderful backcloth for an old country tale, of a child suckled by wolves, perhaps, or of wolves nursed by a woman.

Then he determinedly set his face towards the town and tramped onwards.

'If I look back again,' he thought with a last gasp of superstitious terror, 'I shall turn into a pillar of salt.'

Ellen Gilchrist

Revenge

It was the summer of the Broad Jump Pit.

The Broad Jump Pit, how shall I describe it! It was a bright orange rectangle in the middle of a green pasture. It was three feet deep, filled with river sand and sawdust. A real cinder track led up to it, ending where tall poles for pole-vaulting rose forever in the still Delta air.

I am looking through the old binoculars. I am watching Bunky coming at a run down the cinder path, pausing expertly at the jump-off line, then rising into the air, heels stretched far out in front of him, landing in the sawdust. Before the dust has settled Saint John comes running with the tape, calling out measurements in his high, excitable voice.

Next comes my thirteen-year-old brother, Dudley, coming at a brisk jog down the track, the pole-vaulting pole held lightly in his delicate hands, then vaulting, high into the sky. His skinny tanned legs make a last, desperate surge, and he is clear and over.

Think how it looked from my lonely exile atop the chicken house. I was ten years old, the only girl in a house full of cousins. There were six of us, shipped to the Delta for the summer, dumped on my grandmother right in the middle of a world war.

They built this wonder in answer to a V-Mail letter from my father in Europe. The war was going well, my father wrote, within a year the Allies would triumph over the forces of evil, the world would be at peace, and the Olympic torch would again be brought down from its mountain and carried to Zurich or Amsterdam or London or Mexico City, wherever free men lived and worshipped sports. My father had been a participant in an Olympic event when he was young.

Therefore, the letter continued, Dudley and Bunky and Philip and Saint John and Oliver were to begin training. The United States would need athletes now, not soldiers.

They were to train for broad jumping and pole-vaulting and

332

discus throwing, for fifty-, one-hundred-, and four-hundred-yard dashes, for high and low hurdles. The letter included instructions for building the pit, for making pole-vaulting poles out of cane, and for converting ordinary sawhorses into hurdles. It ended with a page of tips for proper eating and admonished Dudley to take good care of me as I was my father's own dear sweet little girl.

The letter came one afternoon. Early the next morning they began construction. Around noon I wandered out to the pasture to see how they were coming along. I picked up a shovel.

'Put that down, Rhoda,' Dudley said. 'Don't bother us now. We're working.'

'I know it,' I said. 'I'm going to help.'

'No, you're not,' Bunky said. 'This is the Broad Jump Pit. We're starting our training.'

'I'm going to do it too,' I said. 'I'm going to be in training.'

'Get out of here now,' Dudley said. 'This is only for boys, Rhoda. This isn't a game.'

'I'm going to dig it if I want to,' I said, picking up a shovelful of dirt and throwing it on Philip. On second thought I picked up another shovelful and threw it on Bunky.

'Get out of here, Ratface,' Philip yelled at me. 'You German spy.' He was referring to the initials on my Girl Scout uniform.

'You goddamn niggers,' I yelled. 'You niggers. I'm digging this if I want to and you can't stop me, you nasty niggers, you Japs, you Jews.' I was throwing dirt on everyone now. Dudley grabbed the shovel and wrestled me to the ground. He held my arms down in the coarse grass and peered into my face.

'Rhoda, you're not having anything to do with this Broad Jump Pit. And if you set foot inside this pasture or come around here and touch anything we will break your legs and drown you in the bayou with a crowbar around your neck.' He was twisting my leg until it creaked at the joints. 'Do you get it, Rhoda? Do you understand me?'

'Let me up,' I was screaming, my rage threatening to split open my skull. 'Let me up, you goddamn nigger, you Jap, you spy. I'm telling Grannie and you're going to get the worst whipping of your life. And you better quit digging this hole for the horses to fall in. Let me up, let me up. Let me go.'

'You've been ruining everything we've thought up all summer,'

Dudley said, 'And you're not setting foot inside this pasture.'

In the end they dragged me back to the house, and I ran screaming into the kitchen where Grannie and Calvin, the black man who did the cooking, tried to comfort me, feeding me pound cake and offering to let me help with the mayonnaise.

'You be a sweet girl, Rhoda,' my grandmother said, 'and this afternoon we'll go over to Eisenglas Plantation to play with Miss Ann Wentzel.'

'I don't want to play with Miss Ann Wentzel,' I screamed. 'I hate Miss Ann Wentzel. She's fat and she calls me a Yankee. She said my socks were ugly.'

'Why, Rhoda,' my grandmother said. 'I'm surprised at you. Miss Ann Wentzel is your own sweet friend. Her momma was your momma's roommate at All Saints'. How can you talk like that?'

'She's a nigger,' I screamed. 'She's a goddamned nigger German spy.'

'Now it's coming. Here comes the temper,' Calvin said, rolling his eyes back in their sockets to make me madder. I threw my second fit of the morning, beating my fists into a door frame. My grandmother seized me in soft arms. She led me to a bedroom where I sobbed myself to sleep in a sea of down pillows.

The construction went on for several weeks. As soon as they finished breakfast every morning they started out for the pasture. Wood had to be burned to make cinders, sawdust brought from the sawmill, sand hauled up from the riverbank by wheelbarrow.

When the pit was finished the savage training began. From my several vantage points I watched them. Up and down, up and down they ran, dove, flew, sprinted. Drenched with sweat they wrestled each other to the ground in bitter feuds over distances and times and fractions of inches.

Dudley was their self-appointed leader. He drove them like a demon. They began each morning by running around the edge of the pasture several times, then practising their hurdles and dashes, then on to discus throwing and callisthenics. Then on to the Broad Jump Pit with its endless challenges.

They even pressed the old mare into service. Saint John was from New Orleans and knew the British ambassador and was thinking of being a polo player. Up and down the pasture he drove the poor old creature, leaning far out of the saddle, swatting a basketball with my grandaddy's cane.

I spied on them from the swing that went out over the bayou, and from the roof of the chicken house, and sometimes from the pasture fence itself, calling out insults or attempts to make them jealous.

'Guess what,' I would yell, 'I'm going to town to the Chinaman's store.' 'Guess what, I'm getting to go to the beauty parlour.' 'Doctor Biggs says you're adopted.'

They ignored me. At meals they sat together at one end of the table, making jokes about my temper and my red hair, opening their mouths so I could see their half-chewed food, burping loudly in my direction.

At night they pulled their cots together on the sleeping porch, plotting against me while I slept beneath my grandmother's window, listening to the soft assurance of her snoring.

I began to pray the Japs would win the war, would come marching into Issaquena County and take them prisoners, starving and torturing them, sticking bamboo splinters under their fingernails. I saw myself in the Japanese colonel's office, turning them in, writing their names down, myself being treated like an honoured guest, drinking tea from tiny blue cups like the ones the Chinaman had in his store.

They would be outside, tied up with wire. There would be Dudley, begging for mercy. What good to him now his loyal gang, his photographic memory, his trick magnet dogs, his perfect pitch, his camp shorts, his Baby Brownie camera.

I prayed they would get polio, would be consigned forever to iron lungs. I put myself to sleep at night imagining their laboured breathing, their five little wheelchairs lined up by the store as I drove by in my father's Packard, my arm around the jacket of his blue uniform, on my way to Hollywood for my screen test.

Meanwhile, I practised dancing. My grandmother had a black housekeeper named Baby Doll who was a wonderful dancer. In the mornings I followed her around while she dusted, begging for dancing lessons. She was a big woman, as tall as a man, and gave off a dark rich smell, an unforgettable incense, a combination of Evening in Paris and the sweet perfume of the cabins.

Baby Doll wore bright skirts and on her blouses a pin that said REMEMBER, then a real pearl, then HARBOR. She was engaged to a sailor and was going to California to be rich as soon as the war was over.

I would put a stack of heavy, scratched records on the record player, and Baby Doll and I would dance through the parlours to the music of Glenn Miller or Guy Lombardo or Tommy Dorsey.

Sometimes I stood on a stool in front of the fire-place and made up lyrics while Baby Doll acted them out, moving lightly across the old dark rugs, turning and swooping and shaking and gliding.

Outside the summer sun beat down on the Delta, beating down a million volts a minute, feeding the soybeans and cotton and clover, sucking Steele's Bayou up into the clouds, beating down on the road and the store, on the pecans and elms and magnolias, on the men at work in the fields, on the athletes at work in the pasture.

Inside Baby Doll and I would be dancing. Or Guy Lombardo would be playing 'Begin the Beguine' and I would be belting out lyrics.

> 'Oh, let them begin ... we don't care,
> America all ... ways does its share,
> We'll be there with plenty of ammo,
> Allies ... don't ever despair ...'

Baby Doll thought I was a genius. If I was having an especially creative morning she would go running out to the kitchen and bring anyone she could find to hear me.

'Oh, let them begin any warrr ...' I would be singing, tapping one foot against the fire-place tiles, waving my arms around like a conductor.

> 'Uncle Sam will fight
> for the underrr ... doggg.
> Never fear, Allies, never fear.'

A new record would drop. Baby Doll would swoop me into her fragrant arms, and we would break into an improvisation on Tommy Dorsey's 'Boogie-Woogie.'

But the Broad Jump Pit would not go away. It loomed in my dreams. If I walked to the store I had to pass the pasture. If I stood on the porch or looked out my grandmother's window, there it was, shimmering in the sunlight, constantly guarded by one of the Olympians.

Things went from bad to worse between me and Dudley. If we so much as passed each other in the hall a fight began. He would hold up his fists and dance around, trying to look like a fighter. When I came flailing at him he would reach underneath my arms and punch me in the stomach.

I considered poisoning him. There was a box of white powder in the toolshed with a skull and crossbones above the label. Several times I took it down and held it in my hands, shuddering at the power it gave me. Only the thought of the electric chair kept me from using it.

Every day Dudley gathered his troops and headed out for the pasture. Every day my hatred grew and festered. Then, just about the time I could stand it no longer, a diversion occurred.

One afternoon about four o'clock an official-looking sedan clattered across the bridge and came roaring down the road to the house.

It was my cousin, Lauralee Manning, wearing her WAVE uniform and smoking Camels in an ivory holder. Lauralee had been widowed at the beginning of the war when her young husband crashed his Navy training plane into the Pacific.

Lauralee dried her tears, joined the WAVES, and went off to avenge his death. I had not seen this paragon since I was a small child, but I had memorized the photograph Miss Onnie Maud, who was Lauralee's mother, kept on her dresser. It was a photograph of Lauralee leaning against the rail of a destroyer.

Not that Lauralee ever went to sea on a destroyer. She was spending the war in Pensacola, Florida, being secretary to an admiral.

Now, out of a clear blue sky, here was Lauralee, home on leave with a two-carat diamond ring and the news that she was getting married.

'You might have called and given some warning,' Miss Onnie Maud said, turning Lauralee into a mass of wrinkles with her embraces. 'You could have softened the blow with a letter.'

'Who's the groom,' my grandmother said. 'I only hope he's not a pilot.'

'Is he an admiral?' I said, 'or a colonel or a major or a commander?'

'My fiancé's not in uniform, honey,' Lauralee said. 'He's in real estate. He runs the war-bond effort for the whole state of Florida.

Last year he collected half a million dollars.'

'In real estate!' Miss Onnie Maud said, gasping. 'What religion is he?'

'He's Unitarian,' she said. 'His name is Donald Marcus. He's best friends with Admiral Semmes, that's how I met him. And he's coming a week from Saturday, and that's all the time we have to get ready for the wedding.'

'Unitarian!' Miss Onnie Maud said. 'I don't think I've ever met a Unitarian.'

'Why isn't he in uniform?' I insisted.

'He has flat feet,' Lauralee said gaily. 'But you'll love him when you see him.'

Later that afternoon Lauralee took me off by myself for a ride in the sedan.

'Your mother is my favourite cousin,' she said, touching my face with gentle fingers. 'You'll look just like her when you grow up and get your figure.'

I moved closer, admiring the brass buttons on her starched uniform and the brisk way she shifted and braked and put in the clutch and accelerated.

We drove down the river road and out to the bootlegger's shack where Lauralee bought a pint of Jack Daniel's and two Cokes. She poured out half of her Coke, filled it with whiskey, and we roared off down the road with the radio playing.

We drove along in the lengthening day. Lauralee was chain-smoking, lighting one Camel after another, tossing the butts out the window, taking sips from her bourbon and Coke. I sat beside her, pretending to smoke a piece of rolled-up paper, making little noises into the mouth of my Coke bottle.

We drove up to a picnic spot on the levee and sat under a tree to look out at the river.

'I miss this old river,' she said. 'When I'm sad I dream about it licking the tops of the levees.'

I didn't know what to say to that. To tell the truth I was afraid to say much of anything to Lauralee. She seemed so splendid. It was enough to be allowed to sit by her on the levee.

'Now, Rhoda,' she said, 'your mother was matron of honour in my wedding to Buddy, and I want you, her own little daughter, to be maid of honour in my second wedding.'

I could hardly believe my ears! While I was trying to think of something to say to this wonderful news I saw that Lauralee was crying, great tears were forming in her blue eyes.

'Under this very tree is where Buddy and I got engaged,' she said. Now the tears were really starting to roll, falling all over the front of her uniform. 'He gave me my ring right where we're sitting.'

'The maid of honour?' I said, patting her on the shoulder, trying to be of some comfort. 'You really mean the maid of honour?'

'Now he's gone from the world,' she continued, 'and I'm marrying a wonderful man, but that doesn't make it any easier. Oh, Rhoda, they never even found his body, never even found his body.'

I was patting her on the head now, afraid she would forget her offer in the midst of her sorrow.

'You mean I get to be the real maid of honour?'

'Oh, yes, Rhoda, honey,' she said. 'The maid of honour, my only attendant.' She blew her nose on a lace-trimmed handkerchief and sat up straighter, taking a drink from the Coke bottle.

'Not only that, but I have decided to let you pick out your own dress. We'll go to Greenville and you can try on every dress at Nell's and Blum's and you can have the one you like the most.'

I threw my arms around her, burning with happiness, smelling her whiskey and Camels and the dark Tabu perfume that was her signature. Over her shoulder and through the low branches of the trees the afternoon sun was going down in an orgy of reds and blues and purples and violets, falling from sight, going all the way to China.

Let them keep their nasty Broad Jump Pit I thought. Wait till they hear about this. Wait till they find out I'm maid of honour in a military wedding.

Finding the dress was another matter. Early the next morning Miss Onnie Maud and my grandmother and Lauralee and I set out for Greenville.

As we passed the pasture I hung out the back window making faces at the athletes. This time they only pretended to ignore me. They couldn't ignore this wedding. It was going to be in the parlour instead of the church so they wouldn't even get to be altar boys. They wouldn't get to light a candle.

'I don't know why you care what's going on in that pasture,' my grandmother said. 'Even if they let you play with them all it would do is make you a lot of ugly muscles.'

'Then you'd have big old ugly arms like Weegie Toler,' Miss Onnie Maud said. 'Lauralee, you remember Weegie Toler, that was a swimmer. Her arms got so big no one would take her to a dance, much less marry her.'

'Well, I don't want to get married anyway,' I said. 'I'm never getting married. I'm going to New York City and be a lawyer.'

'Where does she get those ideas?' Miss Onnie Maud said.

'When you get older you'll want to get married,' Lauralee said. 'Look at how much fun you're having being in my wedding.'

'Well, I'm never getting married,' I said. 'And I'm never having any children. I'm going to New York and be a lawyer and save people from the electric chair.'

'It's the movies,' Miss Onnie Maud said. 'They let her watch anything she likes in Indiana.'

We walked into Nell's and Blum's Department Store and took up the largest dressing-room. My grandmother and Miss Onnie Maud were seated on brocade chairs and every saleslady in the store came crowding around trying to get in on the wedding.

I refused to even consider the dresses they brought from the 'girls'' department.

'I told her she could wear whatever she wanted,' Lauralee said, 'and I'm keeping my promise.'

'Well, she's not wearing green satin or I'm not coming,' my grandmother said, indicating the dress I had found on a rack and was clutching against me.

'At least let her try it on,' Lauralee said. 'Let her see for herself.' She zipped me into the green satin. It came down to my ankles and fit around my midsection like a girdle, making my waist seem smaller than my stomach. I admired myself in the mirror. It was almost perfect. I looked exactly like a nightclub singer.

'This one's fine,' I said. 'This is the one I want.'

'It looks marvellous, Rhoda,' Lauralee said, 'but it's the wrong colour for the wedding. Remember I'm wearing blue.'

'I believe the child's colour-blind,' Miss Onnie Maud said. 'It runs in her father's family.'

'I am not colour-blind,' I said, reaching behind me and unzipping the dress. 'I have twenty-twenty vision.'

'Let her try on some more,' Lauralee said. 'Let her try on everything in the store.'

I proceeded to do just that, with the salesladies getting grumpier

340

and grumpier. I tried on a gold gabardine dress with a rhinestone-studded cummerbund, I tried on a pink ballerina-length formal and a lavender voile tea dress and several silk suits. Somehow nothing looked right.

'Maybe we'll have to make her something,' my grandmother said.

'But there's no time,' Miss Onnie Maud said. 'Besides first we'd have to find out what she wants. Rhoda, please tell us what you're looking for.'

Their faces all turned to mine, waiting for an answer. But I didn't know the answer.

The dress I wanted was a secret. The dress I wanted was dark and tall and thin as a reed. There was a word for what I wanted, a word I had seen in magazines. But what was that word? I could not remember.

'I want something dark,' I said at last. 'Something dark and silky.'

'Wait right there,' the saleslady said. 'Wait just a minute.' Then, from out of a pre-war storage closet she brought a black-watch plaid recital dress with spaghetti straps and a white piqué jacket. It was made of taffeta and rustled when I touched it. There was a label sewn into the collar of the jacket. *Little Miss Sophisticate*, it said. *Sophisticate*, that was the word I was seeking.

I put on the dress and stood triumphant in a sea of ladies and dresses and hangers.

'This is the dress,' I said. 'This is the dress I'm wearing.'

'It's perfect,' Lauralee said. 'Start hemming it up. She'll be the prettiest maid of honour in the whole world.'

All the way home I held the box on my lap thinking about how I would look in the dress. Wait till they see me like this, I was thinking. Wait till they see what I really look like.

I fell in love with the groom. The moment I laid eyes on him I forgot he was flat-footed. He arrived bearing gifts of music and perfume and candy, a warm dark-skinned man with eyes the colour of walnuts.

He laughed out loud when he saw me, standing on the porch with my hands on my hips.

'This must be Rhoda,' he exclaimed, 'the famous red-haired maid of honour.' He came running up the steps, gave me a slow, exciting hug, and presented me with a whole album of Xavier Cugat records. I had never owned a record of my own, much less an album.

Before the evening was over I put on a red formal I found in a trunk and did a South American dance for him to Xavier Cugat's 'Poinciana'. He said he had never seen anything like it in his whole life.

The wedding itself was a disappointment. No one came but the immediate family and there was no aisle to march down and the only music was Onnie Maud playing 'Liebstraum'.

Dudley and Philip and Saint John and Oliver and Bunky were dressed in long pants and white shirts and ties. They had fresh military crew cuts and looked like a nest of new birds, huddled together on the blue velvet sofa, trying to keep their hands to themselves, trying to figure out how to act at a wedding.

The elderly Episcopal priest read out the ceremony in a gravelly smoker's voice, ruining all the good parts by coughing. He was in a bad mood because Lauralee and Mr Marcus hadn't found time to come to him for marriage instruction.

Still, I got to hold the bride's flowers while he gave her the ring and stood so close to her during the ceremony I could hear her breathing.

The reception was better. People came from all over the Delta. There were tables with candles set up around the porches and sprays of greenery in every corner. There were gentlemen sweating in linen suits and the record player playing every minute. In the back hall Calvin had set up a real professional bar with tall, permanently frosted glasses and ice and mint and lemons and every kind of whiskey and liqueur in the world.

I stood in the receiving line getting compliments on my dress, then wandered around the rooms eating cake and letting people hug me. After a while I got bored with that and went out to the back hall and began to fix myself a drink at the bar.

I took one of the frosted glasses and began filling it from different bottles, tasting as I went along. I used plenty of crème de menthe and soon had something that tasted heavenly. I filled the glass with crushed ice, added three straws, and went out to sit on the back steps and cool off.

I was feeling wonderful. A full moon was caught like a kite in the pecan trees across the river. I sipped along on my drink. Then, without planning it, I did something I had never dreamed of doing. I left the porch alone at night. Usually I was in terror of the dark. My grandmother had told me that alligators come out of the bayou to eat children who wander alone at night.

I walked out across the yard, the huge moon giving so much light I almost cast a shadow. When I was nearly to the water's edge I turned and looked back toward the house. It shimmered in the moonlight like a jukebox alive in a meadow, seemed to pulsate with music and laughter and people, beautiful and foreign, not a part of me.

I looked out at the water, then down the road to the pasture. The Broad Jump Pit! There it was, perfect and unguarded. Why had I never thought of doing this before?

I began to run toward the road. I ran as fast as my Mary Jane pumps would allow me. I pulled my dress up around my waist and climbed the fence in one motion, dropping lightly down on the other side. I was sweating heavily, alone with the moon and my wonderful courage.

I knew exactly what to do first. I picked up the pole and hoisted it over my head. It felt solid and balanced and alive. I hoisted it up and down a few times as I had seen Dudley do, getting the feel of it.

Then I laid it ceremoniously down on the ground, reached behind me, and unhooked the plaid formal. I left it lying in a heap on the ground. There I stood, in my cotton underpants, ready to take up pole-vaulting.

I lifted the pole and carried it back to the end of the cinder path. I ran slowly down the path, stuck the pole in the wooden cup, and attempted throwing my body into the air, using it as a lever.

Something was wrong. It was more difficult than it appeared from a distance. I tried again. Nothing happened. I sat down with the pole across my legs to think things over.

Then I remembered something I had watched Dudley doing through the binoculars. He measured down from the end of the pole with his fingers spread wide. That was it, I had to hold it closer to the end.

I tried it again. This time the pole lifted me several feet off the ground. My body sailed across the grass in a neat arc and I landed on my toes. I was a natural!

I do not know how long I was out there, running up and down

the cinder path, thrusting my body further and further through space, tossing myself into the pit like a mussel shell thrown across the bayou.

At last I decided I was ready for the real test. I had to vault over a cane barrier. I examined the pegs on the wooden poles and chose one that came up to my shoulder.

I put the barrier pole in place, spit over my left shoulder, and marched back to the end of the path. Suck up your guts, I told myself. It's only a pole. It won't get stuck in your stomach and tear out your insides. It won't kill you.

I stood at the end of the path eyeballing the barrier. Then, above the incessant racket of the crickets, I heard my name being called. Rhoda . . . the voices were calling. Rhoda . . . Rhoda . . . Rhoda . . . Rhoda.

I turned toward the house and saw them coming. Mr Marcus and Dudley and Bunky and Calvin and Lauralee and what looked like half the wedding. They were climbing the fence, calling my name, and coming to get me. Rhoda . . . they called out. Where on earth have you been? What on earth are you doing?

I hoisted the pole up to my shoulders and began to run down the path, running into the light from the moon. I picked up speed, thrust the pole into the cup, and threw myself into the sky, into the still Delta night. I sailed up and was clear and over the barrier.

I let go of the pole and began my fall, which seemed to last a long, long time. It was like falling through clear water. I dropped into the sawdust and lay very still, waiting for them to reach me.

Sometimes I think whatever has happened since has been of no real interest to me.

JANET FRAME

Swans

They were ready to go. Mother and Fay and Totty, standing by the gate in their next best to Sunday best, Mother with her straw hat on with shells on it and Fay with her check dress that Mother had made and Totty, well where was Totty a moment ago she was here?

'Totty,' Mother called. 'If you don't hurry, we'll miss the train, it leaves in ten minutes. And we're not to forget to get off at Beach Street. At least I think Dad said Beach Street. But hurry Totty.'

Totty came running from the wash-house round the back.

'Mum quick I've found Gypsy and her head's down like all the other cats and she's dying I think. She's in the wash-house. Mum quick,' she cried urgently.

Mother looked flurried. 'Hurry up, Totty and come back Fay, pussy will be all right. We'll give her some milk now there's some in the pot and we'll wrap her in a piece of blanket and she'll be all right till we get home.'

The three of them hurried back to the wash-house. It was dark with no light except what came through the small square window which had been cracked and pasted over with brown paper. The cat lay on a pile of sacks in a corner near the copper. Her head was down and her eyes were bright with a fever or poison or something but she was alive. They found an old clean tin lid and poured warm milk in it and from one of the shelves they pulled a dusty piece of blanket. The folds stuck to one another all green and hairy and a slater with hills and valleys on his back fell to the floor and moved slowly along the cracked concrete floor to a little secret place by the wall. Totty even forgot to collect him. She collected things, slaters and earwigs and spiders though you had to be careful with earwigs for when you were lying in the grass asleep they crept into your ear and built their nest there and you had to go to the doctor and have your ear lanced.

They covered Gypsy and each one patted her. Don't worry Gypsy they said. We'll be back to look after you tonight. We're

345

going to the Beach now. Goodbye Gypsy.

And there was Mother waiting impatiently again at the gate. 'Do hurry. Pussy'll be all right now.'

Mother always said things would be all right, cats and birds and people even as if she knew and she did know too, Mother knew always.

But Fay crept back once more to look inside the wash-house. 'I promise,' she called to the cat. 'We'll be back, just you see.'

And the next moment the three Mother and Fay and Totty were outside the gate and Mother with a broom-like motion of her arms was sweeping the two little girls before her.

O the train and the coloured pictures on the station, South America and Australia, and the bottle of fizzy drink that you could only half finish because you were too full, and the ham sandwiches that curled up at the edges, because they were stale, Dad said, and he *knew*, and the rabbits and cows and bulls outside in the paddocks, and the sheep running away from the noise and the houses that came and went like a dream, clackety-clack, Kaitangata, Kaitangata, and the train stopping and panting and the man with the stick tapping the wheels and the huge rubber hose to give the engine a drink, and the voices of the people in the carriage on and on and waiting.

'Don't forget Beach Street, Mum,' Dad had said. Dad was away at work up at six o'clock early and couldn't come. It was strange without him for he always managed. He got the tea and the fizzy drinks and the sandwiches and he knew which station was which and where and why and how, but Mother didn't. Mother was often too late for the fizzy drinks and she coughed before she spoke to the children and then in a whisper in case the people in the carriage should hear and think things, and she said I'm sure I don't know kiddies when they asked about the station, but she was big and warm and knew about cats and little ring-eyes, and Father was hard and bony and his face prickled when he kissed you.

O look the beach coming it must be coming.

The train stopped with a jerk and a cloud of smoke as if it had died and finished and would never go anywhere else just stay by the sea though you couldn't see the water from here, and the carriages would be empty and slowly rusting as if the people in them had come to an end and could never go back as if they had found what they were looking for after years and years of travelling on and on. But they were disturbed and peeved at being forced to move. The taste of smoke lingered in their mouths, they had to reach up for hat and coat and case, and comb their hair and make up their face again, certainly they had arrived but you have to be neat arriving with your shoes brushed and your hair in place and the shine off your nose. Fay and Totty watched the little cases being snipped open and shut and the two little girls knew for sure that never would they grow up and be people in bulgy dresses, people knitting purl and plain with the ball of wool hanging safe and clean from a neat brown bag with hollyhocks and poppies on it. Hollyhocks and poppies and a big red initial, to show that you were you and not the somebody else you feared you might be, but Fay and Totty didn't worry they were going to the Beach.

The Beach. Why wasn't everyone going to the Beach? It seemed they were the only ones for when they set off down the fir-bordered road that led to the sound the sea kept making forever now in their ears, there was no one else going. Where had the others gone? Why weren't there other people?

'Why Mum?'

'It's a week-day chicken,' said Mum smiling and fat now the rushing was over. 'The others have gone to work I suppose. I don't know. But here we are. Tired?' She looked at them both in the way they loved, the way she looked at them at night at other people's places when they were weary of cousins and hide the thimble and wanted to go home to bed. Tired? she would say. And Fay and Totty would yawn as if nothing in the world would keep them awake and Mother would say knowingly and fondly The dust-man's coming to someone. But no they weren't tired now for it was day and the sun though a watery sad sun was up and the birds, the day was for waking in and the night was for sleeping in.

They raced on ahead of Mother eager to turn the desolate crying sound of sea to the more comforting and near sight of long green and white waves coming and going forever on the sand. They had never been here before, not to this sea. They had been to other seas, near merry-go-rounds and swings and slides, among people, other girls and boys and mothers, mine are so fond of the water the mothers would say, talking about mine and yours and he, that meant father, or the old man if they did not much care but Mother cared always.

The road was stony and the little girls carrying the basket had skiffed toes by the time they came to the end, but it was all fun and yet strange for they were by themselves no other families and

Fay thought for a moment what if there is no sea either and no nothing?

But the sea roared in their ears it was true sea, look it was breaking white on the sand and the seagulls crying and skimming and the bits of white flying and look at all of the coloured shells, look a little pink one like a fan, and a cat's eye. Gypsy. And look at the seaweed look I've found a round piece that plops, you tread on it and it plops, you plop this one, see it plops, and the little girls running up and down plopping and plopping and picking and prying and touching and listening, and Mother plopping the seaweed too, look Mum's doing it and Mum's got a crab.

But it cannot go on for ever.

'Where is the place to put our things and the merry-go-rounds and the place to undress and that, and the place to get ice-creams?'

There's no place, only a little shed with forms that have bird-dirt on them and old pieces of newspapers stuffed in the corner and writing on the walls, rude writing.

'Mum, have we come to the wrong sea?'

Mother looked bewildered. 'I don't know kiddies, I'm sure.'

'Is it the wrong sea?' Totty took up the cry.

It was the wrong sea. 'Yes kiddies,' Mother said, 'now that's strange I'm sure I remembered what your Father told me but I couldn't have but I'm sure I remembered. Isn't it funny. I didn't know it would be like this. Oh things are never like you think they're different and sad. I don't know.'

'Look, I've found the biggest plop of all,' cried Fay who had wandered away intent on plopping. 'The biggest plop of all,' she repeated, justifying things. 'Come on.'

So it was all right really it was a good sea, you could pick up the foam before it turned yellow and take off your shoes and sink your feet down in the wet sand almost until you might disappear and come up in Spain, that was where you came up if you sank. And there was the little shed to eat in and behind the rushes to undress but you couldn't go in swimming.

'Not in this sea,' Mother said firmly.

They felt proud. It was a distinguished sea oh and a lovely one noisy in your ears and green and blue and brown where the seaweed floated. Whales? Sharks? Seals? It was the right kind of sea.

All day on the sand, racing and jumping and turning head over heels and finding shells galore and making castles and getting buried and unburied, going dead and coming alive like the people in the Bible. And eating in the little shed for the sky had clouded over and a cold wind had come shaking the heads of the fir-trees as if to say I'll teach you, springing them backwards and forwards in a devilish exercise.

Tomatoes, and a fire blowing in your face. The smoke burst out and you wished. Aladdin and the genie. What did you wish?

I wish today is always but Father too jumping us up and down on his knee. This is the maiden all forlorn that milked the cow.

'Totty, it's my turn, isn't it Dad?'

'It's both of your turns. Come on, sacks on the mill and *more on still.*' Not Father away at work but Father here making the fire and breaking sticks, quickly and surely, and Father showing this and that and telling why. Why? Did anyone in the world ever know why? Or did they just pretend to know because they didn't like anyone else to know that they didn't know? Why?

They were going home when they saw the swans. 'We'll go this quicker way,' said Mother, who had been exploring. 'We'll walk across the lagoon over this strip of land and soon we'll be at the station and then home to bed.' She smiled and put her arms round them both. Everything was warm and secure and near, and the darker the world outside got the safer you felt for there were Mother and Father always, for ever.

They began to walk across the lagoon. It was growing dark now quickly and dark sneaks in. Oh home in the train with the guard lighting the lamps and the shiny slippery seat growing hard and your eyes scarcely able to keep open, the sea in your ears, and your little bagful of shells dropped somewhere down the back of the seat, crushed and sandy and wet, and your baby crab dead and salty and stiff fallen on the floor.

'We'll soon be home,' Mother said, and was silent.

It was dark black water, secret, and the air was filled with murmurings and rustlings, it was as if they were walking into another world that had been kept secret from everyone and now they had found it. The darkness lay massed across the water and over to the east, thick as if you could touch it, soon it would swell and fill the earth.

The children didn't speak now, they were tired with the dustman really coming, and Mother was sad and quiet, the wrong sea troubled her, what had she done, she had been sure she would find things different, as she had said they would be, merry-go-rounds and swings and slides for the kiddies, and other mothers to show the kiddies off to, they were quite bright for their age, what had she done?

They looked across the lagoon then and saw the swans, black and shining, as if the visiting dark tiring of its form, had changed to birds, hundreds of them resting and moving softly about on the water. Why, the lagoon was filled with swans, like secret sad ships, secret and quiet. Hush-sh the water said; rush-hush, the wind passed over the top of the water; no other sound but the shaking of rushes and far away now it seemed the roar of the sea like a secret sea that had crept inside your head for ever. And the swans, they were there too, inside you, peaceful and quiet watching and sleeping and watching, there was nothing but peace and warmth and calm, everything found, train and sea and Mother and Father and earwig and slater and spider.

And Gypsy?

But when they got home Gypsy was dead.

AHDAF SOUEIF

The Wedding of Zeina

'I was fifteen,' Zeina began. 'He was nineteen and already doing well. He was a tailor like his father and worked with him. One day my grandmother came and called me. She took me to one side and said,

' "Zeina, you're going to marry Sobhi."

' "But, Setti, how do I marry him?" I asked.

'He was my cousin: the son of my dead mother's sister, but I knew nothing of marriage.

' "You'll be his wife and he'll be your husband and you'll serve him and do what he tells you."

'I started to cry.

' "Will I have to leave you, Setti?"

'The old woman took me in her arms:

' "No, no, you'll have your own room in the house and I'll always be with you. You're a big girl now. You can cook and clean and look after a man and he's your cousin, child, he's not a stranger."

'Well . . . I went out to the other girls in the yard but my heart was full of my new importance. I didn't say anything but in a few hours everyone knew anyway and Sobhi stopped coming to our part of the house. From the time Setti told me, I only saw him again on the wedding night.'

The sound of a bicycle bell rang through the darkness and Zeina refolded her legs and settled more comfortably against the balustrade.

'My bridal box had been ready for years and my uncle arranged for the painters to come and decorate a room on the roof of the house. It had a little bathroom next to it with a toilet, a basin and a shower and I was to cook in the big kitchen downstairs with my grandmother and aunt. They painted the room a very pretty pink and we put in a red rug and a bed and a cupboard and a chair and a little mirror.'

The little girl listening smiled. It sounded lovely. Her grandfather's house had a room on the roof. They kept rabbits there and she was allowed sometimes to go up and play with them. They were all different colours—

'When the day before the wedding came the younger children were all put out into the yard and the Mashta was sent for—'

'Mashta?'

'Yes, she's the woman who comes to adorn the bride. They fetched her from the baths and she hurried in, trilling her joy-cries from the top of the street. "A thousand congratulations, Zeina," she cried, letting out another joy-cry before she took off her *tarha* and hugged me, kissing me on the mouth. I clung closer to my grandmother. "They say he's a fine young man," she said, laughing, and pinched me, then took off her slippers and her outer black dress, rolled up her sleeves and went into the kitchen to prepare the sugar. I had seen the older women use it before—'

'Sugar?'

'It's what you take out your hair with.'

'Why would you take out your hair?' the little girl wondered, gazing at her nurse's rich head of shiny black hair. Dada Zeina usually wore it bundled under a white kerchief like all the other nannies in the club, but tonight was Wednesday and it had been washed in olive-oil soap and was drying round her shoulders. That too was part of the magic of these nights.

'The hair on your legs and on your body, to make you nice and smooth for the bridegroom.'

Her nurse looked at her meaningfully and the child thrilled. Here she was: an accomplice, a grown-up. Her baby sister and brother were asleep inside, but she was eight years old and sitting up on the balcony listening to her nanny's story. And it would be like this every Wednesday night when her parents went out. So long, of course, as she was careful and kept the secret. 'She's a good girl,' Nanny always said to the other nurses in the club, 'she never carries tales to her mother.' And although in some deep corner inside she was uneasy, feeling the bribe in the words, she still felt proud, and anxious to keep those privileged story-telling hours. Besides, she didn't want to carry tales. She had asked her mother once how women did the joy-cry and her father had frowned and said it was something that only vulgar people did.

'They told me to undress and I was so shy,' said Zeina, laughing. 'I held on to my grandmother, but she pulled up my shift and my aunt took it off me, and my undershift too, and sat me down on the straw mat. The Mashta was kneading the sugar in her hands and as it crackled and popped she'd say, "Listen to that. How he must love her if the sugar's popping like this. What a lucky girl you are!" and let out another joy-cry. She smoothed the paste on to my leg, muttered the name of God and tore it off. I howled and jumped up but they pulled me down again:

' "Don't be a child, now."

' "Your body will go numb in a moment and you won't feel the pain."

' "It's all so you can please your man."

' "What's he got to do with my legs?" I cried. I was so foolish.' Zeina laughed.

The little girl noticed then the soft down on her own arms and legs but, anxious to stay a grown-up, she laughed too.

'Well, they plucked my legs and thighs and armpits and arms and my face too, for good measure, then the Mashta said, "Come on, bride, take your knickers off," and I was so startled I cringed into myself and couldn't move.'

The little girl sat very still. She had the strangest, warmest, gentlest, tinging feeling between her legs and her heart was pounding in both fear and pleasure. This was forbidden. Her parents never ever said 'knickers', always 'culottes' and her nurse, in deference to them, said 'kollott' but now, now she was using the other, the 'vulgar' word.

' "Come on, Zeina don't be a spoilt child", my aunt said, and tugged my knickers off. They spread the paste on the hair—'

What hair? wondered the child but she would not stop the flow for anything now.

'—and pulled. It was fire. I tried to struggle up but they held me down and the Mashta went on spreading the paste and tearing it off while I cried and screamed until I was completely clean. Then they heated water and poured it into the large brass tub and I sat in it stark naked while the Mashta rubbed me all over with a rough cloth, trilling her joy-cries all the while. Then she dried me and my grandmother fetched me a clean shift and sent me to lie down and rest.'

Aisha was quiet. 'We ought to go to bed before your parents come back,' said her nanny. 'Oh no,' eyes enormous, 'they're at the ballet. They won't be back before twelve at least. Please, *please* go on. What happened next?'

'Next day they brought up a hundred chairs to the roof. The

neighbours came and helped with the cooking and we cleaned out the room and the bathroom.'

'Was your room on the roof like my grandfather's?'

'What?'

'Where they keep the rabbits.'

'What rabbits?'

'Oh Nanny, you know, on top of my grandfather's house, where the *rabbits* are.'

'Oh. Yes, well, but it was clean and pink and had furniture—'

Rabbits didn't need furniture but perhaps they would like pink walls. Perhaps if she persuaded her grandfather they would be happier, he would have the walls painted pink? But maybe grown-ups didn't really care about rabbits being happy. A treacherous wave of misery hit her as she remembered playing with the rabbits one day when her nurse casually caught one of them. She held him by the ears and he hung and quivered, huge eyes rolled back. When she slit his throat the blood spurted and he kicked and danced around before finally going limp, defeated. She had hated Dada Zeina then.

'I had a beautiful pink dress with sequins and a pink veil and I forgot about being a bride and sat and laughed with my girlfriends. But Setti came and took me away and took me to my uncle. My uncles were butchers and they're very tough men. My uncle had a gun in one hand and he held me by the other. I was scared of the gun because I'd heard of some girl they'd shot on her wedding night, but he led me to the new room. My aunt was there and my grandmother came in. Then the bridegroom came, my cousin. He had a thick white bandage wrapped round the middle finger of his right hand and I thought he had hurt it. I was so foolish. My uncle said, "I'll be right outside", and closed the door but I could still hear the drums and flutes as loud as though they were in the room with us. My aunt put her hand on my shoulder and said, "Take off your knickers, child, and lie down on the rug." I stared at her without understanding. She shook me a little: "Come on, girl, your uncles are waiting." I still stood there. "Tell him to get out," I said pointing at the man.

' "The girl is mad," said my aunt.

' "He's your husband," said my grandmother gently.

' "I won't undress in front of him," I said.

'My aunt suddenly tried to pull me to the floor but I fought her. *He* just stood watching with his finger in the bandage. My aunt opened the door and went out. I could hear my uncle's voice raised angrily, then my aunt came back in with two women.

' "The girl is hard-headed," said one.

' "She's still young and foolish," said my grandmother. "Don't scare her lest her blood should disappear."

'Suddenly the four women surrounded me and pulled me to the floor. One pinned down my shoulders while the other held on to my waist and my aunt and grandmother pulled off my knickers. I struggled and clamped my legs together tight. My aunt was pinching my thighs, trying to get me to open up. I was yelling and screaming but I kept my thighs tight together. My uncle hammered on the door: "What the Hell's going on in there? Curse you all. Shall I come in and shoot the bitch?" "It's all right, brother, have patience," cried my aunt and bent down suddenly and bit my upper thigh so hard I jerked it away and they immediately pulled my legs apart and held them and *he* stepped forward and squatted between them. I managed to wrench a leg away and as he leaned forward I gave him a mighty kick that sent him sprawling on his backside. He looked so funny sitting there on his bum, surprised, then he jumped up and came at me and slapped my face, then using all his man's strength he forced my thighs open, threaded one of my arms behind each knee and drew them up to my head. The women held my arms and I lay there squirming and crying in gasps as he knelt down and forced his bandaged finger into me, working it round and round and in and out as I choked and screamed. Finally he took it out. The bandage was soaked with blood. They let go of me and Setti drew my wedding dress down and I lay shivering and crying. Then he went out. I heard my uncle fire his gun into the air and my other uncles' guns answering it from around the house and the street. Then the drumming went up very loud and the joy-cries filled the air and through the door I could see them unwrapping the bandage from around his finger. My uncle wound it round his head, blood and all, and danced slowly and proudly into the crowd, using his gun like a cane to dance with and calling out, "Our Honour, Our daughter's Honour, Our family's Honour."

'Afterwards Setti explained that he was my husband and any time he wanted to do anything to me I must let him and not fight him. But I did,' Zeina said, laughing. 'I fought him every time for a month, but in the end he mastered me.'

'Did you hate him, Nanny?' the child asked gently.

Zeina laughed again, easily. 'No, of course not. He was a strong man, bless him. And besides he was as big as a bull.'

BOBBIE ANN MASON

Shiloh

Leroy Moffitt's wife, Norma Jean, is working on her pectorals. She lifts three-pound dumb-bells to warm up, then progresses to a twenty-pound barbell. Standing with her legs apart, she reminds Leroy of Wonder Woman.

'I'd give anything if I could just get these muscles to where they're real hard,' says Norma Jean. 'Feel this arm. It's not as hard as the other one.'

'That's 'cause you're right-handed,' says Leroy, dodging as she swings the barbell in an arc.

'Do you think so?'

'Sure.'

Leroy is a truckdriver. He injured his leg in a highway accident four months ago, and his physical therapy, which involves weights and a pulley, prompted Norma Jean to try building herself up. Now she is attending a body-building class. Leroy has been collecting temporary disability since his tractor-trailer jackknifed in Missouri, badly twisting his left leg in its socket. He has a steel pin in his hip. He will probably not be able to drive his rig again. It sits in the backyard, like a gigantic bird that has flown home to roost. Leroy has been home in Kentucky for three months, and his leg is almost healed, but the accident frightened him and he does not want to drive any more long hauls. He is not sure what to do next. In the meantime, he makes things from craft kits. He started by building a miniature log cabin from notched Popsicle sticks. He varnished it and placed it on the TV set, where it remains. It reminds him of a rustic Nativity scene. Then he tried string art (sailing ships on black velvet), a macramé owl kit, a snap-together B-17 Flying Fortress, and a lamp made out of a model truck, with a light fixture screwed in the top of the cab. At first the kits were diversions, something to kill time, but now he is thinking about building a full-scale log house from a kit. It would be considerably cheaper than building a regular house, and besides, Leroy has grown to appreciate how things are put together. He has begun to realize that in all the years he was on the road he never took time to examine anything. He was always flying past scenery.

'They won't let you build a log cabin in any of the new sub-divisions,' Norma Jean tells him.

'They will if I tell them it's for you,' he says, teasing her. Ever since they were married, he has promised Norma Jean he would build her a new home one day. They have always rented, and the house they live in is small and nondescript. It does not even feel like a home, Leroy realizes now.

Norma Jean works at the Rexall drugstore, and she has acquired an amazing amount of information about cosmetics. When she explains to Leroy the three stages of complexion care, involving creams, toners, and moisturizers, he thinks happily of other pet-roleum products—axle grease, diesel fuel. This is a connection between him and Norma Jean. Since he has been home, he has felt unusually tender about his wife and guilty over his long absences. But he can't tell what she feels about him. Norma Jean has never complained about his travelling; she has never made hurt remarks, like calling his truck a 'widow-maker'. He is reasonably certain she has been faithful to him, but he wishes she would celebrate his permanent homecoming more happily. Norma Jean is often startled to find Leroy at home, and he thinks she seems a little disappointed about it. Perhaps he reminds her too much of the early days of their marriage, before he went on the road. They had a child who died as an infant, years ago. They never speak about their memories of Randy, which have almost faded, but now that Leroy is home all the time, they sometimes feel awkward around each other, and Leroy wonders if one of them should mention the child. He has the feeling that they are waking up out of a dream together—that they must create a new marriage, start afresh. They are lucky they are still married. Leroy has read that for most people losing a child destroys the marriage—or else he heard this on *Donahue*. He can't always remember where he learns things anymore.

At Christmas, Leroy bought an electric organ for Norma Jean. She used to play the piano when she was in high school. 'It don't leave you,' she told him once. 'It's like riding a bicycle.'

The new instrument had so many keys and buttons that she was bewildered by it at first. She touched the keys tentatively, pushed some buttons, then pecked out 'Chopsticks'. It came out in an amplified fox-trot rhythm, with marimba sounds.

'It's an orchestra!' she cried.

The organ had a pecan-look finish and eighteen preset chords, with optional flute, violin, trumpet, clarinet, and banjo accompaniments. Norma Jean mastered the organ almost immediately. At first she played Christmas songs. Then she bought *The Sixties Songbook* and learned every tune in it, adding variations to each with the rows of brightly coloured buttons.

'I didn't like these old songs back then,' she said. 'But I have this crazy feeling I missed something.'

'You didn't miss a thing,' said Leroy.

Leroy likes to lie on the couch and smoke a joint and listen to Norma Jean play 'Can't Take My Eyes Off You' and 'I'll Be Back'. He is back again. After fifteen years on the road, he is finally settling down with the woman he loves. She is still pretty. Her skin is flawless. Her frosted curls resemble pencil trimmings.

Now that Leroy has come home to stay, he notices how much the town has changed. Subdivisions are spreading across western Kentucky like an oil slick. The sign at the edge of town says 'Pop: 11,500'—only seven hundred more than it said twenty years before. Leroy can't figure out who is living in all the new houses. The farmers who used to gather around the courthouse square on Saturday afternoons to play checkers and spit tobacco juice have gone. It has been years since Leroy has thought about the farmers, and they have disappeared without his noticing.

Leroy meets a kid named Stevie Hamilton in the parking lot at the new shopping centre. While they pretend to be strangers meeting over a stalled car, Stevie tosses an ounce of marijuana under the front seat of Leroy's car. Stevie is wearing orange jogging shoes and a T-shirt that says CHATTAHOOCHEE SUPER-RAT. His father is a prominent doctor who lives in one of the expensive subdivisions in a new white-columned brick house that looks like a funeral parlour. In the phone book under his name there is a separate number, with the listing 'Teenagers'.

'Where do you get this stuff?' asks Leroy. 'From your pappy?'

'That's for me to know and you to find out,' Stevie says. He is slit-eyed and skinny.

'What else you got?'

'What you interested in?'

'Nothing special. Just wondered.'

Leroy used to take speed on the road. Now he has to go slowly. He needs to be mellow. He leans back against the car and says, 'I'm aiming to build me a log house, soon as I get time. My wife, though, I don't think she likes the idea.'

'Well, let me know when you want me again,' Stevie says. He has a cigarette in his cupped palm, as though sheltering it from the wind. He takes a long drag, then stomps it on the asphalt and slouches away.

Stevie's father was two years ahead of Leroy in high school. Leroy is thirty-four. He married Norma Jean when they were both eighteen, and their child Randy was born a few months later, but he died at the age of four months and three days. He would be about Stevie's age now. Norma Jean and Leroy were at the drive-in, watching a double feature (*Dr Strangelove* and *Lover Come Back*), and the baby was sleeping in the back seat. When the first movie ended, the baby was dead. It was the sudden infant death syndrome. Leroy remembers handing Randy to a nurse at the emergency room, as though he were offering her a large doll as a present. A dead baby feels like a sack of flour. 'It just happens sometimes,' said the doctor, in what Leroy always recalls as a nonchalant tone. Leroy can hardly remember the child anymore, but he still sees vividly a scene from *Dr Strangelove* in which the President of the United States was talking in a folksy voice on the hot line to the Soviet premier about the bomber accidentally headed toward Russia. He was in the War Room, and the world map was lit up. Leroy remembers Norma Jean standing catatonically beside him in the hospital and himself thinking: Who is this strange girl? He had forgotten who she was. Now scientists are saying that crib death is caused by a virus. Nobody knows anything, Leroy thinks. The answers are always changing.

When Leroy gets home from the shopping centre, Norma Jean's mother, Mabel Beasley, is there. Until this year, Leroy has not realized how much time she spends with Norma Jean. When she visits, she inspects the closets and then the plants, informing Norma Jean when a plant is droopy or yellow. Mabel calls the plants 'flowers', although there are never any blooms. She always notices if Norma Jean's laundry is piling up. Mabel is a short, overweight woman whose tight, brown-dyed curls look more like a wig than the actual wig she sometimes wears. Today she has brought Norma Jean an off-white dust ruffle she made for the bed; Mabel works in a custom-upholstery shop.

'This is the tenth one I made this year,' Mabel says. 'I got started and couldn't stop.'

'It's real pretty,' says Norma Jean.

'Now we can hide things under the bed,' says Leroy, who gets along with his mother-in-law primarily by joking with her. Mabel has never really forgiven him for disgracing her by getting Norma Jean pregnant. When the baby died, she said that fate was mocking her.

'What's that thing?' Mabel says to Leroy in a loud voice, pointing to a tangle of yarn on a piece of canvas.

Leroy holds it up for Mabel to see. 'It's my needlepoint,' he explains. 'This is a *Star Trek* pillow cover.'

'That's what a woman would do,' says Mabel. 'Great day in the morning!'

'All the big football players on TV do it,' he says.

'Why, Leroy, you're always trying to fool me. I don't believe you for one minute. You don't know what to do with yourself—that's the whole trouble. Sewing!'

'I'm aiming to build us a log house,' says Leroy. 'Soon as my plans come.'

'Like *heck* you are,' says Norma Jean. She takes Leroy's needlepoint and shoves it into a drawer. 'You have to find a job first. Nobody can afford to build now anyway.'

Mabel straightens her girdle and says, 'I still think before you get tied down y'all ought to take a little run to Shiloh.'

'One of these days, Mama,' Norma Jean says impatiently.

Mabel is talking about Shiloh, Tennessee. For the past few years, she has been urging Leroy and Norma Jean to visit the Civil War battleground there. Mabel went there on her honeymoon—the only real trip she ever took. Her husband died of a perforated ulcer when Norma Jean was ten, but Mabel, who was accepted into the United Daughters of the Confederacy in 1975, is still preoccupied with going back to Shiloh.

'I've been to kingdom come and back in that truck out yonder,' Leroy says to Mabel, 'but we never yet set foot in that battleground. Ain't that something? How did I miss it?'

'It's not even that far,' Mabel says.

After Mabel leaves, Norma Jean reads to Leroy from a list she has made. 'Things you could do,' she announces. 'You could get a job as a guard at Union Carbide, where they'd let you set on a stool. You could get on at the lumberyard. You could do a little carpenter work, if you want to build so bad. You could—'

'I can't do something where I'd have to stand up all day.'

'You ought to try standing up all day behind a cosmetics counter. It's amazing that I have strong feet, coming from two parents that never had strong feet at all.' At the moment Norma Jean is holding on to the kitchen counter, raising her knees one at a time as she talks. She is wearing two-pound ankle weights.

'Don't worry,' says Leroy. 'I'll do something.'

'You could truck calves to slaughter for somebody. You wouldn't have to drive any big old truck for that.'

'I'm going to build you this house,' says Leroy. 'I want to make you a real home.'

'I don't want to live in any log cabin.'

'It's not a cabin. It's a house.'

'I don't care. It looks like a cabin.'

'You and me together could lift those logs. It's just like lifting weights.'

Norma Jean doesn't answer. Under her breath, she is counting. Now she is marching through the kitchen. She is doing goose steps.

Before his accident, when Leroy came home he used to stay in the house with Norma Jean, watching TV in bed and playing cards. She would cook fried chicken, picnic ham, chocolate pie—all his favourites. Now he is home alone much of the time. In the mornings, Norma Jean disappears, leaving a cooling place in the bed. She eats a cereal called Body Buddies, and she leaves the bowl on the table, with the soggy tan balls floating in a milk puddle. He sees things about Norma Jean that he never realized before. When she chops onions, she stares off into a corner, as if she can't bear to look. She puts on her house slippers almost precisely at nine o'clock every evening and nudges her jogging shoes under the couch. She saves bread heels for the birds. Leroy watches the birds at the feeder. He notices the peculiar way goldfinches fly past the window. They close their wings, then fall, then spread their wings to catch and lift themselves. He wonders if they close their eyes when they fall. Norma Jean closes her eyes when they are in bed. She wants the lights turned out. Even then, he is sure she closes her eyes.

He goes for long drives around town. He tends to drive a car rather carelessly. Power steering and an automatic shift make a car feel so small and inconsequential that his body is hardly involved in the driving process. His injured leg stretches out comfortably. Once or twice he has almost hit something, but even the prospect of an accident seems minor in a car. He cruises the new subdivisions, feeling like a criminal rehearsing for a robbery. Norma Jean is probably right about a log house being inappropriate here in the new subdivisions. All the houses look grand and complicated. They depress him.

One day when Leroy comes home from a drive he finds Norma Jean in tears. She is in the kitchen making a potato and mushroom-soup casserole, with grated-cheese topping. She is crying because her mother caught her smoking.

'I didn't hear her coming. I was standing here puffing away pretty as you please,' Norma Jean says, wiping her eyes.

'I knew it would happen sooner or later,' says Leroy, putting his arm around her.

'She don't know the meaning of the word "knock"', says Norma Jean. 'It's a wonder she hadn't caught me years ago.'

'Think of it this way,' Leroy says. 'What if she caught me with a joint?'

'You better not let her!' Norma Jean shrieks. 'I'm warning you, Leroy Moffitt!'

'I'm just kidding. Here, play me a tune. That'll help you relax.'

Norma Jean puts the casserole in the oven and sets the timer. Then she plays a ragtime tune, with horns and banjo, as Leroy lights up a joint and lies on the couch, laughing to himself about Mabel's catching him at it. He thinks of Stevie Hamilton—a doctor's son pushing grass. Everything is funny. The whole town seems crazy and small. He is reminded of Virgil Mathis, a boastful policeman Leroy used to shoot pool with. Virgil recently led a drug bust in a back room at a bowling alley, where he seized ten thousand dollars' worth of marijuana. The newspaper had a picture of him holding up the bags of grass and grinning widely. Right now, Leroy can imagine Virgil breaking down the door and arresting him with a lungful of smoke. Virgil would probably have been alerted to the scene because of all the racket Norma Jean is making. Now she sounds like a hard-rock band. Norma Jean is terrific. When she switches to a Latin-rhythm version of 'Sunshine Superman', Leroy hums along. Norma Jean's foot goes up and down, up and down.

'Well, what do you think?' Leroy says, when Norma Jean pauses to search through her music.

'What do I think about what?'

His mind has gone blank. Then he says, 'I'll sell my rig and build us a house.' That wasn't what he wanted to say. He wanted to know what she thought—what she *really* thought—about them.

'Don't start in on that again,' says Norma Jean. She begins playing 'Who'll Be the Next in Line?'

Leroy used to tell hitchhikers his whole life story—about his travels, his home town, the baby. He would end with a question: 'Well, what do you think?' It was just a rhetorical question. In time, he had the feeling that he'd been telling the same story over and over to the same hitchhikers. He quit talking to hitchhikers when he realized how his voice sounded—whining and self-pitying, like some teenage-tragedy song. Now Leroy has the sudden impulse to tell Norma Jean about himself, as if he had just met her. They have known each other so long they have forgotten a lot about each other. They could become reacquainted. But when the oven timer goes off and she runs to the kitchen, he forgets why he wants to do this.

The next day, Mabel drops by. It is Saturday and Norma Jean is cleaning. Leroy is studying the plans of his log house, which have finally come in the mail. He has them spread out on the table—big sheets of stiff blue paper, with diagrams and numbers printed in white. While Norma Jean runs the vacuum, Mabel drinks coffee. She sets her coffee cup on a blueprint.

'I'm just waiting for time to pass,' she says to Leroy, drumming her fingers on the table.

As soon as Norma Jean switches off the vacuum, Mabel says in a loud voice, 'Did you hear about the datsun dog that killed the baby?'

Norma Jean says, 'The word is "dachshund".'

'They put the dog on trial. It chewed the baby's legs off. The mother was in the next room all the time.' She raises her voice. 'They thought it was neglect.'

Norma Jean is holding her ears. Leroy manages to open the refrigerator and get some Diet Pepsi to offer Mabel. Mabel still has some coffee and she waves away the Pepsi.

'Datsuns are like that,' Mabel says. 'They're jealous dogs. They'll tear a place to pieces if you don't keep an eye on them.'

'You better watch out what you're saying, Mabel,' says Leroy.

'Well, facts is facts.'

Leroy looks out the window at his rig. It is like a huge piece of furniture gathering dust in the backyard. Pretty soon it will be an antique. He hears the vacuum cleaner. Norma Jean seems to be cleaning the living-room rug again.

Later, she says to Leroy, 'She just said that about the baby because she caught me smoking. She's trying to pay me back.'

'What are you talking about?' Leroy says, nervously shuffling blueprints.

'You know good and well,' Norma Jean says. She is sitting in a kitchen chair with her feet up and her arms wrapped around her knees. She looks small and helpless. She says, 'The very idea, her bringing up a subject like that! Saying it was neglect.'

'She didn't mean that,' Leroy says.

'She might not have *thought* she meant it. She always says things like that. You don't know how she goes on.'

'But she didn't really mean it. She was just talking.'

Leroy opens a king-sized bottle of beer and pours it into two glasses, dividing it carefully. He hands a glass to Norma Jean and she takes it from him mechanically. For a long time, they sit by the kitchen window watching the birds at the feeder.

Something is happening. Norma Jean is going to night school. She has graduated from her six-week body-building course and now she is taking an adult-education course in composition at Paducah Community College. She spends her evenings outlining paragraphs.

'First you have a topic sentence,' she explains to Leroy. 'Then you divide it up. Your secondary topic has to be connected to your primary topic.'

To Leroy this sounds intimidating. 'I never was any good in English,' he says.

'It makes a lot of sense.'

'What are you doing this for, anyhow?'

She shrugs. 'It's something to do.' She stands up and lifts her dumbbells a few times.

'Driving a rig, nobody cared about my English.'

'I'm not criticizing your English.'

Norma Jean used to say, 'If I lose ten minutes' sleep, I just drag all day.' Now she stays up late, writing compositions. She got a B on her first paper—a how-to theme on soup-based casseroles. Recently Norma Jean has been cooking unusual foods—tacos, lasagna, Bombay chicken. She doesn't play the organ anymore, though her second paper was called 'Why Music Is Important to Me'. She sits at the kitchen table, concentrating on her outlines, while Leroy plays with his log house plans, practising with a set of Lincoln Logs. The thought of getting a truckload of notched, numbered logs scares him, and he wants to be prepared. As he and Norma Jean work together at the kitchen table, Leroy has the hopeful thought that they are sharing something, but he knows he is a fool to think this. Norma Jean is miles away. He knows he is going to lose her. Like Mabel, he is just waiting for time to pass.

One day, Mabel is there before Norma Jean gets home from work, and Leroy finds himself confiding in her. Mabel, he realizes, must know Norma Jean better than he does.

'I don't know what's got into that girl,' Mabel says. 'She used to go to bed with the chickens. Now you say she's up all hours. Plus her a-smoking. I like to died.'

'I want to make her this beautiful home,' Leroy says, indicating the Lincoln Logs. 'I don't think she even wants it. Maybe she was happier with me gone.'

'She don't know what to make of you, coming home like this.'

'Is that it?'

Mabel takes the roof off his Lincoln Log cabin. 'You couldn't get *me* in a log cabin,' she says. 'I was raised in one. It's no picnic, let me tell you.'

'They're different now,' says Leroy.

'I tell you what,' Mabel says, smiling oddly at Leroy.

'What?'

'Take her on down to Shiloh. Y'all need to get out together, stir a little. Her brain's all balled up over them books.'

Leroy can see traces of Norma Jean's features in her mother's face. Mabel's worn face has the texture of crinkled cotton, but suddenly she looks pretty. It occurs to Leroy that Mabel has been hinting all along that she wants them to take her with them to Shiloh.

'Let's all go to Shiloh,' he says. 'You and me and her. Come Sunday.'

Mabel throws up her hands in protest. 'Oh, no, not me. Young folks want to be by theirselves.'

When Norma Jean comes in with groceries, Leroy says excitedly, 'Your mama here's been dying to go to Shiloh for thirty-five years. It's about time we went, don't you think?'

'I'm not going to butt in on anybody's second honeymoon,' Mabel says.

'Who's going on a honeymoon, for Christ's sake?' Norma Jean says loudly.

'I never raised no daughter of mine to talk that-a-way,' Mabel says.

'You ain't seen nothing yet,' says Norma Jean. She starts putting away boxes and cans, slamming cabinet doors.

'There's a log cabin at Shiloh,' Mabel says. 'It was there during the battle. There's bullet holes in it.'

'When are you going to *shut up* about Shiloh, Mama?' asks Norma Jean.

'I always thought Shiloh was the prettiest place, so full of history,' Mabel goes on. 'I just hoped y'all could see it once before I die, so you could tell me about it.' Later, she whispers to Leroy, 'You do what I said. A little change is what she needs.'

'Your name means "the king",' Norma Jean says to Leroy that evening. He is trying to get her to go to Shiloh, and she is reading a book about another century.

'Well, I reckon I ought to be right proud.'

'I guess so.'

'Am I still king around here?'

Norma Jean flexes her biceps and feels them for hardness. 'I'm not fooling around with anybody, if that's what you mean,' she says.

'Would you tell me if you were?'

'I don't know.'

'What does *your* name mean?'

'It was Marilyn Monroe's real name.'

'No kidding!'

'Norma comes from the Normans. They were invaders,' she says. She closes her book and looks hard at Leroy. 'I'll go to Shiloh with you if you'll stop staring at me.'

On Sunday, Norma Jean packs a picnic and they go to Shiloh. To Leroy's relief, Mabel says she does not want to come with them. Norma Jean drives, and Leroy, sitting beside her, feels like some boring hitchhiker she has picked up. He tries some conversation, but she answers him in monosyllables. At Shiloh, she drives aimlessly through the park, past bluffs and trails and steep ravines. Shiloh is an immense place, and Leroy cannot see it as a battleground. It is not what he expected. He thought it would look like a golf course. Monuments are everywhere, showing through the thick clusters of trees. Norma Jean passes the log cabin Mabel mentioned. It is surrounded by tourists looking for bullet holes.

'That's not the kind of log house I've got in mind,' says Leroy apologetically.

'I know *that*.'

'This is a pretty place. Your mama was right.'

'It's OK,' says Norma Jean. 'Well, we've seen it. I hope she's satisfied.'

They burst out laughing together.

At the park museum, a movie on Shiloh is shown every half hour, but they decide that they don't want to see it. They buy a souvenir Confederate flag for Mabel, and then they find a picnic spot near the cemetery. Norma Jean has brought a picnic cooler, with pimiento sandwiches, soft drinks, and Yodels. Leroy eats a sandwich and then smokes a joint, hiding it behind the picnic cooler. Norma Jean has quit smoking altogether. She is picking cake crumbs from the cellophane wrapper, like a fussy bird.

Leroy says, 'So the boys in grey ended up in Corinth. The Union soldiers zapped 'em finally. April 7, 1862.'

They both know that he doesn't know any history. He is just talking about some of the historical plaques they have read. He feels awkward, like a boy on a date with an older girl. They are still just making conversation.

'Corinth is where Mama eloped to,' says Norma Jean.

They sit in silence and stare at the cemetery for the Union dead and, beyond, at a tall cluster of trees. Campers are parked nearby, bumper to bumper, and small children in bright clothing are cavorting and squealing. Norma Jean wads up the cake wrapper and squeezes it tightly in her hand. Without looking at Leroy, she says, 'I want to leave you.'

Leroy takes a bottle of Coke out of the cooler and flips off the cap. He holds the bottle poised near his mouth but cannot remember to take a drink. Finally he says, 'No, you don't.'

'Yes, I do.'

'I won't let you.'

'You can't stop me.'

'Don't do me that way.'

Leroy knows Norma Jean will have her own way. 'Didn't I promise to be home from now on?' he says.

'In some ways, a woman prefers a man who wanders,' says

Norma Jean. 'That sounds crazy, I know.'

'You're not crazy.'

Leroy remembers to drink from his Coke. Then he says, 'Yes, you *are* crazy. You and me could start all over again. Right back at the beginning.'

'We *have* started all over again,' says Norma Jean. 'And this is how it turned out.'

'What did I do wrong?'

'Nothing.'

'Is this one of those women's lib things?' Leroy asks.

'Don't be funny.'

The cemetery, a green slope dotted with white markers, looks like a subdivision site. Leroy is trying to comprehend that his marriage is breaking up, but for some reason he is wondering about white slabs in a graveyard.

'Everything was fine till Mama caught me smoking,' says Norma Jean, standing up. 'That set something off.'

'What are you talking about?'

'She won't leave me alone—*you* won't leave me alone.' Norma Jean seems to be crying, but she is looking away from him. 'I feel eighteen again. I can't face that all over again.' She starts walking away. 'No, it *wasn't* fine. I don't know what I'm saying. Forget it.'

Leroy takes a lungful of smoke and closes his eyes as Norma Jean's words sink in. He tries to focus on the fact that thirty-five hundred soldiers died on the grounds around him. He can only think of that war as a board game with plastic soldiers. Leroy almost smiles, as he compares the Confederates' daring attack on the Union camps and Virgil Mathis's raid on the bowling alley. General Grant, drunk and furious, shoved the Southerners back to Corinth, where Mabel and Jet Beasley were married years later, when Mabel was still thin and good-looking. The next day, Mabel and Jet visited the battleground, and then Norma Jean was born, and then she married Leroy and they had a baby, which they lost, and now Leroy and Norma Jean are here at the same battleground. Leroy knows he is leaving out a lot. He is leaving out the insides of history. History was always just names and dates to him. It occurs to him that building a house out of logs is similarly empty—too simple. And the real inner workings of a marriage, like most of history, have escaped him. Now he sees that building a log house is the dumbest idea he could have had. It was clumsy of him to think Norma Jean would want a log house. It was a crazy idea. He'll have to think of something else, quickly. He will wad the blueprints into tight balls and fling them into the lake. Then he'll get moving again. He opens his eyes. Norma Jean has moved away and is walking through the cemetery, following a serpentine brick path.

Leroy gets up to follow his wife, but his good leg is asleep and his bad leg still hurts him. Norma Jean is far away, walking rapidly toward the bluff by the river, and he tries to hobble toward her. Some children run past him, screaming noisily. Norma Jean has reached the bluff, and she is looking out over the Tennessee River. Now she turns toward Leroy and waves her arms. Is she beckoning to him? She seems to be doing an exercise for her chest muscles. The sky is unusually pale—the colour of the dust ruffle Mabel made for their bed.

MARGARET ATWOOD

Happy Endings

John and Mary meet.
What happens next?
If you want a happy ending, try A.

A. John and Mary fall in love and get married. They both have worthwhile and remunerative jobs which they find stimulating and challenging. They buy a charming house. Real estate values go up. Eventually, when they can afford live-in help, they have two children, to whom they are devoted. The children turn out well. John and Mary have a stimulating and challenging sex life and worthwhile friends. They go on fun vacations together. They retire. They both have hobbies which they find stimulating and challenging. Eventually they die. This is the end of the story.

B. Mary falls in love with John but John doesn't fall in love with Mary. He merely uses her body for selfish pleasure and ego gratification of a tepid kind. He comes to her apartment twice a week and she cooks him dinner, you'll notice that he doesn't even consider her worth the price of a dinner out, and after he's eaten the dinner he fucks her and after that he falls asleep, while she does the dishes so he won't think she's untidy, having all those dirty dishes lying around, and puts on fresh lipstick so she'll look good when he wakes up, but when he wakes up he doesn't even notice, he puts on his socks and his shorts and his pants and his shirt and his tie and his shoes, the reverse order from the one in which he took them off. He doesn't take off Mary's clothes, she takes them off herself, she acts as if she's dying for it every time, not because she likes sex exactly, she doesn't, but she wants John to think she does because if they do it often enough surely he'll get used to her, he'll come to depend on her and they will get married, but John goes out the door with hardly so much as a goodnight and three days later he turns up at six o'clock and they do the whole thing over again.

Mary gets run down. Crying is bad for your face, everyone knows that and so does Mary but she can't stop. People at work notice. Her friends tell her John is a rat, a pig, a dog, he isn't good enough for her, but she can't believe it. Inside John, she thinks, is another John, who is much nicer. This other John will emerge like a butterfly from a cocoon, a Jack from a box, a pit from a prune, if the first John is only squeezed enough.

One evening John complains about the food. He has never complained about the food before. Mary is hurt.

Her friends tell her they've seen him in a restaurant with another woman, whose name is Madge. It's not even Madge that finally gets to Mary: it's the restaurant. John has never taken Mary to a restaurant. Mary collects all the sleeping pills and aspirins she can find, and takes them and half a bottle of sherry. You can see what kind of a woman she is by the fact that it's not even whiskey. She leaves a note for John. She hopes he'll discover her and get her to the hospital in time and repent and then they can get married, but this fails to happen and she dies.

John marries Madge and everything continues as in A.

C. John, who is an older man, falls in love with Mary, and Mary, who is only twenty-two, feels sorry for him because he's worried about his hair falling out. She sleeps with him even though she's not in love with him. She met him at work. She's in love with someone called James, who is twenty-two also and not yet ready to settle down.

John on the contrary settled down long ago: this is what is bothering him. John has a steady respectable job and is getting ahead in his field, but Mary isn't impressed by him, she's impressed by James, who has a motorcycle and a fabulous record collection. But James is often away on his motorcycle, being free. Freedom isn't the same for girls, so in the meantime Mary spends Thursday evenings with John. Thursdays are the only days John can get away.

John is married to a woman called Madge and they have two children, a charming house which they bought just before the real estate values went up, and hobbies which they find stimulating and challenging, when they have the time. John tells Mary how important she is to him, but of course he can't leave his wife because a commitment is a commitment. He goes on about this more than is necessary and Mary finds it boring, but older men can keep it up longer so on the whole she has a fairly good time.

One day James breezes in on his motorcycle with some top grade California hybrid and James and Mary get higher than you'd believe possible and they climb into bed. Everything becomes very underwater, but along comes John, who has a key to Mary's apartment. He finds them stoned and entwined. He's hardly in any position to be jealous, considering Madge, but nevertheless he's overcome with despair. Finally he's middle-aged, in two years he'll be bald as an egg and he can't stand it. He purchases a handgun, saying he needs it for target practice—this is the thin part of the plot, but it can be dealt with later—and shoots the two of them and himself.

Madge, after a suitable period of mourning, marries an under-standing man called Fred and everything continues as in A, but under different names.

D. Fred and Madge have no problems. They get along exceptionally well and are good at working out any little difficulties that may arise. But their charming house is by the seashore and one day a giant tidal wave approaches. Real estate values go down. The rest of the story is about what caused the tidal wave and how they escape from it. They do, though thousands drown. Some of the story is about how the thousands drown, but Fred and Madge are virtuous and lucky. Finally on high ground they clasp each other, wet and dripping and grateful, and continue as in A.

E. Yes, but Fred has a bad heart. The rest of the story is about how kind and understanding they both are until Fred dies. Then Madge devotes herself to charity work until the end of A. If you like, it can be 'Madge', 'cancer', 'guilty and confused', and 'bird watching'.

F. If you think this is all too bourgeois, make John a revolutionary and Mary a counterespionage agent and see how far that gets you. Remember, this is Canada. You'll still end up with A, though in between you may get a lustful brawling saga of passionate involvement, a chronicle of our times, sort of.

You'll have to face it, the endings are the same however you slice it. Don't be deluded by any other endings, they're all fake, either deliberately fake, with malicious intent to deceive, or just motivated by excessive optimism if not by downright sentimentality.

The only authentic ending is the one provided here:

John and Mary die. John and Mary die. John and Mary die.

So much for endings. Beginnings are always more fun. True connoisseurs, however, are known to favour the stretch in between, since it's the hardest to do anything with.

That's about all that can be said for plots, which anyway are just one thing after another, a what and a what and a what.

Now try How and Why.

BIOGRAPHICAL NOTES

MARGARET ATWOOD (1939–), a Canadian writer of world-wide reputation, was born in Ottawa, Canada, has lived in the USA, Britain, France, and Italy, and now lives in Ontario. She has written seven novels, including *Surfacing* (1972), *The Handmaid's Tale* (1985), and *Cat's Eye* (1988), and three collections of stories, *Dancing Girls* (1982), *Bluebeard's Egg* (1988), and *Wilderness Tips* (1991). She has also written poetry, plays, children's books, and a controversial study of Canadian literature, *Survival* (1972).

ELIZABETH BOWEN (1899–1973) was born in Dublin and brought up there and in the Anglo-Irish family home, Bowen's Court in County Cork. She spent most of the rest of her life in Oxford and London and in later years visited America regularly. Her novels include *The Last September* (1929), *The Death of the Heart* (1938) and *The Heat of the Day* (1949), and she published seven volumes of short stories, including *Look At All Those Roses* (1941) and *The Demon Lover* (1945). Her non-fiction, edited by Hermione Lee, was published as *The Mulberry Tree* in 1986.

ANGELA CARTER (1940–1992) was a London writer, though she spent parts of her life in Japan, the USA, and Australia. She wrote nine novels, including *The Magic Toyshop* (1967), *The Passion of New Eve* (1977), *Nights at the Circus* (1984) and *Wise Children* (1991). She published four collections of stories, *Fireworks* (1974), *The Bloody Chamber* (1979), *Black Venus* (1985), and *American Ghosts and Old World Wonders* (published posthumously in 1993), and three collections of non-fiction, *The Sadeian Woman* (1979), *Nothing Sacred* (1982) and *Expletives Deleted* (published posthumously in 1992). She also wrote screenplays (*The Company of Wolves* with Neil Jordan and an adaptation of *The Magic Toyshop*), and edited anthologies: *Wayward Girls and Wicked Women* (1986), and *The Virago Book of Fairy Tales* (1990).

WILLA CATHER (1873–1947) was born in Virginia and grew up in Nebraska. She was a journalist, poet, essayist, novelist and short

374

story writer. Her novels include *My Antonia* (1918), *A Lost Lady* (1923), *The Professor's House* (1925), *Death Comes for the Archbishop* (1927) and *Shadows on the Rock* (1931). A selection of her stories, edited by Hermione Lee, was published by Virago in 1989.

ELSPETH DAVIE (1920–), short story writer and novelist, was born in Edinburgh and still lives in Scotland. She taught painting before becoming a writer. Her novels are *Providings* (1965), *Creating a Scene* (1971), *Climbers on a Stair* (1978) and *Coming to Light* (1989). She has written stories since the 1950s and her collections include *The Spark and Other Stories* (1968), and *The High Tide Talker* (1976).

ANITA DESAI (1937–) was born in India, the daughter of a Bengali father and a German mother. She was educated in Delhi and now lives in Bombay. Her publications include the short stories *Games at Twilight* (1978) and the novels *Fire on the Mountain* (1977), *Clear Light of Day* (1980), *In Custody* (1984) and *Baumgartner's Bombay* (1988). She has also written several children's books.

JANET FRAME (1924–) was born near Dunedin, New Zealand, and has worked as a teacher and a nurse-companion. Her first collection of stories, *The Lagoon*, appeared in 1951. She has written ten novels, including *Owls do Cry* (1957), *Faces in the Water* (1961), *Scented Gardens for the Blind* (1963), and *Living in the Maniototo* (1980). Her autobiographies, *To the Is-Land* (1983), *An Angel at My Table* (1984) and *The Envoy from Mirror City* (1986), were published in one volume as *An Autobiography* (1990) and filmed as *An Angel at My Table* (1991). Her stories include *You Are Now Entering the Human Heart* (1983) and in 1993 she published a volume of poems, *The Pocket Mirror* (1993).

ELLEN GILCHRIST (1935–) grew up in the Mississippi Delta and now lives in Fayetteville, Arkansas. She is best known as a short story writer, and has published several collections: *In the Land of the Dreamy Dreams* (1981), *Victory Over Japan* (1985), *Drunk With Love* (1986), *The Light Can Be Both Wave and Particle* (1989), *I Cannot Get You Close Enough* (1990) and *The Blue-Eyed Buddhist*. She has also written three novels: *The Annunciation* (1983), *The Anna Papers* (1989) and *Net of Jewels* (1992).

NADINE GORDIMER (1923–), who was awarded the Nobel Prize for Literature in 1991, and is the recipient of prizes, honorary degrees and awards world-wide, lives in Johannesburg, the city near where she grew up, though she has travelled widely in Europe and the USA. Among her novels are *A World of Strangers* (1958), *Occasion for Loving* (1963), *The Conservationist* (1974), *Burger's Daughter* (1979), *July's People* (1981), *A Sport of Nature* (1987), *My Son's Story* (1990) and *Jump* (1991). Her collections of stories include *The Soft Voice of the Serpent* (1952), *Six Feet of the Country* (1956), *Friday's Footprints* (1960), *Livingstone's Companions* (1971), *Some Monday For Sure* (1976), *Something Out There* (1984), and *Crimes of Conscience* (1991). She has also written essays (including *The Essential Gesture* (1988)) and television plays.

ELIZABETH JANE HOWARD (1923–) was an actress and a reviewer before turning to fiction. Her first novel *The Beautiful Visit* was published in 1950; other novels include *The Long View* (1956), *The Sea Change* (1959), *After Julius* (1965), *Getting it Right* (1982) and the novels of *The Cazalet Chronicle*, which are *The Light Years* (1990) and *Marking Time* (1991). She has published a collection of short stories, *Mr Wrong* (1975), and *Green Shades* (1991), an anthology of garden writing.

RUTH PRAWER JHABVALA (1927–) was born in Germany of Polish parents and came to England at the age of 12. Since then she has lived in India, America and Europe. Her short story collections include *A Stronger Climate* (1968) and *How I Became a Holy Mother* (1976), and among her novels are *The Nature of Passion* (1956), *The Householder* (1960), *A Backward Place* (1965), *Heat and Dust* (1975), *In Search of Love and Beauty* (1983) and *Three Continents* (1987). She is famous for her screenplays, which include *Shakespeare Wallah, The Europeans, A Room With a View* and *Howards End*.

MARY LAVIN (1912–) was born in Massachussetts, but grew up and now lives in Ireland. Her novels are *The House in Clewe St* (1945) and *Mary O'Grady* (1950), but she is best known for her short stories, published in many volumes between the 1940s and the 1980s, and including *Tales From Bective Bridge* (1943), *The Long Ago* (1944), *A Single Lady* (1951), *Happiness* (1969), *The Shrine* (1977), *A Family Likeness* (1985) and the three volume *Stories of Mary Lavin* (1964–1985).

DORIS LESSING (1919–) was born in Iran of British parents and grew up in Southern Rhodesia, now Zimbabwe. She came to England in 1949 with the manuscript of her first novel, *The Grass is Singing* (1950). Her publications since then include *The Golden*

Notebook (1962), the tetralogy *Children of Violence* (1952–69), *Briefing for a Descent into Hell* (1971), the *Canopus in Argos Archives* sequence which began in 1979, *The Good Terrorist* (1985) and *The Fifth Child* (1988). She has published plays, poems, essays, writings on places (most recently *London Observed* (1992) and *African Laughter: Four Visits to Zimbabwe* (1992)), pseudonymous novels as "Jane Somers", and numerous volumes of short stories. These include *A Man and Two Women* (1965) and *The Story of A Non-Marrying Man* (1972). They were collected in *Collected African Stories* (2 vols., 1973) and *Collected Stories* (2 vols., 1978) entitled *To Room Nineteen* and *The Temptation of Jack Orkney.*

KATHERINE MANSFIELD (1888–1923), one of the world's greatest short story writers, was born in Wellington, New Zealand, and came to live in London in 1908, though her search for a cure for tuberculosis took her frequently to Europe, where she died. Short stories published in her lifetime were *In a German Pension* (1911), *Prelude* (1918), *Bliss and Other Stories* (1920), and *The Garden Party and Other Stories* (1922). *The Dove's Nest and Other Stories* (1923), as well as letters and journals, were published posthumously.

BOBBIE ANN MASON (1940–) was raised on a farm in Kentucky and now lives in Pennsylvania. Her first collection of stories, *Shiloh and Other Stories*, was published in 1983. Since then she has published *In Country* (1985), *Spence + Lila*, and another collection of stories, *Love Life* (1989).

ALICE MUNRO (1931–) was born in Wingham, Ontario, and went to the University of Western Ontario. She started writing in her teens and her first collection of stories was *Dance of the Happy Shades* (1968). Since then she has published *Lives of the Girls and Women* (1971), a series of linked stories; *Something I've Been Meaning to Tell You* (1974), *Who Do You Think You Are?* (1978), *The Moons of Jupiter* (1982), *The Progress of Love* (1986) and *Friend of My Youth* (1990).

JOYCE CAROL OATES (1938–), author of more than 55 books of novels, stories, poetry, plays, and essays, grew up in rural New York State, and has taught at the Universities of Detroit, Windsor Ontario, and Princeton, where she now works. Her novels include *With Shuddering Fall* (1964), *them* (1969), *Do With Me What You Will* (1973), *Angel of Light* (1981), *Marya: a Life* (1987), *American Appetites* (1989), *Because It Is Bitter and Because It Is My Heart* (1990), and *Black Water* (1992). She has also written thrillers and essays (including *On Boxing* (1987)) and a very large number of short stories, including *The Wheel of Love* (1970), *Crossing the Border* (1976), *Night-Side* (1977), *A Middle-Class Education* (1980), *Wild Nights* (1985) and *The Assignation* (1988).

FLANNERY O'CONNOR (1925–1964) was born in Savannah, Georgia, and spent most of her life, cut short by illness, on her mother's farm in Milledgeville, Georgia. She wrote two novels, *Wise Blood* (1952) and *The Violent Bear It Away* (1960), and two collections of stories, *A Good Man is Hard to Find* (1955) and *Everything that Rises Must Converge* (1965). Her essays and letters were published posthumously. Her collected stories were published by Faber in 1991.

GRACE PALEY (1922–) was born and grew up in the Russian-Jewish immigrant area of New York; she still lives in the city. She has published three volumes of short stories: *The Little Disturbances of Man* (1959), *Enormous Changes at the Last Minute* (1974), and *Later the Same Day* (1985). She has also published the non-fiction *365 Reasons Not to Have Another War* (1989) and *Long Walks and Intimate Talks* (1991).

DOROTHY PARKER (1893–1967), humorist, poet and journalist, was born in New Jersey and lived for most of her life in New York. She worked on *Vogue, Vanity Fair* and *The New Yorker*. Her books of poems include *Enough Rope* (1926) and *Not So Deep As A Well* (1936), and among her volumes of short stories are *Laments for the Living* (1930) and *Here Lies* (1939).

JAYNE ANNE PHILLIPS (1952–) was born in West Virginia and grew up in the Appalachians; she now lives in California. She has published several collections of stories, *Sweethearts* (1967), *Counting* (1978), *Black Tickets* (1979), *How Mickey Made It* (1981), and *Fast Lanes* (1984), and one novel, *Machine Dreams* (1984).

KATHERINE ANNE PORTER (1890–1980) was born on a farm at Indian Creek, Texas, and worked as an actress, reporter, and entertainer. She travelled widely and taught writing at many universities. Her first collection of stories, *Flowering Judas*, was published in 1930. This was followed by *Pale Horse, Pale Rider* (1939) and *The Leaning Tower* (1944). Her novel, *Ship of Fools*, appeared in 1962.

'JEAN RHYS' (1890–1979), pseudonym of Ellen Gwendolen Rees Williams, was born and brought up in Dominica, West Indies. She came to Europe when she was 16. Her first novels and stories, *The Left Bank* (1927), *Postures* (1928, later *Quartet*), *After Leaving Mr M.* (1930), *Voyage in the Dark* (1934) and *Good Morning Midnight* (1939), are set against the background of life in London and Paris in the 1920s and 1930s. After 1939 she disappeared for nearly twenty years, until she was rediscovered living in Cornwall. *Wide Sargasso Sea* was published in 1966, and was followed by two collections of stories, *Tigers Are Better-Looking* (1968) and *Sleep it Off, Lady* (1976). In 1979 she published *Smile Please: An Unfinished Autobiography*.

PAULINE SMITH (1882–1959) was born in Oudtshoorn, the Little Karoo, South Africa, daughter of the first resident doctor in the area. She went to school in England in 1895 and spent the rest of her life in England and Scotland, returning to South Africa on regular visits. Her short story collections are *The Little Karoo* (1925, reissued with additions in 1930) and *Platkops Children* (1935); she wrote one novel, *The Beadle* (1926). Her *South African Journal 1913–1914* was published in 1983.

AHDAF SOUEIF (1950–) was born in Cairo and educated in Egypt and England, where she now lives. She has published one collection of linked stories, *Aisha* (1983). In 1992 she published her vast post-imperial Anglo-Egyptian novel, *In the Eye of the Sun*.

MURIEL SPARK (1918–) *2006* was born and educated in Edinburgh, spent some time in Africa and now lives in Italy. She began her writing career as an editor and biographer. Her first novel, *The Comforters,* appeared in 1957. Other novels include *The Prime of Miss Jean Brodie* (1961), *The Girls of Slender Means* (1963), *Loitering with Intent* (1981), *The Only Problem* (1984), *A Far Cry from Kensington* (1988) and *Symposium* (1990). *The Stories of Muriel Spark* were published in 1987. Her book on Mary Shelley, *Child of Light* (1951), was reissued in 1987. She published her autobiography, *Curriculum Vitae,* in 1992.

JEAN STAFFORD (1915–79) was born in California and brought up in Colorado. Her novels are *Boston Adventure* (1944), *The Mountain Lion* (1947), *The Catherine Wheel* (1952) and *A Winter's Tale* (1954) but she was better known for her stories (some of which draw on her troubled marriage with the poet Robert Lowell), which were collected in 1969 and won the 1970 Pulitzer Prize. She also published a book of interviews with Lee Harvey Oswald's mother, *A Mother in History* (1966).

GERTRUDE STEIN (1874–1946) influential experimental expatriate American writer, was born in Pennsylvania, studied psychology with William James at Radcliffe, and lived from 1902 in Paris where her home in the rue de Fleurus was a salon for modern writers and painters. Her first fiction, *Three Lives* (1909), was followed by avant-garde writings including her 'poems', *Tender Buttons* (1914), her 'family history', *The Making of Americans* (1925) and her 'biography', *The Autobiography of Alice B. Toklas* (1933).

ELIZABETH TAYLOR (1912–75) was born in Reading, Berkshire, and worked as a governess and a librarian for a time. Her novels include *At Mrs Lippincote's* (1945), *A Wreath of Roses* (1949) and *Mrs Palfrey at the Claremont* (1972). Among her short story collections are *Hester Lilly* (1954), *A Dedicated Man* (1965) and *The Devastating Boys* (1972).

ALICE WALKER (1944–) was born in Eatonton, Georgia, into a family of sharecroppers. She has been active in the civil rights movement and in the teaching of Black studies and is America's most famous 'womanist' black writer. She has published several volumes of poems, two books of short stories, *In Love and Trouble* (1973) and *You Can't Keep a Good Woman Down* (1981), five novels, including the Pulitzer Prize-winning *The Color Purple* (1983), *The Temple of My Familiar* (1989) and *Possessing the Secret of Joy* (1992). She has also written collections of essays and edited a Zora Neale Hurston reader.

SYLVIA TOWNSEND WARNER (1893–1978), short story writer, musicologist, novelist, poet and biographer, the daughter of a schoolteacher, was involved with left-wing politics and went to Spain with the Red Cross in the Civil War. She began writing poetry, with *The Espalier* (1925); her *Collected Poems* were published in 1982. Her novels include *Lolly Willowes* (1926), *Mr Fortune's Maggot* (1927), *The Salutation* (1932), *A Garland of Straw* (1943) and *The Corner That Held Them* (1948). Among her short story collections are *The Cat's Cradle Book* (1960), *A Spirit Rises* (1962) and *A Stranger With a Bag* (1966). She also wrote a biography of T. H. White and edited the 10 volume *History of Tudor Church Music*. Her *Selected Stories* were published by Virago in 1990.

EUDORA WELTY (1909–), novelist, short story writer, and recipient of many awards including the Pulitzer Prize, was born in Jackson, Mississippi, where she has lived all her life. Her short story collections include *A Curtain of Green* (1941), *The Wide Net*

(1943) and *The Golden Apples* (1949); her *Collected Stories* were published in 1980. She has published five novels, including *Delta Wedding* (1946), *Losing Battles* (1970) and *The Optimist's Daughter* (1972). Her non-fiction work includes a volume of essays, *The Eye of The Story* (1978) and an autobiography, *One Writer's Beginnings* (1984).

ACKNOWLEDGEMENTS

The editor is grateful for advice and suggestions from John Barnard, Pat Kavanagh and Jenny Uglow.

Acknowledgements are due to the following for permission to include the stories which appear in this book: The Estate of Pauline Smith and Jonathan Cape Ltd for 'The Sisters' from *The Little Karoo* (Jonathan Cape Ltd, 1925); The Estate of Dorothy Parker and Gerald Duckworth & Co Ltd for 'Here We Are' (1933) from *The Collected Dorothy Parker* (Duckworth, 1952); Alfred A. Knopf, Inc for 'Coming, Aphrodite!' by Willa Cather from *Youth and the Bright Medusa* (Alfred Knopf, 1920); the Estate of Gertrude Stein and Vintage Books for 'As a Wife Has a Cow: A Love Story' (1926) from *Selected Writings* (Vintage Books, 1962); the Estate of Elizabeth Bowen and Jonathan Cape Ltd for 'Her Table Spread' from *The Cat Jumps* (Jonathan Cape Ltd, 1934); the Estate of Sylvia Townsend Warner and Chatto & Windus Ltd for 'A Correspondence in *The Times*' (1938) from *Scenes From Childhood* (Chatto & Windus Ltd, 1981); the Estate of Katherine Anne Porter and Jonathan Cape Ltd for 'Rope' (1936) from *The Collected Stories of Katherine Anne Porter* (Jonathan Cape Ltd, 1964); Mary Lavin for 'Love Is For Lovers' from *Tales From Bective Bridge* (Michael Joseph, 1943); Eudora Welty and Marion Boyars Publishers Ltd for 'Livvie' (1943) from *The Collected Stories* (Marion Boyars, 1981); Jonathan Clowes Ltd, London, on behalf of Doris Lessing for 'The De Wets Come to Kloof Grange' from *This Was the Old Chief's Country* (Michael Joseph, 1951); the Estate of Jean Stafford for 'A Summer Day', first published in *The New Yorker*, 11 September 1948; Nadine Gordimer for 'Six Feet of the Country' from *Six Feet of the Country* (Victor Gollancz Ltd, 1956); Grace Paley and Abner Stein Ltd for 'The Loudest Voice' from *The Little Disturbances of Man* (Farrar, Straus & Giroux, 1959); the Estate of Jean Rhys and Andre Deutsch Ltd for 'Let them Call it Jazz' (1962) from *Tigers are Better-Looking* (Andre Deutsch, 1968); A D Peters & Co Ltd for 'Revelation' by Flannery O'Connor from *Everything that Rises Must Converge* (Faber and Faber Ltd, 1966); Virago Press Ltd for 'Mr Wharton' by Elizabeth Taylor from *A Dedicated Man* (Chatto & Windus Ltd, 1965); Penguin Books Ltd for 'The Time of Death' (1968) by Alice Munro from *Dance of the Happy Shades* (King Penguin, 1983, pp 89–99); Alice Walker and The Women's

ACKNOWLEDGEMENTS

Press for 'Everyday Use' (1973) from *In Love and Trouble* (Women's
Press, 1984); Elizabeth Jane Howard and Jonathan Cape Ltd for 'Child's
Play' from *Mr Wrong* (Jonathan Cape Ltd, 1975); Harold Ober Associates
Incorporated for 'The First Year of My Life' by Muriel Spark, first
published in *The New Yorker*, 1975; Ruth Prawer Jhabvala and John
Murray Ltd for 'How I Became a Holy Mother' from *How I Became a
Holy Mother* (John Murray Ltd, 1976); Joyce Carol Oates and Vanguard
Press for 'Small Avalanches' from *The Goddess and Other Women* (Victor
Gollancz Ltd, 1975); Anita Desai and William Heinemann Ltd for 'Private
Tuition by Mr Bose' from *Games at Twilight* (William Heinemann Ltd,
1978); Anthony Sheil Associates Ltd for 'The Time-Keeper' by Elspeth
Davie from *The Night of the Funny Hats* (Hamish Hamilton Ltd, 1980);
Penguin Books Ltd for 'Mamasita' by Jayne Anne Phillips from *Black
Tickets* (King Penguin, 1981, pp 47–8); Angela Carter and Chatto &
Windus Ltd for 'Peter and the Wolf' (1982) from *Black Venus* (Chatto &
Windus Ltd, 1985); Faber and Faber Ltd for 'Revenge' by Ellen Gilchrist
from *In the Land of Dreamy Dreams* (Faber and Faber Ltd, 1981); Curtis
Brown Ltd on behalf of Janet Frame for 'Swans' from *You ~~are Now~~
Entering the Human Heart* (Women's Press, 1983); Ahdaf Soueif and
Jonathan Cape Ltd for 'The Wedding of Zeina' from *Aisha* (Jonathan Cape
Ltd, 1983); Bobbie Ann Mason and Chatto & Windus Ltd for 'Shiloh'
from *Shiloh and Other Stories* (Chatto & Windus Ltd, 1983); Margaret
Atwood and Jonathan Cape Ltd for 'Happy Endings' from *Murder in the
Dark* (Jonathan Cape Ltd, 1984).

The copyright in the individual stories is as follows: 'The Sisters' © Estate
of Pauline Smith 1925; 'Here We Are' © the Estate of Dorothy Parker
1933; 'Coming, Aphrodite!' copyright 1920 by Willa Cather and renewed
1948 by the Executors of the Estate of Willa Cather; 'As a Wife Has a Cow:
A Love Story' © Gertrude Stein 1926, renewed Alice B Toklas 1960; 'Her
Table Spread' © Estate of Elizabeth Bowen 1934; 'A Correspondence in
The Times' © Estate of Sylvia Townsend Warner 1938; 'Rope' © Estate of
Katherine Anne Porter 1936, 1964; 'Love Is For Lovers' © Mary Lavin
1943; 'Livvie' © Estate of Eudora Welty 1943; 'The De Wets Come to
Kloof Grange' copyright 1951 Doris Lessing; 'A Summer Day' © the
Estate of Jean Stafford 1948; 'Six Feet of the Country' © Nadine Gordimer
1956; 'The Loudest Voice' © Grace Paley 1959; 'Let them Call it Jazz' ©
the Estate of Jean Rhys 1962; 'Revelation' © 1961, 1965 by Estate of
Mary Flannery O'Connor; 'Mr Wharton' © Elizabeth Taylor 1965; 'The
Time of Death' copyright © Alice Munro 1968; 'Everyday Use' © Alice
Walker 1973; 'Child's Play' © Elizabeth Jane Howard 1975; 'The First
Year of My Life' © 1975 by Copyright Administration Limited; 'How I
Became a Holy Mother' © Ruth Prawer Jhabvala 1976; 'Small Avalan-
ches' © Joyce Carol Oates 1975; 'Private Tuition by Mr Bose' © Anita

383

Desai 1978; 'The Time-Keeper' © Elspeth Davie 1980; 'Mamasita' copyright © Jayne Anne Phillips, 1975, 1976, 1977, 1978, 1979; 'Peter and the Wolf' © Angela Carter 1982; 'Revenge' © Ellen Gilchrist 1981; 'You are Now Entering the Human Heart' © 1983 by Janet Frame; 'The Wedding of Zeina' © Ahdaf Soueif 1983; 'Shiloh' © Bobbie Ann Mason 1983; 'Happy Endings' © Margaret Atwood 1984.